D0385329

RESEARCH IN ORGANIZATIONAL CHANGE AND DEVELOPMENT

RESEARCH IN ORGANIZATIONAL CHANGE AND DEVELOPMENT

Series Editors: William A. Pasmore,
Abraham B. (Rami) Shani and
Richard W. Woodman

Previous Volumes:

Volumes 1–17: Research in Organizational Change and Development

RESEARCH IN ORGANIZATIONAL CHANGE AND
DEVELOPMENT VOLUME 18

RESEARCH IN ORGANIZATIONAL CHANGE AND DEVELOPMENT

EDITED BY

WILLIAM A. PASMORE
Center for Creative Leadership, Greensboro, North Carolina, USA

ABRAHAM B. (RAMI) SHANI
California Polytechnic State University, San Luis Obispo, CA, USA and Politecnico di Milano, Milan, Italy

RICHARD W. WOODMAN
Texas A&M University, College Station, Texas, USA

United Kingdom – North America – Japan
India – Malaysia – China

Emerald Group Publishing Limited
Howard House, Wagon Lane, Bingley BD16 1WA, UK

First edition 2010

British Library Cataloguing in Publication Data
A catalogue record for this book is available from the British Library

ISBN: 978-0-85724-191-7
ISSN: 0897-3016 (Series)

Awarded in recognition of
Emerald's production
department's adherence to
quality systems and processes
when preparing scholarly
journals for print

CONTENTS

LIST OF CONTRIBUTORS *vii*

PREFACE *ix*

BUILT TO CHANGE ORGANIZATIONS AND RESPONSIBLE PROGRESS: TWIN PILLARS OF SUSTAINABLE SUCCESS
Christopher G. Worley and Edward E. Lawler, III *1*

BREAKING OUT OF STRATEGY VECTORS: REINTRODUCING CULTURE
Julia Balogun and Steven W. Floyd *51*

TRANSCENDING PARADOX: MOVEMENT AS A MEANS FOR SUSTAINING HIGH PERFORMANCE
Jason A. Wolf *77*

RELATIONAL SPACE AND LEARNING EXPERIMENTS: THE HEART OF SUSTAINABILITY COLLABORATIONS
Hilary Bradbury-Huang, Benyamin Lichtenstein, John S. Carroll and Peter M. Senge *109*

SEEKING COMMON GROUND IN THE DIVERSITY AND DIFFUSION OF ACTION RESEARCH AND COLLABORATIVE MANAGEMENT RESEARCH ACTION MODALITIES: TOWARD A GENERAL EMPIRICAL METHOD
David Coghlan *149*

ART OR ARTIST? AN ANALYSIS OF EIGHT LARGE-GROUP METHODS FOR DRIVING LARGE-SCALE CHANGE
Svetlana Shmulyian, Barry Bateman, Ruth G. Philpott and Neelu K. Gulri *183*

THAT'S NOT HOW I SEE IT: HOW TRUST IN THE ORGANIZATION, LEADERSHIP, PROCESS, AND OUTCOME INFLUENCE INDIVIDUAL RESPONSES TO ORGANIZATIONAL CHANGE
Robert M. Sloyan and James D. Ludema *233*

THE IMPACT OF TRUST ON THE ORGANIZATIONAL MERGER PROCESS
Paul Michalenko *279*

THE MATURE WORKFORCE AND THE CHANGING NATURE OF WORK
Kay F. Quam *315*

ABOUT THE AUTHORS *367*

LIST OF CONTRIBUTORS

Julia Balogun	Lancaster University Management School, Lancaster, UK
Barry Bateman	Managing Partner, Sapience Organizational Consulting, Reston, VA, USA
Hilary Bradbury-Huang	University of Southern California, Center for Sustainable Cities, Los Angeles, CA, USA
John S. Carroll	MIT Sloan School of Management, Cambridge, MA, USA
David Coghlan	Trinity College, University of Dublin, Dublin, Ireland
Steven W. Floyd	Institute of Management, University of St Gallen, St Gallen, Switzerland
Neelu K. Gulri	Organization and Leadership Department, Teachers College, Columbia University, New York, NY, USA
Edward E. Lawler, III	Center for Effective Organizations, University of Southern California, Los Angeles, CA, USA
Benyamin Lichtenstein	University of Massachusetts, Boston, MA, USA
James D. Ludema	Center for Values-Driven Leadership, Benedictine University, Lisle, IL, USA
Paul Michalenko	Independent Consultant, Chicago, IL, USA

Ruth G. Philpott	Organization and Leadership Department, Teachers College, Columbia University, New York, NY, USA
Kay F. Quam	Organizational Management Consultant, Reston, VA, USA
Peter M. Senge	Society for Organizational Learning and MIT Sloan School of Management, Cambridge, MA, USA
Svetlana Shmulyian	Organization and Leadership Department, Teachers College, Columbia University, New York, NY, USA
Robert M. Sloyan	Benedictine University, Lisle, IL, USA
Jason A. Wolf	The Beryl Institute and American University, Washington, DC, USA
Christopher G. Worley	Center for Effective Organizations, University of Southern California, Los Angeles, CA, USA

PREFACE

The first annual volume of Research in Organization Change and Development was published by JAI Press in 1987. Since then, ROCD has provided a special platform for scholars and practitioners to share new research-based insights. Volume eighteen continues the tradition of providing insightful and thought provoking chapters. The chapters in the volume represent a commitment to maintaining the high quality of work that our readers have come to expect from this publication.

Authors of contributions to Volume 18 did their writing during one of the most severe global economic crises in the past century. Some of their papers reflect the urgency of change that many leaders of organizations currently feel. Whereas in the booming 1970s and late 1990s, it was difficult for some to push change to the front of the agenda, very few organizations have escaped the need to undertake unprecedented, dramatic actions to stabilize their futures. The need for more efficient and effective approaches to change has never been greater. Not only must we increase our success rates in change projects dramatically over the thirty-three percent level that many studies point to for major change success today, we must also produce more change in less time and with less cost. The crisis has clarified the need for change and has been used as a hammer to force people through unpleasant changes by some leaders. We believe that how leaders respond to a crisis like the one we are experiencing will influence the culture of their organization for years to come. Handled properly, the changes can create greater effectiveness, engagement, and rapid recovery. Handled poorly, the same changes might produce a weakened culture, decreased loyalty, and difficulty in returning to previous levels of success. The "new normal" for a particular organization will be determined in part by the state of the world economy, but also in part by the actions of its leaders during the crisis as well. Change researchers need to accept that the adoption of our approaches to change are not immune to the influences of the broader context. Unless we provide leaders with more efficient and effective approaches to change, leaders may feel forced to adopt measures that are less costly and less time consuming even knowing that the long-term effects they produce could be detrimental.

Against this backdrop, it is not surprising that several papers in Volume 18 address issues of trust and sustainability. Other papers review approaches to change to see if we can discern whether some approaches are more effective than others. Still others explore culture and relationships, since change must ultimately come down to people. Whether we make progress at all, and then what impact a change has on the long-term viability of an organization will always be a function of how well we understand what is happening in human systems as our interventions perturb them.

Christopher G. Worley and Edward E. Lawler argue that the pace and uncertainty of change in today's world, spurred by increased globalization, technological innovation, and the emergence of new concerns, such as ecological sustainability and human rights, creates the necessity for a new approach. They advance an organizational effectiveness model built on the assumption that continuous change is simply business as usual and the best way to sustainable success, and the belief that it should include social and ecological concerns. Toward that end, they propose a model of organization agility – the built to change model – with a revised perspective of organization effectiveness. The new approach represents a framework for OD practitioners to share and build relevant practice in a more cohesive fashion. They argue that such an approach can help to restore and mend some of the fragmented views of theory and practice in organization development and change.

Julia Balogun and Steven W. Floyd focus on understanding how an organization can break out of a strategic lock-in. The authors expand our understanding of strategy vectors and explore the linkages between strategy, culture, and strategic change in order to build a more comprehensive picture of the structural context. A proposed model demonstrates the extent of interconnectedness between the "hard" (e.g., control systems, organization structure) and "soft" (e.g., beliefs, symbols, stories) components, and that development of new required capabilities is dependent on a holistic shift in all these aspects of the structural context, including, therefore, change in the organization's culture.

Sustaining high performance is the subject of the next paper by Jason A. Wolf. The study was conducted in 12 hospitals, 9 of which were categorized as "sustaining" and three of which as "non-sustaining." Three paradoxes that must be managed dynamically during change were identified by Wolf in his work. The three paradoxes are agility/consistency, informative/inquiry, and collective/individualism. In addition, nine key actions that assist in addressing these paradoxes were found helpful in sustaining high performance. The author suggests that sustaining high performance seems to be embedded in the willingness to hold the three movements in dynamic tension through which the power of sustainability as movement is realized.

Hilary Bradbury-Huang, Benyamin Lichtenstein, John S. Carroll, and Peter M. Senge address the need to develop methods that can help companies address complex global sustainability challenges. They propose "the sustainability consortium" as a mechanism that allows corporations to address such multilayer issues. This multi-organizational consortium creates "relational space" in which collaborative projects emerge and are nurtured. The authors provide an in-depth case study of such sustainability consortium. The collaborative projects that evolved generated creative solutions that enhanced the competitive advantage of the corporations involved.

Some of our most powerful tools for learning about change involve collaborative research with client organizations. David Coghlan calls our attention to the continuous and emerging variety of action research and collaborative research methodologies. He argues that as the field of action-oriented research becomes increasingly diffuse and diverse, it is important to identify common ground across the multiple modalities of action research and collaborative management research. Coghlan proposes to ground our practice in the recognizable structure of human knowing by paying attention to observable data (experience), envisaging possible explanations of that data (understanding), and preferring as probable or certain the explanations which provide the best account for the data (judgment). The paper seeks to illustrate how different research modalities engage these operations of human knowing.

More concern with the sustainability of our efforts is evident in Shmulyian, Bateman, Philpott, and Gulri's paper, which focuses on large-scale interventions. The effectiveness of eight different types of large-scale interventions is compared. Case studies in a number of companies are used as the database for examining the outcomes of each type of large-scale intervention. In speaking with both practitioners and their clients, they learned that both the method and the skill of the practitioner involved affect the outcomes achieved. In looking a bit deeper, the authors found that having the right individuals in the room, the right issues under consideration, the right information available, the right infrastructure to support the process, and the right design for the intervention all were critical factors in determining intervention success. This paper also transcends earlier overviews of large-group methods to examine the long-term impact or what actually happened after the interventions took place.

Robert M. Sloyan and James D. Ludema focus on a deeper level investigation of individual responses to change and their influence on the success of organizational change initiatives. The implementations of organization development initiatives at five business units within the same corporation provide the empirical data for the study. The authors found that as people engaged sensemaking, they assessed the changes they experienced against four aspects of trust: trust in the organization, trust in their leadership, trust in the change process, and trust in the outcomes. The authors illustrate how managers can frame the four trusts to their advantage during change efforts and conclude by providing further implications for research and practice.

Mergers continue to be an integral component of emerging markets. Paul Michalenko's paper advances our understanding the processes and dynamics of successful merger initiatives. Michalenko investigates the characteristics of successful mergers within the context of religious provinces. Eight merged organizations provided the empirical data for the study. Three essential elements were found to be critical to the success of mergers, namely clear mission driven purpose, authentic leadership, and inclusive engagement. These elements set the context for building trust among members and organization that enhance organizational renewal.

Finally, Kay Quam's paper calls our attention to the changing nature of work and the maturing of the workforce. The author argues that Web 2.0 technologies fundamentally reshape the nature of work as we know it. Meeting the challenges is not simply a matter of re-skilling or even up-skilling. Rather, what is required are new means of constructing work so that mature workers can contribute in ways that meet their desires and needs and so that organizations can enlist the necessary people to perform in the new work environment. Systemic and holistic action research initiatives, approaches, and specific steps are proposed.

While these papers alone will not lift the world out of the current financial crisis, the level of thoughtfulness they demonstrate provides hope that our field can contribute its part to the solutions organizations seek. Since change is no longer an option, high rates of failure are simply not acceptable. Building more change-ready organizations, leading change with an eye toward the dynamics of trust, focusing on sustainability, and using more effective and efficient approaches will help our world get back on its feet.

William A. Pasmore
Abraham B. (Rami) Shani
Richard W. Woodman
Editors

BUILT TO CHANGE ORGANIZATIONS AND RESPONSIBLE PROGRESS: TWIN PILLARS OF SUSTAINABLE SUCCESS

Christopher G. Worley and Edward E. Lawler, III

ABSTRACT

The increasing interest in economic, social, and ecological sustainability has important implications for the traditional views on organization effectiveness, organization design, and organization development. Managers need to design organizations to achieve a "triple bottom line." A review of the organization effectiveness literature suggests that no single model seems to provide the necessary guidance, and there is a clear need for creation, revision, and integration. Organization effectiveness criteria in the future require a clearer modeling of the multistakeholder demands so that organization designers can specify appropriate strategies, structures, systems, and processes as well as the changes necessary to develop them. We propose an integration called "responsible progress" and suggest that it represents an important new stream of organization development theory. The relationships between this new criterion of organization effectiveness and the design features necessary to pursue them must be tested.

Research in Organizational Change and Development, Volume 18, 1–49

ISSN: 0897-3016/doi:10.1108/S0897-3016(2010)0000018005

The increasing interest in economic, social, and ecological sustainability raises important implications for the traditional views on organization effectiveness, organization design, and organization development (OD). Judging by how surprised most organizations were by the recent economic recession, and the relative lack of socially and ecologically relevant capabilities in most organizations, there is evidence aplenty that the organization design features we have relied on for years have outlived their usefulness. *Organizations that rely on traditional design principles and measures of effectiveness are not able to respond to demands for change and to calls for new economic, social, and ecological outcomes. Traditional design principles and measures of financial performance divert our attention away from what organizations need to do to be agile and sustainable*. To paraphrase Hanna (1988), "organizations are perfectly designed to get the results they get." If the goal is being financially viable, socially relevant, and ecologically responsible over time, we need different design options.

The purpose of this chapter is to propose a model of organization effectiveness and agility that incorporates a broad range of effectiveness criteria. The model represents a radical departure from the traditional perspectives on organization effectiveness – more radical than it might first appear – along two dimensions. First, a fundamental restatement of organization effectiveness criterion is required since most effectiveness frameworks gloss over the socially related effectiveness criterion and frankly do not address ecological sustainability. Second, a significant shift in the principles guiding organization design and the business models underlying strategies is required since prior principles and models rely on stability as the driver of performance. In describing this model, we hope to reinvigorate the discussion of organization effectiveness and generate a new OD research agenda.

We begin with a review of the traditional organization effectiveness perspectives as well as more recent extensions, including models of agility. In addition, we review the economic and ecological effectiveness perspectives. This review supports the conclusion that the demands facing organizations are increasing in both number and intensity, and that traditional models of organization design are not only ill-equipped to handle the rates of change implied by these increases but reflect the pursuit of a narrow set of effectiveness criteria. Our models of organization effectiveness have not kept up with environmental changes, especially with respect to sustainability.

We then turn to the problem of integrating these diverse perspectives into a new model of organization effectiveness criterion. Prior models of effectiveness have tended to be singular in their focus (e.g., financial or ecological). We describe the responsible progress framework that has four different effectiveness criteria.

Finally, we make the case that the only way organizations can be sustainably successful is for them to change and that the only way to ensure that organizations will be able to change is to build them to change (Lawler & Worley, 2006). We argue that sustainable success requires creating organizations that love changing within the context of "responsible progress" (Worley & McCloskey, 2006). We conclude the chapter by describing revisions to the built to change (B2C) model and showing how it supports responsible progress. The proposed model provides a blueprint for research and evolution in the field of OD and change.

MODELS OF ORGANIZATION EFFECTIVENESS

Traditional Models of Effectiveness

There is a long history in organization theory concerning the conceptualization and measurement of organization effectiveness (OE). It was once a thriving research area (cf., Yuchtman & Seashore, 1967; Campbell, 1977; Miles, 1980; Steers, 1975; Cameron, 1980; Quinn & Rohrbaugh, 1983). Over the course of about 20 years, a variety of models were developed to capture the OE construct, including rational, goal-oriented models (Perrow, 1972; March & Simon, 1958), systems-resource models (Yuchtman & Seashore, 1967; Katz & Kahn, 1978), and competing values models (Quinn & Rohrbaugh, 1983). Born partly out of the emerging themes in organization theory, such as natural, open, and rational systems (Scott, 1981), the role of strategic choice vs. environmental determinism (Child, 1972; Pfeffer & Salancik, 1978; Hannan & Freeman, 1975), and the human relations movement (Roethlisberger & Dickson, 1939), these models tried to capture the indicators or criteria of effectiveness. Unfortunately, these perspectives tend to gloss over social responsibility, especially regarding concerns that go beyond the issue of workforce satisfaction, and ignore measures of ecological health altogether.

The OE research stream was codified by two studies in the mid-1970s. Campbell (1977) generated a list of 30 variables representing "serious" indicators of effectiveness. Steers (1975) reviewed 17 effectiveness studies generating a list of 14 indicators that were used by at least 2 different research efforts (Table 1). Adaptability/flexibility was the topmost criterion mentioned in 10 of the 17 studies. Five studies cited productivity and job

Table 1. Traditional Criteria of Organization Effectiveness.

Source: Campbell (1977)	Source: Steers (1975)
• Overall effectiveness	• Adaptability (10)[a]
• Productivity	• Productivity (6)
• Efficiency	• Satisfaction (5)
• Profit	• Profitability (3)
• Product/Service quality	• Resource acquisition (3)
• Accidents	• Absence of strain (2)
• Growth	• Control over environment (2)
• Absenteeism	• Development (2)
• Turnover	• Efficiency (2)
• Job satisfaction	• Employee retention (2)
• Motivation	• Growth (2)
• Morale	• Integration (2)
• Control	• Open communications (2)
• Conflict/Cohesion	• Survival (2)
• Flexibility/adaptability	
• Planning and goal setting	
• Goal consensus	
• Internalization of organizational goals	
• Role and norm congruence	
• Managerial interpersonal skills	
• Managerial task skills	
• Information management and communication	
• Readiness	
• Utilization of environment	
• Evaluations by external entities	
• Stability	
• Value of human resources	
• Participation and shared influence	
• Training and development emphasis	
• Achievement emphasis	

[a]Frequency of use out of 17 empirical studies of organization effectiveness.

satisfaction. Given the popularity and power of the population ecology model (e.g., Hannan & Freeman, 1975), it is interesting that "survival" was on Steers' list but not Campbell's.[1]

Quinn and Rohrbaugh (1983) asked OE researchers to sort Campbell's criteria in an effort to determine whether there was an implicit OE theory in researchers' minds. They found three consistent dimensions related to structure, perspectives, and means/ends logics. Effective organizations were associated with structural preferences (centralized or decentralized) and decision-making perspectives (internal or external focus). Measures of effectiveness associated with a centralized orientation included control, stability, goal consensus, and role and norm congruence. Decentralized effectiveness measures included motivation, participation and shared influence, and flexibility/adaptation. Externally focused decision-making variables included evaluations by external entities, profitability, and utilization of the environment while internal measures were job satisfaction, morale, and turnover. There was, then, a strong contingency flavor. Effectiveness was a function of alignment between the organization and its environment or among the internal features of the organization itself (Lawrence & Lorsch, 1967; Galbraith, 2001).

In line with goal-oriented vs. systems models, some measures were more likely to serve as means (e.g., planning and goal setting) and others as ends (e.g., financial performance). The means–end dimension overlapped with the first two dimensions and, in fact, some variables were mentioned as both (Cameron, 1980), including growth, flexibility/adaptability, stability, quality, and job satisfaction.

Almost from its beginning, OE theory and research has faced serious criticism. Proponents of goal-oriented models were criticized over the objectivity of goals (actual vs. espoused goals) as well as their measurement (Yuchtman & Seashore, 1967). Proponents of a systems resource version of OE were criticized because different constituencies used different measures and there was no objective way of prioritizing them (Cameron, 1980; Pennings & Goodman, 1977; Zammuto, 1982). This led to the observation that managers attend to goals in a sequential manner (Cyert & March, 1992). In addition, Cameron and Whetten (1983) and others found that goals and measures of effectiveness shifted over time and in line with stages in the organization's life cycle. Finally, supposedly cumulative lists such as those of Campbell and Steers were criticized for containing seemingly contradictory measures, such as evaluations by external entities vs. morale and job satisfaction.

In reviewing the field, Lewin & Minton (1986) suggested that much of the criticism stemmed from no clear answer to the question, "what's the best measure of effectiveness?" The answer was always, "it depends," and Hitt (1988) worried that organizations were defaulting to traditional, short-term measures of effectiveness that mortgaged long-term performance. "If executives are using inappropriate measures of effectiveness, they may be making inaccurate decisions" (p. 29).[2] Miles (1980) labeled the whole stream of research an "effectiveness jungle," while Quinn and his colleagues (Quinn & Rohrbaugh, 1983; Quinn & Cameron, 1988) argued for a competing values approach. They saw effectiveness and organization culture as deriving from the reconciliation of the internal/external, people/results, and flexibility/stability conundrums.

Agility Models of Effectiveness

Building on traditional models of effectiveness, acknowledging the increased pace and complexity of change, and reconciling some of the conundrums and criticisms of the traditional stream, a different set of effectiveness models has emerged. Instead of trying to specify the criteria of effectiveness, agility models described the organization design features that are necessary to deliver on any of the various criteria proposed. These models warrant particular attention because of their newness and relevance to sustainability.

Organization agility occupies a middle ground between models of adaptability and planned change. It has been the subject of increasing research (Brown & Eisenhardt, 1997; Volberda, 1999; Haeckel, 1999; Doz & Kosonen, 2008; Beer, 2009) and several calls for a better understanding of its genesis and consequences (e.g., Rudis, 2006). For example, adaptability refers to the organization's capability to respond to changes in environmental demands. Organization evolution (Tushman & Romanelli, 1985), absorptive capacity (Zahra & George, 2002), and population ecology (Aldrich, 1979; Hannan & Freeman, 1975) describe how organizations interpret and enact (Weick, 1969) environmental change and translate those beliefs into organization action and transformation.

Theoretical work in organization adaptation helped to reconcile some conundrums. Stage models (e.g., Greiner, 1967) and punctuated equilibrium models (Tushman & Romanelli, 1985; Miller & Friesen, 1980) suggested that long-term organization effectiveness was a function of both the ability to converge on a given strategic orientation over relatively long periods (stability) and the ability to execute reorientations when significant internal or external events warranted such "transformations" (flexibility). Miller and Friesen (1980) operationalized stability as "continuity in the direction of change and transformation as reversals in the direction of change across a wide variety of organizational features." Data from Romanelli and Tushman (1994), Lant, Milliken, and Batra (1992), and Miller and Friesen (1980) empirically supported this pattern of organization change. Organization performance depended on long periods of relative stability where the organization could learn how best to operate a particular design.

Occasionally, the interplay of various internal and external forces resulted in a violent transformation.

Organization development (Cummings & Worley, 2009), planned change (Beckhard & Harris, 1977), and change management (Paton & McCalman, 2000; Hayes, 2002; Burnes, 2004) all address the activities involved in intentionally moving an organization or subsystem from one state to another. Beckhard and Harris (1977), for example, describe the activities associated with defining the current state, the future state, and the action planning and intervention processes associated with the transition. Models of planned change are not effectiveness models per se. Instead, they argue that in the face of complex and uncertain environmental changes, effective organizations are able to make the transition from one relatively stable state to another because they can plan and execute change as well as sense and respond to it.

While much work has been done on the various pieces of organizational agility, there has not been a cohesive and integrated statement of agile organization design principles. For example, Doz and Kosonen (2008) examined the issues of flexible and dynamic strategy, Hatch and Schultz (2002) explored how organization identities can facilitate or hinder organization change, and Galbraith (2001) and Tushman and O'Reilly (1996) described how reconfigurable and ambidextrous structures can operate. Drawing on these various threads of research and practice, Lawler and Worley (2006) presented an integrated and comprehensive view of organization agility. The basic features of the B2C model are the three core processes of strategizing, organizing, and creating value.

Strategizing: Crafting a Series of Momentary Advantages

Strategizing is the first core process in a B2C organization. It describes how an organization achieves and maintains "proximity," a concept that refers to how "close" an organization's outputs are to the demands of its environment. As environments shift and change, the organization's responses must shift and change (Haeckel, 1999; Aldrich, 1999). Instead of pursuing a single sustainable advantage as supported by the competitive strategy school (Porter, 1980) a B2C organization seeks a *series* of momentary advantages. The other two core processes – creating value and designing – are what allow the organization to capture value from new advantages.

Economic Logic. The strategizing process in agile organizations relies on a fundamentally different economic logic than exists in a traditional organization. Whereas traditional organizations leverage stability and sustainable competitive advantages to drive performance (e.g., economies of scope and scale or static entry barriers), agile organizations believe that long-term performance derives from cumulative rent appropriation in each momentary advantage it pursues. In other words, the ability to change drives performance because no single advantage lasts long enough to warrant the investment.

Momentary advantages have a "hit and run" or "entry and exit" logic with roots in contestability theory (Bailey & Baumol, 1984; Levine, 1987). According to contestability theory,[3] a credible threat of entry by other organizations is enough to induce firms in a market to behave competitively. If a market can be entered (and exited) easily, incumbent organizations will keep their prices at the lowest levels at which profit is possible lest they have to defend their market share from newcomers. From the strategy perspective, when an opportunity to profitably offer new or existing products/services appears, the agile organization will do so. For example, Garmin, the leading global positioning satellite firm, recently entered the mobile telephone market, adapting their handheld GPS units. Lured by the profit potential in this market and the relatively low mobility barriers they face, Garmin is attempting to carve out a niche position leveraging their GPS applications. Should they fail in their attempt, they can easily exit the market and retreat into their traditionally profitable GPS business. However, unlike traditional firms – where this same logic can apply – the organization's change capability (see below) allows the firm to say "yes" often and quickly.

Both competitive and contestable markets are dynamic. However, profit making according to industrial organization theory relies on taking advantage of relatively stable structural and market imperfections to achieve sustainable advantage (Porter, 1980). The nature of these imperfections changes when knowledge becomes the source of advantage – entry and exit barriers are largely reduced and firms have access to scale efficiencies that are independent of size and physical assets. There are fewer sunk costs, and markets are more "contestable" in that a firm can enter and exit at costs that do not exceed revenue and meet the opportunity cost of capital requirements.

Contrary to a traditionally organized firm, where stability leads to effectiveness through efficiency, alignment, and growth, an agile organization expects change to lead to effectiveness through temporary advantages and the speed and elegance with which it orchestrates change. This economic logic represents a significant shift in the fundamental drivers of organization design principles.

Strong Future Focus. To achieve and maintain proximity, B2C organizations have the ability to consider potential alternative futures and create a variety of short- and long-term scenarios (Schwartz, 1991; Schoemaker, 1995). There is no assumption that the B2C organization can predict the future, only that it consciously develops and applies the capability to look at and play with the future. As a result, it is much less surprised by external events, and when change occurs, its conversations about what might happen have created more options with which to respond. Choosing which opportunities to pursue (or not) is still largely a matter of judgment (Tichy & Bennis, 2007). Developing scenarios is easier for B2C organizations because their members are in close contact with the external environment and are able to identify trends. In addition, the flexibility created by the change capability of B2C organizations gives them an advantage in being able to recover from bad choices.

Robust Strategies. Success in a range of possible future environments requires B2C organizations to seek a *robust* strategy that can deliver results under varying environmental conditions. Porter's (1980) generic strategies – differentiation and low cost – are examples of robust strategies because they can achieve above industry-average returns even as any of the forces of industry structure intensify.[4]

Robust strategies have two major components: identity and intent. The organization's identity is what keeps the organization from being whipsawed by environmental demands for change. It is an integration of the organization's internal culture and external brand, image, and reputation, and represents a long-term value proposition for the organization. It is also a central concept in the B2C approach because it is the most stable element (Hatch & Schultz, 2002; Lawler & Worley, 2006). Like an individual's personality, an organization's identity is a defining characteristic that changes very slowly, if at all.

Organizations that are built to change have a clear sense of who they are and what they stand for, and this helps guide what they pursue. In this sense, identity is very much in line with the core values concept that Collins and Porras discuss in *Built to Last* (1994) but differs in its reconciliation with image, brand, and reputation. When organizations know their identity, they are less likely to propose adjustments to strategic intent that will not be supported by the organization's culture or are not in line with its brand image. When new ideas bubble up that honor identity, they are easily supported and implemented. As the new CEO of American Express, Harvey Golub spent a lot of time developing future leaders in the organization by asking them, "Does that strategy sound like 'American Express?'" He was teaching his managers to leverage the power of identity and propose strategies that would be understood, at a gut level, by the people who would implement them.

When B2C organizations say they are changing their strategy, they are not referring to their identity but to their intent. A strategic intent is a short- to medium-term statement of how the organization will win in the marketplace. In B2C organizations, strategic intent is operationalized by tinkering with its breadth, aggressiveness, and differentiation (Hambrick & Frederickson, 2005; Carroll & Hannan, 1995). These three dimensions provide flexibility in describing the content of change in an organization's strategy. Breadth refers to the range of products and services offered, the number of different markets served, the scope of the distribution network, or the different types of technologies that represent the organization's core competencies. Aggressiveness describes the amount of urgency, enthusiasm, and resources the organization throws behind the communication, marketing, and execution of its strategy and with which it pursues advantages. Finally, differentiation describes the product and service features that distinguish the organization's offerings from competitors, including price, quality, warranty, after-sale support, and other characteristics.

Thus, for any set of product/service features, an organization can have a broad or narrow product line and can be relatively aggressive or passive in its approach. For example, WD40 relies on its difficult-to-imitate product features and strong brand reputation for differentiation, but is narrow in breadth and relatively passive in its market approach. Disney, however, leverages its strong brand across a broad range of products, services, and markets in a relatively aggressive manner. Importantly, these elements can be changed quickly to proactively create a momentary advantage or reactively protect an existing advantage. Whereas identity defines the long-term value proposition that exists between the firm and its environment, intent defines how momentary advantages will be monetized. When with a combined strong future focus, they give an organization the elements of a flexible strategy that can maintain proximity with environmental demands over time.

Creating Value: Leveraging Learning and Leadership

The second core process, creating value, is concerned with how organizational competencies and capabilities support the organization's strategy, how those capabilities evolve over time, and how leadership supports them (Barney, 1991; Peteraf, 1993; Zollo & Winter, 2001). In keeping with the economic logic of an agile firm, B2C firms need to be as effective in executing their current strategic intent as they are in executing the transition to the next competitive advantage. Their operational competencies and capabilities are not the drivers of long-term performance per se, whereas these are the key drivers of short-term performance. What creates value and drives long-term performance over a series of momentary advantages is the ability to shift from one advantage to another.

The key to B2C thinking is the integration of organizational competencies and capabilities with learning. Instead of "What do we do well?" a B2C firm asks, "What do we need to learn?", "How do our capabilities need to evolve?", "What new capabilities do we need to develop?" and "What do we need to do better so that we can add value in the future?" The primary creating value processes are the orchestration and learning capabilities of the organization (Beer & Eisenstat, 1996; Worley & Lawler, 2009; Zollo & Winter, 2001; Senge, 2006; Argyris & Schon, 1996). They deliver on short-term objectives, and map out and execute the changes necessary to move from one strategic intent (constellation of breadth, aggressiveness, and differentiation) to another. A B2C firm effectively balances and trades off resource allocations for present performance against investments that will create future fitness, what Brown and Eisenhardt (1998) called "low cost probes." These trade-offs are made as organizations think through a series of "make or buy" decisions to add, modify, or delete elements in their portfolio of capabilities.

The second element in the creating value process is shared leadership or what Mark Hurd, the CEO of Hewlett-Packard, has described as "leadership as a team sport." Viewing CEOs at the helm of a big ship setting direction and ordering people around is the wrong metaphor (Lawler, 2008). A better analogy is to think of the corporation as a community of people spread over miles of hills, fields, and forests. Agile, B2C organizations disperse competent leaders across the countryside, all connected by a shared understanding of identity and purpose.

Shared leadership has four advantages. First, it effectively substitutes for hierarchy and supports the structural features described below. Spreading knowledge and power across many people allows an organization to process and respond to information quickly without requiring a tremendous amount of top-down direction. Second, it builds a deep cadre of leadership talent. By involving everyone in strategizing and orchestration activities, an organization can develop the leadership and management skills of many employees. Third, it leads to people below the executive level seeing important trends that call for corporate change. Finally, and most importantly, shared leadership supports orchestration. In any change effort, there is typically more to do than a single leader or a few leaders can handle. Change efforts that are led by a single hero leader are fragile entities; if that individual falters, is overwhelmed with all there is to do, or leaves, the change effort stalls. With shared leadership, competent others are available to keep the momentum going.

Designing: Implementing Strategic Intent

Designing is the third core process and the most flexible. B2C organizations are defined by their maximum surface area structures, transparent information and decision-making processes, and flexible talent and reward systems. Together, they capture value from the current competitive advantage and support orchestration over time. The designing process has four features that support the implementation and reimplementation of a robust strategy as a continuous and normal process.

First, B2C organizations adopt structures that maximize the "surface area" of the firm by connecting as many employees as possible with the external environment. Organizations that accomplish this increase the external focus of their members; bring in critical information about trends, opportunities, and issues; support the creation of a strong future focus; and prevent people from becoming ossified in their roles. As many employees as possible should be near to or have direct contact with regulators, suppliers, the local community, watchdog groups and, most importantly, customers (and potential customers). When the time comes to alter the organization, everyone moves together based on a common understanding and felt need for the change.

A variety of companies have increased their surface area by adopting front-back, process-based, ambidextrous, or network structures that increase the centrality of customer and other external demands (Galbraith, 2005; O'Reilly, Harreld, & Tushman, 2009). Other companies have maximized their surface area by deploying multiple independent business units, outsourcing, and matrix relationships. For instance, Berkshire Hathaway, with its wide range of autonomous business units faces multiple markets and can adjust its corporate portfolio relatively easily without the angst and grief associated with traditional downsizings and resizings of integrated divisions. Similarly, W.L. Gore's small, interrelated divisions design ensures that each unit is maximally exposed to its relevant market. Internal matrix relationships can also increase an organization's surface area because, when employees from different functions or programs interact, they often must deal with a variety of alternative market perspectives.

Second, B2C organizations adopt transparent information systems and decision-making processes. Performance-based information systems are a particularly effective way to motivate and empower employees in a B2C organization because they facilitate moving decision making to wherever decisions can best be made and implemented. A good example is mySiebel, a personalized information system created by Siebel Systems before its acquisition by Oracle. Each employee could log onto mySiebel and gain access to corporate, market, and competitor information; data on current projects; and quarterly objectives for any individual in the organization (including Tom Siebel, the CEO). This widely available information allowed everyone throughout the organization to make customer-related decisions with up-to-the-minute data, and it helped people to align their individual behaviors with corporate objectives. The system facilitated a timely and inclusive goal-setting, performance-review, and reward process.

Third, B2C organizations adopt flexible talent management and reward systems. For example, B2C organizations can adopt either "commitment to development" or "travel light" talent management strategies (Lawler, 2008). In the commitment to development approach, B2C organizations are keen to recruit individuals who are quick learners and like change; encourage people to find out what needs to be done instead of telling them what their "job" is; and use frequent goal-setting reviews help establish what individuals and teams are expected to accomplish in the near future. Commitment to development organizations have an employment contract that states change is expected and support for change is a condition of long-term employment. In the travel light approach, the employment deal achieves flexibility by clearly articulating that the hiring and laying off employees happens according to a work/talent availability and performance scenario that is constantly changing.

B2C organizations utilize a variety of reward practices, including bonuses, stock, and "person-based pay," that encourage both current performance and change. Bonus systems are used as motivators during periods of change by establishing a clear line of sight between change and rewards. Individual plans that offer relatively large bonuses provide powerful incentives for employees to perform well and to alter their individual behaviors when a shift in strategic intent calls for it. Group and business-unit bonuses are helpful in focusing team performance and creating a shared need for change.

In comparison to bonuses, stock plans are less effective in motivating change because the line-of-sight between the desired behavior and reward is less clear. But broad-based stock ownership can provide executives with a platform on which to stand and talk about the advantages of change.

When only senior managers have stock options, employees cannot be faulted for thinking, "Why should I listen to calls for change that only benefit those at the top?" When they own stock there is a reason for them to change.

Finally, B2C organizations shift the basis of pay from the job (and seniority) to the individual (and what he or she can do). In work environments that call for changing task assignments and the need to develop new skills and competencies, paying the person is a much more effective approach, particularly when it comes to retaining the right people. Instead of the organization rewarding people for expanding their jobs or for moving up the hierarchy, it recognizes them for increasing their skills and for developing themselves. This reinforces a culture that values growth and personal development; the result is a highly talented workforce that is receptive to change.

Conclusions

The newer OE models reconcile some of the contradictions in the earlier ones, but create others. For example, punctuated equilibrium models showed how both stability and change could contribute to effectiveness but the predominance of convergence and stability retarded the development of agility-oriented organization models (e.g., complexity-related organization models remain largely underdeveloped) and the evaluation of change (Lacey & Tompkins, 2007). Agile organizations, in contrast, achieve success through their ability to create or react to opportunities and string together a series of momentary advantages that keep them proximate with environmental demands over time. The organization's structure, capabilities, and processes are designed to support this logic. However, all of these models continue to support relatively narrow effectiveness measures, such as financial performance, cost, and satisfaction. In fact, ecological outcomes are not mentioned at all, and social issues are only given slight mention if we include stakeholder satisfaction and external evaluations in this category.

Economic Models of Effectiveness

A second class of effectiveness models – economic models – also focus primarily on financial sustainability in profit-seeking firms, and provide another important perspective on the concept of effectiveness. For our purposes, the most relevant model of economic effectiveness is the structure-conduct-performance model (Bain, 1968; Scherer, 1980). It draws on concepts from traditional microeconomics and the underlying theory of industrial organization. Industrial organization economics – the foundational discipline for competitive strategy (e.g., Porter, 1980) – proposes that an economic system's performance can be assessed according to efficiency, innovation, employment, and risk/return criteria (Scherer, 1980). That is, rather than describing how an organization should be designed, economic models specify the criteria by which organization effectiveness should be judged, including:

a. Efficiency: Decisions as to what, how much, and how to produce should be efficient in two respects – scarce resources should not be wasted outright and production decisions should be responsive qualitatively and quantitatively to consumer demands.
b. Innovation: The operations of producers should be progressive, taking advantage of opportunities opened up by science and technology to increase output per unit of input and to provide consumers with superior new products, in both ways contributing to the long-run growth of real income per capita.
c. Employment: The operations of producers should facilitate stable, full employment of resources, especially human resources.
d. Risk/Return: The distribution of income should be equitable…implying that producers do not secure rewards far in excess of what is needed to call forth the amount of services supplied (Scherer, 1980, pp. 5–6).

The efficiency criterion is strongly represented in traditional organizational models of effectiveness. That is, resources and capital, such as land, natural resources, people, and cash, are assumed to be scarce, and an important criterion of systems effectiveness is the extent to which they are used productively to maximize profit for individuals, firms, and benefit the social system as a whole. The innovation criterion is typically operationalized in terms of the extent to which new products/services are being developed and introduced over time, with science and technology being key drivers. Christensen (1997) and Chesbrough (2007), for example, have recently explored the shifting patterns of innovation activity whereas Rogers' (2003) studies of innovation diffusion have been a staple in organization research for decades. The third criterion is the extent to which human capital is fully employed. "Full" employment has at least two connotations, including the *number* of people employed and the *quality of work life* enjoyed by employees, and this is the most socially relevant of the four criteria. The fourth criterion is the risk/return principle and suggests that people or firms who take the biggest risks and succeed should be allocated the biggest returns. This entrepreneurial criterion supports the innovation criterion.

When environments are relatively stable, markets are competitive, and resources are allowed to operate freely, the economic model of effectiveness works well, including the pursuit of social and even ecological sustainability (Scherer, 1980). Drawing on concepts from traditional microeconomics, theories of perfect competition, and the dynamic interactions of producers, suppliers, buyers, and technologies, economists can easily address how long-run sustainability in economic, social, and ecological outcomes should be achieved (Reisman, 1996). For example, sustainability should enter into effectiveness decisions through either resource scarcity or consumer demands to pursue efficiency or full-employment criteria. Dwindling supplies of coal and oil should shift input costs up and drive the search for alternative fuels. Similarly, consumer demand for more ecologically friendly or socially relevant outputs should incent organizations to shift their products/services.

However, various market conditions (e.g., asymmetric information flows, mobility barriers, government tax policies) and market failures (e.g., decreasing marginal costs, unaccounted for environmental and social externalities, sticky assets) can warp those criteria. For example, current calculations of profit and loss do not fully recognize environmental externalities and social costs. To be sure, organizations have had to attend to these costs because of non-governmental organizations (NGOs), regulatory action, and government policy, but their full cost is not generally accounted for and decision-making processes are therefore not optimized across all the dimensions of sustainability. Moreover, most organizations resist such efforts by colluding with the market; they note that such cost recognition will almost certainly increase prices, and they can rightfully claim that despite the increasing attention to green products and social issues, many consumers are not yet willing to pay extra for such goods and services. In addition, although the model supports a social sustainability perspective in that the risk/return criterion explicitly suggests that such rewards should not be "far in excess," the concern over CEO pay and the gap between the "haves and the have nots" suggest that the definition of excess has shifted.

The perspective of the economic model is definitely broad. It is concerned with the performance of the individual firm as well as the quality of social fabric in which the firm exists. But the race toward globalization has very few mechanisms in place that balance decisions regarding financial, social, and ecological outcomes (Friedman, 2007; Perkins, 2005; Chua, 2004; Korten, 1995; Korten, 2007). Hawken and his colleagues have noted that a variety of governmental policies, tax incentives, organizational practices, and reward systems actually promote the irrational use of natural capital (Hawken, Lovins, & Lovins, 2008). As a result, short-term economic criteria frequently become prepotent over long-term social and ecological criteria.

Sustainability Models of Effectiveness

Sustainability models are a third type of organizational effectiveness model that have emerged partly because the other models systematically ignore the ecological environment and partly because markets have not addressed critical externalities. As Hawken et al. (2008) argue, most organizational balance sheets account for the resources (e.g., oil, gas, minerals) provided by the ecology but do not account for the services provided by the ecosystem (e.g., generating and cleaning the air, water, and habitat). Sustainability models of organizational effectiveness tend to be unidimensional – focused on meeting ecological criteria of effectiveness – although they are quick to point out the long-run economic advantages of their perspective (Hawken et al., 2008).

Sustainability models overlap to a great degree with models of corporate social responsibility in that there is a conscious integration of firm-level decision making with larger social and environmental issues. Three of the more common sustainability frameworks – the CERES Principles (Cogan, 2006), the Natural Step (Nattrass & Altomare, 1999; Robert, 2008), and Natural Capitalism (Hawken et al., 2008) – are shown in Table 2. Each model has a slightly different purpose.

The CERES Principles were born from efforts to encourage corporations to report on their carbon footprint and to do so in a standardized way. The CERES organization works with corporations to comply with the principles and makes changes in line with the principles.

The Natural Step (TNS) begins with the premise that current economic models based on the assumption of growth cannot reconcile the increasing demand for and decreasing supply of finite and fundamental natural resources. The sooner this incompatibility is recognized and addressed, the larger the number of available and socially acceptable solutions.

Finally, Natural Capitalism defines sustainability in terms of services or products competing in the marketplace because they deliver goods and services that reduce energy consumption, pollution, and other forms of environmental damage. In this framework, sustainability is an economic state where the demands placed upon the environment by people and

Table 2. A Comparison of Sustainability Models.

Dimension	CERES Principles	The Natural Step	Natural Capitalism
Purpose of the framework	Standardized reporting	Guide to strategizing	Rectifying economic and ecological ends
Principles	• Protection of the biosphere • Sustainable use of natural resources • Reduction and disposal of wastes • Energy conservation • Risk reduction • Safe products and services • Environmental restoration • Informing the public • Management commitment • Audits and reports	(1) Substances from within the earth must not systematically increase in the ecosphere (2) Substances produced by society must not systematically increase in the ecosphere (3) The physical ability of nature to renew itself must not be diminished (4) The basic human needs of all people need to be met with fairness and efficiency	• Dramatically increase the productivity of natural resources • Shift to biologically inspired production models • Move to a solutions-based business model • Reinvest in natural capital

commerce can be met without reducing the capacity of the environment to provide for future generations.

Like the economic models of effectiveness, sustainability models tend to describe the criteria of effectiveness and are not organizational models per se. The dimensions or principles listed in the three models are very similar. All three models have a clear and strong focus on protecting and restoring the natural ecology. The CERES Principles focus on protection of the biosphere, reduction of waste disposal, and environmental restoration. TNS addresses the rate of resource extraction and the ability of the environment to renew itself, and Natural Capitalism recommends reinvestment in natural capital. Similarly, all models recognize that economics should play a role in sustainability. The CERES Principles call for safe products and services, TNS recognizes that meeting diverse human needs will require trade-offs in fairness and efficiency, and Natural Capitalism calls for shifts in the business models to make these trade-offs explicit. Finally, all three models address issues of productivity by referring it to conservation and sustainable use of natural resources, transformation processes that increase nonnatural substances into the ecosphere, and biologically inspired production models. All three sustainability models report case studies of organizations adopting their principles and improving their sustainability, but there have not been any large-scale evaluation efforts of these models.

The CERES model, owing to its purpose as a standard for organizations, is unique in calling out of organization system requirements such as management commitment, public reporting, and audit processes. TNS and Natural Capitalism both acknowledge the need for changes in organization design and financial systems, but are relatively silent on the specifics. Natural Capitalism, for example, is concerned that tax policies and organization reward systems may tacitly or explicitly reward organization members for decisions that misuse natural capital but does not offer alternatives.

Almost by definition, sustainability models have focused on ecological issues in an attempt to balance the perspectives in other OE models. To their credit, they have not ignored the economic implications of their perspectives. However, they spend very little time and effort spelling out the organizational implications (Worley et al., 2009).

OE Models: Conclusions

Traditional OE models highlight measures related to financial performance, productivity, employee satisfaction, and customer loyalty but systematically (although probably unconsciously) ignore the criterion related to sustainability. Economic models can explain multistakeholder sustainability in theory, but in the presence of market failures are unable to generate practical results. Sustainability models have a singular focus on ecological outcomes but oddly ignore social issues in an effort to be seen as economically palatable and have little in the way of organizational solutions to support their recommendations.

There are two important implications of this review. First, much of the organizational effectiveness theorizing and all of the economic and sustainability effectiveness models focus on the output criteria of effectiveness. That is, how is one to know if an organization is effective or not? Second, the organizational effectiveness perspectives taken together support the conclusion that the environmental demands an organization must address no longer consist of just maximizing profits or pleasing demanding customers or focusing on being a great place to work or for that matter doing all three. Organizations must now give equal attention to all of these demands in addition to ever changing community concerns, social obligations, and ecological realities. All told, the clear message looking across these models is that organizations are increasingly expected to satisfy all three classes of demands – economic, social, and ecological – in what is becoming known as the "triple bottom line" (Elkington, 1994).

The interaction of the complex demands organizations face means that the pace of change will continue to increase. For example, when an organization is faced with increasing pressure for better economic performance from the financial markets and for increasing ecological performance from the environmental NGOs watching the industry, it has to possess the capability to identify potentially competing goals, make important trade-offs in allocating resources, and conduct multiple, integrated change efforts quickly to achieve them.

No single model seems to provide the necessary guidance to organizations, and there is a clear need for creation, revision, and integration. Organization effectiveness criteria in the future will require a clearer modeling of the demands so that organization designers can specify appropriate levels of achievement as well as the changes necessary to reach them. In addition, managers and executives will need to plan their strategies, structures, and process designs against a revised model of organization design that acknowledges multiple stakeholder demands. To address the issue of an integrated criteria set, we propose the "responsible progress" framework (Worley & McCloskey, 2006).

INTEGRATING OE PERSPECTIVES: THE RESPONSIBLE PROGRESS FRAMEWORK

Responsible progress is an integration and relabeling of the organizational, economic, and sustainability frameworks. Our labeling of the framework – responsible progress – is derived from the concern that definitions of sustainability have been overly associated with the ecological perspective (World Commission on Environment and Development, 1987; Docherty, Kira, & Shani, 2009) and subsequent treatments have show more emphasis on this dimensions than social or economic sustainability. A recent TV ad demonstrates the point. A middle manager is presenting a "sustainability" strategy to a dour set of executives only interested in the "bottom line." Their attacks on the plan are cynical and hostile (e.g., "we aren't tree huggers") until the manager says that the plan will cut energy costs by 40%. The black and white commercial turns to color, voices sing, and the executives dance. The point is clear: executives are very interested in "sustainability" if the economic bottom line is the first among equals in the triple bottom line.

The integration and relabeling of these frameworks therefore leans heavily on the economic model as a starting point. By grounding the responsible progress framework in traditional economic thought, it is hoped that traction can be gained in terms of social and ecological outcomes as well as signaling the organization design features that are needed. Most attempts at describing the triple bottom line, however, have not provided any theoretical mechanism for balancing these criteria. The responsible progress model does this.

The responsible progress prescription calls for businesses, governments, NGOs, and other stakeholders to jointly optimize economic development, technological innovation, cultural diversity, and ecological health to achieve sustainable global effectiveness (Table 3). Responsible progress is influenced by the joint optimization principle from sociotechnical systems theory and recognizes that each of the elements alone is insufficient to produce responsible progress; the pursuit of each element's goal has to be achieved within the bounds of the other three (Cummings & Srivastva, 1977). For example, Murrell (2004) proposed that people be treated as ends and that organizations should drive for performance as an important outcome, address the tension between trying to achieve both people and performance outcomes, and be designed for sustainability. Similarly, a responsible progress policy was influenced by the "triple bottom line" that focused on the economic, social, and ecological value added or destroyed by governments, organizations, and individuals. The triple bottom line, however, is overly focused on outputs (ends) whereas responsible progress suggests that

Table 3. Dimensions of Responsible Progress.

Dimension of Responsible Progress	Definition and Boundary
Technological innovation	• New and better ideas for progress should be generated • Guided by diversity, development, and sustainability
Economic development	• Economic systems should be productive and effective • Balanced by innovation, diversity, and sustainability
Cultural diversity	• Human and cultural dignity are valued in their own right • Supported by innovation, development, and sustainability
Ecological sustainability	• The ecology should have standing in all decisions • Founded on innovation, development, and diversity

each element is both a means and an end (Quinn & Rohrbaugh, 1983). We present a brief description of each element below and propose these as *the* design challenge for today's organizations.

Technological Innovation

Technological innovation is an important element in all models of effectiveness and supports the goal of new and better ideas for progress. It is the economic power train of responsible progress and is focused by the principles of ecological health and cultural diversity. Technological innovation as used here differs from its use in the economic model. First, without the ecological health and cultural diversity goals in the original model, the guideposts for technological innovation are both too narrow (focused on financial performance) and too broad (no explicit constraint to social and ecological impact).

Investment decisions prior to the responsible progress criteria often have favored incremental innovations with higher likelihoods of generating incremental profits over riskier innovations with great potential (Mensch, 1979). Too often, these incremental investments are easier to justify on a cost/benefit basis because they are associated with existing fossil fuel-based paradigms, unconsciously increase commitments to an oil-based economic model, and do not have to fully account for social and ecological externalities. The automobile industry's commitment to SUVs serve as a case in point. They were clearly revenue positive but diverted attention away from electric, hybrid, and fuel cell development.

Often, traditional change implementation processes make the false assumption that people and cultures are more similar than different; and that diffusion is both easy and desirable. For example, many US high-technology manufacturers and software developers have tried to extend their fast-paced and confrontation-oriented operational practices to their Asian subsidiaries (Hughes, 2009). The operational progress that is achieved is often fleeting and in a direction that unconsciously supports cultural homogenization. Hughes found that the skills employees developed at work were carried over into personal and social arenas where they hurt the long-standing social order.

In contrast, the responsible progress criteria encourage organizations to adopt a more specific set of guidelines when choosing technologies, products, and services to support, pursue, develop, and deploy. Organizations should recognize and reward managers and employees who identify and develop clean technologies, substitute clean technology for fossil fuel-based business models, and leverage technology to preserve cultural diversity. The NGO community has led the way in creating a civil society, developing a cadre of social entrepreneurs, and promoting technologies of empowerment (Cooperrider & Dutton, 1999; Bornstein, 2004). The for-profit community could learn from their example, although the short-term view of most financial markets and the short tenures of many senior managers are important constraints to acknowledge and address.

Economic Success

The economic success criterion integrates the efficiency criterion with the full employment criterion from the economic model of effectiveness. Both organization and economic models of effectiveness overstate the value of efficiency and predictability as indicators of and contributors to effectiveness. Adam Smith's original definition of efficiency as specialization in task performance meant that work could be performed at high levels of reliability and effectiveness. The resulting machine metaphor of efficiency became a staple in organization theory (Morgan, 1997).

In modern times, efficiency and predictability have had a prominent place in management thinking. Weber noted, "from a purely technical point of view, a bureaucracy is capable of attaining the highest degree of efficiency.... It is superior to any other form in precision, in stability, in the stringency of its discipline, and in its reliability" (Rheinstein, 1968, p. 223). In their classic book *The Social Psychology of Organizations*, Katz and Kahn (1978, p. 41) note, "one can define the core problem of any social system as reducing the variability and instability of human actions to uniform and dependable patterns." Toward that end, organizations have spent millions of dollars implementing six sigma, lean, reengineering, and other improvement programs in an effort to be more efficient and to get their processes "under control." The financial markets, shareholders, and customers also base their judgments of effectiveness on the expectation that organizations will deliver on their forecasts. The continued popularity of process improvement programs provides ample evidence of the consuming desire for predictability and efficiency as a means of producing stability and high levels of performance.

Efficiency and predictability have not turned out to be the strategic weapons that were originally envisioned. For example, of the 16 Malcolm Baldrige quality award recipients between 1994 and 2003, only one outperformed the S&P 500 during that time period. These organizations showed millions of dollars of savings through their continuous improvement effort, but did not post commensurate increases in profits. In fast changing environments, an overzealous pursuit of efficiency slows change and threatens long-term effectiveness (Van Alstyne, 1997). Efficiency and predictability abhor variation, which is essential for innovation and adaptation. The efficiency-obsessed organization often mortgages sustainability for current performance.

The economic success criterion supports the belief that organizations, governments, and societies should operate effectively and provide employment guided by the principles of cultural diversity and ecological health. Whereas the technological innovation plank is the economic driver of responsible progress, the economic development plank recognizes that firms, NGOs, and governments should operate where revenues/benefits exceed expenses/costs. Technological innovations are deployed to create effective organizations, productive countries, and a robust global economy.

However, the economic success criterion challenges the traditional definitions and measures of effectiveness with respect to growth. To understand this perspective we must first differentiate between growth as a goal and growth as a strategy. Growth, for example, can be a strategy (a way or means) of achieving employee satisfaction by providing more career paths and opportunities for advancement. As a goal, growth in profit or other financial measures is almost the sine qua non of effectiveness. At some level, any strategy is being adopted because of its potential to support growth. We are more concerned here about growth as a goal.

In addition, we need to differentiate between aggressive growth that is considerably above industry average and a rate of growth that matches natural levels. Overall population increases, changes in technology, and shifts in the definition of "quality of life" all support a natural level of growth in organizations, industries, and economies. For example, globally, the growth rate of the human population in 2007 was 1.19% per annum. In contrast, the average annual GDP growth rate was about 3.3% between 1990 and 2006 according to IMF's World Economic Outlook database.

Economists and social scientists agree that while some growth improves the quality of life, there is a rate of growth that obstructs sustainable living (Beddoe et al., 2009). Despite these markers, many organizations publicly pursue growth goals that far exceed this natural level or the growth rate of their industries.

The economic success criterion recommends that revenue growth goals be consistent with natural market evolutions; profit growth goals need to be aligned with competitor and capability realities; and value added goals need to be consistent with returns on living capital. The consequences of overly aggressive goals, big hairy audacious goals (BHAGs), and stretch goals are a cycle of boom and bust – not inconsistent with the punctuated equilibrium model – that traditionally designed organizations are ill-equipped to handle and that utilize resources disproportionately to the earth's ability to generate them. As described by punctuated equilibrium theory, growth is one of the reasons organizations build up pressure and commitment to the status quo. Growth results in a certain way of doing things that is rewarded and reinforced.

When individuals are focused on achieving specific tasks, they tend to misread or ignore signals that suggest the need for change (Simons & Chabris, 1999; Taleb, 2007). Absent perceptive employees who stay in touch with environmental change, the momentum of growth and the consequences of tighter alignment, more efficiency, and more predictability encourage organizations to continue the same practices well after they lose their ability to contribute to effectiveness. In response, organizations commit more resources to the existing strategy and continue to do so long after their recipe for success is no longer useful. This type of disproportionate reaction is more than the market (boom) can support which leads to the need for a retrenchment/downsizing and transformation (bust) which leads to the need for a turnaround (prelude to the next boom). The inevitable outcome from a period of overly aggressive growth is a period of retrenchment.

We are not saying growth is bad. Far from it. For example, Align Technologies' "invisible" orthodontics product is disruptive to the traditional concept of realigning teeth with metal braces. Success requires aggressive growth to establish legitimacy and market share, but to do so without a eye on the future will commit the organization to a strategy and design that cannot be sustained, and the violent transformation into maturity without the requisite change capabilities will likely consume the profits generated during growth. Thus, periods of convergence and stability and the pursuit of effectiveness are not inconsistent with growth. However, we are saying that a singular focus on aggressive growth will not lead to responsible progress. Starbuck's recent history of overly aggressive growth in the number of stores and the revenue/store clearly demonstrates this nonsustainable pattern.

Ecological Health

Ecological health supports the goal of living within the environment's ability to support life over the long run and contribute to cultural diversity and economic development. It is a link pin value in the responsible progress framework and suggests that business strategies built around the productive use of natural resources can solve environmental problems at a profit (Hawken et al., 2008). The principles and propositions of TNS and Natural Capitalism apply here and now have the support of a framework beyond the simple pursuit of ecological health. Recognizing and addressing the achievement of economic, social, and ecological outcomes as part of the responsible progress criteria creates a larger number of available and socially acceptable solutions (Nattrass & Altomare, 1999).

For example, organizations, driven by social pressures, a set of internal cultural values, or enlightened economic thinking, are beginning the process of understanding how their operations impact the natural environment. The largest single framework is the concept of a "carbon footprint." Organizations as diverse as UPS, DaVita, Northrop Grumman, and the Gap are developing metrics and processes for understanding how a variety of activities and assets, including office buildings, commuting patterns, air travel, supply chain operations and externalities, and production facilities, are depleting the ecology and contributing to global warming.

This work must continue, but it is not enough to support responsible progress. Organizations must find ways to change their operations to not only achieve appropriate levels of economic success but to do so in ways that are ecologically and socially healthy. This is no small feat. A 2008 sustainability conference sponsored by USC's Center for Effective Organizations, attended by more than 20 organizations, found that most firms have little knowledge and even fewer frameworks and experience with organization designs and strategy that can produce all three outcomes of the triple bottom line.

Cultural Diversity

We use the term cultural diversity to reflect not only a global and systemic perspective of human and cultural dignity but an important long-term adaptability strategy. Friedman's *The World is Flat* (2007) and his more recent *Hot, Flat and Crowded* (2009) have gone well beyond the descriptions of globalization that characterized his *Lexus and the Olive Tree* (2000). Friedman and others (Korten, 1995 , 2007; Sen, 2000) are now advocating a more values-driven and conscious set of practices. Key among the values is an appreciation of the cultural diversity that exists and a desire to preserve that diversity because of its contributions to the quality of life.

In this sense, we are not referring to cultural diversity programs within organizations that promote more inclusive views of the workforce and an appreciation of how cultural differences can contribute to one's fulfillment. These are good and positive approaches, but they are shortsighted from a responsible progress perspective. Cultural diversity cannot be an end – a program to be implemented, a quota to be met, or a personal approach to life – it must be seen as a strategy or means to achieve a much broader and more relevant purpose. In particular, cultural diversity should be leveraged to drive technical and managerial innovation. For example, Prahalad's (2006) bottom of the pyramid approach is an important business model innovation driven by an appreciation of different economic and cultural contexts.

Prahalad's arguments suggest that cultural diversity and economic differences should be the source of innovation rather than a constraint to the expansion and implementation of traditional business models. Traditional models of economic growth and globalization have consciously or unconsciously sought predictability, efficiency, and control over operations through standardization. Standardized operating procedures and technological platforms are difficult to optimize within cultural norms that vary across global subsidiaries. As a result, adopting a standard culture is preferred and encouraged in a variety of ways.

Cultural diversity in this view is a source of innovation for economic development and ecological health. Adapting network structures allows local organizations to leverage and develop local suppliers (economic and ecologically sound and contributing to the maintenance of diversity) and ways of operation that create a best of the best organization and contribute to global effectiveness. Even when large-scale integration is a key to success, such an approach can work. Intel has adapted its "global factory" concept with a worldwide supply chain of plants, transportation and distribution systems, R&D facilities, and sales organizations that depends on tight integration. Each of the facilities is required to meet strict operational requirements that facilitate integration but they are also encouraged to take advantage of local cultural customs. Although cultural diversity is important in its own right, it clearly needs to support other elements of the responsible progress policy. The cultural diversity principle elevates the importance of increasing diversity awareness and asks decisions makers to commit to the health of this long-term source of development and innovation.

REVISING THE AGILITY MODEL TO SUPPORT RESPONSIBLE PROGRESS

With a more comprehensive organization effectiveness framework to guide decisions, the second part of an integrated model of effectiveness is a description of the organization design features that will support responsible progress. We propose that agility models, in particular the B2C model, can operationalize sustainable organization design features quite well. Organizations with the ability to sense and respond to environmental pressures and to proactively create opportunities ought to be better able to adopt a more responsible stance than firms designed in traditional ways. Table 4 summarizes how a B2C organization contributes to responsible progress, which will be discussed in the following section with some changes. Each of the core processes can leverage or achieve the organization effectiveness criteria in the responsible progress approach.

The Role of Strategizing in Responsible Progress

Creating a B2C organization designed for responsible progress begins with the strategizing process. Because strategy reflects the values of the organization, this is undoubtedly the most pivotal set of systems and processes in setting the organization's direction. Revising the strategizing process to support responsible progress involves adjustments to the future focusing process and the definitions of the organization's robust strategy.

In terms of their future focus, most organizations have some form of forecasting or environmental sensing, and agile firms have stronger sensing capabilities than non-agile firms. Organizations built for responsible progress expand this capability by developing specific scenarios about social and ecological issues as well as integrating these perspectives into economic scenarios. Organizations designed for agility and responsible progress add NGO activities, changing government policies related to social and ecological issues, and monitoring social trends to their future focus data collection and sensing activities. This increases the amount of social and ecological information available to decision-making processes, and can be accomplished in one of two ways.

First, the existing environmental scanning processes can be expanded to include search routines in areas beyond market demand, customer requirements, and regulatory trends to include social and community impacts and ecological implications. Second, specialized units, such as corporate social

Table 4. Built to Change Design Features Support Responsible Progress.

		Built to Change Core Processes (Means)		
		Strategizing	Creating value	Designing
Dimensions of responsible progress (ends)	Technological innovation	• A strong future focus identifies viable and emerging green technologies, diversity-friendly innovations (technological and managerial)	• Learning is a key source of innovation	• Flexible organizations[a] can adapt to new innovations more quickly
	Economic success	• Future focus identifies momentary advantages that contribute to sustainable success and ideally obviate need for episodic boom/bust cycles of change • A series of momentary advantages and reasonable growth goals support long-term economic success	• Change capability helps shifts between advantages • Learning makes strategies more effective sooner	• Flexible organizations support momentary competitive advantages as an agile economic logic
	Cultural diversity	• Change-friendly identities raise cultural diversity as a source of innovation	• Diversity is a source of creativity and learning	• Flexible organizations are able to adjust to different cultural contexts without loss of productivity
	Ecological health	• Future focus and robust strategies see ecological health as a source of innovation and business opportunity • Change-friendly identities support shifts to "green" products, services, and business models	• New business models • Seeing the environment as an opportunity	• Maximum surface area structures and transparent processes make it easier to incorporate eco-friendly practices

[a]To simplify the table, we use the term flexible organization to refer to a firm with a maximum surface area structure, transparent information and decision-making processes, a clear human capital strategy, and flexible performance management systems.

responsibility departments, can be charged with gathering these data and bringing them for integration with traditional data during strategizing meetings.

Second, the strategizing process must be revised with respect to the robustness of the organization's strategy, how it achieves objectives over a long period of time, and the features that support or thwart responsible progress. As described earlier, robust strategies have a long-term value proposition that is expressed as organization identity and a near-term rent appropriation proposition that is expressed as strategic intent.

Organization identities are usually manifested as a metaphor that describes what the organization is and how it relates to its environment. It is relatively easy for an organization to project an image of sustainability through its advertising messages about green products and the social issues it supports through sponsorships and other philanthropy. The real key is whether such messages line up with the actual behavior of the organization and the values that influence the way employees behave. For example, Starbuck's identity of creating great experiences, Microsoft's identity of persistence, or Capital One's identity of test and learn represent powerful metaphors that not only indicate something about their cultures and reputations, but also how each organization explains success (and why performance declines when they become distracted). However, these identities do not necessarily reflect a stance toward social or ecological issues. This represents an additional standard that agile, responsible organizations have to meet.

Agile organizations have change-friendly identities; but agile, responsible progress organizations also develop identities that support "doing well and doing good over the long run." To achieve that integration, one of the most impactful interventions an organization can initiate is a conversation among the people who understand and have their fingers on the pulse of the culture, the messages sent through advertising/marketing, the opinions of external customers/critics/analysts, the perspectives of ecological and broader community members, and other stakeholders. To what extent do these perspectives share views about who the organization is, what it stands for, and how it behaves as a system? Is there alignment or contradiction between (a) who we say we are and how we behave and (b) the perceptions of customers, competitors, the ecology, the communities in which the organization operates, and other external stakeholders? Do we have an identity that supports change as routine and respects and drives social and ecological objectives?

At DaVita, the nation's largest kidney dialysis and treatment provider, their "we're a village first and a company second" identity reflects this integrated conversation between their values-in-use and their image, brand, and reputation. Internally, there is a clear understanding that taking care of patients and each other – maintaining the village – will reap rewards of revenue, profit, and other business outcomes. Externally, analysts know that the first five minutes of the quarterly earnings call will begin, not with financial results, but with clinical outcomes. The village metaphor can be easily extended to convey DaVita's relationship to the community and the environment around it. DaVita has internal employee support programs as well as external philanthropy efforts that focus on social accountability and extend to an understanding of its ecological responsibilities. DaVita is consciously concerned about the ecological impacts of its clinical treatments (current dialysis treatment technologies result in a number of toxic wastes), how it relates to its local communities, and to health care reforms. To do otherwise would poison the local water well (figuratively) and fail to create the conditions for long-term survival.

Once the identity metaphor is understood, an organization's strategic intents can be explored. Intent generates advantages that drive current performance and is characterized by its breadth, aggressiveness, and differentiation. These dimensions must be explored for their relationship to responsible progress. Although breadth is not expected to be closely related to responsible progress, product/service, technological, and market breadth can reflect a positive or negative stance to social, ecological, or economic concerns. For example, the breadth of the markets an organization chooses to participate in – especially with respect to global markets – is an important input to the organization's "footprint" and represents an opportunity to contribute to or detract from social and ecological outcomes. In this sense, the organization's identity can help to guide choices that will promote positive outcomes. Whenever Intel opens a new plant in Asia, there are intentional conversations about which parts of the organization's culture are critical for economic success and which parts of the operational footprint and culture can be adapted to support local customs, local suppliers – especially local labor pools – and local energy and ecological concerns.

The aggressiveness dimension of strategy has a clear relationship to responsible progress, and argues for moderate levels. Rather than aggressive growth goals and BHAGs that encourage the firm to "reach beyond its grasp" for motivation, agile and responsible organizations take an accountable approach to goals that can be defended from ecological and social as well as economic perspectives. As we are writing this in late 2009, Honda's response to Toyota's missteps are instructive.

Toyota, long since an example of agility and consistency, has made a couple of rare missteps in its expansion in Asia, its response to quality problems, its capacity additions in the North America, and its lobbying in the United States for less strict mileage requirements. Together, these missteps – in combination with the global recession – have resulted in uncommon losses, overcapacity, a tarnished reputation, and the need for some retrenchment. It would appear to be a perfect opportunity for Honda to step on Toyota while it is down. To date, Honda's response has been quite measured with little increase in advertising, expanded production, sales incentives, or other tactics. Honda is sticking to its message and its way of operating. It will no doubt experience some short-term gains, and perhaps some longer-term benefits as well, but it does not appear that it will overstep the opportunity and be overly greedy. Such a response is in keeping with a responsible progress approach.

Finally, the differentiation dimension of strategy is important because an organization can choose from a variety of product/service features that are more ecologically or socially sensitive. Supporting their strategic intent of customer intimacy and emotional connection, the Victoria's Secret (VS) division of Limited Brands has a sophisticated set of potential and actual differentiation advantages. By constantly asking, "what's new, what's next?" VS creates a stream of innovations in its core intimate apparel line that maintains a strong emotional connection to their customers. In addition, VS has an intricate supply chain that involves a variety of plants located throughout the world that must address local labor laws and social situations. By utilizing sound and fair practices, VS can make important connections with customers who are looking for responsible operational decisions.

Supporting VS's marketing differentiation involves printed catalogues and other paper materials. When VS was challenged by the NGO Forest Ethics for using paper from nonsustainable growth forests, they had a choice to fight the NGO or adjust their strategy to create a new momentary advantage. Choosing the latter and working with Forest Ethics, they shifted their paper supply policies and began promoting responsible practices. Similarly, it continues to work with textile suppliers and manufacturers to use materials that are ecologically friendly and at the same time test the market for the extent to which the deep emotional connection and intimacy is strengthened by the use of such materials.

As shown in Table 4, a revised strategizing process can contribute to the goals of responsible progress. A strong future focus increases an organization's exposure to technological innovations and business opportunities that will supply a series of momentary advantages for long-term economic sustainability. Guided by a socially and ecologically relevant identity, the exploration of present and future environments and the development of culturally and ecologically relevant scenarios can help an organization look for appropriate innovation opportunities. Such a view can help the process to be more efficient by narrowing the range of options and alternatives, and it can direct the search process toward often underexplored sources of both innovation and economic advantage. Different cultures provide a variety of new perspectives to see problems in new ways and views ecological sustainability as an opportunity rather than a constraint for innovation.

Strategizing supports long-term economic success by setting reasonable growth goals and laying out a road map of strategic intents and momentary advantages that smooth out the boom/bust cycles that are the result of episodic change. B2C organizations – in attempting to maintain proximity with their environments – are less likely to pursue growth for its own sake. To do so places an organization on a path full of highs and lows in performance. Sustainable success recognizes that consistently above-average performance is more desirable than extraordinary performance followed by periods of retrenchment and loss as a new competitive advantage is sought. In combination with a strong future focus, a responsible progress organization moves with flexibility from one advantage to the next, taking profit from the opportunity but not overreaching the limits of a particular advantage.

Strategizing also supports both cultural diversity and ecological health through identity formation. Consciously attending to its identity forces the organization to reconcile its internal values and external brand, image, and reputation. Organizations that operate with internal values that do not support ecological sustainability cultural diversity and human capital development will create a variety of problems and dissonance for organization members who hear their organization talk about their community efforts, green policies, and socially responsible practices. Increasing environmental pressures and information availability allow the NGO community to quickly note when organizations do not live up to their promises. Identity serves as an important tool for ensuring that organizations "walk the talk" with respect to sustainable practices. B2C organizations understand their identity and the responsible progress policy suggests that all organizations should think through the implications of their identity with respect to promoting human development and ecological sustainability.

Creating Value in Responsible Progress

Revising the creating value process in agile organizations to achieve the goals of responsible progress involves minor changes in the orchestration process but more substantive revisions to its innovation/learning capabilities and its shared leadership capacity. Although change and learning are quite similar – all learning involves change – they are focused on two very different areas.

First, a B2C organization designed for responsible progress needs a strong – if somewhat generic – orchestration capability. The change or orchestration capability needs to focus on supporting a strategizing process, which strings together a series of momentary advantages. These two B2C elements – strategizing and orchestration – need to work hand in hand to generate both short-term (momentary advantage) and longer-term (a series of advantages) success. Because a B2C organization does not depend on a single, sustainable advantage for a long period of time, it can ill afford the drop in productivity and effectiveness associated with inefficient large-scale transformations.

Capital One Financial did an excellent job of building a change capability and has, to date, leveraged the capability to build a stronger customer experience, integrate recent bank mergers, and avoid many of the negative economic consequences that have fallen to other financial services firms. It recently received a positive "stress test" evaluation and has repaid federal TARP funds (Worley & Lawler, 2009). Agile organizations, and especially B2C organizations designed for responsible progress, expect to generate performance through change rather than treating it as a necessary evil. Although generic, an orchestration capability can contribute to responsible progress by raising people's awareness of the social and ecological consequences of the choices that are made during change.

The responsible progress framework lists innovation as a key criterion and a key driver of economic development that is fed by the goals of ecological health and cultural diversity. Learning is a key capability in the B2C agility framework and an important driver of innovation (Sahal, 1981). Thus, we see a great deal of complimentarity in the two approaches. In an agile, responsible progress organization, sourcing new product/service ideas based on environmentally friendly principles, cultural differences, social trends, or best practices in different operating units represents a large and largely untapped economic opportunity. Working with technologies and applying them in different markets, scales, and contexts can generate knowledge and experience that can be applied to both product and process improvements. Even existing technologies deployed in new markets or on different scales with a clear eye toward the extent to which they promote economic, social, and ecological ends can represent important sources of new revenue. In combination with the orchestration capability, learning capabilities effectively shorten the cycle time between strategy formulation and implementation and allow organizations to capture profit possibilities more quickly.

The Gap has applied a learning process to working with NGOs and others in its supply chain to build a social problem solving and network collaboration advantage. In working with the NGO Social Accountability International (SAI), they have developed alliance relationships that foster social credibility and compliment their economic and ecological goals. In addition, Hawken, Lovins, and Lovins' Natural Capitalism model strongly asserts the need for innovation in business models. Their primary suggestion is the shift from a "purchase our product" model to a "rent our services" model. They describe how Interface carpet, United Technologies, DOW Chemical, and others have shifted their business model to embrace a services and solutions mindset that improves economic success and lowers ecological harm.

A revised shared leadership capability compliments the change and learning capabilities in creating value. Under a shared identity that is change friendly and responsible progress aware, pushing leadership responsibilities to a broad set of organizational associates creates the capacity for quick responses and coordinated change that support a more sustainable organization along social, ecological, and economic dimensions. This can be accomplished by rotating people through foreign assignments to increase their awareness of alternative cultures and to expose them to sources of innovation. It supports the future focus process and the achievement of a maximum surface area structure. Managers in foreign subsidiaries can be brought into the formal leadership development process to increase the subject matter diversity and cultural perspectives in conversations. Finally, local managers can be encouraged to leverage local practices within clear operational boundaries and provided opportunities to share best practices and results.

A revised creating value process contributes to the goal of responsible progress (Table 4). B2C organizations with a strong learning and change capability understand there is a strong reciprocal interdependency between these capabilities and cultural diversity. With experience, learning and change activities occur much more fluidly and quickly in the presence of alternative points of view, and diversity represents an important source of innovation, creativity, and learning in its own right. Creating value contributes to cultural diversity by leveraging different knowledge and new perspectives to fuel innovation and appreciating these sources of economic opportunity to solve problems. Local talent and new perspectives represent an important source of learning.

Finally, creating value processes helps drive ecological health. A bias toward creating value and learning views ecological sustainability as a huge opportunity. In combination with a strong future focus, creating value capabilities can identify and monetize new innovations that are ecologically and socially relevant.

Designing Processes in Responsible Progress

The designing process in an agile, responsible progress organization is about supporting the value shifts that organizations make in the strategizing process when they use responsible progress as the criterion for effectiveness. The nimble, responsible progress organization leverages a maximum surface area structure to support a strong future-focused strategizing process. The more that people are connected to the external environment, and are coached and guided to look for information about future trends in economically related areas but also in socially and ecologically related areas, the more information the organization will have to think about alternatives, new capacities to build, and new trends to consider. An organization's surface area can be expanded through role definitions that explicitly include gathering information from the external environment all the way to structural choices about flattening the hierarchy, creating small business units, and increasing the virtual nature of work.

Alegent Health has developed an innovation capability that involves the use of large-group interventions called decision accelerators (DA). The DAs routinely bring together health system employees as well as relevant outside stakeholders to design new clinical services, plan organizational changes, or accelerate execution. Recently, Alegent used its innovation capability to develop a sustainability strategy. Community members, physicians, health care regulators, supplier and partner organizations as well as Alegent employees who were passionate about the organization's ecological footprint were brought together to craft a vision and strategy. By integrating educational models in the DA, the whole system became more aware of Alegent's operations vis-à-vis the triple bottom line. By arranging for organization members and outside stakeholders to interact, Alegent gave its employees and managers direct access to environmental issues and knowledge and an immediate opportunity to apply that information to organizational operations. Its innovation capability fosters transparency in information flows and rapid decision making in support of responsible progress. It has used its innovation capability to implement a variety of clinical, social, and ecological innovations in a short period of time.

Traditional firms need to revise their performance management systems to support responsible progress. First, the talent procurement process needs to be altered to recruit and hire individuals with both the technical competence necessary to add economic value and the personal attitudes and beliefs that support the triple bottom line. Second, people in the organization need to be evaluated and given feedback on their awareness of economic, social, and ecological issues related to the organization's strategic intent. They also need to be rewarded for innovative ideas that further the strategic intent in responsible ways.

Managers and executives at the Limited Brands are encouraged to think about the "shadow" they cast as a leader; do their actions and words reflect the values and beliefs of a responsible organization? CEO Les Wexner encourages and rewards managers and employees who work with community and non-profit organizations and get involved in ecological issues. Such rewards have the secondary benefit of bringing in relevant trends and ideas that can be integrated with future-focused scanning, innovation, and identity processes.

The designing process is the most flexible of the B2C core processes. It impacts important enablers of the responsible progress goals. First, the designing process supports organizations capable of moving from one momentary advantage to another easily and routinely. By implementing maximum surface area structures, flexible performance management systems, transparent decision-making practices, and nimble reward processes, B2C organizations are able to implement ecologically friendly innovations more quickly, execute complex strategies that leverage local cultural customs and knowledge and still integrate organizational structures on a global basis, and change – not just grow – more easily. Leveraging local assets means a better hiring and retention environment, better in-country image and reputation, and better resources for faster learning. Together, implementing innovations and integrating global structures that leverage local assets clearly contribute to economic success.

Socially, economically, and ecologically relevant innovations – in a world that is changing quickly – must be deployed and implemented quickly to generate revenue and returns for as long as practicable. A flexible design that allows resources and management focus to shift quickly through orchestration processes, rewards people for not only executing change but driving the right results, and continues to gather information about what might happen next is a signatory element of agility. The nimble, responsible progress firm does so with the added element of sustainability.

Agile organizations are able to adjust their designs to align with different cultural contexts and still meet local and corporate revenue and productivity targets. Philips – a global health and well-being products organization – uses its storied technology capabilities and a strong country manager network to balance a "One Philips" view of the portfolio with local customization of lighting, consumer, and health care products. Finally, maximum surface area structures and transparent information processes make it easy to identify ecological opportunities and reflect strong ecological practices.

Conclusion

The proposed revisions to the B2C agility model reflect an updated view of organization effectiveness. It is based on the view that an organization's effectiveness should be defined by its ability to jointly optimize economic success, technological innovation, cultural diversity, and ecological health. The model proposes that the best organization framework to generate these outcomes is based in agility.

As described here, the revised B2C agility model is supported by some recent research. For example, the revised B2C model is similar in intent to De Geus's (2002) "living company." As part of an internal study at Royal Dutch Shell to understand why some organizations were able to survive over long periods of time, four dimensions were identified: (1) sensitivity to the environment, (2) cohesiveness and a strong sense of identity, (3) tolerance, and (4) conservative financing. The first dimension is clearly related to our concept of a strong future focus; long-lived companies had developed stronger scenario capabilities as well as the systems and processes to overcome several psychological tendencies that make enacting environments problematic (Weick, 1969). The second dimension of cohesion and identity is related to our concept of identity, although De Geus's definition is decidedly more anthropomorphic. Based on a theory of Personalismus by German psychologist William Stern, De Geuss suggested that identity was *unitas multiplex* or that organizations were viewed as one when seen from the outside, but as differentiated parts when viewed from within. Thus, organizations develop shorthand descriptions of its persona to describe its behaviors, such as "we are a learning organization" or the "competitor's moves made us feel defensive."

Our reading of De Geus's third characteristic, tolerance, is that it is the most design-oriented feature and focuses on decentralization and learning. The revised B2C agility model goes much farther in its description of organization design features and gives special attention to structural surface area, which can be partially achieved through decentralization. Similarly, we call out learning and change capabilities whereas De Geus only suggests that these are good characteristics to have.

Finally, the conservative financing perspective of De Geus provides a unique and specific functional strategy. It is not part of the B2C model although aligns neatly with our view that strategizing processes used to achieve responsible progress should not be overly aggressive.

Despite these important similarities, the revised B2C model is different from the living company model in terms of its effectiveness priorities. De Geus looked at organizations that were "long lived" and without regard to performance per se. In fact, he traded off performance for survival as the key effectiveness metric. The revised B2C model and the criteria of responsible progress set the goal of above-average economic performance that is achieved because of a focus on cultural diversity, ecological health, and appropriate innovation. In addition, and as noted above, the living company model contained mostly broad assertions about organization design features but few specifics to guide executives in choices about how to support responsible progress and agility.

The revised B2C model also has important parallels with Beer's "high commitment, high performance" (HCHP) organizations (Beer, 2009). These organizations are characterized by performance alignment, psychological alignment, and the capacity for learning and change. Performance alignment reflects many of the same design issues in the B2C model, including flexible structures, transparent management processes, and empowering human resource practices. However, Beer makes the learning and change capability a stand-alone characteristic rather than a part of performance alignment. His psychological alignment addresses similar issues to our shared leadership dimension and specifically addresses issues of power, a unique strength of the HCHP model.

The HCHP model differs from the model presented here in some important ways in that it does not call out ecological sustainability. There is a clear emphasis in the HCHP model on working with and addressing multiple stakeholders, but the ecological dimension is absent. In addition, he treats culture in more traditional ways and does not deal with the more complex notions of identity. Overall, the B2C agility model and the criteria of responsible progress not only extend and reconcile much of the organization effectiveness research, they integrate well with some of the recent organization design models.

IMPLICATIONS FOR ORGANIZATION DEVELOPMENT AND CHANGE

A primary motivation for writing this chapter was to reinvigorate research and practice that is focused on organization effectiveness. The revised B2C agility model and the proposed OE criteria represent a significant and new opportunity for OD and change. OD is not a profession but a field of practice and research (Jamieson & Worley, 2008) that is struggling to find purpose, cohesion, and identity (Worley & Feyerherm, 2003; Worren, Ruddle, & Moore, 1999; Farias & Johnson, 2001). We believe the B2C agility model and the responsible progress criteria can invigorate and repurpose the field.

Implications for Research

From a research perspective, the new models presented here need testing and suggest a number of research questions that warrant substantial effort. Theoretically and empirically, we need to know whether the revised B2C model and the responsible progress criteria hold up. Both frameworks are young and have yet to be systematically subjected to criticism and tested against objective data.

With respect to the agility model, we are currently engaged in a program of research aimed at refining methods for assessing organizations against the B2C dimensions (Worley & Lawler, in press). There are a variety of assumptions in the model that need to be validated. For example, is the alternative economic logic of a series of temporary advantages viable? How do the relationships among strategizing, designing, and creating value work together to create proximity? What is the contribution of learning and change capabilities to the design's flexibility? Perhaps most importantly, is agility related to the different dimensions of effectiveness implied by responsible progress?

With respect to the responsible progress framework, do the relationships among economic development, innovation, cultural diversity, and ecological health make sense? For example, is diversity the right indicator of social sustainability? How will ecological health be measured since a carbon footprint is only a measure of activity? Can managers effectively make decisions in the face of such a complex set of criteria? Will they pursue the goals sequentially or can they jointly optimize at the risk of not maximizing on the economic criterion? Similarly, can the financial markets embrace such a criteria set?

There is a clear and wide-open new research arena here. These questions speak to a new and exciting stream of research in OD and change. The B2C model of agility and the responsible progress framework provide important theories that can be tested to determine whether their implementation and pursuit can make real differences.

Implications for Practice

From a practice perspective, we believe that the proposed agility model and responsible progress criteria will challenge OD practitioners. It is easy to like and agree with the principles of responsible progress. They represent politically correct objectives: Who would not want to see a world of economic success, cultural diversity, and ecological health driven by new and better products and services? One real question that will be faced by OD practitioners is "how?" How do we make these goals appealing beyond a "wink and a nod" and what are the best methods for achieving these ends?

Our answer is, "slowly." Change begins with a conversation, and all organization change is preceded by a personal one (Worley & Vick, 2005). Organizations that are not on the path of agility and responsible progress must first begin a conversation about it. Our guess is that this is already happening in both ways – large and small, formal and informal. It is hard to get away from it even in today's environment of anxiety and concern over the economic crisis. So there is already a good start and the next step is one of raising the bar by formally introducing the issues and implications of responsible progress in decision-making meetings.

In the past, social diversity and ecological health issues may have taken a back seat in decisions about technological or market development, growth, and ways of working. Now, the conversation needs to shift to one where these things are considered and their legitimacy established. We suspect that this is already happening in organizations where individuals have changed or there are significant proportions of sustainability-minded members who want their employers to understand its importance. Ultimately, this will lead to substantive change in policy and behavior. Such a process may be too slow for ecological zealots, but it is occurring and it will gain momentum. This time, rather than a random walk toward a globalized economy that is guided only by a narrow and restricted view of economic concern, we will achieve success that is sustainable.

We need to know a great deal more about the transformation to agility and the pursuit of responsible progress. Docherty et al. (2009) review several methods and propose a process for the transition to sustainable work systems, and many of the sustainability models reviewed earlier have implied transformation steps. There are a few cases of the transformation. DaVita's emergence from bankruptcy (Pfeffer, 2006), IBM's transformation from products to solutions (Applegate, Austin, & Collins, 2006; Applegate, Heckscher, Michael, & Collins, 2006), the insurance company case study presented by Todd, Parker, and Sullivan (2009), and Beer's case studies (Beer, 2009) provide glimpses of the process, but do not yet cumulate to answer many of the most important process and practice questions. Those questions include, should the definition and transformation of identity precede decisions on organization design features and what are the tools for diagnosing and changing these elements? Is the process of transformation to agility and responsible progress any different from traditional methods of transformation? Does an organization need to have a change capability before the transformation to agility or can it be developed at the same time? These are important, practical questions that effective and responsible executives will want to know the answers to as they think about committing their organizations to such a fundamental change.

Implications for the Field

An examination of OD's history (Kleiner, 1996; Cummings & Worley, 2009) suggests that the field was a more powerful force for change when it had a clear and cohesive purpose. For example, early in its life cycle and in the wake of learnings from World War II, OD practitioners were united in their view that organization effectiveness could be improved by liberating human potential from overorganized bureaucracies. OD practitioners across the board worked, in their own way, to influence organization strategy, structure, process, and culture. Today, there is no clear purpose characterizing the field and coordinating the action of practitioners.

The elaboration, discussion, and implementation of the agility model and the responsible progress criteria could give OD a common voice in shaping and influencing significant social and organizational change. Because these models embrace and integrate the traditional and pragmatic parts of OD's history and leverage the strengths of OD's diverse perspectives, they promise to place OD in the center of debate about the future of organizations as opposed to its marginal position during the reengineering, downsizing, and total quality management periods.

If the OD community begins adapting and promulgating agility and the responsible progress criteria in publications, conversations, and practice, it can begin shaping organizational strategies, structures, and processes. Professional associations within OD can assist by sponsoring large multi-governmental, multiorganizational, and multicountry conferences on cultural contributions to innovation, alternative energy integration, government–business coordination, sustainability, network structures, and other transorganizational problems in line with the responsible progress criteria. The results will be difficult to see at first but will accelerate over time as a critical mass of thought and practice occurs. Globalization will move in a valued direction where more and more people become involved with and benefit from diversity, innovation, development, and ecological health. The trends in economic, social, political, and technological environments – and trends within OD itself – all contain the seeds of an integrative and influential force that is capable of shaping a more positive future for our world.

NOTES

1. Population ecology's measure of change is entry and exit. We are concerned with survival only to the extent that it is a prima facie case of agility over time.

2. In as much as the most referred to lists of criteria were produced in 1975 and 1977, it is important to ask, "has anything changed?" A quick search through the past five years of Strategic Management Journal, the Journal of Applied Behavioral Science, Management Science, the Academy of Management Journal, Organizational Dynamics, and Organization Science returned five hits where the term "organization(al) effectiveness" was included in the abstract since 2000, only one article was related to effectiveness per se.

3. A number of criticisms of contestability theory have been raised, and its assumptions regarding "super free" entry and exit challenged (Cairns & Mahabir, 1987; Shepherd, 1984). As a result, we are left with at least three theories – perfect competition, industrial organization, and contestability theories – none of which are flawless. Our use of contestability theory derives from its alternative economic logic – entry and exit vs. sustainable advantage – and its support of agility and sustainability.

4. It may be splitting hairs, but Porter defines differentiation or low cost as two potential sustainable competitive advantages whereas we argue that these are robust strategies – or means to an end – and any particular advantage does change or morph over time. Few firms with a "differentiation" advantage would say that the advantage itself – quality or speed for example – is static. The very nature of the advantage must shift in response to customer changes, technological advances, and general industry evolution. Moreover, a low-cost strategy is just one way of differentiating. Thus, our definition of strategy, without denying the benefits of the competitive strategy approach, is more in line with that proposed by Hambrick and Frederickson as well as the views of the population ecologists who describe aggressiveness and specialization (Carroll & Hannan, 1995).

REFERENCES

Aldrich, H. (1999). *Organizations evolving*. Thousand Oaks, CA: Sage Publications.

Aldrich, H. E. (1979). *Organizations and environments*. Englewood Cliffs, NJ: Prentice-Hall.

Applegate, L., Austin, R., & Collins, E. (2006). *IBM's decade of transformation (A): The turnaround* (9-805-130). Boston: Harvard Business School Publishing.

Applegate, L., Heckscher, C., Michael, B., & Collins, E. (2006). *IBM's decade of transformation: Uniting vision and values* (9-807-030). Boston: Harvard Business School Publishing.

Argyris, C., & Schon, D. A. (1996). *Organizational learning II*. Reading, MA: Addison-Wesley.

Bailey, E., & Baumol, W. (1984). Deregulation and the theory of contestable markets. *Yale Journal on Regulation*, *1*, 111–137.

Bain, J. (1968). *Industrial organization*. New York: Wiley.

Barney, J. (1991). Firm resources and sustained competitive advantage. *Journal of Management*, *17*, 99–120.

Beckhard, R., & Harris, D. (1977). *Organization transitions: Managing complex change*. Reading, MA: Addison-Wesley.

Beddoe, R., Costanza, R., Farley, J., Garza, E., Kent, J., Kubiszewski, I., Martinez, L., Mccowen, T., Murphy, K., Myers, N., Ogden, Z., Stapleton, K., & Woodward, J. (2009). Overcoming systemic roadblocks to sustainability: The evolutionary redesign of worldviews, institutions, and technologies. *Proceedings of the National Academy of Sciences of the United States of America*, *106*(8), 2483–2489.

Beer, M. (2009). *High commitment, high performance*. San Francisco: Jossey-Bass.

Beer, M., & Eisenstat, R. (1996). Developing an organization capable of implementing strategy and learning. *Human Relations*, *49*, 597–619.

Bornstein, D. (2004). *How to change the world: Social entrepreneurs and the power of new ideas*. New York: Oxford University Press.

Brown, S., & Eisenhardt, K. (1998). *Competing on the edge*. Boston: Harvard Business School Press.

Brown, S. L., & Eisenhardt, K. M. (1997). The art of continuous change: Linking complexity theory and time-paced evolution in relentlessly shifting organizations. *Administrative Science Quarterly*, *42*, 1–24.

Burnes, B. (2004). *Managing change* (4th ed.). Essex, England: Prentice-Hall.

Cairns, R., & Mahabir, D. (1987). Contestability: A revisionist view. *Economica*, *55*, 269–276.

Cameron, K. (1980). Critical questions in assessing organization effectiveness. *Organization Dynamics*, *9*, 66–80.

Cameron, K., & Whetten, D. (1983). *Organization effectiveness: A comparison of multiple models*. New York: Academic Press.

Campbell, J. P. (1977). On the nature of organizational effectiveness. In: P. S. Goodman & J. M. Pennings (Eds), *New perspectives on organizational effectiveness*. San Francisco: Jossey-Bass.

Carroll, G., & Hannan, M. (1995). *Organizations in industry: Strategy, structure, and selection*. New York: Oxford University Press.

Chesbrough, H. (2007). *Open business models: How to thrive in the new innovation landscape*. Boston: Harvard Business School Press.

Child, J. (1972). Organizational structure, environment, and performance: The role of strategic choice. *Sociology*, *6*(1), 1–22.

Christensen, C. (1997). *The innovator's dilemma*. Boston: Harvard Business School Press.

Chua, A. (2004). *World on fire*. London: Doubleday Broadway Publishing.

Cogan, D. G. (2006). *Corporate governance and climate change: Making the connection*. Boston: CERES.

Collins, J., & Porras, J. (1994). *Built to last*. New York: HarperCollins.

Cooperrider, D., & Dutton, J. (1999). *Organizational dimensions of global change*. Thousand Oaks, CA: Sage Publications.

Cummings, T., & Srivastva, S. (1977). *Management of work*. Kent: Comparative Administration Research Institute (distributed by Kent State University Press).

Cummings, T., & Worley, C. (2009). *Organization development and change* (9th ed.). Mason, OH: Cengage Publishing.

Cyert, R., & March, J. (1992). *A behavioral theory of the firm*. Oxford: Blackwell.

De Geus, A. (2002). *The living company*. Boston: Harvard Business School Press.

Docherty, P., Kira, M., & Shani, A. B. (2009). Organizational development for social sustainability in work systems. In: R. Woodman, R. Passmore & A. B. Shani (Eds), *Research in organizational change and development* (Vol. 17, pp. 77–144). Amsterdam: JAI Press.

Doz, Y., & Kosonen, M. (2008). *Fast strategy*. Harlow, UK: Wharton School Publishing.

Elkington, J. (1994). Towards the sustainable corporation: Win-win-win business strategies for sustainable development. *California Management Review*, *36*(2), 90–100.

Farias, G., & Johnson, H. (2001). Organizational development and change management: Setting the record straight. *Journal of Applied Behavioral Science*, *36*, 376–379.

Friedman, T. (2000). *The lexus and the olive tree*. Garden City, NY: Anchor Books.

Friedman, T. (2007). *The world is flat*. New York: Picador.

Friedman, T. (2009). *Hot, flat, and crowded*. New York: Picador.

Galbraith, J. R. (2001). *Designing organizations: An executive guide to strategy, structure, and process*. San Francisco: Jossey-Bass.

Galbraith, J. R. (2005). *Designing the customer-centric organization: A guide to strategy, structure, and process*. San Francisco: Jossey-Bass.

Greiner, L. (1967). Patterns of organizational design change. *Harvard Business Review*, *45*, 119–130.

Haeckel, S. (1999). *Adaptive enterprise: Creating and leading sense-and-respond organizations*. Boston: Harvard Business School Press.

Hambrick, D. C., & Frederickson, J. W. (2005). Are you sure you have a strategy? *Academy of Management Executive*, *19*(4).

Hanna, D. (1988). *Designing organizations for high performance*. Reading, MA: Addison-Wesley.

Hannan, T. M., & Freeman, J. (1975). Growth and decline processes in organizations. *American Sociological Review*, *40*, 215–228.

Hatch, M., & Schultz, M. (2002). The dynamics of organizational identity. *Human Relations*, *55*, 989–1019.

Hawken, P., Lovins, A., & Lovins, L. (2008). *Natural capitalism: Creating the next industrial revolution*. Boston: Back Bay Books.

Hayes, J. (2002). *The theory and practice of change management*. New York: Palgrave.

Hitt, M. (1988). The measuring of organizational effectiveness: Multiple domains and constituencies. *Management International Review*, *28*, 28–40.

Hughes, N. (2009). Changing faces: Adaptation of highly skilled Chinese workers to a high-tech multinational corporation. *Journal of Applied Behavioral Science*, *45*(2), 212.

Jamieson, D., & Worley, C. (2008). The practice of organization development. In: T. Cummings (Ed.), *Handbook of organization development* (pp. 99–122). Thousand Oaks, CA: Sage Publications.

Katz, D., & Kahn, R. (1978). *The social psychology of organizations* (2nd ed.). Hoboken, NJ: Wiley.

Kleiner, A. (1996). *The age of heretics*. New York: Doubleday.

Korten, D. (1995). *When corporations rule the world*. San Francisco: Berrett-Koehler.

Korten, D. (2007). *The great turning: From empire to earth community*. San Francisco: Berrett-Koehler.

Lacey, M., & Tompkins, T. (2007). Analysis of best practices in internal consulting. *Organization Development Journal*, *25*(3), 123–131.

Lant, T. K., Milliken, F. J., & Batra, B. (1992). The role of managerial learning and interpretation in strategic persistence and reorientation: An empirical exploration. *Strategic Management Journal*, *13*, 585–608.

Lawler, E. E. (2008). *Talent*. San Francisco: Jossey-Bass.

Lawler, E. E., & Worley, C. (2006). *Built to change: How to achieve sustained organizational effectiveness*. San Francisco: Jossey-Bass.

Lawrence, P., & Lorsch, J. (1967). Differentiation and integration in complex organizations. *Administrative Science Quarterly*, *12*, 1–30.

Levine, M. (1987). Airline competition in deregulated markets: Theory, firm strategy, and public policy. *Yale Journal on Regulation*, *4*, 393–494.

Lewin, A. Y., & Minton, J. W. (1986). Determining organizational effectiveness: Another look, and an agenda for research. *Management Science*, *32*(5), 514–538.

March, J. G., & Simon, H. A. (1958). *Organizations*. Wiley.

Mensch, G. (1979). *Stalemate in technology*. Cambridge: Ballinger Publishing Co.

Miles, R. (1980). *Macro organizational behavior*. Santa Monica, CA: Goodyear Publishing.

Miller, D., & Friesen, P. H. (1980). Momentum and revolution in organizational adaptation. *Academy of Management Journal*, *23*(4), 591–614.

Morgan, G. (1997). *Images of organization*. Thousand Oaks, CA: Sage Publications.

Murrell, K. (2004). Hope: Our intended OD legacy for 2050. *Organization Development Journal*, *22*(2), 21–28.

Nattrass, B., & Altomare, M. (1999). *The natural step for business*. Gabriola Island, BC: New Society Publishers.

O'Reilly, C., Harreld, J., & Tushman, M. (2009). Organizational ambidexterity: IBM and emerging business opportunities. *California Management Review*, *51*(4), 75–99.

Paton, R., & McCalman, J. (2000). *Change management* (2nd ed.). London: Sage Publications.

Pennings, J. M., & Goodman, P. S. (Eds). (1977). *New perspectives on organizational effectiveness*. San Francisco: Jossey-Bass.

Perkins, J. (2005). *Confessions of an economic hit man*. San Francisco: Berrett-Koehler.

Perrow, C. (1972). *Complex organizations: A critical essay* (2nd ed.). New York: Random House.

Peteraf, M. (1993). Cornerstones of competitive advantage: A resource-based view. *Strategic Management Journal*, *14*, 179–192.

Pfeffer, J. (2006). *Kent Thiry and DaVita: Leadership challenges in building and growing a great company* (OB-54). Santa Clara, CA: Stanford Graduate School of Business.

Pfeffer, J., & Salancik, G. R. (1978). *The external control of organizations: A resource dependence perspective*. New York: Harper and Row.

Porter, M. E. (1980). *Competitive strategy*. New York: The Free Press.

Prahalad, C. K. (2006). *The fortune at the bottom of the pyramid: Eradicating poverty through profits*. Philadelphia: Wharton School Publications.

Quinn, R., & Cameron, S. (1988). *Paradox and transformation: Towards a theory of change in organizations*. Cambridge, MA: Ballinger Publishing.

Quinn, R. E., & Rohrbaugh, J. (1983). A spatial model of effectiveness criteria: Towards a competing values approach to organizational analysis. *Management Science*, *29*, 363–377.

Reisman, G. (1996). *Capitalism: A treatise on economics*. Ottawa, IL: Jameson Books.

Rheinstein, M. (Ed.), (1968). *Max Weber on law in economy and society* (E. Shils & M. Rheinstein, Trans.). New York: Simon and Schuster.

Robert, K. (2008). *The natural step story: Seeding a quiet revolution*. Gabriola Island, BC: New Society Publishers.

Roethlisberger, F., & Dickson, W. (1939). *Management and the worker*. Cambridge, MA: Harvard University Press.

Rogers, E. (2003). *Diffusion of innovations*. New York: Free Press.

Romanelli, E., & Tushman, M. (1994). Organizational transformation as punctuated equilibrium: An empirical test. *Academy of Management Journal*, *37*(5), 1141–1166.

Rudis, E. (2006). *CEO challenge 2006: Perspectives and analysis*. New York: Conference Board.

Sahal, D. (1981). *Patterns of technological innovation*. Reading, MA: Addison-Wesley.

Scherer, F. M. (1980). *Industrial market structure and economic performance*. Chicago: Rand McNally.

Schoemaker, P. (1995). Scenario planning: A tool for strategic thinking. *Sloan Management Review*, *36*, 25–41.

Schwartz, P. (1991). *The art of the long view*. New York: Doubleday.

Scott, W. R. (1981). *Organizations: Rational, natural, and open systems*. New York: Prentice Hall.

Sen, A. (2000). *Development as freedom*. New York: Anchor Books.

Senge, P. M. (2006). *The fifth discipline: The art and practice of the learning organization*. New York: Doubleday.

Shepherd, W. G. (1984). 'Contestability' vs. competition. *American Economic Review*, *74*, 572–587.

Simons, D., & Chabris, C. (1999). Gorillas in our midst: Sustained inattentional blindness for dynamic events. *Perception, 28*, 1059–1074.

Steers, S. S. (1975). Problems in the measurement of organization effectiveness. *Administrative Science Quarterly, 10*, 546–558.

Taleb, N. (2007). *The black swan: The impact of the highly improbable*. New York: Random House.

Tichy, N., & Bennis, W. (2007). *Judgment: How winning leaders make great calls*. New York: Portfolio.

Todd, J., Parker, J., & Sullivan, A. (2009). Whole system transformation: Becoming radically different. In: W. Rothwell, J. Stavros, R. Sullivan & A. Sullivan (Eds), *Practicing organization development* (pp. 594–607). San Diego: Pfeiffer.

Tushman, M. L., & O'Reilly, C. A. (1996). Ambidextrous organizations: Managing evolutionary and revolutionary change. *California Management Review, 38*(4), 8–29.

Tushman, M. L., & Romanelli, E. (1985). Organization evolution: A metamorphosis model of convergence and reorientation. In: B. Staw & L. L. Cummings (Eds), *Research in organizational behavior* (Vol. 7, pp. 171–222). Greenwich, CT: JAI Press.

Van Alstyne, M. (1997). The state of network organizations: A survey in three frameworks. *Journal of Organizational Computing and Electronic Commerce, 7*, 83–151.

Volberda, H. (1999). *Building the flexible firm*. New York: Oxford.

Weick, K. (1969). *The social psychology of organizing*. New York: McGraw Hill.

World Commission on Environment and Development. (1987). *Our common future*. New York: Oxford University Press.

Worley, C., & Feyerherm, A. (2003). Reflections on the future of organization development. *Journal of Applied Behavioral Science, 39*(1), 97–115.

Worley, C., & Lawler, E. (2009). Building a change capability at capital one financial. *Organizational Dynamics, 38*(4), 245–251.

Worley, C., & Lawler, E. (2010). Agility and organization design: A diagnostic framework. *Organizational Dynamics, 39*(2), 194–204.

Worley, C., & McCloskey, A. (2006). A positive vision of OD's future. In: B. B. Jones & M. Brazzel (Eds), *The NTL handbook of organization development and change: Principles, practices and perspectives*. San Diego, CA: Pfeiffer.

Worley, C., Mohrman, S., Bradbury-Huang, H., Feyerherm, A., Docherty, P., Lifvergren, S., & Parker, S. (2009). *Organizing for sustainability*. All-Academy Theme Symposium presented at the annual Academy of Management Meeting, Chicago.

Worley, C., & Vick, Y.H. (2005). Leading and managing change: Leading change management involves some simple, but too often forgotten rules. *Graziadio Business Report*. Vol. 8 No. 2, Pepperdine University.

Worren, N., Ruddle, K., & Moore, K. (1999). From organizational development to change management: The emergence of a new profession. *Journal of Applied Behavioral Science, 35*(3), 273–286.

Yuchtman, E., & Seashore, S. E. (1967). A system resource approach to organizational effectiveness. *American Sociological Review, 32*, 891–903.

Zahra, S. A., & George, G. (2002). Absorptive capacity: A review, reconceptualization, and extension. *Academy of Management Review, 27*(2), 185–203.

Zammuto, R. (1982). *Assessing organization effectiveness*. New York: SUNY Press.

Zollo, M., & Winter, S. (2001). Deliberate learning and the evolution of dynamic capabilities. *Organization Science, 13*, 339–351.

FURTHER READING

Baumol, W., Panzar, J., & Willig, R. (1979). *Contestable markets and the theory of industry structure*. New York: Harcourt.

Cairns, R., & Mahabir, D. (1999). Contestability: A revisionist view. *Economica, 55*, 269–276.

Dosi, G., Nelson, R., & Winter, S. (2006). *The nature and dynamics of organization capabilities*. Oxford: Oxford University Press.

Hamel, G., & Prahalad, C. (2006). *Competing for the future*. Boston: Harvard Business School Press.

Hornstein, H. (1996). Organizational development and change management: Don't throw the baby out with the bath water. *Journal of Applied Behavioral Science, 37*(2), 223–226.

Teece, D., Pisano, G., & Shuen, A. (1984). Dynamic capabilities and strategic management. *Strategic Management Journal, 18*(7), 509–534.

BREAKING OUT OF STRATEGY VECTORS: REINTRODUCING CULTURE

Julia Balogun and Steven W. Floyd

ABSTRACT

There is considerable evidence that long periods of success in organisations can lead to ossification of strategy and strategic inertia. Burgelman (2002) shows how co-evolutionary lock-in occurs through the creation of a strategy vector. He demonstrates that the internal selection environment can become configured to create sources of inertia that dampen the autonomous strategy process, driving out unrelated exploration and creating a dominance of the induced, top-down strategy process. While this study shows how lock-in occurs, it does not address how a company breaks out *of co-evolutionary lock-in. This is the focus of this paper. We argue that to understand how an organisation breaks out of a strategy vector a more complete conceptualisation of the structural context, and in particular the under specified cultural mechanisms, is required. It also requires an understanding of the linkages between the structural context and the new core capabilities required for breakout. Thus we first expand on what is known about strategy vectors and review research from the strategy process tradition that explores the linkages between strategy, culture and strategic change, to build a more comprehensive picture of the structural context. Our model demonstrates the extent of interconnectedness between the 'hard' (e.g., control systems and organisation*

Research in Organizational Change and Development, Volume 18, 51–76

ISSN: 0897-3016/doi:10.1108/S0897-3016(2010)0000018006

structure) and 'soft' (e.g. beliefs, symbols and stories) components, and that development of new required capabilities is dependent on a holistic shift in all these aspects of the structural context, including, therefore, change in the organisation's culture. We then illustrate the link between lock-in, capability development and culture change through the case of the famous Formula One team, Ferrari. We finish with a discussion of the implications of our findings for strategic change.

INTRODUCTION

Despite the debates about whether evolutionary and continuous models of change or punctuated equilibrium models more accurately capture how organisations undergo change and long-term adaptation, there is evidence that long periods of success in organisations can lead to ossification of strategy, and strategic inertia (Burgelman, 2002; Johnson, 1987, 1988; Miller, 1990a, 1990b, 1992, 1994; Miller & Friesen, 1980; Prahalad & Bettis, 1986; Tushman & Romanelli, 1985). Burgelman (2002) shows how co-evolutionary lock-in occurs through the creation of a strategy vector. He demonstrates that the internal selection environment can become configured to create sources of inertia that dampen the autonomous strategy process, drive out exploration and lead to the dominance of an induced, top-down strategy process.

Whilst Burgelman's (2002) study along with other studies (e.g. Johnson, 1987, 1988; Miller, 1990b), provide insight into how lock-in occurs, these studies fail to address the follow-on question: How does an organisation break out of co-evolutionary lock-in? What happens when renewal is not enough and discontinuous change is needed? These questions are the focus of this paper. Understanding how to avoid lock-in may be wise. The failure rate of strategic change is cited to run at rates as high as 70–80% (Beer & Nohria, 2000; Burnes, 2004, 2005). Yet, too many companies get trapped in strategy vectors for researchers to ignore the issue of breaking out. This paper is by no means the only paper to raise this issue. Much has been written recently about ambidextrous organisations, for example, as the solution to the tendency of successful firms to move towards lock-in (O'Reilly & Tushman, 2004). However, again these studies don't really consider how an organisation that is already in lock-in recovers.

The need to break out of co-evolutionary lock-in implies a need for variation. This cannot come autonomously as proposed in Burgelman's earlier work (see, e.g. Burgelman, 1991, 1994) since lock-in has shut down the strategic context that allows for autonomous initiatives and renewal. This is likely to require top-down direction in the form of a new strategic intent, but any new intent must be accompanied by simultaneous efforts to change the structural context, or the latter will select out strategic initiatives aimed at realizing the intent (Burgelman, 1994, 1996; Noda & Bower, 1996). To be able to change the structural context, however, one must first be able to conceptualise it.

Those adopting the evolutionary approach to strategic change define the structural context in terms of administrative and cultural mechanisms (Burgelman, 1991, 1994, 1996, 2002; Noda & Bower, 1996; Lovas & Ghoshal, 2000) . Yet empirically they focus primarily on the selection and retention properties of administrative mechanisms in the form of, for example, strategic planning, resource allocation, measurement and reward systems and hierarchical positions and responsibilities. The cultural mechanisms remain underspecified, with conceptual references limited to aspects such as socialisation rituals and behavioural norms (do's and don'ts) (Burgelman, 1991) and occasional empirical consideration of aspects such as constructive confrontation (Burgelman, 1994). The same is true of change research from a punctuated equilibrium perspective (e.g. Tushman & Romanelli, 1985; Romanelli & Tushman, 1994; Miller & Friesen, 1982), since empirically these authors also focus on what Burgelman refers to as the administrative mechanisms. In addition, neither of these literatures adequately links to more recent research from the resource-based view (e.g. Leonard-Barton, 1992) to consider how administrative and cultural mechanisms influence the development of the new core capabilities needed to deliver significant strategic change. The concept of core capabilities is important to our understanding of lock-in because it provides a way to connect the basis of competitive advantage with the value systems (i.e. culture) of the organisation.

To conceptualise how an organisation breaks out of lock-in, we first describe the link between the administrative and cultural mechanisms within the structural context and the development of new core capabilities. We expand on what is known about strategy vectors, review research from the strategy process tradition that explores the linkages between strategy, culture and strategic change, and use this to build a more comprehensive understanding of the changes needed to deliver breakout. The central argument is that breaking out of lock-in requires the development of new capabilities and that this, in turn, requires change in the structural context including change in the organisation's culture. Then to illustrate the link between lock-in, capability development and culture change we draw on the case of Ferrari.

Most people know Ferrari to be both an Italian manufacturer of sports cars, and a famous Formula One (F1) race team. Here, we are looking at the F1 operation. Ferrari was the leading F1 team in the 1950s and 1960s, but lost their dominant position after a brief period of rejuvenation in the 1970s, not to return as a serious contender until the late 1990s. The case provides interesting insights into how competitiveness can be re-established despite lock-in, and also enables connections to be made between administrative and cultural mechanisms and the development of new core capabilities. The case demonstrates the interconnectedness of the 'hard' (control systems and organisation structure) and 'soft' (beliefs, symbols, power structures and myths) sides of the structural context and shows how the development of new core capabilities is dependent on a holistic shift in organisational culture.

The focus on culture as a critical ingredient in breaking out of strategy vectors is supported by high profile cases such as IBM, and British Airways in the 1980s. IBMs repeated efforts to refocus on PCs, software and services were frustrated until the organisation experienced a complete cultural meltdown, structural shakedown and the appointment of Lou Gerstner. It nearly killed them, but cultural transformation was required before they really changed. Similarly, British Airways in the 1980s not only required a financial turnaround to restore their profitability under Lord King, but also a cultural transformation under Colin Marshall to change the company from an airline that was less about transportation and more about customer services. We finish the chapter with a consideration of the implications of our findings.

GETTING IN AND OUT OF LOCK-IN: CONCEPTUALISING THE STRUCTURAL CONTEXT

Burgelman (2002) argues that complex and reciprocal interactions between a CEO's strategic intent and the structures and processes put in place to align strategy and action, results in co-evolutionary lock-in that impedes exploratory activity and therefore new business development. Within the internal selection environment, sources of renewal are choked off as the strategic context is suppressed by the tight coupling between the structural context and induced strategic action. This prevents the retention, if not the selection, of autonomous strategic actions. As long as an organisation's competitive market place remains relatively stable, this may not be a problem. Ongoing induced strategic actions should be sufficient to maintain an organisation's competitive position (Johnson, 1988). However, if there is a shift in the viable basis of competitive advantage in the external environment so that the organisation's existing capability base no longer serves to add economic value (Leonard-Barton, 1992) (such as would be precipitated by, e.g. change in the forms and/or means of delivery of products/services), induced strategic actions that leverage existing capabilities are no longer adequate. Instead, responding to such change requires renewal of the capability base. The bottom-up, autonomous initiative required to produce renewal is not possible as the strategic context has been dampened by lock-in (Burgelman, 2002). Furthermore, even if induced actions that are consistent with the new intent are introduced, these will be selected out by the tight fit between the existing structural context and the existing strategy (Burgelman, 1994, 1996; Noda & Bower, 1996; Johnson, 1987).

Thus, on its own, articulating a new strategic intent will be insufficient to break out of lock-in. Furthermore, reorientation based on existing core capabilities is not likely an option. The shift in the viable basis of competitive advantage requires new ways of competing in existing product markets and therefore the development of new core capabilities. Moreover, if the new intent includes domain change, this, too, requires the development of new capabilities. Therefore, for the organisation to survive and break out of co-evolutionary lock-in, the structural context itself must change to enable the selection and retention of induced strategic actions, and to reinvigorate the engine of autonomous strategic initiatives, both of which are the source of new capability development.[1] As argued by models of punctuated equilibrium, the necessary transformation involves a fundamental realignment of 'an organization's strategies, power, structure, and systems ... toward the purposive actions of executive leaders' (Tushman & Romanelli, 1985, p. 173).

Therefore, consistent with the argument above, for an organisation's strategy to change in the face of lock-in, it is necessary to realign everything else to support the new strategic intent. This then leads to the question posed in the introduction – how can the structural context be defined in order to understand how to change it? Whilst both those adopting evolutionary and punctuated equilibrium perspectives consistently point to the importance of structures, systems and culture, empirically they focus almost exclusively on what Burgelman refers to as the administrative mechanisms, leaving culture as an unopened 'black box'. Furthermore, neither of these perspectives makes adequate linkages to research on core capabilities. According to this view, change is conceptualised as the improvement of existing or the development of new core capabilities, i.e. those capacities required to develop and/or sustain a competitive advantage in line with conditions in the competitive environment (Maritan, 2001; Helfat & Peteraf, 2003; Teece & Pisano, 1997). It is worth noting that organisations experiencing lock-in may have little problem with improving existing capabilities, i.e. enhancing the basis of their current competitive advantage (Burgelman, 2002). Lock-in becomes a problem when improvements in existing core capabilities are insufficient to respond either to a new way of competing in existing product markets, or to the need for a domain change requiring the development of new core capabilities.

For example, changing competitive conditions may dictate that an organization needs to bring new products to market faster by accelerating its development process to continue to grow market share. Significant shifts in speed to market require the development of new core capabilities. To take another example, for global organisations to remain competitive, capabilities to do with local responsiveness must be augmented by capabilities in strategic integration across geographies (Bartlett & Ghoshal, 1993). Thus significant change on the basis of competitive advantage requires new administrative and cultural mechanisms to enable the development of new core capabilities, which in turn underpin the new products and services that deliver competitive advantage. Yet again, however, whilst the role of values and culture in capability development has been identified (e.g. Leonard-Barton, 1992; Teece, 2007), specifying the nature of the needed shift in value systems or, in other words, culture, has largely been neglected. 'Culture change' has become the property of organisational change and HR theorists while strategy scholars talk in other terms, with the result that the two fields often appear to be talking past each other.

Linking Strategy, Culture and Strategic Change

An alternative way to conceptualise the problem of change in the face of lock-in is to return to the language of Mintzberg (1978) and think in terms of realised strategies. He argues that 'strategy can be viewed as the set of consistent behaviours by which the organization establishes for a time its place in its environment' (Mintzberg, 1978, p. 941), and then therefore views the implementation of strategy as 'their translation into collective action' (Mintzberg & Waters, 1985, p. 259). This suggests a more distributed view in which a realised strategy is embedded throughout the organisation in the ways people behave, interact, talk and negotiate. This view is consistent with the findings of the sources of organisational inertia by both Miller (1990b, 1992) and Johnson (1987, 1988). They put the 'Icarus paradox' or the 'paradigm trap' down to the way top management intent in successful organisations becomes embedded in, and recursively related to, an organisation's culture. In order to introduce a new strategic intent, therefore, it is necessary to change the patterns of behaviours and interactions within an organisation – or in Johnson and Miller's terms, to change the embedded cultural routines, rituals and programs including the power structures that underpin these practices.

More specifically, Johnson (1987) describes the structural context in terms of organisational and power structures, control systems, symbols, rituals, stories and myths and unwritten norms of behaviour, all of which reinforce and support shared assumptions and beliefs. The interconnectedness of these elements is a key feature of Johnson's formulation, captured in what he calls a 'cultural web'.

However, the focus of these authors, like Burgelman, is more to consider how to avoid lock-in rather than how to break out of it. Furthermore, this research largely predates the work in the strategy field on core capabilities. Thus whilst the concern of Johnson and Miller, and others such as Balogun and Hope Hailey (2008), is to show the linkages between 'culture' and strategy, and therefore the need to deliver cultural change as a part of strategic change, there is a lack of linkage to considerations of new capability development. Yet, the view of Leonard-Barton (1992) that core capabilities are underpinned by an organisation's values does hint at a link to the culture web. Similarly, the components used by Johnson in his web connect to the cultural elements proposed by both those working from punctuated equilibrium and evolutionary perspectives. Thus, it seems to us that a more complete conceptualisation of breaking out of lock-in requires a reintroduction of culture. Fig. 1 suggests one way to see the link between culture and lock-in. What this figure suggests is that for a new strategic intent to succeed in delivering required new capabilities, the 'realised strategy' of the organisation embedded in the ways people behave, interact, talk and negotiate, needs to change. This, in turn, requires a shift in not just administrative components, but the cultural system. Such holistic change is required to develop the new core capabilities needed to adapt to a shift in the basis of competitive advantage. It is this sequence of changes that we propose as a tentative description of the process associated with breaking out of co-evolutionary lock-in.

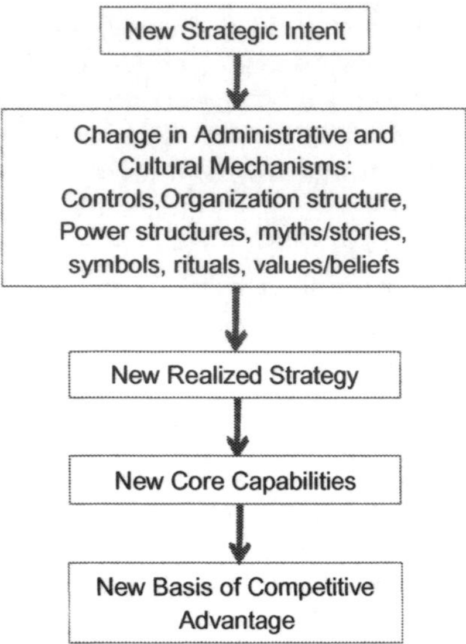

Fig. 1. Linking Strategic Intent.

A response to this argument might be: 'If it is so easy, how come all organisations facing the need for renewal aren't doing this?' The culture web provides some indications as to where the difficulties might lie. First, the web shows that in fact the administrative and cultural mechanisms are tightly interlinked and interdependent, and that both are unpinned and linked to the central values and beliefs of the organisation. As such, 'cultural mechanisms' are not something that can be changed separately. Second, much change becomes mired in politics; the assumptions and beliefs of those who are most powerful underpin the administrative and cultural mechanisms in an organisation; thus, power dependencies (Ranson & Hinings et al., 1980) must shift for change to be possible. Connected to issues of power dependency are issues of leadership. Without a shift in the focus and behaviours of senior leaders, all of which underpin what sits in the administrative and particularly cultural mechanisms, a shift in the elements of the cultural system will not be possible (Balogun & Hope Hailey, 2008; McGuire & Rhodes, 2009). Leadership patterns are inherently inert due to their self-reinforcing nature. This coupled with the interconnectedness of these elements with the rest of the web means that change relies on a painful revolution usually involving significant change in who is leading the organisation. Since the environmental shift inevitably occurs on the watch of the 'old guard', where is the motivation for such change to come from? Finally, there are also process issues to do with communication, training, personal development and so on. In reality, the complexity of what Fig. 1 proposes is, of course, huge. We therefore hope to illustrate the utility of our basic proposition with reference to a short case study.

DELIVERING CHANGE IN FORMULA ONE: THE CASE OF FERRARI

Ferrari was formed by Enzo Ferrari, himself once a racing driver. Ferrari is probably the most famous name in Formula One and Enzo Ferrari is himself an icon. Quotes equating Ferrari with style, Italy and passion such as the following are typical:

> 'Internationally famous as the bright red racing team and as a commercial motoring brand and style icon, with a long history of colourful and glamorous cars, drivers and adventures, everyone understands the meaning of Ferrari. So well known, it is virtually synonymous with Italy and Italian fashion chic as well as power, beauty and macho speed. Founded by Enzo Ferrari as a sports car production firm that also raced with style and success, Ferrari built up a reputation around original manufacturing home at Modena. Ferrari himself became a symbol of his team with his individualism, ambition, dark glasses and habit of rarely, if at all, travelling to races'.[2]

Table 1 provides an overview of the track record of Ferrari between 1950 and its renaissance in the late 1990s. The drivers column shows the years in which one of the Ferrari drivers won the drivers' championship. This is an annual award for the single driver who has the most race points at the end of the season. The constructors column shows the years in which Ferrari won the constructors' championship. This is awarded to the most successful Formula One constructor over a season, as determined by a points system based on Grand Prix results calculated by adding points scored in each race by any driver for that constructor. (Each team typically has 2 drivers.) In the 1950s, Italy was the leader in motorsport engineering and Ferrari had a lot of success in this period. (There was no Constructors Championship at this point in time.) There was also another period of success in the 1970s, but then Ferrari lost its leadership position until the end of the 1990s.

Enzo managed Ferrari in a particular way with a focus on the car. Drivers were dispensable, and drove for the honour of driving a red Ferrari. He rarely left Modena where Ferrari was based, and managed the team in a political way informed by what his advisors told him about performance

Table 1. Ferrari Drivers and Constructors Championship.

Date	Drivers	Constructors
1952	✓	
1953	✓	
1956	✓	
1958	✓	
1961	✓	✓
1964	✓	✓
1975	✓	✓
1976		✓
1977	✓	✓
1979	✓	✓
1982		✓
1983		✓
1999		✓
2000	✓	✓
2001	✓	✓
2002	✓	✓
2003	✓	✓
2004	✓	✓
2007	✓	✓
2008	2nd & 3rd	✓

Source: Available at http://www.formula1.com. Retrieved on April 2010.

away from Modena (Jenkins, 2001). Ferrari's dominance began to wane in the early 1960s with the ascendancy of the British constructors, who changed the nature of the racing cars to have the engine behind the driver rather than in front as was traditional. Ferrari resisted the changes introduced by the British 'assemblatori' or 'garagistes' as he called them since the 'horse always pulled the cart', until their dominance in the 1960s became so clear that Ferrari had no choice but to follow (Jenkins, 2005). The Ferrari designers who were by tradition engine designers did come up with a very successful rear-mounted engine winning Ferrari an additional world title, but meanwhile technology was changing and the British were becoming experts in chassis design using aerodynamics to build faster speed.

A rescue package appeared in the shape of an acquisition by Fiat in the late 1960s. This provided much-needed investment resources (enabling the building of a test race track at Modena, for example) and some professional management in the form of Luca Montezemolo for a period of time. Clearer team leadership under Montezemolo that broke away from the

Enzo Ferrari leadership style of 'divide and conquer' and a focus again on engine design with the recall of the old technical director, delivered another period of success from 1975–1979 in terms of driver and constructor championships (Jenkins, 2001, 2005).

Despite extensive investment (through Fiat), Ferrari continued to lose out since the new developments in aerodynamics and use of composite materials had originated, and was based, in the United Kingdom's motorsport valley (Jenkins, 2005). Enzo Ferrari did acknowledge this and took on a British designer, John Barnard. Barnard recognised the advantages of space age materials long before most were prepared to contemplate such a drastic departure and created the McLaren which dominated Formula One in the mid-eighties.[3] When Barnard joined Ferrari the team had won only two Grands Prix in the last two seasons. The designer was able to name his terms and was given a large sum of money to set up a design office in England, the Ferrari Guildford Technical Office (GTO) and began work on returning Ferrari to regular winning.[4] Although in charge of the technical direction of Ferrari, Barnard's location in the United Kingdom led to factions in Ferrari. Furthermore, Enzo died in 1988 leaving 90% of Ferrari in Fiat's hands and interference led to Barnard's departure in 1989 (Denison & Henderson, 2003; Jenkins, 2005).

However, in 1991, Luca Montezemolo returned to run Ferrari. He broke Ferrari into smaller departments and reappointed John Barnard to combine competence in engine design with competence in chassis design. Barnard formed Ferrari Design & Development in England (Denison & Henderson, 2003) employing British and Italians. This didn't ultimately work as Barnard left again. However, new professional team management had been put in place with the arrival of John Todt. Todt was a team player, as was Michael Schumacher who Todt then recruited in 1996, whereas Barnard was a brilliant engineer and not a team person.[5] Michael Schumacher then encouraged Todt to recruit designers Ross Brawn and Rory Byrne from his old team Benetton to fill the space left by Barnard's departure.[6] Between them these individuals set about establishing a team environment at Ferrari and ushered in a period of long-term stability.

Montezemolo also put in place many breaks with the past (see Denison & Henderson, 2003; Jenkins, 2005). Cars were now to be numbered on the year of racing, rather than the characteristics of the engine. The driver's position in the team was made central instead of incidental with the use of Nicki Lauder as an adviser. Schumacher's recruitment was made possible by a commercial deal with Phillip Morris to use the Ferrari cars to advertise Marlboro cigarettes. Morris paid Schumacher's salary and in exchange the colour of the Ferrari cars was changed from a blood red to the Marlboro orange red. Other commercial partnerships (different to the traditional 'selling of space on cars to advertise' arrangements) with Shell and Bridgestone tyres brought additional financial and technical support to Ferrari.

The newly created team environment with the driver as the central pivot in the team, and a strong relationship between engine design and chassis development, drove Ferrari to success once more. Come 1999, Ferrari started to dominate again.

ANALYSING FERRARI: LINKING CAPABILITY DEVELOPMENT TO MORE FUNDAMENTAL CHANGE

This case outline shows how the changing nature of the F1 environment required Ferrari to move away from its reliance on capabilities based in engine design to not only a broader set of capabilities to do with car and engine design, but also team performance where the driver worked in partnership with all other members of the Ferrari team rather than as adjunct of secondary importance to the car. The case also shows that Enzo Ferrari did recognise this in the 1980s with the establishment of GTO in the UK, but that car design and teamwork was never really incorporated into the philosophy of Ferrari. Furthermore, when Fiat took more control following the death of Enzo there was a lack of management knowledge as to how to run an F1 company, let alone how to deliver performance winning change at Ferrari.

Fig. 2 captures the way Ferrari would have looked prior to the return of Luca Montezemolo in the 1990s, through the cultural web. It shows how the *whole* Ferrari system hangs together as one concerned with engines as the basis of success, dominated by romantic notions of the past stemming from Enzo as the founder and his particular brand of leadership. There are not just issues of engine design, but also loyalty to the blood red, the prancing horse as a symbol and linkages to Italian pride and in particular 'being Italian':

> There's no question the passion for it is immense in Italy and Ferrari is the national team … It's something people over here, working in English Formula One teams, don't understand. You go there, you see it, you begin to feel it and you realise what you are into. People don't walk around the streets with their heads down in this country if

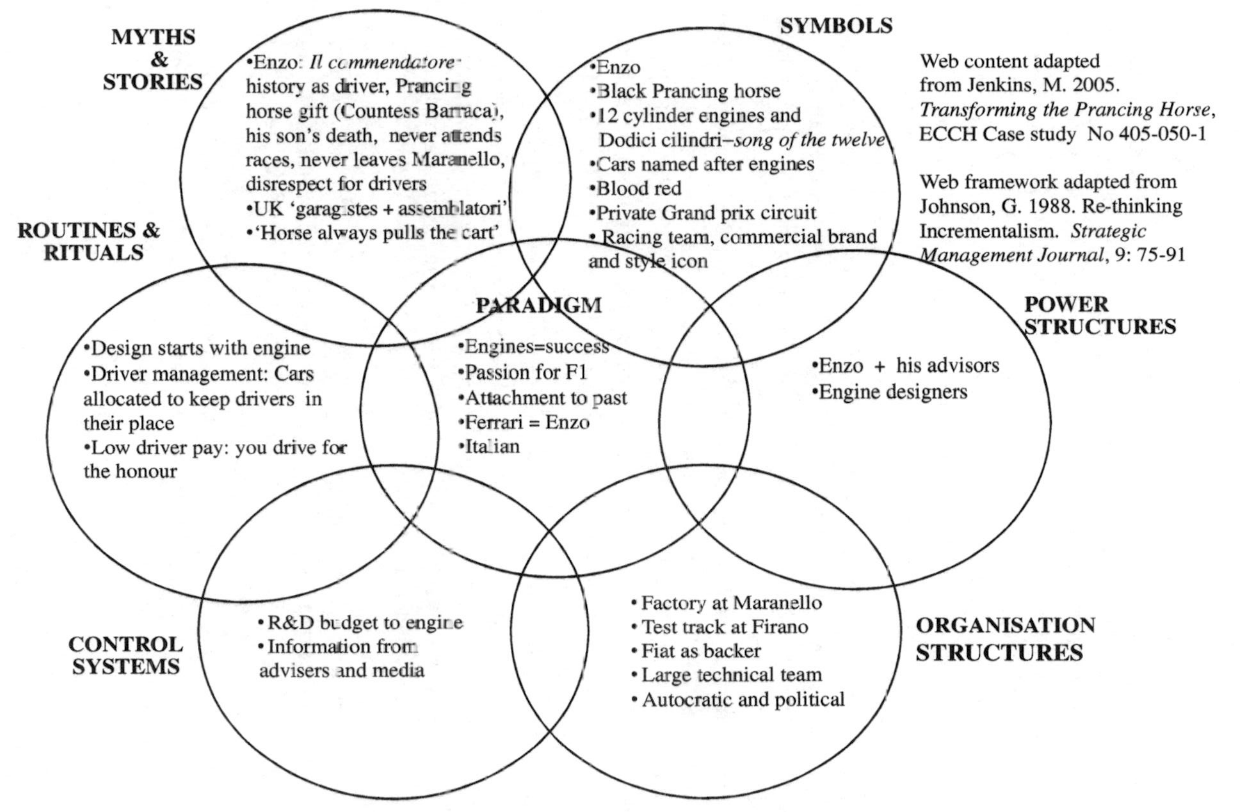

Fig. 2. Culture Web of Ferrari up to the 1980s.

> Williams or McLaren have had a bad weekend. They do in Italy if Ferrari has had a bad one. (John Bernard quoted in Allsop, 1995)

Fig. 2 also shows that to incorporate new capabilities around something other than engine design, and to make Ferrari a modern day racing company concerned with 'performance' and 'winning' above loyalty to traditions of the past, all aspects of the organisation had to change. Attachment of additional capabilities through, for example, GTO, UK would not be enough as the tightness of the existing organisational components would not allow for its integration. As argued in the introduction, any new intent has to be accompanied by simultaneous efforts to change the structural context, or the structural context will select out any new strategic initiatives (Burgelman, 1994, 1996; Noda & Bower, 1996). Enzo's death alone would not be enough either, as his founding principles were embedded through the organisation in a way that extended beyond him personally, in legend, symbols and so on.

Fig. 3 shows a new cultural web for Ferrari from 1999 onwards. What is noticeable is that Montezemolo has introduced a team concept that allows for incorporation of new capabilities with old capabilities, but has also allowed dramatic breaks from the historical and romantic past in things such as car colour and engine numbering. It is not just structures and systems that have been changed, but also the carriers of the old cultural value system that prevented a breakout from this way of thinking. Table 2 tracks the difference in the new and old organisations to show how these changes impacted on Ferrari, and ultimately these changes permeate the shared assumptions and beliefs of the organisation. Note that despite the changes, enough of the glorious days of the past were retained to maintain pride and make people want to work for Ferrari. The cars' colour changed but with their distinctive prancing black horse emblem the cars remained a cultural icon: a racing car and a glamorous commercial brand. The fantastic facilities of Ferrari remained in place at Maranello and Firano, with the Ferrari-owned private Grand Prix circuit.

Of course, power during the change process was crucial, not just in terms of Montezemolo, but also the people he recruited such as Todt, Bryne and Brawn and Schumacher, who shared his vision, and therefore created a new power dependency with a new set of assumptions and beliefs that could be used to drive through Montezemolo's vision. This links back to Leonard-Barton to show that *individual* capabilities are an important additional component to core competence, and that this capability may be technical, managerial or both. Fig. 1 needs to be augmented to capture this.

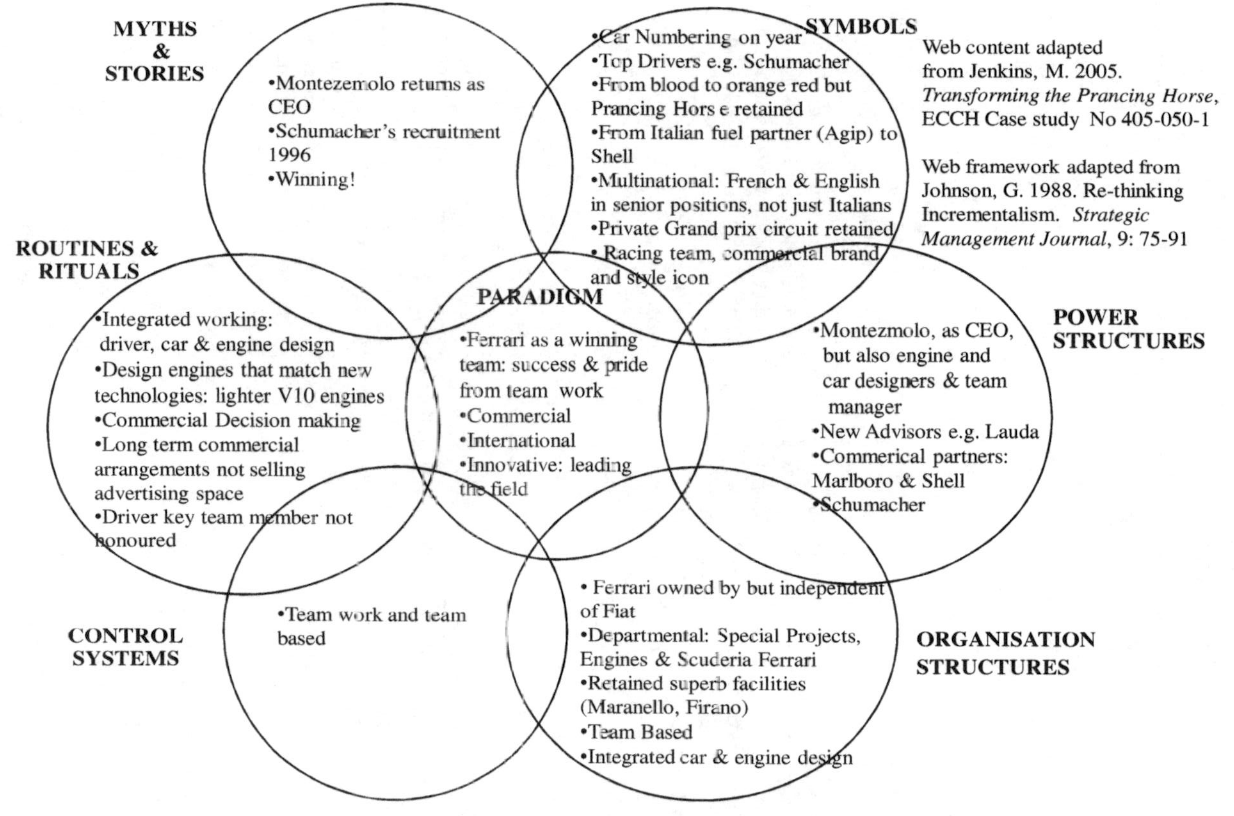

Fig. 3. Culture Web of Ferrari from 1999 Onwards.

Table 2. Changing Ferrari.

Old Ferrari	New Ferrari	Impact on Organizational Operation
Organisation structure • Factory at Maranello • Test track at Firano • Fiat as backer • Large technical team • Autocratic and political	Organisation structure • Ferrari owned by but independent of Fiat • Departmental: special projects, engines & Scuderia Ferrari • Retained superb facilities (Maranello, Firano) • Team based • Integrated car and engine design	The organization was changed radically and quite fast from a monolithic autocratic structure to something departmental and team based, sowing the seeds for (1) integrated working between car & engine design, but also (2) co-operation within teams rather than the prior politicised environment. This structural change is linked with power through the assignment of roles and responsibilities. (See Power Structures.)
Power structures • Enzo and his advisors • Engine designers	Power structures • Montezemolo, as CEO, but also chief engineer and car designer • New advisors, for example, Lauda • Commerical partners: Marlboro & Shell • Schumacher	For the new structure to work, the individuals holding key roles and their working styles and relationships were critical. It required a guiding coalition who were willing to adopt the types of team-based behaviours and integrative design principles the structure required to work. Individuals like Schumacher, but also Todt, Brawn and Byrne were key in this, as was Montezemolo's own willingness to let a team environment develop. It is these individuals that completed the structure by building the more informal 'ways we do things around here' reflected in the routines. Other influences also came into Ferrari with the new advisors Montezemolo used rather than governing autocratically as had Enzo. In addition, commercial partnerships started to play an important role as they provided much needed finance for a cash hungry operation.
Control systems • R&D budget to engine • Information from advisers and media	Control systems • Teamwork and team based	Control moved away from the politically based information regime that had been run by Enzo (he managed based on what his advisers and the press told him about performance away from Modena), leaving the organisation fragmented with individuals working for themselves. Instead the new regime focussed on more team-based controls and team loyalty and stability.

Table 2. *(Continued)*

Old Ferrari	New Ferrari	Impact on Organizational Operation
Routines and rituals • Design starts with engine • Driver management: cars allocated to keep drivers in their place • Low driver pay: you drive for the honour	Routines and rituals • Integrated working: driver, car and engine design • Design engines that match new technologies: lighter V10 engines • Commercial rather than political decision-making • Long-term commercial arrangements not selling advertising space • Driver key team member not honoured	The new design principles put in place by Montezemolo and reinforced by the new engineers and team manager were about giving the engine and car equal priority. Although Enzo had recognised this, since the whole organization had never been shifted away from the priority placed on the engine, prior attempts to deliver better car design had never led to integration of design. Now under the leadership of new individuals integrated design routines were put in place, and the engine engineers were allowed to design engines that matched new technologies. In addition, the way the driver worked with those designing and building the car and the engine became critical. The driver was no longer an add-on there just to drive. The driver was there to provide feedback and as a pivotal member of the team. In addition, the move to long-term commercial relationships to acquire finance rather than the selling of advertising space on the car also started to change the way things worked in the whole F1 industry.
Symbols • Enzo • Black prancing horse • 12 cylinder engines and Dodici cilindri – *song of the twelve* • Cars named after engines • Blood red • Private Grand Prix circuit • Racing team, commercial brand and style icon	Symbols • Car Numbering on year • Top Drivers e.g. Schumacher • From blood to orange red but Prancing horse retained • From Italian fuel partner (Agip) to Shell • Multinational: French & English in senior positions, not just Italians • Private Grand Prix circuit retained • Racing team, commercial brand and style icon	Communication doesn't just occur through the spoken and written word. Many of the things done indicated serious breaks from the past: numbering cars after the year not the engine indicated the lesser importance of the engine, the shift to orange red showed a more commercial and less historical and sentimental style of operating, the importance now attached to drivers made them into strong icons embodying the new found success of Ferrari and the greater range of nationalities involved suggested that Ferrari was no longer as Italian as it used to be. Again, what mattered was the commercial decision: who was the best person for the job.

Table 2. (*Continued*)

Old Ferrari	New Ferrari	Impact on Organizational Operation
Stories and myths • Enzo: *Il commendatore:* history as driver, prancing horse gift (Countess Barraca), his son's death, never attends races, never leaves Maranello, disrespect for drivers • UK 'garagistes' and 'assemblatori' • 'Horse always pulls the cart'	Stories and myths • Montezemolo returns as CEO • Schumacher's recruitment 1996 • Winning	Enzo's hold over Ferrari was always reinforced through the legends and stories about him. Similarly these stories perpetuated his views. Who would believe he was serious about the English designers when he still called them 'garagistes' & 'assemblatori'? Or that he was serious about attaching equal weight to the car when he kept his focus on the engine? However, with Enzo's death, and the arrival of Montezemolo and the clear breaks with the past he put in place, these stories ceased to have relevance, and the organization moved on to worship new heroes such as Schumacher.

Thus we can see how for new capabilities to deliver a new competitive performance mandate (with the product as the car and an integrated team performance), change was needed in all elements of the structural context to support and drive through a fundamental shift in the assumptions and beliefs of the organisation. Crucially, this change started with a change in leadership and power dependencies. Furthermore, the assumptions and beliefs of Ferrari were never targeted directly by this new leadership team. A fundamental shift occurred gradually through the use of the other elements of the structural context.

DISCUSSION

We can describe the change that occurred at Ferrari in many different ways: breaking out of a strategy vector, developing new capabilities, as a transformation or even as a culture change. The Ferrari case shows these things to be different facets of the same phenomena. For Ferrari to deliver a new strategy to do with dominating F1 once more, and through a vision of teamwork to enable a group of gifted individuals working in harmony to deliver more than was possible through the addition of their discrete contributions,[7] demanded a new set of capabilities. These capabilities were technical in the sense of engineering excellence beyond engine design, but also managerial to enable the different functional capacities and capabilities to work together. This in turn required a shift in the structural context of Ferrari – both administrative and cultural. This also meant a challenge to some of the taken-for-granted assumptions that underpinned the old Ferrari model.

In addition to showing the need for a change in strategy which is based on the development of new capabilities to be underpinned by changes to both technical and cultural aspects of organisations, the case of Ferrari also raises questions about some of the assumptions underpinning earlier models of transformation. The premise of punctuated equilibrium models of change, for example, is that for radical change to occur a revolution is needed, in which it is necessary to change all aspects of the organisation in a short timescale. This case study shows that this isn't necessarily the case. In fact, the range of organisational components considered in the Ferrari case would suggest that changing all of these components 'at once' (i.e. in a short timescale) as suggested by punctuated equilibrium models is probably impossible – particularly in large organisations. This leads us to a more nuanced systems' perspective in which components first need to be broken apart and then rewoven (Schilling, 2000; Siggelkow, 2002; Rivkin, 2000).

Schilling (2000) argues that modularity, which describes the degree to which a system's components can be segregated and recombined and the tightness of coupling, is a general property of systems. Furthermore, this property of modularity enables systems to be broken up and recombined in different ways to create different configurations. Yet 'synergistic specificity' does also exist where there are extensive interactions between components a change in one component will require accompanying changes in the other components for the system to continue to function effectively. Siggelkow (2001) suggests that this is as true of organisational systems as any other systems. Therefore, when an organisation's fit with the external environment declines, managers of a firm need to change a whole range of elements in a mutually supportive manner to enable the organisation to play a new game, thereby treating the structural context as a number of interlinked and interdependent components. Achieving *internal fit* between components is critical (Siggelkow, 2001). This doesn't differ from the punctuated equilibrium models in terms of conception, but it does allow for the components to be decoupled and changed at different speeds. Thus, intended strategy, leadership and power dependencies and structure may be changed up front in a kind of 'big-bang' fashion to kick start the breakout from a strategy vector, but then other components need to follow in a more evolutionary and supportive manner as at Ferrari.

This notion of hard then soft change is supported by other research which explores paths of change (Balogun & Hope Hailey, 2008; Beer & Nohria, 2000). These writers argue that it is necessary for senior managers to rebuild their organisations physically through a focus on the tangible, before focussing on the softer and less tangible elements to drive through the longer term transformation. Restructuring may deliver a temporary uplift in performance, but without the focus on the latter, longer term transformation won't occur. Authors such as Huy (2001) quite rightly link the different approaches that can be taken to change to the theories underlying them (such as rational design assumptions, or a 'guided learning approach'). This provides us with insight into why top managers leading change may choose one approach over another and also insight into the range of different approaches that exist and their potential suitability for different types of change. However, importantly, this does not provide adequate acknowledgement of the fact that different approaches may be suited to different phases of change, or of the need to use different approaches in combination to impact on different modules of the organisational system. At times of breakout, the initial big-bang change to intended strategy, leadership and structure may require senior managers to follow rational design assumptions, whereas as change in other components then follows on, change approaches that are more targeted at values and beliefs (e.g., socialising and teaching Huy, 2001), may be needed.

Whilst it would be possible to look at the Ferrari case and argue that the predominant approach was based on rational design assumptions, in fact there is evidence of significant symbolic activity to create breaks with the past and indications of what the future is about. Symbolic activity is about the management of meaning and involves the manipulation of organisational artefacts, use of metaphors and new language, sharing of new stories, the obvious break with myths of the past (through symbolic behaviour, including role modelling) and use of ritual (Trice & Beyer, 1984, 1985). Symbols are any object, event, quality or relation that serves as a vehicle for conveying meaning, usually by representing another thing (Trice & Beyer, 1984). They are a communication vehicle, and cue-scripted action (Gioia, 1986). Symbolism refers to 'those aspects of an organisation that its members use to reveal or make comprehendable the unconscious feelings, images, and values that are inherent in that organization' (Dandridge, Mitroff, & Joyce, 1980, p. 77). As such, they are powerful because they link into the organisational ideology and value system. Since symbolic activity is a type of non-verbal language (Morgan, Frost, & Pondy, 1983), arguably, any signs or signals, sent by objects, events, activities or behaviours triggering sensemaking, can influence how individuals interpret what is expected of them – and indeed do (Balogun & Johnson, 2004, 2005). Whilst a significant body of prior literature focused on the role of symbolic activity in change and the management of meaning, this emphasis has largely disappeared from the literature of strategy and change, with some exceptions (Zott & Huy, 2007). Yet the Ferrari case shows its significance.

CONCLUSION

At one level this paper could be said to simply repackage old models and concepts – and this is partly true. However, it is also attempting to reintroduce thinking that has disappeared from the fields of strategic management and organization development and change: to show the way forward we need to look backward. We currently have two fields talking past each other through the use of different languages and different concepts (such as capabilities and lock-in) which add richness to our conceptualisation of organisations, yet are also creating a fragmented view of the system with different fields working on different components of the whole without adequate recognition of the linkages. To return to Mintzberg's analogy of the blind men and the elephant, integration is required for organisations to break out of lock-in rather than feeling one part of the elephant. For the organisational change literature to be able to provide insight into how top managers implement strategy, there is a need for more links between the strategies and strategic context driving the need for change and the design of the change process. Similarly, for the strategic change literature to be able to provide more insight on how top managers lead strategy, there needs to be more cognisance of the prior learning in the field of organisational change. For both fields to move forward requires more explicit attempts to share and link learning.

The juxtaposing of concepts such as realised strategy alongside strategic intent and capability first shows that delivery of a new strategic intent is about the alignment of not just structures and systems (the administrative mechanisms), but also the way people are going about their work (which has more to do with the underspecified cultural mechanisms). As such, Fig. 1 is consistent with earlier models such as Nadler and Tushman's (1989) congruence model which argues that various organisation components need to be aligned with one another to implement a new strategy and achieve improved business performance. We need to distinguish between what is the planned or intended strategy of an organisation and the actual realised strategy of that organisation as captured in what people are actually doing. Once the problem of strategic change is framed in these terms it becomes clear that implementation is about far more than writing a plan, issuing new objectives and communicating a clear direction. To implement strategic change it is necessary to understand and change the *realised* strategy of the organisation, what people are currently doing, to align it with the *intended* strategy. This means changing the way people think and behave on a day-to-day basis, thereby changing the pattern in the actual stream of decisions and actions over time.

Livne-Tarandach and Bartunek (2009) argue that scholarly attention to only one of planned or emergent change, or just one of these at a time, creates a one-sided view of the change challenge. Their paper highlights the danger of a focus on only one component of change as do we. Our paper argues against an exclusive focus on just the administrative mechanisms of an organisation, insisting instead on a dual focus on the administrative and cultural mechanisms. It then argues for the need to work simultaneously with intended and realised strategies. The former represents only a vision of the future; the latter represents the current state of the organisation. The change challenge is to close the gap between the two. This is also likely to require an ongoing focus on both planned and emergent as change progresses.

Of course, not all planned strategies require a fundamental reappraisal, but herein lies a second issue highlighted by the juxtaposing of concepts such as realised and intended strategies. Without an understanding of the gap that often exists in organisations between the intended and the realised, senior executives regularly underestimate the extent of change demanded by the new strategies they have formulated. In other words, problems with implementation start with formulation. There is talk of the development of new core capabilities, and new ways of operating or of reaching customers or of defeating the competition, without a realisation of the way the old capabilities and old ways are underpinned by existing beliefs, values, habits and routines. Ironically, most executives would simultaneously acknowledge that existing value systems underpin much of what happens in their organisation. For example, Lou Gerstner is on record as saying, 'I came to see in my time at IBM that culture isn't just one aspect of the game, it *is* the game'. Similarly Carl-Henrik Svanberg, CEO of Ericsson, has said 'culture always defeats strategy'. Despite these acknowledgements, there is a fear of intangibles like 'culture', 'values' and 'behaviours', which leads to a focus on changing only structures, control systems and work processes, which in turn limits the development of new capabilities.

The case of Ferrari is the case of a small organisation operating in a particularly fast moving competitive context. We may question the extent to which ideas from this context can be translated into larger and more complex companies. The case also dodges many issues that continue to plague the field of strategy and change. What are the conditions, other than crisis, that enable a new power dependency to take control and start to effect change? How does a handful of strategic leaders effect change in huge and complex organisations? On the other hand, the analysis of the Ferrari case also shows that we cannot continue to discuss change in terms of purely 'capabilities', or 'administrative and cultural mechanisms' or 'routines' as the literature on strategic renewal has a tendency to do. To really understand how to break out of lock-in, the understanding we have developed from studying these things in isolation needs to be used in a far more integrative fashion. 'Culture' is a mechanism that enables us to do this, so it needs to be moved from the 'too hard' box and put back into the mainstream.

NOTES

1. This pattern is consistent with a punctuated equilibrium model of change (Tushman & Romanelli, 1985). However, as Van de Ven and Poole (1995) point out, this is not inconsistent with an evolutionary approach. The punctuated equilibrium model incorporates evolutionary motors of change in convergent, evolutionary periods and teleological motors of change in divergent periods of discontinuous change.
2. (http://f1.uk.reuters.com/team/ferrari/profile.php?refresh = true: 22 September, 2008).
3. Barnard focuses Ferrari on war, Independent, The (London), Jul 15, 1995 by Derick Allsop.
4. http://en.wikipedia.org/wiki/John_Barnard
5. Inside Ferrari, autosport.com, April 17 2008.
6. Inside Ferrari, autosport.com, April 17 2008.
7. Inside Ferrari, autosport.com, April 17 2008.

ACKNOWLEDGMENTS

We would like to thank Mark Jenkins and Julie Verity for giving us the inspiration to use the Ferrari case to illustrate the points we wished to make in this paper. We would also like to thank Bill Passmore and Dick

Woodman for their constructive comments on early drafts of this paper. The authors gratefully acknowledge financial support in the preparation of this manuscript from the UK ESRC/EPSRC/Advanced Institute of Management (AIM) Research: RES-331-25-3014.

REFERENCES

Allsop, D. (1995). Barnard focuses Ferrari on war. *The Independent (London), July 15th.*

Balogun, J., & Hope Hailey, V. (2008). *Exploring strategic change*. Harlow, Essex: Financial Times Prentice Hall.

Balogun, J., & Johnson, G. (2004). Organizational restructuring: The impact of manager sensemaking. *Academy of Management Journal*, *47*(4), 523–549.

Balogun, J., & Johnson, G. (2005). From intended strategies to unintended outcomes: The impact of change recipient sensemaking. *Organization Studies*, *26*(11), 1573–1601.

Bartlett, C., & Ghoshal, S. (1993). Beyond the M-form: Toward a managerial theory of the firm. *Strategic Management Journal*, *14*(Winter), 23–46.

Beer, M., & Nohria, N. (2000). Cracking the code of change. *Harvard Business Review*, *78*(3), 133.

Burgelman, R. A. (1991). Intraorganizational ecology of strategy making and organizational adaptation: Theory and filed research. *Organization Science*, *2*(3), 239–262.

Burgelman, R. A. (1994). Dynamics of competitive strategy. *Administrative Science Quarterly*, *39*(3), 523.

Burgelman, R. A. (1996). A process model of strategic business exit: Implications for an evolutionary perspective on strategy. *Strategic Management Journal*, *17*(Special Issue), 193–214.

Burgelman, R. A. (2002). Strategy as vector and the inertia of coevolutionary lock-in. *Administrative Science Quarterly*, *47*, 325–358.

Burnes, B. (2004). *Managing change: A strategic approach to organisational dynamics* (4th ed.). Harlow, Essex: Financial Times Prentice Hall.

Burnes, B. (2005). Complexity theories and organizational change. *International Journal of Management Reviews*, *7*(2), 73–90.

Dandridge, T. C., Mitroff, I., & Joyce, W. F. (1980). Organizational symbolism: A topic to expand organizational analysis. *Academy of Management Review*, *5*(1), 77–82.

Denison, D., & Henderson, J. (2003). *The Ferrari Renaissance*. IMD case study, Ref. No. IMD-4-0276.

Gioia, D. A. (1986). Symbols, scripts, and sensemaking: Creating meaning in the organizational experience. In: H. P. Sims & D. A. Gioia (Eds), *The Thinking Organization*. San Francisco: Jossey-Bass.

Helfat, C. E., & Peteraf, M. A. (2003). The dynamic resource-based view: Capability lifecycles. *Strategic Management Journal*, *24*(10), 997–1010.

Huy, Q. N. (2001). Time, temporal capability and planned change. *Academy of Management Review*, *26*(4), 601–623.

Jenkins, M. (2001). Formula One constructors: Combined case. ECCH Case Study. Ref. No. 301-056-1.

Jenkins, M. (2005). *Transforming the Prancing Horse: Ferrari 1950–2004*, ECCH case study, Reference No. 405-050-1.
Johnson, G. (1987). *Strategic change and the management process*. Oxford.
Johnson, G. (1988). Re-thinking incrementalism. *Strategic Management Journal, 9*, 75–91.
Leonard-Barton, D. (1992). Core capabilities and core rigidities: A paradox in managing new product development. *Strategic Management Journal, 13*, 111–125.
Livne-Tarandach, R., & Bartunek, J. (2009). A new horizon for organization development and change scholarship: Connecting planned and emergent change. *Research in Organization Development and Change, 17*, 1–35.
Lovas, B., & Ghoshal, S. (2000). Strategy as guided evolution. *Strategic Management Journal, 21*, 875–896.
Maritan, CA. (2001). Capital investment as investing in organizational capabilities: An empirically grounded process model. *Academy of Management Journal, 44*(3), 513–531.
McGuire, J. B., & Rhodes, G. B. (2009). *Transforming your leadership culture*. San Francisco: Wiley.
Miller, D. (1990a). Organizational configurations: cohesion, change and prediction. *Human Relations, 43*(8), 771–789.
Miller, D. (1990b). *The Icarus paradox*. New York.
Miller, D. (1992). The Icarus paradox: How exceptional companies bring about their own downfall. *Business Horizons*, Jan–Feb.
Miller, D. (1994). What happens after success: The perils of excellence. *Journal of Management Studies, 31*(3), 326–358.
Miller, D., & Friesen, P. (1980). Momentum and revolution in organisational adaptation. *Academy of Management Journal, 23*(4), 591–614.
Miller, D., & Friesen, P. (1982). Structural change and performance: Quantum versus piecemeal-incremental approaches. *Academy of Management Journal, 25*(4), 867–892.
Mintzberg, H. (1978). Patterns in strategy formation. *Management Science, 24*, 934–948.
Mintzberg, H., & Waters, J. A. (1985). Of strategies deliberate and emergent. *Strategic Management Journal, 6*(3), 257–272.
Morgan, G., Frost, P. J., & Pondy, L. R. (1983). Organizational symbolism. In: L. R. Pondy, P. J. Frost, G. Morgan & T. C. Dandridge (Eds), *Organizational symbolism* (pp. 3–35). Greenwich, CT: JAI.
Nadler, D. A., & Tushman, M. L. (1989). Organizational frame bending: Principles for managing reorientation. *Academy of Management Executive, 3*(3), 194–204.
Noda, T., & Bower, J. L. (1996). Strategy making as iterated processes of resource allocation. *Strategic Management Journal, 17*, 159–192.
O'Reilly, C. A. III, & Tushman, M. (2004). The ambidextrous organization. *Harvard Business Review, 4*, 74–81.
Prahalad, C. K., & Bettis, R. A. (1986). The dominant logic: A new linkage between diversity and performance. *Strategic Management Journal, 7*, 485–502.
Ranson, S., Hinings, C. R., et al. (1980). The structuring of organizational structures. *Administrative Science Quarterly, 25*(1), 1–17.
Rivkin, J. W. (2000). Imitation of complex strategies. *Management Science, 46*(6), 824–844.
Romanelli, E., & Tushman, M. L. (1994). Organizational transformation as punctuated equilibrium: An empirical test. *Academy of Management Journal, 37*, 1141–1166.
Schilling, M. (2000). Toward a general modular systems theory and its application to interfirm product modularity. *Academy of Management Review, 25*(2), 312–334.

Siggelkow, N. (2001). Change in the presence of fit: The rise, the fall, and the renaissance of Liz Clairborne. *Academy of Management Journal, 44*(4), 838–857.

Siggelkow, N. (2002). Evolution towards fit. *Administrative Science Quarterly, 41*(1), 125–159.

Teece, D. J. (2007). Explicating dynamic capabilities: The nature and microfoundations of (sustainable) enterprise performance. *Strategic Management Journal, 28*, 1319–1350.

Teece, D. J., Pisano, G., et al. (1997). Dynamic capabilities and strategic management. *Strategic Management Journal, 18*, 509–533.

Trice, H. M., & Beyer, J. (1984). Studying organizational cultures through rites and ceremonies. *Academy of Management Review, 9*, 653–669.

Trice, H. M., & Beyer, J. (1985). Using six organizational rites to change culture. In: R. H. Kilman, M. J. Saxton & R. Serpa (Eds), *Gaining control of the corporate culture*. San Francisco: Jossey-Bass.

Tushman, M., & Romanelli, E. (1985). Organizational evolution: A metamorphosis model of convergence and reorientation. In: L. Cummings & B. M. Staw (Eds), *Research in Organisational Behaviour* (Vol. 7, pp. 171–222). Greenwich, CT: JAI.

Van de Ven, A. H., & Poole, M. S. (1995). Explaining development and change in organizations. *Academy of Management Review, 20*(3), 510–540.

Zott, C., & Huy, Q. (2007). How entrepreneurs use symbolic management to acquire resources. *Administrative Science Quarterly, 52*, 70–105.

TRANSCENDING PARADOX: MOVEMENT AS A MEANS FOR SUSTAINING HIGH PERFORMANCE

Jason A. Wolf

INTRODUCTION: A STUDY OF SUSTAINED HIGH PERFORMANCE

> All things change, nothing is extinguished.... There is nothing in the whole world which is permanent. Everything flows onward; all things are brought into being with a changing nature; the ages themselves glide by in constant movement. (Ovid)

As Ovid said, "There is nothing in the whole world which is permanent." It is this very premise that frames the discoveries in this paper and the compelling paradox it raises. The research discussed herein began with the simple question: *what supports the sustainability of high performance?* The findings suggest the sustainability of high performance is not a permanent state to be achieved, i.e., sustaining is not about maintaining. Rather, the paradox uncovered offers that sustaining is about being, as Ovid asserts, "in constant movement."

This idea of sustainability as movement is predicated on the ability of organizational members to move beyond the typical experience of paradox as an impediment to progress. By holding three critical "movements" – *agile/consistency*, *informative/inquiry*, and *collective/individualism* – as active

Research in Organizational Change and Development, Volume 18, 77–107

ISSN: 0897-3016/doi:10.1108/S0897-3016(2010)0000018007

polarities, the organizations in the study were able to transcend paradox and take active steps to continuous achievement in outperforming their peers. The study reveals powerful stories of care and service, of the profound grace of human capacity, and of clear actions taken to create significant results. All of this was achieved in an environment of great volatility, which is perhaps why the need to not only be in movement but also capitalize on that movement is critical to success.

THEORETICAL FRAMEWORK

A New Environment of Change

The challenge of change in organizations has been a central point of dialogue in organization science from its very beginning. Yet, the need to address the issue of change has become more and more apparent in an age of "permanent whitewater" (Marshak, 1993; Vaill, 1989; Weisbord, 2004) in which information, technology, markets, and people are emerging and advancing at breakneck speed (Beer, 2001; Marshak, 2002). The challenge of change has significant implications for the field of organization development (OD) itself. While by its early definitions, OD represented a process of planned change (Porras & Bradford, 2004; Weisbord, 2004), the shift to an environment of constant change calls for new models by which change is addressed in organizations. The world no longer moves in incremental steps, but rather in significant leaps that call for new modes of effecting change.

The English statesman, David Lloyd George, once said, *"Don't be afraid to take a big step if one is indicated. You can't cross a chasm in two small jumps."* The simple significance of this thought perhaps best captures one of the greatest challenges facing today's organizations. If organizations become complacent or stationary for too long, it is inevitable that the chasm will continue to widen and our ability to reach the other side will quickly diminish. To remain in shape to make these leaps requires the development of organizational agility (Shafer, 2001) and the need for organizations to be in constant movement.

The shift to an environment of constant change calls for new models and processes by which change is addressed in organizations. The organization that will succeed in this new environment is one that plays the role of destabilizer (Drucker, 1995), meaning it focuses on using knowledge in the moment to guide its actions. The organization for this century must be built to thrive in an environment of continuous change, not simply based on continuous as evolutionary (Porras & Robertson, 1992; Weick & Quinn, 1999) or incremental, but as continuous and transformational.

Woodman (1993) addressed this very issue, warning us to look at the issue of OD and change with a wider lens. He asserted OD's founders built the field to do "BIG OD"; what he described as second-order transformations at the level of strategy and culture. BIG OD is system-wide change and has no beginning or end, but rather provides a "way of managing complex organizations so that they are able to survive in a world of constant change" (p. 72). He raises the potential that change itself is paradoxical, suggesting it is both transformational and continuous, and emphasizing that managing this dynamic tension should be the rallying cause and "battle cry" of all OD practitioners. Woodman summarizes his point in a simple, yet powerfully integrative statement, "Organization development means (and still means) creating adaptive organizations capable of repeatedly transforming and reinventing themselves" (Woodman, 1993, p. 73). This is a model of change predicated on dynamic movement, not simply change management.

Marshak (2004) supports this notion suggesting the need to build organizations capable of continuous whole-system change. He adds that "the emphasis…be on creating and maintaining capability rather than arriving at some preferred or planned end state" (Marshak, 2004, p. 16). We need to look for new language to help us move beyond the embedded assumptions we currently hold in thinking about change as there is still a strong tendency for organizations to strive for a state of permanence, order, and stability. This reinforces the paradox that to sustain actually calls for us to be in movement and places the concept of paradox itself at the heart of this study of sustaining high performance.

This needed shift in the discourse of change calls for a new way of talking, from static to dynamic and from descriptive to active. Lawler and Worley (2006) suggest that this "new" language is at the core of the *built to change* organization. These organizations do not search for the strategy, but are continuously strategizing. They do not attempt to find the organization design, but rather remain in an ongoing process of organizing. As the data revealed, the sustaining high performers had just such an active and dynamic discourse.

> In an increasingly complex world, organizations built on traditional assumptions of stability, equilibrium, alignment and predictability will, more and more, be out of touch and ineffective. Pursuing the latest management fad that is sold as a way to make organizations more efficient, more agile, more reengineered, or more whatever doesn't address the fundamental need for organizations to change more quickly and effectively. (Lawler & Worley, 2006, p. 283)

The speed with which organizations are now called to change is becoming legend (Barczak, Smith, & Wilemon, 1987) and in many ways is ultimately about a continued state of becoming (Kofman & Senge, 1993; Tsoukas & Chia, 2002). It requires the abandonment of past practices (Friedman, 2005), the changing of core processes, and retuning of cultural commitments (Nutt & Backoff, 1997). While addressing the nature of organizations as complex and dynamic systems, these complicated phenomena and the contradictions (paradoxes) they raise are ignored as incongruent, inconsistent, and therefore are often overlooked (Quinn & Cameron, 1988). Underlying this is the tendency in management theory to want to reduce these tensions and reconcile potential paradox. Yet, it is in this body of literature, on "irreconcilable" organizational tensions – on paradox itself – where the core concepts for this study are found and where a fundamental contribution to organization theory can be made.

The Perspective of Paradox

> Why is it that organization theorists should be concerned with the issues of paradox? What insights does it offer to the understanding of organizations that are not available or have not been available though the existing "nonparadoxical" perspectives? For us, the answer to these questions is quite simple: *paradoxes are important because they reflect the underlying tensions that generate and energize organizational change* (italics added)...A focus on paradox, therefore, moves us away from the concept of organizations as static systems coping with problematic environmental fluctuations through deviation counteracting processes to a concept of organizations as continually dynamic systems that carry the seeds of change within themselves. (Ford & Backoff, 1988, p. 82)

In examining the idea that sustainability itself may actually be grounded in action or movement, we are called to examine the very paradoxical nature of organizations themselves. Many writers have identified the importance of paradox in understanding the complexity of organizational performance (Cameron, 1986; Cameron & Quinn, 1988; Marsh & Macalpine, 1999; Pascale, 1990; Peters & Waterman, 1982). Yet paradox as a concept unto itself continues to carry a stigma in current management thinking. Much of the focus of contemporary theory construction is still biased toward the side of permanence, order, and stability (Poole & Van de Ven, 1989). Little has been addressed in looking at the tensions or oppositions (paradoxes) in organizations. Investigations of complex organizational phenomena continue to focus on linear solutions and equilibrium, either ignoring contradictions or identifying one polarity as good and the other bad in order to resolve the issue (Quinn & Cameron, 1988). This suggests there is a still a general discomfort with the idea of, and feeling experienced when facing, paradox.

This avoidance of, and attempt to, resolve paradox seems common to organizational thinking. While acknowledging paradox exists, many continue to suggest it is something to be "managed" (Morgan, 1997; Peters & Waterman, 1982) or "addressed" (Van de Ven & Poole, 1988). In contrast, as paradox has become more prevalent in organizational studies (Lewis, 2000; Poole & Van de Ven, 1989; Quinn, 1988; Quinn & Cameron, 1988), it has also emerged as an effective means to explore what is taking place in organizations (Luscher, Lewis, & Ingram, 2006).

In recognizing paradox we are exposed to, and can more effectively explore, the complexity and ambiguity of organizational life (Cameron & Quinn, 1988). In developing a model for sustaining high performance, paradox presents a powerful means to get at the dynamic factors involved and can serve as a viable path to developing theory (Poole & Van de Ven, 1989). In looking for organizational tensions, we can stimulate the development of broader and more interesting (Bartunek, Rynes, & Ireland, 2006; Davis, 1971) theoretical concepts.

While understanding paradox does not solve problems (Luscher et al., 2006), it creates the potential for new possibilities. The presence of paradox and the tensions raised by their duality creates the potential for action and energizes organizational change (Ford & Backoff, 1988). This supports the ongoing nature of action and continuous movement as a means for creating new opportunities. If we deny the presence of paradox in favor of a stable or consistent framework we in essence restrict the very movement, and therefore the progress, an organization can make.

> If realities are constructed (as is suggested), paradox is a function of how construction is accomplished, and the dualities of paradox provide the energy for change, then it is possible to bring about organizational change through the creation of paradox…It is the creation of paradoxical tension which serves as the basis for change. (Ford & Backoff, 1988, p. 114)

Morgan (1997) suggests successfully managing change in organizations requires the ability to deal with the "contradictory tensions" of paradox. The perspective that tensions are contradictory could stand in the way of change. He dubs this the "inevitable struggle of opposites," adding to lead successful change; managers must be skilled in managing the tensions that arise.

Poole and Van de Ven also suggest the importance of taking on this struggle of opposites, identifying how certain perceptions of and reactions to paradox, can stand in the way of building sound theory (Poole & Van de Ven, 1989; Van de Ven & Poole, 1988).

> If unacknowledged and unresolved, a paradox can drive theorists to emphasize one pole over the other, in an attempt to maintain an elusive consistency. Organization and management theorists have not been immune to this tendency. Most efforts to build theories of organization change have emphasized either action or structure, stability or change, external or internal causality, and have subordinated the other terms. In part, this tendency to deny the existence of paradox may be due to the common quest to achieve coherent, consistent, and parsimonious theories. But this quest often appears to minimize appreciation of the paradoxes inherent in human beings and their social institutions. (Van de Ven & Poole, 1988, p. 21)

Even with the recognition that paradox is part of organizational life and in the face of many who suggest it is in paradox that we find the potential for the greatest outcomes, there still seems to be a tendency toward the resolution of paradox versus living in the paradox in search of new "truths" (Van de Ven & Poole, 1988). To finds these truths and capitalize on paradox, Fiol (2002) suggests that organizations must use "the inherent tensions to one's advantage rather than ignoring or resolving them" (p. 655). She too asserts the tendency of research to avoid or look for a means to resolve these tensions versus exploring how to use them.

While the literature identifies the existence of paradox as an unavoidable part of organizational life, it also suggests that much of the effort in organizations today is focused on reducing paradoxical situations. Lewis (2000) provides an alternative perspective, suggesting rather than attempting to reduce the tension of paradox or rationalize its existence we should use paradox to generate insight and change. She believes that the linear models under which we tend to frame organizational action do a great disservice to the complex organizations today. We cannot turn from paradox and suppress the tensions paradox may reveal.

Lewis discusses three means by which researchers have chosen to address paradox. The first, *acceptance*, is the freedom to live with a paradox, allowing it to exist not as a source of conflict, but acknowledging it as part of organizational life. The second, *confrontation*, is as it suggests, taking on a paradox with the intention of shifting its presence and ultimately reducing the tension it brings. The third, Lewis suggests is *transcendence*, which represents the "capacity to think paradoxically" (Lewis, 2000, p. 764). This is a reframing of thinking that incorporates paradox in an organization's "way of being." Rather than seen as contradictory to action, the tensions associated with paradox are experienced as complementary. Transcendence is not the removal of paradox. It is changing the way in which it is experienced from a potential impediment to a potent and powerful force.

While it is widely recognized that the paradoxes found in organizational life are unavoidable, little has been offered on how organizational change and paradox actually allow for the sustainability of organization vitality and performance. This exploration into what supports the sustainability of performance is grounded in these two very items – paradox and change – and leads us to the critical intersection between them. The literature has provided a grounding in change and a suggestion that BIG OD – continuous, transformational change – has a significant position in exploring what effects organizations today. The literature also expresses the unavoidable challenges paradox poses, as the prevailing tendencies are to manage paradox versus use it as a constructive part of organizational life. Only in Lewis' (2000) suggestion that paradox can be transcended, do we begin to explore a new way to experience and exist with paradox as the regular element of organizational life it is. If sustainability is paradoxically juxtaposed with movement, the possibility for looking at how we lead change and strive for performance outcomes in organizations can be fundamentally impacted. Lewis perhaps summed this up best and begins to frame the potential for an emerging theory in her conclusion.

> The rising intricacy, ambiguity, and diversity of organizations place a premium on researchers' abilities to think paradoxically: to live and even thrive within the plurality and changes of organizational life and help practitioners do likewise. Building this capacity requires confronting our own defenses – the desire to over rationalize and oversimplify the complications of organizational life – and learning to explore the natural ebb and flow of tensions. (2000, p. 774)

Paradoxes both energize change and move us beyond the view of organizations as static systems to the potential of movement itself (Ford & Backoff, 1988). If we deny the presence of paradox or are simply stopped by it, we restrict the very movement an organization can make. Ultimately it is in transcending paradox (Lewis, 2000; Pascale, 1990) through which we discover the potential for the sustaining of organizational performance.

THE RESEARCH JOURNEY

An Initial Exploration and Emerging Question

This paper finds its roots in research initially conducted in 2005 at Healthco (a large hospital company) that was focused on determining the key drivers of business performance. The central questions of the inquiry were what was it that had some facilities rise and stay above the rest; what could we learn from them; and how could we help others achieve the same outcomes? It was believed that performance characteristics could be identified from these "high-performing facilities" and shared among other facilities in the company. (High performers were identified as those facilities that were in the top quartile of all Healthco facilities and/or trending to the top quartile in four core measures – employee engagement, turnover, patient satisfaction, and productivity – as well as outperforming the company in outcomes measures including quality and financial performance.) This foundational study identified seven central characteristics including visionary leadership, consistent and effective communication, selecting for fit and providing ongoing development of staff, maintaining an agile and open culture, ensuring service is job one, supporting constant recognition and community involvement, and creating solid relationships (Wolf, 2008).

In continuing to monitor the performance of the original 12 facilities from the initial inquiry over an extended period from 2002 to 2007, it was discovered that 9 continued to meet the selection criteria established in determining "high performers" and outperformed Healthco on a number of measures. Over that period, these "sustaining" facilities averaged over seven percentage points higher in employee engagement score, over four points lower in turnover percentage, and over five percentage points higher in margin performance. While the qualitative findings in the study discussed below paint a compelling picture about what took place within the organizations sustaining high performance, it is this extended look at the quantitative data that substantiates the validity and reinforces the impact of the findings. It also supports why the question about sustainability has significantly bigger implications than simply new theoretical considerations. Not only do sustaining high performers impact the people they touch, they also impact the critical measures of business success.

The extended data coupled with the ability to identify both "sustaining" and "nonsustaining" (those no longer meeting the original criteria) facilities raised an interesting set of questions. Perhaps it was not just "having" characteristics that caused "high performance," but rather was it possible that the characteristics initially discovered were merely manifestations of a more significant cause driving and sustaining performance. Why did certain facilities continue to thrive while others did not? What allowed these facilities to outperform the remainder of the organization over this extended period of time? And ultimately, the central question of this study: *what supports the sustainability of high performance?*

Methodology

The study followed a qualitative approach (Cresswell, 2007; Glaser & Strauss, 1967; Strauss & Corbin, 1998). It was grounded in the ideas of generative theory (Gergen, 1978), which closely aligns with this exploration of potentially paradoxical concepts. Instead of substantiating "truth," generative theory looks to "unseat the comfortable truths of wide acceptance" (Gergen, p. 1357).

The study was based on 41 interviews conducted at 12 different hospital locations: the 9 "sustaining" and 3 "nonsustaining" facilities. Interviews at the sustaining facilities were held with the CEO, longest tenured executive, longest tenured staff member, a director or manager with tenure from at least 2000 and a staff member with tenure from at least 2000. The interviews were conducted using a semi-structured interview protocol (Rubin & Rubin, 2005), digitally recorded and transcribed resulting in almost 900 pages of data.

Using the conventions of grounded theory (Glaser & Strauss, 1967; Strauss & Corbin, 1998), a comprehensive coding process was conducted including open and axial coding, and outcomes were confirmed via a multi-rater validation. The findings were then compared with those of four research partners to enrich the interpretive process. Once codes were identified (over 1200 raw codes initially) a review of the data was conducted to categorize and identify key themes. The initial code count was reduced to 128 initial categories, which were then grouped into 24 supercategories capturing the main concepts developed in the study. The supercategories were consolidated into 10 key themes. After additional review, the 10 themes were refined into 3 core concepts, representing 3 active polarities – the 3 movements of sustaining high performance – within the subject facilities.

FINDINGS

The findings in this study were drawn from hundreds of stories shared by participants in the hospitals studied. While this paper cannot share every story told, it touches on the compelling and powerful messages they conveyed as represented by the three movements of sustaining high performance uncovered in this study. Each movement is comprised of three key actions (Table 1) that represent what the sustaining high performers revealed as critical to their ability to achieve ongoing performance. The movements and key actions are not items to simply check off. They are actions that must be

Table 1. The Three Movements and Nine Key Actions in Sustaining High Performance (Wolf, 2009).

Movement	Key Actions
Agile/consistency	Acting with clarity of purpose Going above and beyond Challenging the status quo
Informative/inquiry	Caring about our people Seeking input and sharing information Walking the talk
Collective individualism	Committing to who Connecting and caring Acting with ownership and autonomy

taken on relentlessly day after day. Sustaining performance is a never-ending journey that requires great stamina, resolve, and a commitment to these fundamentals.

Agile/Consistency

The first movement, *agile/consistency,* represents the culture, or consciousness, of the organization. It appeared in the data almost 600 times. The stories related to this finding talk about the sustaining high-performing facilities "acting with a clarity in purpose," i.e., a determination and resolute focus on a desired result. They also tell of these facilities balancing this focus with a strong willingness to "challenge the status quo" with a commitment to positive change and continuous improvement. These items were found in the data on almost 400 occasions. *Agile/consistency* represents both a focus on purpose and a balanced commitment to progress that provide people the ability to move toward moments of anxiety, but without fear. This movement represents the capacity to engage in organization efforts and participate in guiding organizational outcomes not as contradictory to purpose, but rather as contributing to cause.

The data provide us insight to a precarious, but potentially important balance. At one end is the need for consistency in organizations as seen in many of the responses of participants who stated "we have clear shared expectations," a "common commitment to purpose," and "we all focus on the same goals." At the other is the need for agility to address the challenges of a rapidly changing world. The recognition of this shows up across the data in phrases such as "we change what needs to be changed," "we make changes quickly," and "we are willing to change as required to be better." This dynamic tension presents itself in the recognition over and over that these facilities are clear about who they are, but realize that the world may call them to adapt at any given moment. The third element that comprises the movement *agile/consistency* is tied directly to the last phrase shared above "as required to be better." The theme of "going above and beyond," which appears almost 200 times in the data, presents that potential balancing point where focus on purpose and a commitment to progress meet.

The first of three key actions under *agile/consistency* is *acting with clarity of purpose*. The data showed these organizations to have a strong sense of collective self and organizational pride supported by a sense of personal connection to the organization and the contributions people could make. This is supported by the second key action, *going above and beyond*, which represents the ability of individuals to do what it takes to create peak experiences for customers and for one another. One CEO annually challenges his staff to list what achievements they will strive for in the year ahead. The goals, such as "Best Place to Work," "Magnet Status," and "Baldridge" are taken on as critical commitments aligned with the purpose of the organization. This is reflected in the significant number of times participants referred to their facility as striving "to be the best." The third key action is *challenging the status quo*. The ability to challenge the status quo is reinforced by an environment that supports people's efforts to try new things. Most importantly it is the ability to do so with the knowledge that mistakes are not career ending, but rather the discoveries they lead to (positive or negative) are seen as organizational gifts. This belief, that it is far better to fail trying than not to do at all, represents the very idea of movement. Following a consistently clear purpose, while maintaining the agility to alter course, trying new ideas and taking on new endeavors is one key movement in sustaining performance.

An example of *agile/consistency* can be seen in the following story, where acting on needs and making appropriate changes trumped long committee-based decision-making processes. The nurse was able to distinguish what made her current facility a sustaining high performer versus her "frustrating" experiences at a previous hospital. What is also provided in this story is an insight shared throughout the data; that "challenging the status quo" is not about change for the sake of change. It seems in situation after situation, as exemplified below, the sought-after changes were aligned with the purpose of the facility.

> One of the things that attracted me to come here to begin with was that I was frustrated at my previous hospital by the fact that in order to get something changed or to do something you had to submit it to this committee. Then it went to this committee and that committee. Our CEO here told me if you need to change it, do it, if it works fine, if it doesn't that's okay too, you tried. If we need something for patient care that improves patient care, you don't have to justify it. I don't even have to tell her what it is, I just tell her what I need and she says well get it. If it's for patient care, for staff, if it is improvement related, we don't have to go through committees or submit a financial statement on why it's important. That was very frustrating at the other facilities, you want to change a process and six months later they may agree to go ahead and let you change. But [our CEO] is like well do it. Everybody knows that, if we want to try something we can, as long as it's for the right reason.

Another interesting takeaway from this story has appeared across the data and is woven into all three movements. It is both the freedom to make decisions on needed change and also the freedom to make mistakes –"if it works fine, if it doesn't that's okay too, you tried." The CEO the subject described also made a comment to this effect during her interview telling me she would rather her people challenge what they do to make it better and mess it up (not too bad of course), than leave things as they are and never achieve their purpose.

This willingness to step up and take on what needs to happen sits at the very balance of *agile/consistency* – where "acting with clarity of purpose" is balanced by "challenging the status quo." In holding this paradox throughout the data, respondents said, "we are ready to change" and "we can make changes quickly." One participant noted, "Our facility is a work in progress." This simple statement perhaps is one the most powerful elements of this entire movement. That though rooted in principle, and committed in direction and purpose, these organizations report in the data that standing still is simply a definition for falling behind.

In comparison, in one of the nonsustainers, a long-tenured leader tells of feeling he has his "hands tied" and does not have the ability to make decisions. This has a significant impact on the ability to have either clarity in purpose or challenge the status quo. The idea in this example that they "would have done things differently," but in essence were unable to, shows how *agile/consistency* was stopped before it could even take root.

> Yeah, well the problem is that from where I sit leadership doesn't always get to make the decisions…so I think if you look at what we do here, would we have done some things differently or maybe a different way? Yeah, I think we would have. Does that lead to some sense of not following through? Yeah, I think so, because I think what ends up happening is we want to do it a certain way and [instead we are told] I'd like to see you do it like this…We're not as independent as we used to be and we can't make our own decisions like we used to.

This statement exemplifies the very fragile nature of *agile/consistency* in these organizations. You can see that while identified as a high performer in the initial study, the manager talks about having a greater sense of autonomy in leadership and the ability to make decisions. Now, identified as a nonsustainer, "we can't make our own decisions like we used to." This limitation in the culture of the organization contracts an individual's ability to strive above and beyond or challenge the status quo. If it is these actions that support the movement needed to sustain high performance, you can begin to see how easy it is to falter.

Informative/Inquiry

The second movement, *informative/inquiry,* represents the important influence of leadership in sustaining organization performance. It was represented in the data over 500 times. The stories representing *informative/ inquiry* express the impact of leadership at all levels of the organization. In particular it touches on the critical balance of two key components. The first, a willingness to inform and share critical information, or as one subject said, "they're willing to share the good, the bad and the ugly"; the second, an openness to inquire, which is different than simply "listening." This sense of inquiry was represented in the data over 150 times. As some participants defined it, it is the accessibility to leadership and the active gathering of input that brings leaders closer to their people. One interviewee said with great pride that "they actually listen," while another expressed that leadership truly "wants to hear from people."

This effort to both actively seek and share information appeared in the data not simply in standard examples such as rounding or an open-door policy, but rather as clear and sometimes very unique efforts of leaders at all levels to engage with and show they care about their people. This idea of caring expressed by leadership showed up over 120 times in the data. As one executive shared, "I have to walk the talk." In the end, the data seem to suggest that it is a very personal and intentional action of building strong relationships.

While this movement focuses on the critical role of leadership in sustaining high performance, it is not directed simply at leadership traits or styles such as "transformational" or "visionary." Rather, this movement suggests it is the constancy of actions from leadership at all levels in the organization that has the most significant impact, not the consistency of individual. One of the most resilient of the sustaining organizations in the study had a change in CEO two times over the course of the six years examined, yet maintained their results. Leadership is not necessarily about the individual, but rather about how the fundamentals of leadership are applied throughout the organization.

The first key action is *caring about people*, which focuses on sincere interest in and respect for people across the organization. This fundamental action carries great weight in supporting the engagement of people in supporting performance. The second action, *seeking input and sharing information*, is more than delivering communication. It represents the consistent effort to reach out to people in the organization for their ideas, concerns, and contributions. Most critical as the data suggested is the informal communication process in which leadership invests the time to personally connect with people, while gathering a broad collection of information from people across the organization. The third key action is *walking the talk*. This may be the core of effective leadership in sustaining high performance. The data suggested that the impact of leaders doing what they say, of living their words through their actions captures the very essence of the simple yet powerful nature of the movements in sustaining high performance. It is in walking the talk that commitment is realized and respect is delivered. It is also where commitment to and respect for leadership is earned. Leadership action has a significant impact in generating the outcomes of sustained performance.

An example of *informative/inquiry* can be seen in the following story told by a longest tenured executive. It is just one example of many from the data in which leadership has had influence through their actions outside of the administrative suite or director's office. In this story, the CEO shows up to work the night shift. In fact, he and his executive team have a commitment with the facility to work rotating shifts throughout the year. In this example we see how walking the talk provides the opportunity for *informative/inquiry* to be realized. The commitment this story expresses is about leadership not just being visible, but about turning visibility into input, and input into results.

> There's simple little things like when [our CEO came in to work] the night shift, he went into the ICU and said hey, how's it going, what do you guys need? We need a microwave. The next day he orders a microwave. How simple, but guess what, how timely was that? They want a microwave, get a microwave and get it in there today. That's a simple example. The ER still talks about the time that he pushed patients down to the room [when he worked a shift in the ER], where he actually said okay, here I am, can you help us move this patient? The CEO of the hospital moving the patient…that is walking the talk.

As this subject says, "that is walking the talk" and perhaps in some ways this concept touches on the core "mechanics" of this movement, walking and talking. The data seem to suggest that we need to be cautious in not accepting the concept of "walking the talk" as simply being visible. The data also seem to show us that what is most appreciated is when leaders engage with their people as a person first, meet them where they work, hear from them where they hurt, and share with them what is critical to move the organization forward.

The differences found in the nonsustainers are exemplified in the following story shared by one facility director. While he makes an effort to connect with his team, he follows this with the fact that "you always hear the administration never comes up." This lack of visibility and the resulting inability to either inform or inquire, make this movement nearly impossible to implement in these facilities.

One positive in the example is that amongst nonsustainers, there seems to be an intentional effort to address this challenge and turn these perceptions around. This action probably springs from the roots of high performance, which remain embedded in the organization from the period of the original study. If properly nurtured, these roots may provide the opportunity for sustained high performance to reestablish itself in the future.

> I know on my unit it helps that I do spend time getting to know them, you always hear that administration never comes up, they don't know us, so on this last survey one of the problems my staff had still was on communication, and that one I jumped on in a staff meeting and said okay, here's your problem that you all have that I can't fix, you have to tell me what this problem is. I said is it a communication problem from the floor level, from me, or are you still talking about administration? And it was administration. I said well, the first thing we're going to do then is every month for our staff meeting we're going to invite somebody different to come to the meeting that you can talk to and get to know, because we do have some people who have been here a fairly short time, we've got a new CFO, and our CNO has been here about a year now, so it just takes a little while, especially on the night shifts, to think they know everybody.

This example still unveils a challenge this facility faces in comparison to what the data reveal about the sustaining high performers. In the subject facilities, leadership, especially at the senior level, was the catalyst and driver of communication. Yet, in the situation described above, it is the department leader who has to reach up to engage the executive leadership in opening lines of communication. Until the administration begins an active effort of outreach to both inform and inquire, the sustainability of high performance for this facility will remain out of reach.

Collective/Individualism

The third movement, *collective/individualism,* represents the powerful element of people in the organizations. It was found in the interviews on almost 800 occasions. The stories related to this finding tell of the accomplishments of strong individual contributors. They expand on these accomplishments as not just an individual achievement, but as exponential successes resulting from the strong collaboration among members of the organization, both across departmental boundaries and spanning the organizational hierarchy. The data provides story after story of both the strengths of the individuals that comprise a facility and the synergy of excellence generated by the connection of these individuals with one another.

This movement represents the polarities of ensuring the right people are part of your organization; people who are aligned with, understand, and are committed to the organization's purpose and direction; people who can serve as strong individual contributors, but who also recognize that in spite of individual strength they can most effectively contribute by using their individual strength in powerfully collaborating across individual and organizational boundaries. This engages us in the systemic perspective of organizations that while they represent a collection of individuals, it is the organization that provides the framework for accomplishment. The idea of collaboration does not diminish individual contribution, but rather expands organizational capability.

This movement is grounded in the fundamental human principles of caring and commitment, directed not only at the organization and its customers but also with great focus on colleagues. The three themes comprising this concept include *committing to who*, *acting with ownership and autonomy*, and *connecting and caring*. The concept of caring appeared in the interviews almost 350 times. Commitment itself appeared just under 300 times, while ownership and autonomy appeared almost 200 times.

The first key action, *committing to who*, is grounded in the idea of getting the right people on board, but it is not only the attraction and acquisition of talent. It also takes us to the next level of our commitment to each of those individuals with an investment in developmental opportunities. *Connecting and caring* is the next key action and is about providing the opportunity for people in the organization to connect with one another, weave a network (that many in the study referred to as "family") that is supportive even in the face of critical work demands. This action is about ensuring someone's basic needs are met, not as mandatory management action, but rather from a groundswell of collegial support. This is not to suggest that every individual will embrace one another in any organizational setting, but the data shows sustaining high performance is solidly grounded on the level of care shown for and among people across the organization, from outreach in moments of crisis to celebrations in moments of joy. The support for and encouragement of personal connection has a profound effect on the sustaining of performance. The last of the key actions is *acting with ownership and autonomy*. This is the freedom and ability of members of the organization to make significant decisions at the point of contact. These actions come from people who feel they are not at risk for doing the wrong thing and given the opportunity continuously do what is right. Decision hierarchies may be necessary for significant expenditures or fundamental strategy shifts, but providing the space for individuals to make contributions through their daily interactions and individual decisions without the fear of retribution or punishment plays a significant role in supporting the movement of *collective/individualism* and its role in sustaining high performance.

An example of *collective/individualism* in action is seen on this final story. It shares the actions of the nurse that exemplify both personal ownership and a freedom to act without the need for "permission." This autonomy literally takes this nurse far from her unit and in essence alters her role from nurse to valet as she strives to provide the best possible experience for this patient.

> This is a story about one of my nurses. She had a patient that was elderly and he had parked in building C, we're in A, and she said to him where did you park? He said I'm out at building C. She said let me push you in the wheelchair over there. So she pushed him way over to building C and she got to the bottom floor and she said now, where's your car? He said it's in the back row. Okay. She pushed him all the way up the hill, all the way to the back row, and she found that the people next to him had parked so close to him that he couldn't get in there with his walker. So she had to leave him locked in the chair, get in his car, back his car out, and then help him get in the car. I thought, you know, that is [our hospital].

This story presents a powerful metaphor of continuing to stretch beyond the boundaries individuals oftentimes feel in their roles, whether by organizational constraints or by the self-imposed thought, "that is not my responsibility." The untold portion of this story, as expressed by the subject sharing this experience, is about what occurred when the nurse returned to the unit after a longer than expected absence. As she began to relay her story to her peers, rather than finger pointing or blaming for her absence, there was collective laughter at the never-ending journey she took on behalf of one of their patients.

As the interviewee shared, "This is an example of the type of facility we want to be. It is what we have been taught and encouraged to do." While there was probably not a formal protocol for taking a patient to his car at the far reaches of the parking lot, let alone pulling his car out of a space to provide easier access, the nurse in the story acted within the "boundaries" of the type of facility they wanted to be. The story provides a glimpse at how a sense of ownership can link with the freedom to act, and in this case provided the nurse the opportunity to have a powerful impact on this patient far beyond direct care. I can only imagine later that day, the elderly gentleman sitting with his family or friends telling the incredible story of the personal nurse/valet service he received. The autonomy and ownership exemplified by this individual had ripple effects well beyond the boundaries of her "job" that day. It exemplifies that the right individual connected to the right sense of commitment to the whole is a critical element in sustaining high performance.

In contrast, an example from a nonsustaining facility paints quite a different picture. A manager describes a situation in which nurses do not get up to respond to call lights due to the belief of "that's not my patient." The story presents conflicts with the very notion of both strong contributors, exemplified in people's unwillingness to act, and collaboration, as it is evident that the individuals are only committed to doing what is specifically assigned to them.

> A lot of times, patients, when they call out to the desk and they need something, there will be three people sitting there, but that's not their patient, so they don't get up. I said the patient doesn't know why you're not getting up. If you're sitting then you need to be answering call lights, because these are all our patients.

While a simple story, it serves as a powerful example of how the actions of *collective/individualism* can easily fall by the wayside in one simple moment. The nurses in the example are just "sitting there" because "that's not their patient." The story provides an example of how people's perspective on their role (*committing to who*), may be linked to these individuals choosing not to *act with ownership or autonomy* to address the situation, and in doing so, potentially misses the mark of *connecting and caring* for one another and even more so for the patients in need. This example shows how fragile the nature of *collective/individualism* is and how easily it can be derailed.

This overview of findings presents the central themes discovered through the voices of people across the facilities in the study. While only a sampling of the stories are shared here, those supporting the three movements signify a consistency in commitment, clarity in purpose, and a focus on action that is reflective of the importance of dynamic movement versus static characteristics. The stories of the nonsustainers paint an even more critical picture, one that expresses the truly fragile nature of sustaining high performance. The movements and key actions discovered represent an active picture of daily life in these facilities. We also see that if we falter on any one, if we become stagnant in our commitment and action, that it is far too easy to slip backwards. The data ultimately suggest constancy in focus and a commitment to action that leads to sustaining. They also offer that it is not one movement alone, but their connected nature that supports these facilities' ability to face the paradox of sustainability as movement and distinguish themselves as sustaining high performers.

DISCUSSION

The Importance of Paradox

In reflecting on the findings of the question, *what supports the sustainability of high performance*, I am struck by the powerful simplicity of the theoretical potential revealed in the data. One may be hard pressed to call the individual components of the findings in this research "unique" if each of them were to stand alone. Yet the findings suggest that in the act of sustaining they do not stand alone. Rather it is in the paradoxical nature of the movements through which the potential for a new conversation on change and sustaining performance emerges.

High performance is not a fixed state to be achieved by following a certain "recipe" (Quinn, 1988) or even an end itself (Pascale, 1990). Quinn (1988) suggests instead, "excellence is a paradoxical phenomenon that emerges under conditions of uncertainty and creative tension" (p. 12). Cameron (1986) contends that to be effective an organization must possess attributes that are "simultaneously contradictory." Without tensions between simultaneous opposites, unproductive "schismogenesis" occurs (a process of self-reinforcement where one action/attribute perpetuates itself and becomes extreme and dysfunctional). Paradox, on the other hand, calls for mutually exclusive opposites (e.g., strong individuals and powerful collaboration as found in *collective-individualism*), not those that are mutually reinforcing (e.g., dominance and submission). Can it be then that paradox itself provides the tension deemed critical to organization performance?

Janstch (1975), as cited in Ford and Backoff (1988), stresses that the potential for action itself is realized in the tensions created by the opposing ends of paradox. Eisenhardt (2000) adds that vibrant organizations drive change and performance by their ability to simultaneously hold the two states in a paradox. She asserts that this action is not simply finding a "bland halfway point" between the two extremes, but rather it is being in constant flux in exploring and capitalizing on this creative tension. This movement, the pursuit of simultaneous contradiction, counters the extreme outcomes of schismogenesis and can serve in supporting organizational effectiveness (Cameron, 1986) and performance.

A Metaphor of Movement

There is more than one way to live in a world of paradox (Smith & Berg, 1987). While stuckness is often the fate faced by groups, there is also the potential that efforts to engage in coexisting opposites will lead to movement. Smith and Berg (1987) define movement as "the exploration of new ground [and] the leaving of old patterns" (p. 215). This definition returns us to some of the very fundamentals organizations face today; the nature and pace of change in today's world requires a continuous, transformational (Marshak, 2002, 2004; Woodman, 1993) capability. Accepting this, the exploring of new ground and leaving old patterns is not just a "nice" thing to do, it is the necessary thing to do in order to compete and sustain performance in this environment. With this, the concept of movement emerges as a critical component for the sustaining of performance.

The question then is how is movement achieved? Smith and Berg (1987) suggest this results from one thing – living within paradox.

> By staying within the paradox, by immersing oneself in the opposing forces, it becomes possible to discover the link between them, the framework that gives meaning to apparent contradictions in the experience. The discovery…of the link provides the release essential for group movement (p. 215).

While Smith and Berg's thoughts focus on group life, I would suggest that these principles show up in a much more significant manner in the core consciousness, representative actions and determined leadership of organizations sustaining performance. The three movements themselves represent not just a way of being for an organization looking to sustain performance, but they encompass the central actions organizations can take to move performance forward.

So how does an organization ensure the transformation of these movements from potential roadblocks to a pathway to sustained success?

I suggest it comes down to the ability of an organization to reframe the paradoxes they face, experiencing them as complementary polarities, as continuums of good organizational behavior, which contribute to success. This starts with the simple choice of being in movement. Yet it calls for one more step in facing paradox, which is found in the ability to reframe it, create a new consciousness in action, and move toward the transcendence (Lewis, 2000; Pascale, 1990; Schumacher, 1977) of paradox itself.

Transcending Paradox: Beyond Contradiction to Continuum

The "paramount attribute characterizing organizations that have the capacity to adapt successfully (to turbulent times) is the presence of paradox" (Cameron, 1986, p. 545). It also is this adaptive capacity that is fundamental to achieving high performance. Cameron's statement in some ways seems contradictory in its own right, in that to adapt organizations actually need to acknowledge and capitalize on the presence of paradox, yet paradox continues to be seen by many as a significant impediment to progress.

Perhaps the simplest step the sustaining high performers take is recognizing the very paradoxes that frame the actions they take. They seem to understand that organizations are, at their core, dynamic entities that live in a world wrought with paradox. The sustainers' very willingness to be in motion and take on simultaneous, complementary actions holds the key to sustaining success. This is the act of transcendence (Lewis, 2000; Pascale, 1990).

The concept of transcendence has significant implications in looking at how organizations sustain high performance. It brings us back to our earlier discussion that high performance is not a state to be achieved, but a perpetual movement. It is the willingness to be in action and to take on levels of broader consciousness. Pascale (1990) offers a challenge to the management principles of the day, warning of the complacency of organizations in today's business environment. He suggests that with operational excellence seemingly an end unto itself, organizations have the tendency to believe they have achieved and in essence stop moving. He believes the biggest challenge we potentially face is the tendency upon reaching perceived achievement to set and stand fast with the status quo that helped us to achieve success. This too contradicts the reality of the turbulent environments we face.

Organizations today often find themselves stuck trying to repeat the one solution that helped them achieve desired results in the past. The "answer" replaces action, and eventually stuckness overcomes movement. If organizations are unwilling to move to keep pace with the constant change we face, it is easy to see how sustaining success would be virtually impossible. The challenge for organizations is to have the willingness to take the bold step into the fray, to address paradox head on, and in doing so transcend its potential drag and thrive in its potential. It is through the ability to transcend (Pascale, 1990) paradox that unleashes the creative possibility found within paradox itself. In transcending paradox the tensions of opposites shift from dualities (either/or) to polarities (ends of a continuum). Interactions shift from "either/or," to "and/also," moving beyond static state to dynamic tension. But how do we make this shift?

Pascale suggests a simple path to reaching this transcendent capacity, asserting the potential rests in our imagination. This is a powerful and profound suggestion; that fundamentally our challenge in organizations has been a failure of imagination. For example, until the four-minute mile barrier was surpassed, we did not have the belief it was possible.

This idea of *transcendent consciousness* allows organizations to make the choice of moving toward either a state of stability (a convergent solution that restricts capacity) or a mindset of dynamic tension, which is the capability of a system to absorb change and effectively adapt. This is reflected by the continuous, transformational "state" of change that sustaining high performers have purposefully chosen.

> Paradox lives and moves in this realm; it is the art of balancing opposites in such a way that they do not cancel each other but shoot sparks of light across their points of polarity. It looks at our desperate either/ors and tells us they are really both/ands – that life is larger than any of our concepts and can, if we let it, embrace our contradictions. (Mary Morrison cited in Smith & Berg, 1987, p. 3)

The idea of *transcending* paradox shifts the thinking from that of convergent problem solving to a reframing of the inherent tensions. Instead, contradictions become complementary and integrated polarities. The link between potentially opposing forces allows for dynamic movement and an oscillation between two continuous poles (Smith & Berg, 1987) – the ebb and flow between polarities. Ford and Backoff (1988) suggest, "the steering of a viable course requires that opposites…be balanced dynamically, rather than hold to one side or the other" (p. 88). This supports the findings that in continually balancing agility and consistency, collectivism and individuality, and informing and inquiring these organizations take on sustaining itself as movement.

Can we then say that sustaining itself is about movement? I would suggest we must.

> Thus being long lasting does not mean being in a fixed or definitive state. Being fixed and definitive, a thing cannot last long. The way to be constant is to change according to circumstance. (I Ch'eng as translated by Chan, cited by Marshak, 1993, p. 402)

A MODEL FOR SUSTAINING HIGH PERFORMANCE

In framing a model for sustaining high performance, we first ground it in an understanding of the power of an almost unconscious, continuous, transformational (Marshak, 1993; Tushman & O'Reilly, 1996; Weick & Quinn, 1999; Woodman, 1993), and morphogenic (Marshak, 2004) change process. We incorporate an understanding of the relational nature of humanness (Gergen, 1999; Gergen & Walter, 1998; Homans, 1951/1992) and dynamic balance (Bertalanffy, 1950; Evans, 1992; Guerra, 2005; Katz & Kahn, 1966; Smith & Berg, 1987), and include the recognition of unity in polarity (Durlabhji, 2004; Karcher, 1999; Marshak, 1993; Sun, 1999).

The result is the connection of the three central movements, *collective/individualism*, *agile/consistency*, *and informative/inquiry*, as individual polarities linked in a state of dynamic balancing and ongoing interaction.

As represented in the model (Fig. 1), each movement maintains the unity of its own "trilarity" of key actions, while contributing to the overall whole. Each part of the model represents movement and the continuous balancing of polarities. As the data show, the power of *collective/individualism* (people) enables strong individuals to interact and collaborate in powerful ways. The strength of *agile/consistency* (culture) provides unwavering purpose and the ability to rapidly respond in a moment's notice. The reach of *informative/inquiry* (leadership) supports an internal dialogue that not only informs, but continually learns and supports the very ability of its counterparts to operate most effectively.

Central to the model is that the movements coexist and are in a mode of continuous action. While at times one movement or another may ebb and flow, it is only together that they are effective in sustaining high performance. It is through the very complementary nature of the movements and the interconnectedness of their individual contributions that the system gets its power and the potential exists for the sustaining of performance.

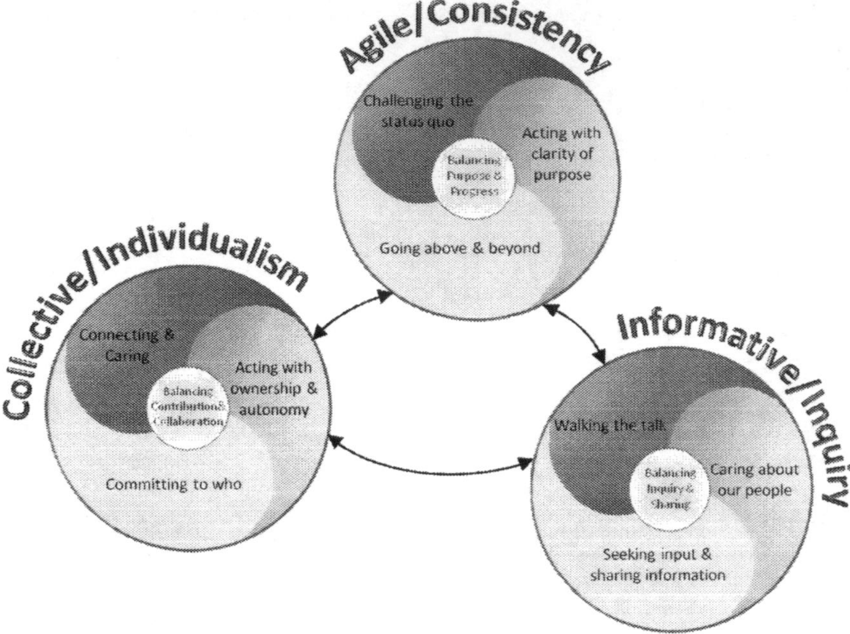

Fig. 1. A Model for the Sustaining of High Performance (Wolf, 2009).

The model is grounded in the challenges posed by paradox in organizations and is supported by the potential that there is more that can be accomplished than simply managing paradox. If we shift perspective and begin to look at these extremes, not as contradictory impediments, but as polar complements, we reframe the ability for organizations to address these seemingly conflicting issues.

This represents a shift in organizational consciousness, driven by a focus on key actions. Transcending paradox is about a willingness to be in a state of continuous balancing and disequilibrium. The elements of the model, the three movements of sustaining high performance, provide a framework of possibility for organizations to do just that. As one hospital CEO injected, this is not "*rocket science*"; it is rather about intentional action and the willingness to maintain focus on the key actions found in the data as part of what the organization does every day.

> When we transcend a paradox there is often a quality of obviousness that produces a shock of recognition. No longer held captive by the old way of thinking, we are liberated

> to see things we have known all along, but couldn't assemble into a useful model for action. (Pascale, 1990, p. 110)

It is true some could say this model represents things we have known of organizations, management, and leadership for some time. While on the surface it would be hard to argue, those holding that frame of reference should be cautious before setting off again on the trail of checklists and shallow assumptions. As the research suggests, there is a significant distinction between establishing a set of "successful" characteristics and actually taking action to ensure the three movements flourish in an organization. The process requires an intentional choice, an unwavering focus, and a lasting commitment. As the literature framed and the data exemplified, to be in movement toward sustaining performance is a never-ending journey requiring hard work on the part of every member of the organization.

IMPLICATIONS FOR PRACTICE

In returning to an important commitment of this study – making the findings accessible and relevant to practice, we are posed with the dilemma of translating a theoretical framework to potential for action. A key consideration in discussing implications for practice is the realization that while providing critical steps in the process, this information is more than a simple checklist of activities. It is imperative that the implementation of these items be part of a comprehensive organizational strategy that is in movement on all key actions. As one facility CEO noted, it takes "*unbelievable courage*" to be willing to put these seemingly paradoxical ideas in motion.

The general tendency of organizations will continue to focus on reducing tension and to drive linear cause and effect problem solving. Getting in to action around transcending paradox and moving toward sustaining high performance requires a bold leap in the face of these deep-seeded tendencies. While dynamic tensions will always exist, we must resist the desire to remove, manage, or avoid them. Instead what is required is a commitment to and focus on continuous action in each of the three movements.

Using the movements as a guiding framework, the key actions themselves can serve as core steps an organization can take on the road to sustaining performance. The data pulled from the stories also revealed a collection of simple actions that can help spark an organizational journey toward transcending paradox. These suggestions are offered to provoke thought and catalyze action.

Collective/Individualism

- People are introduced to and sign off on behavioral standards as part of the hiring process.
- Strong orientation and on-boarding processes are put in place to ensure new employees are quickly integrated into the organizational culture.
- Positive cross-departmental and interpersonal communications are required and reinforced.
- Space is provided for social interaction both formally and informally to create strong intra-staff connections, support relationships, and build trust.
- Broad cross-sections of people are involved in both solving critical problems and planning for longer-term solutions.
- Opportunities to take ownership for outcomes are provided and parameters for making decisions are established at all levels of the organization.
- People are made aware of what resources exist across the organization that can assist in accomplishing goals.

Agile/Consistency

- Clear organizational mission in place that guides the daily actions and decisions of the organization.
- People can easily see the connection of their role to the organizational mission and understand how the contributions they make support both purpose and goals.
- Performance is not measured simply by achieving goals, but rather by efforts to exceed them.
- Problems are addressed as they occur in real time by the people necessary to resolve the issue.
- Organization structure is not an excuse for inaction and the need for control and/or organizational politics are not impediments to expediency.
- An environment of "risk-taking" is encouraged by consistently supporting and recognizing efforts, rather than punishing failures.

- Current processes are seen as dynamic, malleable, and replaceable at the moment that new ideas and/or better ways of doing things emerge.
- Service is not just an initiative, it is a way of being; it is simple and focused and is not only about caring for the "customer" but also exemplified in caring for colleagues and peers.

Informative/Inquiry

- Leaders perform consistent rounding (walking the floors and engaging employees in the work environment) and show a clear and continuous presence (versus "management by fly-by").
- Employee input is sought and encouraged, both individually and through formal employee groups. More than just an "open door" policy, this is meeting employees where they are, in the units, halls, cafeterias, etc., and engaging in what matters most to them.
- An environment of openness is reinforced ensuring feedback can be delivered to leadership without fear of punishment or retribution.
- There is a commitment to sharing both good and bad news, reinforcing employees' knowledge of, ownership in, and accountability for the organization.
- Leaders engage employees in the work environment expressing appreciation and gaining understanding by taking on employee roles, e.g., unit secretary, transporter, etc., or working different shifts than "normal" work hours.
- Personal connections are made with employees through the use of notes and other direct communications both in moments of celebration and moments of hardship.
- Leaders consistently close the loop with employees, communicating actions taken in the facility and exemplifying a commitment to follow through in formal meetings such as town halls and department meetings.

While moving purposefully toward paradox and balancing the chaos in the midst of polarities may sound potentially intimidating, perhaps it should be the consideration of the consequences of not doing so that should be the true motivating factor. In a world where, as discussed above, the pace of change is now the pulse of organizational life, the ability of an organization to hold tensions as creative opportunities versus impediments to progress will be vital. The subject facilities provide simple yet powerful examples of what is required and the outcomes are painted in story after story shared by staff at all levels of what they have been able to accomplish. Thanks to the discovery of these organizations' rigorous efforts and unwavering commitments beyond basic action plans and performance checklists, the implications for practice can be significant. It all comes down to the courageous choice to act.

CONCLUSION

In discovering the three movements at the heart of sustaining high performance, it is not suggested that the concepts are unique in their own right. Rather, it is in the willingness to hold them in dynamic tension through which the power of sustainability as movement is realized. In transcending paradox, organizations accept the wholeness that each of these concepts and their key actions represent and comfortably find that space in balancing polarities that keeps them forever moving. It is an idea that rises directly from the chaotic nature of the world in which we live today. As discussed at the outset of this work, change now simply "is." It is our choice to accept it. "There is nothing in the whole world that is permanent … the ages themselves glide by in constant movement" (Ovid).

REFERENCES

Barczak, G., Smith, C., & Wilemon, D. (1987). Managing large-scale organizational change. *Organizational Dynamics*, *16*(2), 23–35.

Bartunek, J. M., Rynes, S. L., & Ireland, R. D. (2006). What makes management research interesting, and why does it matter?. *Academy of Management Journal*, *49*(1), 9–15.

Beer, M. (2001). How to develop an organization capable of sustained high performance: Embrace the drive for results-capability development paradox. *Organizational Dynamics*, *29*(4), 233–247.

Bertalanffy, L. V. (1950). The theory of open systems in physics and biology. *Science*, *3*.

Cameron, K. S. (1986). Effectiveness as Paradox: Consensus and conflict in conceptions of organizational effectiveness. *Management Science*, *32*(5), 539–553.

Cameron, K. S., & Quinn, R. E. (1988). Organization Paradox and transformation. In: R. E. Quinn & K. S. Cameron (Eds), *Paradox and transformation: Toward a theory of change in organization and management* (pp. 1–18). Cambridge, MA: Ballinger.

Cresswell, J. W. (2007). *Qualitative inquiry & research design: Choosing among five approaches* (2nd ed.). Thousand Oaks, CA: Sage Publications.

Davis, M. S. (1971). That's interesting! Towards a phenomenology of sociology and a sociology of phenomenology. *Philosophy of the Social Sciences, 1*(2), 309–344.

Drucker, P. (1995). *Managing in a time of great change*. New York: Truman Talley Books.

Durlabhji, S. (2004). The Tao of organization behavior. *Journal of Business Ethics, 52*(4), 401–409.

Eisenhardt, K. M. (2000). Paradox, spirals, ambivalence: The new language of change and pluralism. *Academy of Management Review, 25*(4), 703–705.

Evans, P. A. L. (1992). Balancing continuity and change: The constructive tension in individual and organizational development. In: S. Srivastva & R. E. Fry (Eds), *Executive and organizational continuity: Managing the Paradoxes of stability and change* (pp. 253–283). San Francisco: Jossey-Bass.

Fiol, C. M. (2002). Capitalizing on paradox: The role of language in transforming organizational identities. *Organization Science, 13*(6), 653–666.

Ford, J., & Backoff, R. (1988). Organizational change in and out of dualities and paradox. In: R. E. Quinn & K. S. Cameron (Eds), *Paradox and transformation: Toward a theory of change in organization and management* (pp. 81–121). Cambridge, MA: Ballinger.

Friedman, T. L. (2005). *The world is flat: A brief history of the twenty-first century*. New York: Picador.

Gergen, K. J. (1978). Toward generative theory. *Journal of Personality and Social Psychology, 36*(11), 1344–1360.

Gergen, K. J. (1999). *An invitation to social construction*. London: Sage Publications.

Gergen, K. J., & Walter, R. (1998). Real/izing the relational. *Journal of Social and Personal Relationships, 15*(1), 110.

Glaser, B. G., & Strauss, A. L. (1967). *The discovery of grounded theory. Strategies for qualitative research*. Hawthorne, NY: Aldine de Gruyter.

Guerra, D. (2005). *Super performance: New profound knowledge for corporate leaders*. Houston, TX: Old Live Oak Books.

Homans, G. C. (1951/1992). *The human group*. New Brunswick, NJ: Transaction Publishers.

Janstch, E. (1975). *Design for evolution: Self-organization and planning in the life of human systems*. New York: Braziller.

Karcher, S. (1999). Jung, the Tao, and the classic of change. *Journal of Religion and Health, 38*(4), 287.

Katz, D., & Kahn, R. L. (1966). *The social psychology of organizations*. New York: Wiley.

Kofman, F., & Senge, P. M. (1993). Communities of commitment: The heart of learning organizations. *Organizational Dynamics, 22*(2), 4–23.

Lawler, E. E., & Worley, C. G. (2006). *Built to change: How to achieve sustained organizational effectiveness*. San Francisco: Jossey-Bass.

Lewis, M. W. (2000). Exploring paradox: Toward a more comprehensive guide. *Academy of Management Review, 25*(4), 760–776.

Luscher, L. S., Lewis, M., & Ingram, A. (2006). The social construction of organizational change paradoxes. *Journal of Organizational Change Management, 19*(4), 491–502.

Marsh, S., & Macalpine, M. (1999). The search for reconciling insights: A 'really useful' tool for managing paradox. *Journal of Management Development, 18*(7/8), 642.

Marshak, R. J. (1993). Lewin meets Confucius: A review of the OD model of change. *Journal of Applied Behavioral Science, 29*(4), 393–415.

Marshak, R. J. (2002). Changing the language of change: How new contexts and concepts are challenging the ways we think and talk about organizational change. *Strategic Change, 11*(5), 279–286.

Marshak, R. J. (2004). Morphing: The leading edge of organizational change in the twenty-first century. *Organization Development Journal, 22*(3), 8–21.

Morgan, G. (1997). *Images of organization* (Rev ed.). London: Sage.

Nutt, P. C., & Backoff, R. W. (1997). Organizational transformation. *Journal of Management Inquiry, 6*(3), 235–254.

Pascale, R. (1990). *Managing on the edge: How successful companies use conflict to stay ahead.* New York: Simon and Schuster.

Peters, T. J., & Waterman, R. H. (1982). *In search of excellence: Lessons from America's best-run companies.* New York: Harper & Row.

Poole, M. S., & Van de Ven, A. H. (1989). Using paradox to build management and organization theories. *Academy of Management Review, 14*(4), 562–578.

Porras, J. I., & Bradford, D. L. (2004). A historical view of the future of OD. *Journal of Applied Behavioral Science, 40*(4), 392–402.

Porras, J. L., & Robertson, P. J. (1992). Organizational development: Theory, practice & research. In: M. D. Dunnette & L. M. Hough (Eds), *Handbook of industrial and organizational psychology* (2nd ed., Vol. 3, pp. 719–822). Palo Alto, CA: Consulting Psychologists Press.

Quinn, R. E. (1988). *Beyond rational management: Mastering the Paradoxes and competing demands of high performance.* San Francisco: Jossey-Bass.

Quinn, R. E., & Cameron, K. S. (1988). Paradox and transformation: A framework for viewing organization and management. In: R. E. Quinn & K. S. Cameron (Eds), *Paradox and Transformation: Toward a theory of change in organization and management.* Cambridge, MA: Ballinger.

Rubin, H. J., & Rubin, I. S. (2005). *Qualitative interviewing: The art of hearing data* (2nd ed.). Thousand Oaks, CA: Sage Publications.

Schumacher, E. F. (1977). *A guide for the perplexed.* New York: Harper & Row.

Shafer, R. A. (2001). Crafting a human resource strategy to foster organizational agility: A case study. *Human Resource Management, 3*, 197–211.

Smith, K. K., & Berg, D. N. (1987). *Paradoxes of group life: Understanding conflict, paralysis, and movement in group dynamics.* San Francisco: Jossey-Bass.

Strauss, A., & Corbin, J. (1998). *Basics of qualitative research: Techniques and procedures for developing grounded theory.* Thousand Oaks, CA: Sage Publications.

Sun, H. (1999). Yin-yang theory and its implications for management. *International Journal of Management, 16*(3), 439.

Tsoukas, H., & Chia, R. (2002). On organizational becoming: Rethinking organizational change. *Organization Science, 13*(5), 567–582.

Tushman, M. L., & O'Reilly, C. A. (1996). Ambidextrous organizations: Managing evolutionary and revolutionary change. *California Management Review, 38*(4), 8.

Vaill, P. (1989). *Managing as a performing art.* San Francisco: Jossey-Bass.

Van de Ven, A., & Poole, M. S. (1988). Paradoxical requirements for a theory of organizational change. In: R. E. Quinn & K. S. Cameron (Eds), *Paradox and transformation: Toward a theory of change in organization and management* (pp. 19–63). Cambridge, MA: Ballinger.

Weick, K. E., & Quinn, R. E. (1999). Organizational change and development. *Annual Review of Psychology*, *50*(1), 361.

Weisbord, M. R. (2004). *Productive workplaces revisited: Dignity, meaning, community in the 21st century*. San Francisco: Jossey-Bass.

Wolf, J. A. (2008). Health care, heal thyself! An exploration of what drives (and sustains) high performance in organizations today. *Performance Improvement*, *47*(5), 38–45.

Wolf, J. A. (2009). *Transcending paradox: A metaphor of movement for sustaining high performance*. Ph.D. dissertation, Benedictine University, IL, USA. Retrieved December 11, 2009, from Dissertations & Theses: Full Text. (Publication No. AAT 3349409).

Woodman, R. W. (1993). Observations from the field of organizational change and development from the lunatic fringe. *Organization Development Journal*, *11*(2).

RELATIONAL SPACE AND LEARNING EXPERIMENTS: THE HEART OF SUSTAINABILITY COLLABORATIONS

Hilary Bradbury-Huang, Benyamin Lichtenstein, John S. Carroll and Peter M. Senge

ABSTRACT

Corporations are now collaborating to meet complex global sustainability challenges, which, until recently, were considered beyond the mandate of business leaders. Multi-organizational consortia have formed, not as philanthropic efforts, but to find competitive advantage. To examine the dynamics of an early collaboration of this sort, with a view to suggesting how future inter-organizational projects might be fostered, we pursued an in-depth multi-method case study of "The Sustainability Consortium." The Consortium has convened Fortune 50 senior managers since 1998. Our analysis uncovers the primacy of "Relational Space" – a rich context for aspirational trust and reflective learning across organizational boundaries, which is enabled by, and in turn gives rise to, collaborative projects. Within this space, an ecology of organizational leaders committed to sustainability can accomplish together what would be impossible in their individual organizations. We explain the viability of this collaboration.

Research in Organizational Change and Development, Volume 18, 109–148

ISSN: 0897-3016/doi:10.1108/S0897-3016(2010)0000018008

A new organizational form is emerging: inter-organizational consortia of companies that span multiple industries, through which "business can be a leading force in eradicating poverty, enhancing the environment, and advancing peace – while still prospering financially" (BAWB/AOM Global Forum, 2006; see also Waddock, 2008). Compared to "traditional" R&D consortia (Browning, Beyer, & Shetler, 1995; Faulkner & De Rond, 2000) these multi-sector alliances (Glasbergen, Bierman, & Mol, 2007; Wondolleck & Yaffe, 2000) are addressing issues of unprecedented scope that go well beyond conventional business mandates and market boundaries (Gray, 1989; Austin, 2000, 2007). Of particular interest are "sustainability collaborations" such as the World Business Council for Sustainable Development (WBCSD), the Social Venture Network, and the UN Global Compact, which are composed of large, for-profit companies exploring how to transform their businesses and their societies into more sustainable systems. Although some business participants' primary motive may be to "greenwash" their enterprises with symbolic gestures, for the most part the participants in sustainability consortia sincerely seek unique opportunities to undertake systemic change that is both economically sensible and enables the business to mitigate or improve the environmental and social outcomes of their actions (Senge, Smith, Kruschwitz, Laur, & Schley, 2008).

Such "sustainability collaborations" appear rife with paradox (Huxham & Vangen, 2005). For example, they both aim to foster long-term strategic benefits for their own organizations and seek innovations across industries, sectors, and regions (e.g., Lawrence, Hardy, & Phillips, 2002). Like multi-sector collaborations designed to solve societal problems (Rondinelli & London, 2003; Rangan, Samii, & Van Wassenhove, 2006), these consortia are often driven by benefits that members perceive can be generated by collaboration. However, in contrast to the types of problems focused on by consortia that have been the focus of most research on inter-organizational relationships (Barringer & Harrison, 2000; Cropper, Ebers, Huxham, & Ring, 2008), sustainability consortia tackle more complex, ill-structured problems for which goals are seldom clear at the outset and which may only be tackled successfully by enormously complex innovations (Cooperrider & Dutton, 1999; Glasbergen, Bierman, & Mol, 2007; Roth & Senge, 1996).

To gain insight into the value of such sustainability oriented consortia, the authors studied the early years of the Sustainability Consortium – a voluntary association of about a dozen corporate members, including Ford, Nike, Shell, GM, BP, and Unilever, who were interested in moving their diverse companies and industries toward greater sustainability. The Consortium also included a few smaller firms as well as non-profit organizations, e.g., the World Bank. Initiated through the Society for Organizational Learning (2007) and its founder, Peter Senge (1990), the Consortium aims to apply principles of organizational learning and dialogue to develop new business practices that incorporate broad concerns for social and environmental impacts. We found a sustainable "relational space" at the heart of the collaborative process to be what the participants most valued from the consortium. *We define relational space as a dialogical context of shared trust and learning that precedes the emergence of shared expectations or negotiated projects and that supports project execution.* It may be contrasted with a more transactional goal oriented space, though it contains elements of more formal goal-setting processes.

We introduce this concept by differentiating between sustainability consortia and collaborative innovation more generally, drawing attention to the development of trust and facilitation of learning in relational space. We then introduce our data and analytic methods, and present the results of our analysis – the identification of four dynamic contexts in the Consortium: Relational Space, Collaborative Action, Participant Influences, and Governance. We follow this by examining the interdependence of these contexts, and specific consequences of that interdependence including Aspirational Trust and Dialogical Learning. We conclude with a set of suggestions that crystallize the value we saw and reflect on how the outcomes of the collaborations may also be improved.

TRUST AND LEARNING IN INTER-ORGANIZATIONAL COLLABORATIONS

Distinguishing Business Alliances from Sustainability Collaborations

A wide review of the literature on collaborative innovation in business organizations (Inkpen & Currall, 2004; Olk & Earley, 2000; Rangan, Samii, & Van Wassenhove, 2006; Ring & Van de Ven, 1994) and in multi-sector alliances that seek to solve specific problems (Brown & Ashman, 1999; Gray, 2000; Rondinelli & London, 2003) reveals that most research into inter-organizational alliances and collaborations has involved organizations with obvious common characteristics, be it an industry or product market (Rangan et al., 2006; Ring, Doz, & Olk, 2005), or specific institutional need (Maguire, Hardy, & Lawrence, 2004). Specific projects also catalyze collaborations (Arino & de la Torre, 1998) or "social alliances" (Rondinelli & London, 2003; Berger, Cunningham, & Drumwright, 2004).

In the less commonly studied cases where goals are not articulated in advance, researchers have explored the negotiation process leading to shared beliefs and actions (Gray, 1989, Olk & Earley, 2000). In those cases too, the participants share an industry, market, or region (Wondolleck & Yaffe, 2000; Ring et al., 2005).

By contrast, sustainability consortia are not formed around market commonalities nor institutional risks and threats. Rather, they tend to emerge through a recognition of members' interdependence that goes well beyond the short-term and mid-term issues (or crises) that motivate most other inter-organizational collaborations. They reflect concerns about the ongoing role of business in society writ large, which generates a longer time horizon for leadership and organizational learning (Senge et al., 2008). The longer horizon makes it difficult to define formal goals or deliverables in advance of formation (Gray, 2000; Hart, 1999). Therefore the dynamics of organizing and implementation in these multi-industry, system-wide efforts may be different from the processes in the types of industry-based consortia that have been more widely studied. Important differences include the lack of a formal basis for trust between the firms and significant uncertainty in how knowledge and learning can be generated in these ill-structured contexts (Tenkasi & Mohrman, 1995); next we explore both of these issues.

Trust in Traditional Collaborations

Research has recognized the important role that trust plays in the success of collaborations and strategic alliances that focus on the economic or strategic benefits that accrue to partner firms (Ring & Van de Ven, 1994; Rangan et al., 2006) or on the long-term benefits to the shared industry (Browning et al., 1995; Garud, Sanjay, & Kumaraswamy, 2002). Currall and Inkpen (2000, p. 328) summarize the basis of trust in these circumstances: "Joint venture trust is defined as reliance on another party (i.e., person, group, or firm) under a condition of risk." One party's fate can be determined by the other party(ies); reliance is risky precisely because "a party would experience potentially negative outcomes, i.e. 'injury or loss', from the untrustworthiness of the other party" (*ibid.*, p. 330). Risk and trust are thus conjoined, since "without risk, trust is irrelevant" (*ibid.*). In business alliances that aim to generate knowledge and institutional change, only to the degree that the benefits are truly *shared* will the contributing partners accrue the strategic (economic) gains that motivate their participation.

Some researchers have argued that "calculative trust can make the transition to relational trust, which derives from repeated interactions, and which further can become identity-based trust at its limit" (Bachmann & Zaheer, 2008, p. 537). According to Inkpen and Currall's "co-evolution of trust" model (2004, p. 589), repeated interaction is important in the formative stages of a collaboration: "In newly formed alliances between firms without prior interactions, a basis for trust may be absent and the partners are often suspicious of each other … As interactions increase and individual attachments develop, trust may increase."

According to Social Exchange Theory (Blau, 1964; Muthusamy & White, 2005), early levels of trust may be sparked by specific exchanges (or promises) of resources, e.g., a significant financial commitment. Thus, Social Exchange Theory readily explains the rapid creation of trust in the SEMATECH consortium, an R&D collaboration started in the early 1990s with the result of this reciprocity being a group-based trust that allowed members to cooperate (Browning et al., 1995).

Trust in the Sustainability Consortium

In contrast to SEMATECH, the initial commitments to the Sustainability Consortium were relatively small: an annual fee of $40,000 was used to support the two consultant-leaders of the project. Each company was asked to send up to three people to the Sustainability Consortium's semi-annual meetings; most (but not all) meeting participants also had their travel costs covered by their organizations.

Further, all projects and collaborations that arose from the interactions at these meetings were undertaken by participants. Unlike such forums as WBCSD, the Consortium provided no funding for consultants nor any personnel to pursue project tasks; all such work was to be accomplished by consortium participants on their own time in their companies. Given such a low up-front commitment of time and resources, Social Exchange Theory would predict that initial levels of information sharing and trust might be relatively low.

A different basis for initial trust is membership in social and professional networks (Ring & Van de Ven, 1994). Many (but not all) of the companies in the Sustainability Consortium were members of the Society for Organizational Learning, which convenes a professional network of business people committed to organizational learning from a systems thinking perspective (Senge, 1990). In addition, many of the Consortium's member companies had recognized potential economic benefits of the collaboration in the sense that exploring, and being seen by peer corporations as exploring, sustainability issues could help reduce business risks, e.g., from future regulations such as those developed or developing in Europe.

Even so, the research on trust in collaborations suggests that shared networks and perceived company benefits may not on their own generate enough confidence and trust in a collaboration member who is new to another participant (Arino & de la Torre, 1998; Inkpen, 2000; Inkpen & Currall, 2004). The vast majority of individual participants – executives and middle managers in member companies – had virtually no previous experiences with each other. To start, reputations seemed primarily based on the organizations which the participants hailed from. Moreover, neither agreements nor contracts were developed nor affirmed by participants during the process. Further, although companies may have stated values around sustainability, the actual participants in the Consortium were individuals who had never met with their counterparts from other companies. These factors inform one dimension of our inquiry: On what basis is trust developed in sustainability consortia, and what are the conditions that support the creation of trust and mutual respect in the Sustainability Consortium?

Learning in Sustainability Collaborations

Closely associated with the creation of trust is the generation of learning in sustainability consortia. Organizational learning has been identified as one of the key benefits of business collaborations generally, especially in periods of uncertainty and rapid change (Khanna, Gulati, & Nohria, 1998).

Generally, there are two interrelated types of learning in joint ventures: "learning about" partners, and "learning from" partners (Inkpen & Currall, 2004). *Learning about* a partner "facilitates relational understanding and can provide the foundation for trust development" (Inkpen & Currall, 2004, p. 593). It reflects a type of "behavioral learning" in the alliance (Lubatkin, Florin, & Lane, 2001). *Learning from* a partner may produce knowledge others can exploit to the benefit of their own operations, thus constituting "the private benefits that a firm can earn unilaterally by picking up skills from its partner" (Inkpen & Currall, 2004, p. 593; see also Holmqvist, 2004).[1]

Whereas *learning about* and *learning from* partners are especially relevant to strategic alliances, the broader focus of sustainability collaborations tends to involve "changes in societal institutions and patterns of behavior" (Brown & Ashman, 1999, p. 156). We suggest that it is important to explore the systemic process of learning in this context, focusing on sets of interactions that might lead to the formation of new institutional practices (Lawrence et al., 2002).

The Contexts for Collaborative Learning

There is very little empirical attention on *how* learning occurs within industry-based consortia (Arino & de la Torre, 1998; Lubatkin et al., 2001). For example, Doz, Olk, and Ring's (2000) study of 84 R&D consortia in the United States identified six types of learning by member companies, but does not indicate why such learning took place. In Arino and de la Torre's (1998) detailed study of two product-based collaborations virtually no mention is made of what learning took place and how it was used by the member companies.

We agree with Brown and Ashman (1999) that learning in multi-stakeholder alliances may be generated at the levels of program learning, organizational learning, and social learning. At the early stages of collaboration, however, these three may not be well distinguished. For example, what begins as a negotiation between two organizations may generate a specific project or program, which may lead to practices that disseminate throughout the collaboration, across multiple organizations (Ring & Van de Ven, 1994).

Our analysis focuses on the *context* for learning in sustainability collaborations, and on how organizational learning is described by participants. Others have used specific contexts as the basis for understanding collaborative action and the learning it produces. In their study of social learning in sustainability collaborations, Bouwen and Taillieu (2004, p. 144) identify a "relational practice" as their unit of analysis; they define this context as "any interactive project or exchange between at least two actors." "Interpretive spaces" have been focused as contexts for mutual learning and joint meaning making. Similarly, Bradbury and Lichtenstein (2000) explore "the space between" actors as the locus for interactive efforts including learning. In this study we focus on "collaborative context" as a general unit of analysis.

The complexity of the Consortium's task engenders our expectation that significant time will be spent understanding the sustainability issues *before* any particular projects are defined, negotiated, and executed (Ring & Van de Ven, 1994; Arino & de la Torre, 1998; Bouwen & Taillieu, 2004). Consequently, the process dynamics may be concentrated on relationship-building rather than on project-based action, especially early in the consortium's development. Therefore, we focus attention on the interactions preceding and leading to the creation and execution of collaborative projects.

METHODS

Setting

The Sustainability Consortium was founded in 1999 as a special program within the Society for Organizational Learning (www.solonline.org). Society for Organizational Learning had been, in turn, spun off from MIT where it was called the Center for Organizational Learning. Its purpose and key players remained constant through the transition and focused on doing community action research that brought together business people, researchers, and consultants to inquire and produce actionable knowledge (Senge & Scharmer, 2001). The stated purpose of the Sustainability Consortium was to "... build the learning capacity to achieve economic, ecological and social sustainability [through] a 'learning community' of companies committed to accelerating the creation of knowledge needed to achieve a truly sustainable economy" (Laur & Schley, 2004). As mentioned in the introduction, the Sustainability Consortium is a voluntary collaboration of mostly large corporations and NGOs. Two consultant members of the Society for Organizational Learning participated in the Consortium as paid facilitators. All other participation was without compensation.

Guided by the facilitators, Consortium members established a steering committee, membership fees, and an evolving set of practices around meetings and projects. Member organizations rotate responsibility to host 2- or 3-day semi-annual meetings, typically at or near the host company's corporate headquarters. Approximately 50 participants attend each meeting, one-third of whom were usually there for the first time. Non-member attendees must be invited by a member organization or by the facilitators. Meetings include opportunities to create new collaborations and projects. Projects developed within the Consortium are managed by organizational participants who take them on in addition to their own business tasks; this contrasts with most business consortia in which projects are managed by hired staff.

Sample and Data Collection

Roughly 200 individuals from the member companies participated in meetings between 1999 and 2004, including executives, line managers, engineers, internal consultants, and other individual contributors. The organizational membership was steady with rarely more than a small percentage of new companies attending a consortium. However the individual membership was less steady. What came to be called stalwart members (who attended all meetings) often brought new colleagues to the meetings, seeing in this the opportunity to expose colleagues to useful ideas. As the newcomers usually came "under the wing" of stalwarts they shared at least some of the social capital already developed. Four researchers (including two of the authors) attended Consortium meetings between 1999 and 2004. Their field notes from the meetings were discussed post hoc in regular teleconferences among research team members. Observational data were verified with facilitators and, where appropriate, with participants. During that period, 42 interviews were conducted with participants on the topic of collaboration; interviewees included 29 executives/senior managers in member companies, six managers from non-profits, five internal/external consultants, and the consortium facilitators. All but one of the interviews were audiotaped and transcribed. Demographics of interviewees are in Table 1.

We asked each interviewee to discuss his or her experiences within a "collaborative context," defined as a specific project or a series of interactions that were meaningful to the participant in getting work done. In an approach similar to the "critical events" method (Arino & de la Torre, 1998), each interviewee was asked to describe the characteristics of a "successful" collaborative context in the Consortium, and then an unsuccessful one (Motowidlo & Carter, 1992). Semi-structured interview questions allowed the interviewees to emphasize various aspects of the collaborations and directive probes about who were involved, how they were involved, what seemed to work well, and what things the participant could have done differently elicited a high degree of detail.

The interviews and observation notes supported development of a time-line highlighting key events and the most significant projects to emerge in the first 4 years of collaboration. This time-line is presented in Table 2. Note that although the Consortium had its kick-off meeting in 1998, no formal projects emerged for more than 18 months, not until June 2000. The first round of interviews took place in 2001 and the second in 2002.

Table 1. Demographics of Interviewees.

Code Number	Gender	Participant Category	OrgRank	Mtg Freq	Organization
SE1	F	Senior Executive	Senior	Low	HP
SE2	M	Senior Executive	Senior	High	Plug
SE3	M	Executive	Senior	High	BP
SE4	M	Executive	Senior	High	Harley
SE5	M	Executive	Senior	High	NE Utilities
BK	F	Executive	Senior	Low	BP
BT	M	Executive	Senior	High	Pratt
JM	M	Executive	Senior	Low	Shell Chem
SC02	M	Executive	Senior	High	Ford
SC03	M	Executive	Senior	High	Interface
SC04	M	Executive	Senior	High	Harley
SC05	M	Executive	Senior	High	NE Utilities
SC06	F	Executive	Senior	High	Nike
SC10	F	Executive	Senior	High	Interface
SC13	F	Executive	Senior	Low	Nike
SC14	F	Executive	Senior	High	Schlumberger
SC19	F	Executive	Senior	Low	HP
SC20	M	Executive	Senior	Low	Pratt
MM1	M	Manager	Middle	Low	DTE
SC15	M	Manager	Middle	Low	Interface
SC16	M	Manager	Middle	Low	Plug
SC17	M	Manager	Middle	Low	Harley
CV	M	Manager	Middle	Low	HP
DR	M	Manager	Middle	Low	
RF	M	Manager	Middle	Low	Ford
Sc12	M	Manager	Middle	Low	Ford
SC22	F	Manager	Middle	Low	Visteon
SC18	F	Manager	Junior	Low	Visteon
SC18	M	Manager	Junior	Low	Visteon
037	M	Consultant	Senior	Low	HP
039	M	Consultant	Senior	Low	NativePeoples
045	M	Consultant	Senior	Low	Nike
044	M	Consultant	Middle	Low	Nike
038	M	Consultant	Middle	Low	DTE
SC07	M	Senior Executive, non-profit	Senior	High	S.W.
SC01	M	Manager – non-profit	Senior	High	Sustainer
SC08	F	Manager – non-profit	Senior	High	TNS
043	M	Manager – non-profit	Senior	Low	Mentor program
046	F	Manager – non-profit	Middle	Low	Mentor
050	F	Manager – non-profit	Middle	High	
JC	M	Researcher	Senior	High	MIT
SC11/W	*F*	*Facilitator*	*Senior*	*High*	*SeedSys*
SC09/M	*M*	*Facilitator*	*Senior*	*High*	*SeedSys*
SC21/M	*M*	*Facilitator*	*Senior*	*High*	*SoL*

Table 2. Timeline of Action Projects in the Sustainability Consortium.

Date Started	Event/Project Name	Brief Description	Status in 2008
June 1998	Origin of Consortium	Conversation among representatives from multinational corporations gathered at the Society of Organizational Learning led to a white paper defining the Sustainability Consortium	
January 1999	Semi annual meetings begin	First "official" meeting hosted by a company (Xerox)	Most recent meeting held in May 2008, hosted by Nike in Beaverton, OR
June 2000	Frameworks	Conceptual model describing how sustainability frameworks can be related and operationalized inside companies	Frameworks document has been made public. It is referred to as a common document by participants in the consortium.
December 2000	Proteus	Distributed energy generation using fuel cells to improve economic/socially disadvantaged areas of the world	The group disbanded in 2004, some of the ideas continue to percolate in the more discrete efforts of the customer design focus groups
December 2000	Cool Fuel	Partnership between energy and carpet company to establish energy use and to offset that use; carbon reduction certified by third party	Expanded to other companies after initial success. Continues as a vibrant program between companies and uses a third party certification process
December 2000	Women Leading Sustainability	Dialogue group for women in the consortium	Meets by teleconference every 6 weeks. Hosted its first international meeting April 2006 at Nike with 80 participants, 40 from the developing world. All meetings of the Consortium include a WLS sub-meeting
June 2001	Distributed Energy Generation	Exploring with member companies the value and drawbacks to using distributed generation technology	Small group developed a preliminary framework to inform marketing. Disbanded after learning had been crystallized
June 2002	Materials Pooling	Companies working together on eliminating toxins from their value chain by addressing their market needs to the chemical suppliers	Continues to evolve in regular meetings, teleconference and in person. Emphasis is limited to removal of three primary toxins from shared materials
June 2003	Green Marketing: Cultivating Markets	Companies exploring how to create more customer demand for green products	Group disbanded

Coding and Analysis

In a formal sense, we see the collaborative contexts defined by the interviewees as a series of interactions between two or more participants focusing on a specific project, event, or arena for learning and shared action (Bouwen & Taillieu, 2004). Although 30% of these collaborative contexts were projects (see Table 2), participants described a wide range of other contexts. Overall, the interviewees reported 86 collaborative contexts; these are presented in Table 3.

Our qualitative research process unfolded in several phases, following a traditional grounded theory approach. We performed open coding of each transcript, using words and phrases to identify the issues that appeared to be salient and important to the participants. We paid close attention to (a) the characteristics of the collaborative contexts described by participants; (b) the trust, learning, and other dynamics that emerged within those contexts, and (c) any other qualities that may have influenced the collaborations.

We gained inter-rater reliability in several ways. The first and second author started by coding a subset of the interviews, iteratively reducing codes to a limited number of themes, which were then organized into four main categories (Miles & Huberman, 1994). These two authors then came together to compare their themes; they identified similarities and differences in their coding schemes. They worked out a parsimonious set of 18 themes across four categories that best summarized the qualities and characteristics both authors had identified in their analysis (Miles & Huberman, 1994). The categories and themes are shown in Table 4.

Next, as a means of further increasing coding validity, an MBA research assistant who had not been connected with the project coded another subset of interviews, using the coding scheme developed by the first two authors. Agreement between the third coder and the first two authors was 81.8%. The second author and the third coder then worked together to resolve any differences until 100% agreement was reached. Finally, the third coder coded the rest of the interviews, using the final coding scheme. These codes, developed across all three researchers, became the basis of our results (see Table 4).

Eighteen distinct themes may seem high, but is not surprising.[2] While each theme is conceptually distinct, many are interdependent and each affects the others holistically (Huxham & Vangen, 2005). This is particularly true of the themes within a category.

Table 3. Collaborative Contexts Mentioned by Interviewees.

Collaborative Context	Number (%) of Participants Mentioning
General consortium	**36** (42%)
Consortium projects	**26** (30%)
Proteus project	7
Distributed generation project	6
Materials pooling project	5
Cool fuel project	4
Sustainable transportation	2
Frameworks document	1
Janus	1
Bi-annual meetings	**17** (20%)
Nike meeting	11
Xerox–Lakes meeting	2
Aspen meeting	1
BP meeting	1
Harley Davidson meeting	1
HP Corvalis meeting	1
Internal company projects	**3** (3.5%)
Alliance for regional stewardship	1
EWEB Schools project	1
Seed project	1
Consultants	**2** (2.3%)
Other	**2** (2.3%)
Plug power	1
Honda invitation	1
Total	86

Our primary contribution is aggregation of these themes into four categories (see below) and especially the category of "Relational Space," which was at the heart of successful collaborations in our data.

FINDINGS

Contexts for Collaboration

The three collaborative contexts most often mentioned by interviewees were, in order of noted frequency, the Consortium, which was talked about as the general organization within which meetings and projects happened (42%),

Table 4. Themes of Collaboration, Across Four Categories.

Relational Space	Qualities of Relational Interaction in Participant's Experience of the Consortium
Aspirational trust	I would say that it [trust] was there more at the beginning, just because we were all coming together trying to have this common vision of helping the world, right? (SC02). And so I think that they [our collaborators] have a lot of similar values to us that we would not necessarily find somewhere else. I would say the thing that makes [these collaborations] them happen is just leading with trust, and having that trust fulfilled, warranted, justified, enforced (42). To me the key to building trust and for open sharing of ideas and projects is that truly the companies are coming with no agenda. They're just coming to give their time potentially and/or resources towards a common goal (CV).
Mutual learning	Particularly for a business like ours it's very important for us to be part of interesting conversations … because we are learning what other people are thinking and what other organizations are doing in this area (SE1). [T]he intent was to … come together and to explore the question (41). [We have been] sharing a lot of ideas and learning from each other … (46). This is a special group of people with high capacity for telling the truth, thinking about complexities without oversimplifying. They can see the big picture.
Peer-connect	It really has been, I would use the term, "collaborative" and that we're all in this together, and there not a client–vendor relationship – which is where most of spend our lives – it's more we're on an equal level. We're peers (43). [I]t's very much a peer-like space … Organizationally, the [participants] are not at the same level hierarchically. But in the space of the meeting, that's never [been a particular focus or issue. It appears to me that the level of engagement and trust that exists really, really just washes [that] away… (49).
Helping	And I think, my hope is anyway, that the next time someone wants to do a collaborative effort like we helped [Company Y] to do, that we'll again be able to help them craft the design of their project and help them identify some pitfalls to watch out for and give them some advice. … We get that we are here to help one another …. I get support, both psychological [and] practical advice [from fellow participants] (40). [A fellow participant] called me and he said, "You know, I believe in you. We are going to be successful. I'm going to do my part." So yeah, you feel trust and support by your peers. Validated, understood. And I don't think there's much more support than that that you can get (42). I find the folks are innovative, creative, cooperative. They've tended to support each other. They've tended not to be judgmental and not overly demanding (43).
Commitment to process	It's the process that really builds the trust (SE2). [A]s long as the process is done in a sort of straightforward and respectful way, … the outcome almost becomes immaterial. …And it's the process that really builds the trust. (49) [We] build on personal relationships, build our guiding principals through that, and then out of that comes a specific [project] like this, that we could do. Then… there's a multiplier effect [as others] say "Oh, I want to do the same sort of thing."

Table 4. (*Continued*)

Relational Space	Qualities of Relational Interaction in Participant's Experience of the Consortium
Whole-self presence	So when we were at [one particular meeting]... we virtually had the trusted space because we were all in the same room and over the course of the three days we got to know one another and have a beer together and all that kind of social interaction (40). I don't think you can underestimate still the sort of personal connections that are made at these meetings...when you actually meet someone, the chemistry that takes place [is] incredibly important (39). I didn't understand before the Sustainability Consortium the real power of getting in the room with other folks and actually speaking the truth rather than trying to bullshit each other like we do at conventional business meetings (42). ... Well-intentioned, vulnerable, willing to be vulnerable to some extent. Willing to sort of let their hearts out and be real (50). People check in and out, they talk about their family life, just where they are with what is going on in their lives. We make sure everyone is heard. [Our] emotional reactions are shared, e.g., people are asked to share how they felt about a meeting (JM).
Action Projects	Tangible, Outcome-Oriented Action that Contributes to Consortium-Wide Projects
Tangible goals	And we see that in that kind of opportunity that I mentioned, where there's a clear win-win in terms of the business case and an environmental benefit for the company. I think one of the things that has not been as pronounced, is ... saying "Okay, what are the goals and the desired outcomes of this activity and how do we measure those?" Again, I think that's tended to be more anecdotal or qualitative. We've got to get value, and one way to do that is to provide value through developing projects that address business concerns while evolving some of the social and environmental issues ... On-the-ground type projects, real things that you can touch, feel, show results.
Outcomes	So I think it's very important that you can demonstrate that there are benefits to each of the individual participants who are also wearing their corporate hats otherwise you're not going to make any progress. So it's been a strong... collaboration. As a matter of fact, we're going to be in (X-city) in about a month to sit down and debrief what's worked, what hasn't worked, what we've learned – all with a goal of trying to carry it forward next year either at the same scale or, potentially, I think ideally, on a larger scale. We were really looking for ... basically, we wanted to learn ... we were really concerned about having a product at the end of the day. Our product or what we thought we were going to take away from that was the knowledge we gave and the deeper understanding that we gave.

Table 4. (*Continued*)

Action Projects	Tangible, Outcome-Oriented Action that Contributes to Consortium-Wide Projects
Goal alignment	We found that people who have not been involved in the consortium are just not aligned, so they hear us talk about wanting to learn like we're making a product pitch to them, and don't want to let you in the door. So we really had to learn how to navigate, to talk about this language of collaborative learning that the Consortium is aligned around and it's different from "We want to come try to sell you a project." I would say not only a lot, but the goals have to be common goals. I can't walk into a collaboration and say "Here are the goals of the collaboration." It's got to be common. And you don't have to have unanimous consent, but every person that's involved in the collaboration needs to understand and subscribe to and feel a part of those goals. "I did a lot of trying to come back to, again, what are the goals of the project, which in turn bring back to what are the goals of the Consortium." "I think you can have fairly fuzzy objectives to start with, and then as the conversation evolves you have to probably make the ultimate objectives more and more clear."
Project structure	I think we tried hard to structure tasks and to create [momentum]. If I was frustrated about anything, it's just that in the way of the structure it's hard to get work done between face to face meetings. Getting down to the details is a crucial element of these projects: "For an effective collaboration to happen, logistics need to be very clean, very concise, high quality. Because when that doesn't happen, trust breaks down quickly." At the same time, we saw that senior people pulled in more junior people from their organization as projects began to take off: "Oh well, first of all, you've got to understand that I'm the President and the CEO and I'm not working on a lot of the operational details. There is someone by the name of ___ who has been doing. And she is in a far better position to comment on [project X] than I am."
Resources/risks	"This [project] had been identified as an initiative that a number of companies had felt was … sufficiently important to justify some additional resource [which] they were willing to identify and recruit." On the other hand, sometimes this created internal challenges: There's an issue around how much budget people can commit to these … they profess to be really interested in the starter projects … but they say "Well, I just can't justify that internally and we're going to have make a choice here …" … At the end of the day many of the things that [X-Company] would need to do to make more sustainable [products] would actually put their whole franchise at risk. So, for them it was… how do I deal with sustainability but not destroy my business. "We this as we're trying to mitigate risk by trying to pull together a wider coalition of companies who will share the risk—so it wouldn't just be [Company A] or [Company B] speaking out on global climate change, it would be all of us."

Table 4. *(Continued).*

Participant Influences	Pre-Existing Aspects of Participants' Home Company and Their Own Personal Aspirations, which Affect Behavior within the Consortium.
Organizational context	I think that if you look culturally, [Z-Company] and [our company] were probably the biggest competitors in the room. And although we are very different companies … we also share some cultural values that I think are important to both of us and that make us more willing … to be more open with each other than we might be with a company that didn't share those values. If I go to the meeting and I feel like … the company doesn't support this that really does influence sort of the quality of the collaboration. This is a subject that [our company has] been thinking about – sustainability – for some time. … If you look culturally we share [with our competitor] some cultural values that I think are important to both of us and that make us more willing [to] be more open with each other than we might be with a company that didn't share those values.
Business goals	"In the context of [the] consortium … the concerns that are raised are the concerns I have for [my company] … Me saying "this is something very important to … the company." And lately, the company has in fact invested a lot of resources in trying to understand the [sustainability] issue. And so I think it's becoming less a personal issue and more clearly a business issue. Frankly our goals are pretty modest compared to those of some other companies and so our goals were very much accommodated within the overall curve of the project as it got defined. And lately, [my] company has in fact invested a lot of resources in trying to understand this issue [of sustainability]. And so I think it's becoming less a personal issue and more clearly a business issue.
Personal aspirations	My work is anchored in personal commitment. I need to align my personal values and express those in work. [Attending a special workshop on sustainability] was just something that I was going to do regardless of whether or not [my company] was going to pay for it. Many were champions for sustainability. Their long-standing commitment to these ideals is partly responsible for arguing the business case of sustainability to their executive colleagues, and for putting in the many hours of personal and professional time to help make things happen within any given collaborative event. What I [have] in common with them is, we're all very interested and committed to sustainability…. They're more passionate about sustainability before going in and kind of chose that job as a route to try to express that (42).
Governance	**Control Mechanisms and Structures within the Consortium, Including Meetings, Membership, and the Mix of Participants at Any Given Meeting**
Participant ratio	There were times during the meeting where I felt like … a paid commercial for consulting services. Because it was a very heavy mix, it felt like, of consultants that were in the room [who] were almost dominating the conversation. And the meeting, you know, my desire was to hear more from the businesses, not to hear from the consultants and the market research that they'd done.

Table 4. (*Continued*)

Governance	Control Mechanisms and Structures within the Consortium, Including Meetings, Membership, and the Mix of Participants at Any Given Meeting
	And I was floored that there were more consultants in attendance than there were practitioners. All of a sudden, I was feeling very uncomfortable. And feeling low levels of trust.
	As mentioned earlier, the Consortium was designed to support executives and managers, with a limited number of participants from NGOs. The latter perceived themselves to be less valued than the corporate members: "I'm a non-profit organization. I'm sort of there as a guest, and sort of on the fringe … we're not the real members." As one executive said: "When you get to have as many consultants as companies, I'm clear that they can't all contribute … And that makes me really uncomfortable."
Internal controls	It's hard to understand where you fit in the process. It's ambiguous and somewhat confusing … [and] at the moment [I] feel that that's somewhat the nature of the Consortium, the nature of the beast. And you just learn to live with it and you learn how to work within the context of that kind of an organization. I think all of us know what is a trade-secret and what's not. And obviously we won't go across that line without getting some kind of appropriate assurances. But my sense is this is more of an individual … it's what we're supposed to know as opposed to setting out hard, fast roles.
Meeting structure	Well, there aren't a lot of environments where people truly collaborate. … But at the end of the day, I think that the reason that this group … was more collaborative was that we were put in an environment where collaboration could occur and there weren't a lot of agendas going on and because we all really wanted to and we were all willing to contribute.
	I found that the small groups and the lunch meetings were actually the most productive for me, because it was an opportunity to really interact with a small group of people, really stop and say "What is it that you really, really do?" and "What are some of the challenges that you face within your business?"
	And during the [___] meeting, we were given the opportunity to kind of suggest subjects which we felt were topical and of interest to other members of the consortium. And this [topic was successful], and then a little working group kind of developed around that, during the meeting. [Note: This topic became one of the action projects listed in Table 2.]
Leadership	[The SoL Founder] was involved as a project design coach and he helped with a couple of the key interventions.
	"Well, you have, at [C-Company], you have [___] who is a key player. He has very enthusiastically picked this up …. And I think [___] has a similar amount of enthusiasm. So you have a senior manager [and] a junior manager at [C-Company], that are really very responsive … and the impression that I got is that the [project] has been … terrific."
	But I think people are just so distracted and so time poor that they don't have the ability to, you know, just kind of run with these things without someone taking a very obvious leadership role.

specific Consortium projects (30%), and bi-annual meetings (20%). While it was to be expected that participation in projects and meetings would be noted as collaborative contexts, it was surprising that the Consortium itself was the most relevant and salient locus of collaborative learning and action for so many. We are intrigued by the fact that projects make up less than one-third of all the collaborative events mentioned. Instead, we found that *peer interactions* account for the majority of reported collaborations. Notably, in some cases peer interactions produced projects or other concrete outcomes. Two participants discussed internal company projects whose ideas were catalyzed by peer interactions in the Consortium. A CEO described his interactions with a senior manager in the Consortium – a serendipitous meeting which led the CEO to invite the manager to leave his current organization and join the CEO's executive team. This result was somewhat unexpected, and led us to include reflections on the Consortium in general *as well as* the specific collaborative projects that emerged within it.

Four Categories of Collaboration

Our analysis identified 18 collaboration themes, which we aggregated into four categories: *relational space*, *action projects*, *participant influences*, and *governance*. These four categories, the themes within them, and an example of each theme are found in Table 4.

Category 1: Relational Space. Interviewees consistently noted primarily what they perceived to be qualities of their Consortium relationships including "openness," "respect," "inspiration," "support," "safety," "proximity," and "friendship." These six distinct and interrelated themes in the data reflect an ecology of relationships that we aggregate into the category of Relational Space. Below we describe the themes and suggest how they interact to create Relational Space.

- *Aspirational trust*: A unique form of trust gained as the product of a shared goal to "make the world a better place." Whereas values-based trust depends on *past* actions that demonstrate corporate principles, Aspirational Trust reflects a vision of potential that may transcend one's organization, expressing one's personal, "pro-social" ideology and motivation for action. What is noteworthy here is that while such trust is commonplace in most value driven communities, it is far less common in corporate environments.
- A *mutual learning process*: The opportunity to give open consideration to all ideas and perspectives. Participants noted a "dialogical" process

(Isaacs, 1993) of checking assumptions, building upon each others' thinking, and focusing on learning rather than on problem-solving or negotiation. Learning involved a balance of advocacy and inquiry in conversations.

- *Peer-connect*: Although unusual in most business interactions, peer-like relationships were ubiquitous in the Consortium. Peer-connect is our term for an experience of mutual support that supersedes rank, making most participants feel accepted and heard regardless of the size of their company or their role within their organization.
- *Helping*: People offered help, ideas, and a willingness to share their insights to support each other. The sense of emotional connection in the Sustainability Consortium seemed deeper and more personal than one might expect from traditional business relationships or learning consortia (Dyer & Singh, 1998; Bouwen & Taillieu, 2004).
- *Commitment to process*: Over time participants formed strong, positive relationships that deepened their engagement in the Consortium. Process and temporality thus stood out as a key quality of Relational Space, incorporating specific exercises, face-to-face interaction, and a wealth of iterative interactions among participants.
- *Whole-self presence*: Interviewees referred to the uniqueness of sharing both personal and business goals within and between individual meetings. The acceptance of personal stories and the inclusion of topics relating to one's whole-self – e.g., values, family, feelings, and concerns far beyond one's company – offered a powerful dimension to the meetings which appeared to be fundamental to the creation of Relational Space.

The interdependence of these themes in creating Relational Space is reflected in the following quote: "Collaboration takes a lot longer. It's a lot more uncertain. There's a lot more opinions to deal with .... But the benefits are that people can really inspire one another to do stuff." This participant references *commitment to process* in highlighting the time-dimensions of interactions; the process is inspiring, reflecting the *helping* quality of the collaborative context. Another useful perspective is exemplified by a middle-manager from Ford, who provided the following description of Relational Space – "the environment that we create" – which connects Reflective Learning, Commitment to Process and Whole-Self Presence:

> I don't know if it's the environment that we create or the learning principals, but [fellow participants] do tend to bare their souls more and set a precedence for showing truly what's going on and where the challenges are. And I think there are other collaborations

> where if you don't take the time to adhere to and practice some of the learning principals, that doesn't happen. So … I've seen people be more open and sharing of what they're doing.

Category 2: Action Projects. Most of the interviewees felt tangible outcomes and projects that emerged through the Consortium were important. As one executive explained: "We are not just hoping, we are also engaging in concrete projects." Another participant noted: "Over the time of the consortium, I think the conversation shifted towards action. What are the things that we can start to do with one another … and where might we start to join one another in fairly common projects."

Our analysis of the data showed five themes in the category of Action Projects: *tangible goals*, *outcomes*, *aligning interests*, *project structuring*, and *resources/risks* (see Table 4).

Category 3: Participant Influences. The values, goals, and aspirations of participants and their home organizations set the stage for and shaped interactions within the Consortium. We identified three themes in the category of Participant Influences: *organizational context*, *organizational goals*, and *personal aspirations*.

These are reflected in the following quote:

> This [i.e. sustainability] is something very important to me personally, but it's also, I think, very important to the company. And lately, the company has in fact invested a lot of resources in trying to understand this issue. [Overall this made me] extremely, definitely passionate about going to the Consortium meeting.

Note how this participant's *personal aspiration* for sustainability is reflected as an *organizational goal* that has led to an *organizational context* of investing resources. Together the three qualities are hugely motivating, leading this person to be "extremely, definitely passionate" about the meetings. We were surprised to see the frequency with which personal aspirations surfaced in the data suggesting the important role this theme played in the Consortium, especially when these passions are shared by the individual's sponsoring organization.

Category 4: Governance. We use the term Governance to describe facilitation and administrative routines that characterized the Sustainability Consortium. These are captured in four themes: *internal control*, *meeting structure*, *leadership*, and *participant balance* this last referring to finding the right number of business members vs. consultants and NGOs in Consortium Meetings.

TRUST AND LEARNING IN RELATIONAL SPACE

Aspiration, Trust, and Pro-Social Motivation

The theme of *personal aspiration* may help to explain trust building in the Sustainability Consortium. This aspect of Participant Influence was clearly expressed by a senior manager: "I have great personal aspirations for this work and a sense of pride … Frankly, I think of this as doing God's work." This commitment has been described as the "motivation to make a pro-social difference" (Grant, 2007). The idea was framed by Thompson and Bunderson (2003, p. 572) as "ideological currency … the 'real motivation' for many employees comes from believing that their work has a purpose, and that they are part of a larger effort to achieve something truly worthwhile."

Personal aspiration thus describes participants' passionate commitment to sustainability and their willingness to go far beyond the expected in donating their time and efforts. As explained by one participant: "These people are committed, I mean really committed, beyond what I would have believed if I weren't involved." Research into collaborations for sustainability like this one has found that managers with such strong personal aspiration may be compelled to express it in projects that far exceed their accepted job roles and job scope, a finding recently confirmed in the context of employee support programs (Grant, Dutton, & Rosso, 2008). Like "tempered radicals", the values held by individuals may or may not be reflected in the missions of their host organizations. Yet, as complexity science shows, personal aspiration leads individuals to access a broader range of resources for change, and thereby may help catalyze emergence, as we see in the self-organization of consortium projects.

Aspirational trust: Drawing on this view of *personal aspiration*, we turn to the question of how trust was developed in the Sustainability Consortium? We identified some intriguing patterns of trust development. For example, one participant explained how his trust of participants from a certain company was due to the high degree of technical information they offered to the Consortium, reflecting the effects of Social Exchange Theory:

> And the technical detail provided on behalf of [BigCo] helped build the trust. Me personally, I don't know that much about [product line], but I know enough to know that they're sharing very deeply around the technical content of what they did.

Reflecting the influence of reputation, one senior executive explained that he had previously worked with several of the other CEOs in the consortium, and already held their companies in high esteem:

> They were all people that we had worked with in the past who have high integrity, and I think it makes a big difference. I also think it was the quality of the companies involved as well.

In addition participants described a third form of trust that was extended without projected exchanges or prior reputation. Instead, this form of trust seemed to be founded upon the Personal Aspirations of participants:

> I would say that it [trust] was there more at the beginning [than may be typical], just because we were all coming together trying to have this common vision of helping the world.

> It took [only] about 24 hours before I was really much more open and trusting … I think just the level of openness that other people were exhibiting, how much they were really sharing about their own dreams, their own fears, and their own hopes.

> I would say the thing that makes [these collaborations] happen is just leading with trust, and having that trust fulfilled, warranted, justified, enforced. (42)

Aspirational trust emerged right away – almost instantly – simply by virtue of the broad visions shared and articulated by participants and leaders in the Consortium. It apparently bypassed the period of negotiation which is predicted for broadly based consortia (Ring & Van de Ven, 1994; Inkpen & Currall, 2004); it also goes beyond the "reciprocal trust process" found by Huxham and Vangen (2005) in their practice-oriented model of collaborations.

Some argue that trust can be created through shared values, i.e., due to "one's confidence in another's goodwill … [based on] faith in the moral integrity or goodwill of others" (Ring & Van de Ven, 1994, p. 93). In this case, however, the trust we found seems to be based on shared *aspirations* – the "hopes" and "dreams" for a sustainable world that are expressed by individuals and in many cases by their organizations as well. In this way the presence of Aspirational Trust goes beyond "shared values," thus offering a broader view into how trust may be generated in sustainability consortia.

Learning in Relational Space

Sustainability Consortium participants primarily described "learning with" their peers as they explored and effected sustainability in their organizations. This contrasts with learning after the fact, or more conceptual (rather than practical) learning about someone else's project. In effect participants emphasized what they were *learning together* for mutual benefit. For example:

> So I guess the key learning there was [that] even though it is our project, we wanted to make sure that it was a two-way collaboration ... where knowledge is shared in collaborative efforts [rather than] just coming to us.

> And because of the consortium getting together, we heard about this project ... And then we recruited companies within the consortium to help out. So they were willing to collaborate on learning together. ... this idea of collaborative learning is really pretty different from most people's interactions with suppliers or customers or competitors.

"Learning" here comes close to a synonym for "learning together." Learning is inherently dialogical and mutually supportive, and thus differs from forms of "knowledge creation" that are more opportunistic and focused on the individual firm (e.g., Noteboom, 2008). Like dialogue, learning can engender significant institutional innovations that go beyond the knowledge boundaries of all participants individually (Roth & Senge, 1996; Waddell, 2005). Lubatkin et al. (2001, p. 1362) refer to this as *reciprocal learning*, a new form of collaborative relationship "whose primary intent is to co-experiment and leverage each others' unique, but complementary, knowledge structures."

Another aspect of this type of learning was noted by participants as a form of *learning how to learn* about sustainability in an environment that encourages inquiry about challenging issues. As one participant reported: "My mental model about the consortium is it's companies learning to learn about tough problems. ... the companies are paying to create the learning environment." This kind of shared inquiry leads to personal and professional learning outcomes:

> I want to learn and reflect and think about the hard parts of running the business ... It's the only place I can go with a group of people that I can reflect and utilize all four parts of my learning wheel. ... That's why I'll continue [with] it. ... I like to learn, I like to soak the different views up.

The Primacy of Relational Space

At the heart of Relational Space is trust and mutual action learning – qualities that appear to be interdependent with peer-connections, helping, commitment to process and "whole-self" presence. Together these six qualities of Relational Space reflect an ecology of reflection, trust, and systemic thinking. According to our participants, these interdependent qualities make Relational Space especially useful for exploring the systemic challenge of sustainability. Like all ecologies Relational Space is dynamic and evolving; these dynamics also extend to Action Projects as well as to Participant Influences and Governance.

DYNAMICS OF RELATIONAL SPACE

Although we have insufficient evidence to propose a formal model, our analysis and intimate knowledge of the Consortium leads to a dynamic framework, shown in Fig. 1. This framework summarizes the relationships among Relational Space, Action Projects, Participant Influences, and Governance. By virtue of participants' emphasis, relational space and its characteristics are the centerpiece of organizing in this sustainability collaboration; it is the critical precursor to the emergence of collaborative projects. Relational Space is supported by Participant Influences such as participants' aspirations and the business goals of member organizations, and also by Governance features including the meeting structure, internal controls, and leadership. These inter-connections are modeled in Fig. 1.

Participant Influences → Relational Space

As Zilber (2002) reminds us, meaning attracts actors to action. Some forward-looking participants see the business mandate changing in ways that align more closely with their personal values, providing opportunities to redirect their corporations. As one participant explained, "My work is anchored in personal commitment. I need to align my personal values and express those in work." Connecting personal values to workplace values expands intrinsic motivation, through an increasingly recognized mode of "ideological currency" (Thompson & Bunderson, 2003). Thus, the specific leverage for people convening successfully is a set of shared aspirations. In this sense the work of the sustainability consortium is less like the work

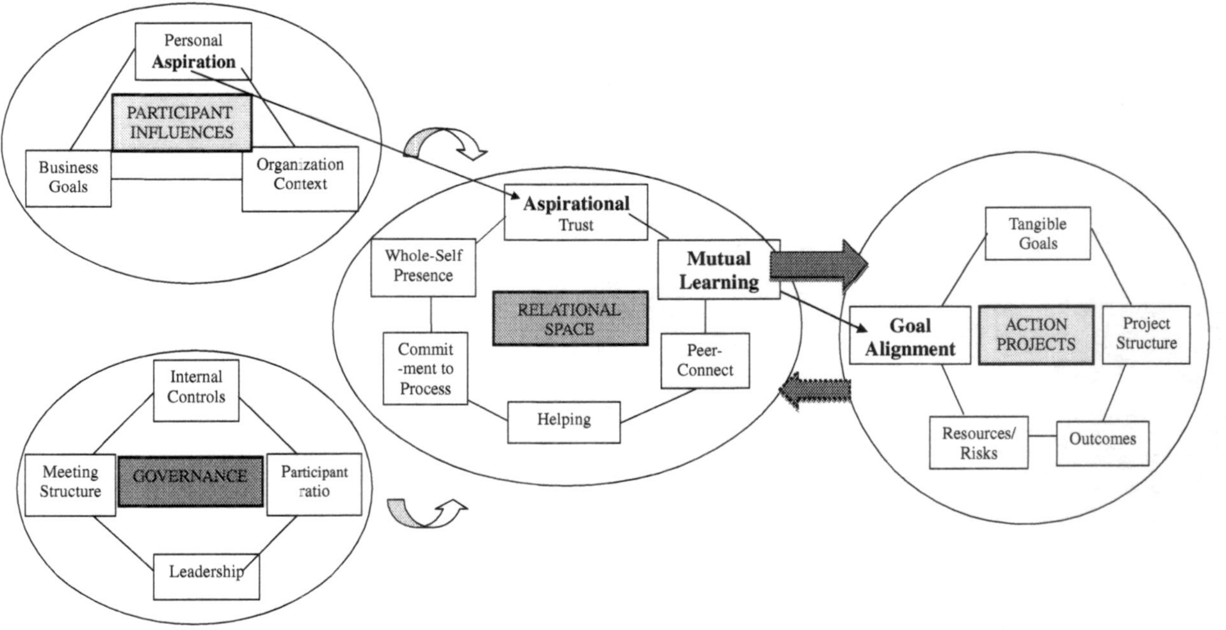

Fig. 1. Dynamics of Interaction in the Sustainability Consortium.

of transactional business consortia and more like the work of a community of commitment, a mission driven community.

Relational Space → Action Projects

Once convened, many participants suggested that the depth of listening and learning about sustainability required Relational Space, which then led to specific collaborations and Action Projects. Thus the specific leverage for mutual learning becoming action projects is the identification of shared goals. For example, one participant showed how *mutual learning,* when done well, rapidly generates Action Projects:

> Collaboration doesn't occur simply by listening. Collaboration in my mind occurs when the listening turns into an understanding of similar goals ... when the group understands that I understand them as tangible targets. And when that occurs, trust immediately is created and collaboration unfolds as project management.

Another made the link between the creation of trust and its application to specific projects:

> How can we work together toward sustainability? We've got this consortium, we've been meeting, we've established a level of trust ... in collaboration and now how do we want to move forward with that? And the whole point of [a key meeting] was to try to come away with some ideas for those types of projects get aligned as to resources.

Finally, several elements of Relational Space are briefly described in this next quote, which recognizes how successful new projects involve a combination of *peer-connecting*, *helping*, *aspirational trust*, and *whole-self presence*:

> I looked at it as a way to build a community of friends who are trying do this work together, learn the best practices in something that's been relatively new ... primarily learning methodologies. Build a network, and then try to work on some real cool projects together to kind of ... to change the world.

Governance → Relational Space

The quality of facilitation and the intensive yet open structure of each meeting enabled a stronger experience of Relational Space and development of trust and commitment. Participants described the role of meeting structure:

> The first day was fairly regimented ... And the next day was in fact loosely structured around dialogue. And I think it's because we were so engaged the first day with actual

> [X-company] issues and successes and failures that the rest of the two days' openness allowed us to engage in conversations that were meaningful.

Likewise, ineffective Governance compromised Relational Space: "And I was floored that there were more consultants in attendance than there were practitioners. All of a sudden, I was feeling very uncomfortable. And feeling low levels of trust." Our findings suggest that the participants' positive experience inside the Sustainability Consortium depended on the presence of Relational Space, on a supportive *organizational context*, on the right mix of participants in the room, and on facilitative but minimal formal controls.

Overall, these examples suggest that Participant Influences and Governance play an important role in the creation of Relational Space; in turn, Relational Space seems to be a foundation for the creation of Action Projects.

THEORETICAL IMPLICATIONS

Whereas researchers of corporate alliances focus more on transactional issues including trust, governance and control, researchers of multi-sector constructive partnerships tend to focus on the relational dynamics of shared values and social exchange (Bouwen & Taillieu, 2004; Muthusamy & White, 2005). Our study of the Sustainability Consortium throws new light on the intersection of these approaches, highlighting several qualities that have not been expressed in this literature. First, we identified a unique form of trust in the Consortium – Aspirational Trust – which was not "earned" in a transactional way, but seemed to be conferred only because of a shared aspiration among participants. Although other forms of trust were present, Aspirational Trust is distinct in that it goes beyond perceptions of *past* behaviors, and relies on the *projected visions* of self and other. We hope this finding helps others explore how aspiration and trust are connected in sustainability collaborations.

Secondly, we identified an expanded kind of learning in the Consortium. Incorporating a less-utilized stream of organizational learning research, this kind of learning involves a balance of advocacy and inquiry (Argyris, Putnam, & Smith, 1985) and reflection-in-action (Schoen, 1983), which can lead to a transformation of both parties (Carlisle, 2004) and potentially of the system itself (Lubatkin et al., 2001). Although we identified more common kinds of learning in the Consortium, we were intrigued by the presence of this mutually beneficial style of learning, especially because it was exemplified in relationship building more than in action projects. We hope others will explore further the role of *learning* in sustainability consortia.

Third, and most importantly, we identified Relational Space – an ecology of high-quality interactions that precedes Action Projects. This finding builds on the recognition that negotiation and direction-setting are always present in inter-organizational collaborations (Ring & Van de Ven, 1994). However, Relational Space extends that idea by showing how trustful, learning-based interactions can be created *before* the existence of formal goals or the emergence of even exploratory projects. Indeed, for the most broadly systemic issues like sustainability, Relational Space may be essential to provide an appropriate "container" for collaboration (Senge, Laur, Schley, & Smith, 2006; Senge et al., 2008).

Although we have not seen Relational Space described formally by others, we believe the concept is present in other studies showing that supportive and respectful interactions play an important role in producing uncommon innovations. For example, the term "relationality" (Bradbury & Lichtenstein, 2000) emphasizes how such high-quality innovations may be generated in this "space between" individuals and organizations. Nonaka and Konno (1998, p. 46) use the term *ba* to describe "a shared space that serves as a foundation for knowledge creation ... [which] includes qualities of care, trust and commitment, interaction and reflection, reconciling mental models, and enacting these qualities in action with others" (1998, pp. 46–48). We believe that Relational Space fits well with the movement toward Positive Organizational Scholarship (Cameron, Dutton, & Quinn, 2003), and that it can be useful as a frame for a range of interdependent qualities – six of which were identified in our study.

IMPLICATIONS FOR SUSTAINABILITY COLLABORATIONS

> There are many things to do to bring about a sustainable world ... whatever you do, do it humbly. Do it not as an immutable policy, but as an experiment. Use your action, whatever it is, to experiment. (Donella Meadows)

In addition to reflecting on our research questions, our work was also motivated by a desire to offer suggestions to business leaders and change agents who are confronted by the complexity of taking action toward more sustainable business models. In the following section we take what we have learned to suggest 10 practical implications for would-be organizational leaders and change agents.

Premise: Sustainability Requires Systems Level Coordination; Fragmentation is an Obstacle

At a rudimentary level, we learned from the Sustainability Consortium that real learning takes place when business people can both meet their own business goals while also advancing collaborative projects with a larger social purpose. The advantage to simply allowing like-minded organizations to convene is that unusual collaborations emerge, which enable companies to address organizationally important tasks that alone they cannot. Where else might companies as different as Nike, DuPont, Harley Davidson, and Ford find much in common, if not as a result of deliberating seeking to pursue mutual interest, e.g., The Materials Pooling Project involved all of them [see Table 2] in an effort to create new "green" chemistry to replace unsustainable chemical feedstock. The consortium illustrates that given the general interdependence of companies, more sustainable industrial ecologies can be fostered. However, such ad hoc emergence of projects in the Sustainability Consortium raises the question of whether other learning experiments might be more effective if populated by companies with a more easily identifiable synergy.

Sustainability presumes healthy levels of financial, social, and environmental capital (Elkington, 2002) in a system. The sustainable organization is therefore presumed to build and balance all three forms of capital, rather than building only financial capital at the expense of social and environmental health. In essence companies engaged with the sustainability challenge are shifting from the industrial era practice of externalizing costs to internalizing them. No one organization may determine itself sustainable, however, unless the value network in which it is located is not also sustainable (Bradbury, 2009). Thus, a whole value chain becomes an important focus of attention when we seek to understand and develop sustainable businesses. In considering how one might best populate an ideal consortium, we must also consider, more practically, who has the requisite invitational power to convene it. Mirvis (2008) describes academic-practitioner learning forums as a new model of inter-organizational research. A university or neutral civil society organization often acts best as a convener for such efforts. Indeed the Society for Organizational Learning which spawned the Sustainability Consortium was itself located originally at MIT. The work, after all, is educational – albeit not in the conventional sense. A learning consortium convened at a university offers conditions for the transformation of knowledge creation. Complementing the practical concerns of practitioners with the propositional concerns of scholars (Bradbury-Huang, 2010), knowledge creation is triggered not in a classroom setting, but in a project.

The following are our suggestions for how to advance sustainability through collaborative learning. They are necessarily interdependent and discussed along a time-line that emphasizes sensitivity to initial conditions:

1. *Universities as conveners*: The absence of coordinated governance and systemic decision making will, in all likelihood, present the greatest challenge to sustainability efforts. A university, with its relative disinterestedness and neutrality however, may bode well for convening many types of stakeholders. The most effective invitation to convene might therefore come from a university whose gravitational pull is related to the number of peer universities and alumni networks in its orbit.

   A university-based learning consortium acts ideally as a meeting place in which business leaders, researchers, and policy makers are enabled to make experimental investment decisions for the whole system. The system may be defined first as a region and/or expanded around a particularly significant supply chain. Bounding a system is as much an art as a science. What is important is having key stakeholders agree to the boundary and become active in convening relevant others.
2. *Learning as co-investment*: As supported by social exchange theorists noted above, it is best to establish from the outset that a collaborative learning experiment will succeed only as *a co-investment* by those involved. Given the multiple agendas of a true learning consortium, learning that is not immediately applicable must also be funded. Therefore funding may be sought from multiple sources and might be a mix of:
   a. R&D budget of companies
   b. Federal grants sponsored by business, but written by university-based researchers
   c. Public agencies.
3. *Include the entire ecology of business*: The Sustainability Consortium suggests that it is very helpful to have, at a minimum, an executive decision maker and a technical expert from each business organization. Of those invited from a particular company, at least one ideally has demonstrated capacity for success and personal commitment to sustainability practices. After co-investment, the decision about who else to invite is an important next step for a learning consortium. It is also an attractive opportunity. As simple as it sounds, it is rare that systems stakeholders get to communicate directly outside transactional

exchanges. As a consequence stakeholders rarely know much about others experience of their shared system.

4. *Systems Vision and Dialogue*: In the Sustainability Consortium we saw a gathering of people with similar aspirations for sustainability. The longevity and multiple projects demonstrate the value of adopting a systems thinking approach. We believe that aspirations can be broadened and elevated if effort is undertaken after initial convening to cohere a shared vision of sustainability, informed by natural science.

   We cannot assume that people of like interests can communicate well, or can see broadly enough to collaborate effectively. Systems thinking exercises that allow participants to explain their own system and to see the systems represented by their colleagues are useful in this regard. Intensive work with building capacity, however, must happen at the individual level, outside the consortium. Once inside the consortium, reference to computer simulation models can ease conversations toward highlighting the collective leverage points for self interested action, in practical terms. To this end, systems thinking and dialogue are ways to change mindsets, approaches that generate collaborative social action (Habermas, 1989).

5. *Carefully Structure Governance*: Good meeting design and light-handed facilitation can help create adequate time for dialogue. Dialogue is itself an intervention, given the fast-paced workflow at the executive level and among line managers and contributors.

   University scholars active in the presentation and shaping of relevant learning can help address the reluctance of many practitioners to engage in learning beyond their personal experience. Substitute and vicarious learning experiences may be especially persuasive for an audience not keen to embrace conceptual knowledge. Experiential and technologically-mediated learning can be brought to the network by the presence of talented educators. Learning facilitators must be aware that the desire to "hurry things along" can subvert optimization of the process and should address this directly.

6. *Crystallize collaborative action projects*: It is important to take time to generate coherent movement toward collaborative action. Dialogue, however, is always only a means, not an end in itself. Therefore only activity that builds toward collaborative action should be undertaken in early efforts to cultivate dialogue. There is no reason not to pursue "early, small wins" as long as the commitment to a longer time horizon is firmly maintained. The more tightly bound to the daily business tasks of those present (as opposed to a good idea for "someone else" to do), the more likely a project can move forward. In deference to the need to

have participants experience their time as directly applicable to their everyday business goals, specific collaboration may be suggested in demonstration projects. A starting list might include:

- Supply chain carbon emission reductions
- Sustainability *footprinting*
- Collective purchasing
- Public education/outreach.

7. *Link individual and collective efforts*: In the Sustainability Consortium we saw that personal aspiration is a key driver of system-wide efforts for change. An essential element of a learning consortium will be a coordinating/developing/delivering a coordinated program.
8. *Long-term thinking*: All the best thinking and goodwill in the world cannot maneuver around current budgetary practices that militate against sustainability in important ways. For example, if ROI is demanded within 3 years, many "systems oriented" sustainability practices which require much longer time horizons, will not qualify for investment. For example, solar panels rarely produce return in less than 5 years. Unless these and similar structural hurdles are reconsidered at the executive level, there cannot be large-scale sustainable investment in new infrastructure. Scholars with financial and accounting expertise must therefore also be part of a learning consortium.
9. *Establish feedback between government and business*: Institutionalize best practices by establishing dynamic feedback loops between government and those regulated. A university learning consortium would have to be overseen and administered by a body with impact at the level of state and possibly federal governments. Strategies that arise in the learning experiment can, in turn, be brought to the attention of policy makers – perhaps by inviting them as participants on a parallel track with the business leaders. These feedback loops allow for moving beyond current unilateral communication between regulators and those regulated. Without representation and the experience of genuine feedback loops in communication, there would be merely a development of another layer of bureaucracy, unlikely to be embraced by business leaders. In operational terms this means creating feedback loops between regulators and the efforts of regional learning systems, using the university's learning consortium as a point of connection. Institutionalization of effort then becomes a form of collaborative policy making, something with precedent in other societies seriously grappling with the challenge of sustainability, e.g., Australia, New Zealand.

10. *Assessment as learning*: The goals and the performance standards used in the decision-making process must be, at least in part, quantified if they are to be used to make funding decisions. Strategies must factually achieve these goals and objectives. On a regular basis, public agencies must measure and report on the progress made in achieving stated goals. In operational terms, useful assessment calls for a balanced scorecard to be defined by a steering committee (Lifvergren, Mohrman, & Docherty, 2009). It should be simple and easily understood by decision makers. The practice of creating a learning history (Roth & Bradbury, 2008) an *evaluation and participant engagement methodology* that has been particularly popular in similar contexts in Europe, may be useful. Starting with quantitative results that define success in meeting targets originally defined, the methodology of the learning history offers promise for engaging new stakeholders in collaborative learning (Gearty, 2009).

In summary, taken together the 10 suggestions above suggest a mechanism for convening a learning experiment among stakeholders of a business network aimed at coordinating action toward sustainability to help overcome their system's fragmentation. Fig. 2 encapsulates the suggestions above, which range over and seek to integrate three levels of learning, namely the institutional, inter-organizational/project, and individual participation levels. Thus, the collaborative learning experiment proposed may reach also to integrate policy making (something that the Sustainability Consortium stopped short of) from the context of inter-organizational projects (which the Consortium generated) predicated on a foundation of individual leadership and learning, fostered by relational space.

Limitations and Extensions

Our study has a number of limitations. First, the data are based on retrospective interviews, although Druskat and Wheeler (2003) indicate that the validity and reliability of retrospective self reports are stronger when events described have occurred within the past year, as ours did. We attempted to mitigate the potential problems with qualitative case-based analysis through the use of multiple coders across multiple stages of analysis (Yin, 1994), as well as through triangulation of the interviews with our longitudinal field notes. Our research team meetings were often lively debates through which we processed our data.

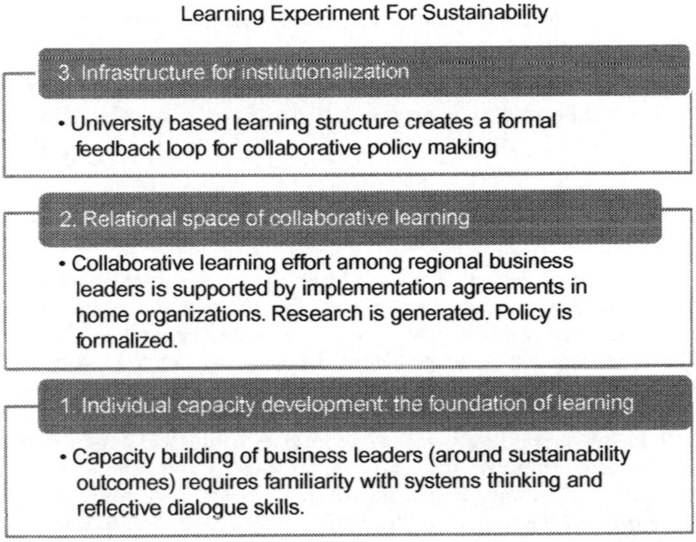

Fig. 2. Integrating Three Levels of Learning.

Moreover, the Sustainability Consortium is only a single case, albeit based on well-known multi-national corporations observed over a multi-year period. Indeed, the capacity of the participants to work together was considerably expanded by the attention to organizational learning practices (e.g., dialogic conversation) and reinforced by the facilitators until they became more automatic. However, the data are highly consistent with other reports of particular types of consortia focused on complex and ambiguous issues and transformational learning (Ring et al., 2005). The difficulties in generalizing notwithstanding (Numagami, 1998), additional studies are required before more formal hypotheses may be developed.

Conclusion

Corporations are recognizing that seemingly intractable system-wide problems can be approached through innovation-based collaborations. Our study suggests that enduring collaborations are founded on an ecology of high-quality interactions, aspirational trust and learning – the combination of which we term Relational Space. We found that Relational Space nourishes collaborative contexts – projects, events, and meetings – that help create sustainability. As business relations are too often defined by economic and technical transactions little place remains for relational "glue" that allows for highly complex, assumption-challenging learning to find new ways to transform competitive relationships into truly sustainable partnerships across multiple stakeholders with tangible benefit for many. Future work will help compare and contrast what we describe here with other efforts.

NOTES

1. These interactions reflect "cognitive learning," through which alliance partners come to understand what resources are available through the relationship (Dyer & Singh, 1998), and the ways in which these resources might be "... blended and leveraged in a manner that is independently meaningful to each, [as they] realize their 'goal interdependence'" (Lubatkin et al., 2001, p. 1371). At the same time, the more valuable the knowledge that is sourced by any partner, the more likely the partner can exploit it for private rather than shared benefit (Noteboom, 2008). Thus, "While many organizations often talk in glowing terms about their alliances' learning potential, learning is a difficult, frustrating, and often misunderstood process" (Inkpen, 2000, p. 777). We would expect that this inherent tension in strategic alliances' learning process will also be felt within multi-sector alliances (Lawrence et al., 2002; London, Rondinelli, & O'Neill, 2004).

2. We note that using a similar theory-generating approach to their 15 years of qualitative data, Huxham and Vangen (2005) identify 17 themes which together describe the key issues in inter-organizational collaborations. Perhaps unsurprisingly, many of their themes are similar to ours; however, we became aware of their themes only after our initial analysis.

ACKNOWLEDGMENT

This manuscript has been developed, in part, with funding from a National Science Foundation Grant # SES NSF 0080643. We are particularly grateful to Ned Powley and Sarah LeRoy for help with data gathering and analysis, and to John Ehrenfeld and Katrin Kaeufer, our colleagues in this work.

REFERENCES

Argyris, C., Putnam, R., & Smith, D. (1985). *Action science*. San Francisco: Jossey-Bass.

Arino, A., & de la Torre, J. (1998). Learning from failure: Towards an evolutionary model of collaborative ventures. *Organization Science*, *9*, 306–325.

Austin, J. E. (2000). Principles for partnership: How cross-sector alliances work for business and communities. *Leader to Leader*, 44–50.

Austin, J. E. (2007). Sustainability through partnering: Conceptualizing partnerships between businesses and NGOs. In: P. Glasbergen, F. Biermann & A. Mol (Eds), *Partnerships, governance and sustainable development*. Cheltenham, UK: Edward Elgar.

Bachmann, R., & Zaheer, A. (2008). Trust in inter-organizational relations. In: S. Cropper, M. Ebers, C. Huxham & P. Smith Ring (Eds), *The Oxford handbook of inter-organizational relations* (pp. 533–554). New York: Oxford University Press.

Barringer, B., & Harrison, J. (2000). Walking a tightrope: Crating value through inter-organizational relationships. *Journal of Management*, *26*, 367–403.

BAWB-Business as an Agent of World Benefit. (2006). *Global forum organized by the Academy of Management, the U.N. Global Compact, and Case Weatherhead School of Management*. Available at: http://www.bawbglobalforum.org/

Berger, I., Cunningham, P., & Drumwright, M. (2004). Social alliances: Company/non-profit collaborations. *California Management Review*, *47*(1), 47–90.

Blau, P. M. (1964). *Exchange and power in social life*. New York: Wiley.

Bouwen, R., & Taillieu, T. (2004). Multi-party collaboration as social learning for interdependence: Developing relational knowing for sustainable natural resource management. *Journal of Community and Applied Social Psychology*, *14*, 137–153.

Bradbury, H. (2009). Three powers of feedback for sustainable multi-organizational learning. In: P. Docherty, J. Forslin & A. B. Shani (Eds), *Creating sustainable work systems: Emerging perspectives and practice*. London and New York: Routledge.

Bradbury, H., & Lichtenstein, B. (2000). Relationality in organizational research: Exploring the "space between". *Organization Science*, *11*, 551–564.

Bradbury-Huang, H. (2010). What is good action research? *Action Research Journal*, *8*(1), 1–11.

Brown, D., & Ashman, D. (1999). Social capital, mutual influence, and social learning in intersectoral problem solving in Africa and Asia. In: D. Cooperrider & J. Dutton (Eds), *Organizational dimensions of global change: No limits to cooperation* (pp. 139–167). Thousand Oaks, CA: SAGE Publications.

Browning, L., Beyer, J., & Shetler, J. (1995). Building cooperation in a competitive industry: SEMATECH and the semiconductor industry. *Academy of Management Journal*, *38*, 113–131.

Cameron, K., Dutton, J., & Quinn, R. E. (Eds). (2003). *Positive organizational scholarship*. San Francisco: Berrett-Koehler.

Carlisle, P. (2004). Transferring, translating, and transforming: An integrative framework for managing knowledge across boundaries. *Organization Science*, *15*, 555–568.

Cooperrider, D., & Dutton, J. (Eds). (1999). *Organizational dimensions of global change: No limits to cooperation*. Thousand Oaks, CA: SAGE Publications.

Cropper, S., Ebers, M., Huxham, C., & Ring, P. S. (Eds). (2008). *The Oxford handbook of inter-organizational relations*. Oxford, UK: Oxford University Press.

Currall, S., & Inkpen, A. (2000). Joint venture trust: Interpersonal, intergroup, and interfirm levels. In: D. O. Faulkner & M. de Rond (Eds), *Cooperative strategies: Economic, business and organizational issues* (pp. 324–340). Oxford, UK: Oxford University Press.

Doz, Y. L., Olk, P., & Ring, K. (2000). Formation processes of R&D consortia: Which path to take? Where does it lead? *Strategic Management Journal*, *21*, 239–266.

Druskat, V. U., & Wheeler, J. V. (2003). Managing from the boundary: The effective leadership of self-managing work teams. *Academy of Management Journal*, *46*, 435–457.

Dyer, J. H., & Singh, H. (1998). The relational view: Cooperative strategy and sources of inter-organizational competitive advantage. *Academy of Management Review*, *23*, 660–679.

Elkington, J. (2002). *Cannibals with forks* (Paperback). London, UK: Conscientious Commerce.

Faulkner, D., & De Rond, M. (Eds). (2000). *Cooperative strategy: Economic, business, and organizational issues*. Oxford, UK: Oxford University Press.

Garud, R., Sanjay, J., & Kumaraswamy, A. (2002). Institutional entrepreneurship in the sponsorship of common technological standards: The case of Sun Microsystems and Java. *Academy of Management Journal, 45*, 196–214.

Gearty, M. R. (2009). *Exploring carbon reduction through tales of vision, chance and determination: Developing learning histories in an inter-organizational context*. Dissertation. University of Bath, UK.

Glasbergen, P., Bierman, F., & Mol, A. (Eds). (2007). *Partnerships, governance and sustainable development*. Cheltenham, UK: Edward Elgar.

Grant, A. (2007). Relational job design and the motivation to make a prosocial difference. *Academy of Management Review, 32*, 393–417.

Grant, A., Dutton, J., & Rosso, B. (2008). Giving commitment: Employee support programs and the prosocial sensemaking process. *Academy of Management Journal, 51*, 898–918.

Gray, B. (1989). *Collaborating: Finding common ground for multiparty problems*. San Francisco: Jossey-Bass.

Gray, B. (2000). Assessing inter-organizational collaboration: Multiple conceptions and multiple methods. In: D. Faulkner & M. De Rond (Eds), *Cooperative strategy* (pp. 243–260). Oxford, UK: Oxford University Press.

Habermas, J. (1989). *The theory of communicative action*. Cambridge: Polity Press.

Hart, S. (1999). Corporations as agents of global sustainability: Beyond competitive strategy. In: D. Cooperrider & J. Dutton (Eds), *Organizational dimensions of global change: No limits to cooperation* (pp. 246–362). Thousand Oaks, CA: SAGE Publications.

Holmqvist, M. (2004). Experiential learning processes of exploitation and exploration within and between organizations: An empirical study of product development. *Organization Science, 15*, 70–81.

Huxham, C., & Vangen, S. (2005). *Managing to collaborate*. New York: Routledge.

Inkpen, A. (2000). A note on the dynamics of learning alliances: Competition, cooperation, and relative scope. *Strategic Management Journal, 21*, 775–779.

Inkpen, A., & Currall, S. (2004). The coevolution of trust, control and learning in joint ventures. *Organization Science, 15*, 586–599.

Isaacs, W. (1993). Taking flight: Dialogue, collective thinking, and organizational learning. *Organizational Dynamics, 22*(2), 24–39.

Khanna, T., Gulati, R., & Nohria, N. (1998). The dynamics of learning alliances: Competition, cooperation, and relative scope. *Strategic Management Journal, 19*, 193–210.

Laur, J., & Schley, S. (2004). *The SoL Sustainability Consortium: Society for Organizational Learning*. Available at: http://www.solsustainability.org/about.htm. Accessed October 2008.

Lawrence, T. B., Hardy, C., & Phillips, N. (2002). Institutional effects of interorganizational collaborations: The emergence of proto-institutions. *Academy of Management Journal, 45*, 281–290.

Lifvergren, S., Mohrman, S. A. & Docherty, P. (2009). The Swedish SkaS development coalition for sustainability. A presentation at "Organizing for Sustainability" symposium. Academy of Management, Chicago, IL, August 9.

London, T., Rondinelli, D., & O'Neill, H. (2004). Exploring uneasy learning alliances between corporations and non-profit organizations. *Academy of Management best paper proceedings*, SIM Division (pp. B1–B6).

Lubatkin, M., Florin, J., & Lane, P. (2001). Learning together and apart: A model of reciprocal interfirm learning. *Human Relations*, *54*, 1353–1382.

Maguire, S., Hardy, C., & Lawrence, T. (2004). Institutional entrepreneurship in emerging fields: HIV/AIDS treatment advocacy in Canada. *Academy of Management Journal*, *47*, 657–680.

Miles, M., & Huberman, M. (1994). *Qualitative data analysis*. Newbury Park, CA: SAG.

Mirvis, P. (2008). Academic-practitioner learning forums: A new model of interorganizational research. In: A. B. Shani, S. A. Mohrman, W. A. Pasmore, B. Stymne & N. Adler (Eds), *Handbook of collaborative management research* (pp. 201–224). Los Angeles and London: SAGE.

Motowidlo, S. J., & Carter, G. W. (1992). Studies of the structured behavioral interview. *Journal of Applied Psychology*, *77*, 571–588.

Muthusamy, S. K., & White, M. (2005). Learning and knowledge transfer in strategic alliances. *Organization Studies*, *26*(3), 415–441.

Nonaka, I., & Konno, J. (1998). The concept of "Ba": Building a foundation for knowledge creation. *California Management Review*, *40*(3), 40–54.

Noteboom, B. (2008). Learning and innovation in inter-organizational relationships. In: S. Cropper, M. Ebers, C. Huxham & P. Ring (Eds), *The Oxford handbook of inter-organizational relations* (pp. 607–634). Oxford, UK: Oxford University Press.

Numagami, T. (1998). The infeasibility of invariant laws in management studies: A reflective dialogue in defense of case studies. *Organization Science*, *9*, 2–15.

Olk, P., & Earley, C. (2000). Interpersonal relationships in international strategic alliances: Cross-cultural exchanges and contextual factors. In: D. Faulkner & M. De Rond (Eds), *Cooperative strategy* (pp. 303–307). Oxford, UK: Oxford University Press.

Rangan, S., Samii, R., & Van Wassenhove, L. (2006). Constructive partnerships: When alliances between private firms and public actors can enable creative strategies. *Academy of Management Review*, *31*, 738–751.

Ring, P. S., & Van de Ven, A. (1994). Developmental processes of cooperative interorganizational relationships. *Academy of Management Review*, *19*, 90–118.

Ring, P. S., Doz, Y., & Olk, P. (2005). Managing formation processes in R&D consortia. *California Management Review*, *47*, 137–156.

Rondinelli, D., & London, T. (2003). How corporations and environmental groups cooperate: Assessing cross-sector alliances and collaborations. *Academy of Management Executive*, *17*(1), 61–76.

Roth, G., & Bradbury, H. (2008). Learning history: An action research practice in support of actionable learning. In: P. Reason & H. Bradbury (Eds), *The handbook of action research: Participative inquiry and practice* (2nd ed.). London & Thousand Oaks, CA: Sage Publishing.

Roth, G., & Senge, P. (1996). From theory to practice: Research territory, processes and structure at an organizational learning centre. *Journal of Organizational Change Management*, *7*(5), 92–106.

Schoen, D. (1983). *The reflective practitioner*. New York: Basic Books.

Senge, P. (1990). *The fifth discipline: The art and practice of the learning organization*. New York: Doubleday Books.

Senge, P., Laur, J., Schley, S., & Smith, B. (2006). *Learning for sustainability*. Cambridge, MA: Society of Organizational Learning.

Senge, P., & Scharmer, O. (2001). Community action research. In: P. Reason & H. Bradbury (Eds), *Handbook of action research*. Thousand Oaks, CA: SAGE Publications.

Senge, P., Smith, B., Kruschwitz, N., Laur, J., & Schley, S. (2008). *The necessary revolution*. NewYork: Doubleday.

Society for Organizational Learning. (2007). Available at: http://www.solonline.org/

Tenkasi, R. V., & Mohrman, S. A. (1995). Technology transfer as collaborative learning. In: T. E. Backer, S. L. David & G. Soucy (Eds), *The behavioral science knowledge base on technology transfer* (pp. 147–168). Rockville, MD: U.S. Department of Health Services.

Thompson, J., & Bunderson, J. S. (2003). Violations of principle: Ideological currency in the psychological contract. *Academy of Management Review*, *28*, 571–586.

Waddell, S. (2005). *Beyond corporate citizenship and social responsibility: Societal learning and change*. Sheffield, UK: Greenleaf Publishing.

Waddock, S. (2008). Building a new institutional infrastructure for corporate responsibility. *Academy of Management Perspectives*, *22*(3), 87–108.

Wondolleck, J., & Yaffe, S. (2000). *Making collaboration work*. Washington, DC: Island Press.

Yin, R. (1994). *Case study research: Design and methods* (2nd ed.). Newbury Park, CA: SAGE Publications.

Zilber, T. B. (2002). Institutionalization as an interplay between actions, meanings, and actors: The case of a rape crisis center in Israel. *Academy of Management Journal*, *45*, 234–254.

SEEKING COMMON GROUND IN THE DIVERSITY AND DIFFUSION OF ACTION RESEARCH AND COLLABORATIVE MANAGEMENT RESEARCH ACTION MODALITIES: TOWARD A GENERAL EMPIRICAL METHOD

David Coghlan

ABSTRACT

As the field of action-oriented research becomes increasingly diffuse and diverse, this paper seeks to identify common ground across the multiple modalities of action research and collaborative management research through articulating and exploring a general empirical method that is grounded in the recognizable structure of human knowing. This method is grounded in: attention to observable data (experience), envisaging possible explanations of that data (understanding), and preferring as probable or certain the explanations, which provide the best account for the data (judgment). Engaging this method requires the dispositions to perform the operations of attentiveness, intelligence, and reasonableness, to which responsibility is added when we seek to take action. This paper

Research in Organizational Change and Development, Volume 18, 149–181

ISSN: 0897-3016/doi:10.1108/S0897-3016(2010)0000018009

seeks to provide insight into the multiple modalities of action research and collaborative management research and to illustrate how each modality engages the recognizable operations of human knowing.

The field of action-oriented research is becoming more increasingly diffuse and diverse. Miller (1994, p. 69) refers to action research as a "bewildering array of activities and methods." Under the term "action research," Reason and Bradbury (2008), for example, outline participatory action research, feminist participatory research, action inquiry, action science, appreciative inquiry, cooperative inquiry, clinical inquiry, action learning, and learning history as expressions within that broad approach. Shani, Mohrman, Pasmore, Stymne, and Adler (2008), working from within a business and organizational context, present "collaborative management research" as the umbrella term. They focus on the dynamics of collaboration between practitioners and academic researchers and between insiders and outsiders as central to the formation of communities of inquiry from these communities of practice and emphasize the generation of actionable knowledge that meets the requirements of both practitioner and academic communities.

Raelin (2009) reflects on the multiplicity of what he refers to as these "action modalities" and identifies a number of similarities. They focus on contextualized and useful theory rather than testing decontextualized and impartial theory. They invite learners to be active participants, leading to change in both self and the system in question. They emphasize reflection-in-action rather than reflection-on-action, the development of double-loop rather than single-loop learning, and meta-competence over competence. Reflection needs to be facilitated rather than taught. They are comfortable with tentativeness rather than certainty. They follow a dialectic, rather than a didactic classroom approach. The normal learning outcomes are often more practice based than theory based.

A further distinctive element of these approaches to research is that quality is judged in terms of dimensions of real-life action, the quality of collaboration, the quality of inquiry in action, and sustainability (Shani & Pasmore, 1985; Levin, 2003; Coghlan & Shani, 2008; Pasmore, Woodman, & Simmons, 2008; Coghlan & Brannick, 2010). A yet further dimension of quality is how emergent choices are weighted and selected (Reason, 2006).

In the face of such diversity and similarity, this chapter seeks to identify common ground across these multiple modalities through exploring how they are grounded in the dynamic structure and operations of human knowing, from which a general empirical method for action research and collaborative management research in the field of organization development and change may be drawn (Coghlan, 2008a). The structure of human knowing is a three-step heuristic process: experience, understanding, and judgment (Lonergan, 1992). Experience is the empirical level of consciousness and is an interaction of data of sense and data of consciousness. Understanding occurs at the intellectual level of consciousness and grasps the intelligible connections between things in answer to questions arising from experience. It also occurs through aesthetics, for example, where artists grasp patterns of color and shapes, sounds, and movements. Judgment occurs at the rational level of consciousness and seeks to verify understanding. The pattern of the three operations is invariant in that all knowing involves experience, understanding, and judgment and applies to all settings whether in the challenges of everyday living or engaging in scientific research. Attending to how we know provides a general method that enables us to engage with the different action modalities and to clarify what we are doing when we engage in any particular modality.

This chapter is directed toward the community of inquiry and practice that works with action modalities through action research and collaborative management research. It seeks to follow the question of what the "bewildering array of activities and methods" might mean and how understanding human cognition provides a framework for collaborative creativity (Mathews, 1981). The aim of this chapter is not to minimize or deflect diversity or to create a single overarching method. Rather, it adopts the perspective of the researcher and seeks to provide insight into each modality and to clarify how the operations of cognitional structure are operative within each modality in order that we may better understand what we are doing when we engage in each one. In this manner, it issues a challenge to the view that the action modalities are identical and to those perspectives that advocate using one modality only with which to address all contexts, the key is to have insight into the context of any particular inquiry and into the insights that underpin each modality.

THE TURN FROM MODERNISM

At issue is modernism's adherence to the split between the knower and the known, where the position on knowing is a matter of a subject "in here" looking at or reflecting on an object "out there." For Descartes, Locke, and Hume, inner perception was conceived by the analogy of taking an inner look at something outside of ourselves and so consciousness was held to be a faculty of inner perception. For Kant, for anything to be an object of knowledge it first had to be the object of sense perception. Modernist social science embedded itself in this perceptualist standpoint on human cognition that found expression in behaviorism and positivism. Where perceptualism fails is in its lack of attention to the world mediated by meaning and to the active role of human consciousness in constructing that world. The postmodern and phenomenological perspective critiqued this focus on immediacy and objectivity, and brought the focus to bear on meaning and value and how this world is constructed through human consciousness and language (Kanaris & Doorley, 2004; Ladkin, 2005).

The distinction between the world of immediacy and the world mediated by meaning is important. We live in a world mediated by meaning, which is constructed by the experiences, understandings, judgments, and decisions of the people and cultures in which we have learned to name things, to interpret them, and live and operate within patterns of relationships and cultures. We can rarely experience the world of immediacy in a pure form, though sensuous sunbathing may be such an instance. Most of the time we make inferences about and add meanings to our immediate sense experience.

Consciousness is not some inward look but rather a quality in the operations of human knowing. So while consciousness is a sense experience, it is also imagination, questioning, understanding, weighing evidence, and so on. There are levels of consciousness paralleling the levels of knowing: empirical consciousness (the extroverted biological consciousness of all animals), intelligent consciousness, rational consciousness, and responsible consciousness. As Lonergan (1988, p. 229) comments, "[I]t is one thing to be to feeling blue and another thing to advert to the fact that you are feeling blue. It is one thing to be in love and another to discover that what has happened to you is that you have fallen in love. Being oneself is prior to knowing oneself." There is a unity in these forms of consciousness, in that what we experience is also what we question, what we seek to verify, and the basis on which we choose to act.

Considering Raelin's (2009) reflections on the characteristics of action modalities listed above, it is evident that internalization of one's own knowing and learning processes is central to engaging in action research and collaborative management research. Such attention, which Marshall (1999, 2001) describes "inquiry as a way of being" and Lonergan (1992) calls "self-appropriation," involves integrating the researcher's own stance and operations as part of what is to be investigated. Such an application takes us to the structure of human knowing.

THE STRUCTURE OF HUMAN KNOWING

How do we know? We know by engaging in a series of operations that begins from experience, which involves questioning that experience, and arriving at some judgment that verifies the answers to our questions, however provisional those answers may be (Dewey, 1933; Kolb, 1984; Lonergan, 1992; Meynell, 1998). Of course, a great deal of our knowing is actually belief, where we accept the work of others, though at times we may need to verify for ourselves. The pattern of the three operations is invariant in that it applies to all settings of cognitional activity.

Experiencing

Experience occurs at the empirical level of consciousness and is an interaction of inner and outer events, or data of sense and data of consciousness. We not only experience external data through our five senses but also experience internal data as we imagine, remember, feel, and think. We also experience ourselves as seeing, hearing, thinking, feeling, remembering, and imagining.

Understanding

Understanding not only names experiences and distinguishes them from one another; it also correlates and associates experiences with one another. Understanding comes through insight, an act that grasps the intelligible connections between things that puzzle us and that occurs at the intellectual level of consciousness. Sensory data are what we experience but do not yet understand. So we ask questions: "What was that noise that I just heard?"; "What does it mean?" Answers to such questions come in the form of insights, which are creative acts of understanding, of grasping and formulating patterns, unities, relationships, and explanations in response to questions posed to our experience. Insights may come in different forms: ideas for the reader, images of color, form and texture for the artist, cadences and harmonies for the composer, shapes for the designer, and so on. In all these situations, the search for understanding is intelligent and is grounded in a particular search. While we might not know yet if a particular current search is intelligent, we anticipate intelligent answers. This act of understanding grasps a pattern in data. There are no recipes, rules, or procedures to follow that lead inevitably to insights. The achievement of insight is unpredictable. It can happen quickly or more slowly. Insight makes the difference between the tantalizing problem and the evident solution. Insofar as it is the act of organizing intelligence, insight is an apprehension of relations and meaning. Every insight goes beyond experience to an explanation. There are also inverse insights, ones for which there are no intelligible answers or patterns. The process of learning involves a series of insights as single insights can cluster and combine to yield further insights and broader applications and deductions, leading to higher viewpoints emerge where we understand patterns. Such learning may also show up the limitations of earlier insights and facilitate learning about our biases.

Judgment

While insights are common they are not always satisfactory answers to our questions. The question then is, does the insight fit the evidence? This opens up a question for reflection. Is it so? Yes or no? Maybe. I don't know. So we move to a new level of the cognitional process, where we marshal and weigh evidence and assess its sufficiency. We are at the rational level of consciousness. We set the judgment up conditionally; if the conditions have been fulfilled, then it is reasonable to judge that this is the case. There may be possible conflicting judgments and we may have to weigh the evidence and choose between them. If we do not think that we have sufficient evidence to assert that our insight fits the data then we may postpone judgment or make a provisional judgment and correct it later when we have more or other evidence.

What makes evidence sufficient depends on the experience of prior judgments. New judgments correct, complement, and criticize former judgments. So we review and criticize prospective judgments in the light of previous judgments. We learn through the accumulation of judgments whereby each successive act of judgment complements the accuracy or uncovers the inaccuracy of those that went before. So we can develop the confidence and skills of being capable of making reasonable judgments and learn to recognize our biases.

There are, of course, such things as stupidity, obtuseness, confusion, divergent views, bias, lack of attention, and a general lack of intelligence. Understanding may not spontaneously flow from experience. Many insights may be wrong. Interpretations of data may be superficial, inaccurate, biased. Judgments may be flawed. We can gain insight into these negative manifestations of knowing by the same three-fold process of knowing.

Taking Action

We are not merely knowers; we also make decisions and act. Decision/action is at the responsible level of consciousness. The process of deciding is a similar process to that of knowing. We experience a situation. Using sensitivity, imagination, and intelligence we seek to answer the question for understanding as to what possible courses of action there might be. At this level we ask what courses of action are open to us and we review options, weight choices, and decide. We reflect on the possible value judgments as to what is the best option and we decide to follow through the best value judgment and we take responsibility for consistency between our knowing and our doing. Accordingly, the responsible level of consciousness is added to the empirical, intellectual, and rational levels.

Taking individual knowing to group and organizational knowing is a complex process. Sharing individual insights that are accepted by others as the basis for joint judgment and action involves participants engaging in conversations as they react to and consider what others put to them (Coghlan, 1997). As a specific framework in this regard, Crossan, Lane, and White (1999) present an organizational learning framework of four *I*s (*i*ntuiting, *i*nterpreting, *i*ntegrating, and *i*nstitutionalizing) that provide insight into this complex process. *Intuiting* is a preconscious recognition of patterns or possibilities inherent in a personal stream of experience, that is, insight. *Interpreting* refers to more conscious elements of explaining an insight. *Integrating* is the process of developing shared understanding among individuals and of taking coordinated action through mutual adjustment. *Institutionalizing* is the process of ensuring that routinized actions occur. Taking the four *I*s to the process of organizational learning, Crossan and colleagues place *intuiting* and *interpreting* in individual learning. They understand group learning as a process of *integrating*, where shared understanding is worked at through conversation among group members in order to attain coherence. They understand the process of *institutionalizing* as being one which makes organizational learning distinctive from individual and group learning, which is a means for organizations to leverage and consolidate the learning of its individual members. The four *I*s framework provides a framework for considering how an individual's experience, understanding, and judgment may become a group and organization's experience, understanding, and judgment.

THE GENERAL EMPIRICAL METHOD

From the cognitional operations of experience, understanding, and judgment, a general empirical method, which is simply the enactment of the knowing process, may be formulated. This method is grounded in:

- Attention to data of sense and of consciousness (experience)
- Envisaging possible explanations of that data (understanding)
- Preferring as probable or certain the explanations, which provide the best account for the data (judgment).

Engaging this method requires the dispositions to perform the operations of attentiveness, intelligence, and reasonableness, to which is added responsibility when we seek to take action (Table 1).

A word about method, particularly as the term tends to have connotations of being applied in a mechanistic and disembodied manner. We might distinguish between a method and a recipe; the latter delivers another instance of the same product. A method is not a set of rules to be followed meticulously; it is a framework for collaborative activity. The key to method is the relationship between questioning and answering; it is a framework for collaborative creativity that deals with different kinds of questions, each with its own focus. So questions for understanding specific data (What is happening here?) have a different focus from questions for reflection (Does this fit?) or from questions of responsibility (What ought I do?). The general empirical method of being attentive, intelligent, reasonable, and responsible is a normative heuristic pattern of related and recurrent operations that yield ongoing and cumulative results. It envisages all data, both of sense and of consciousness. It doesn't treat objects without taking into consideration the subject's operations of experience, understanding and judgment. It is operative in natural science, in human sciences, in spirituality, and in the practical world of the everyday.

Table 1. General Empirical Method.

Experience	Attentiveness (to data of sense and of consciousness)	Empirical level
Understanding	Intelligence (envisaging possible explanations of that data)	Intellectual level
Judgment	Reasonableness (preferring as probable or certain the explanations which provide the best account for the data)	Rational level
Action	Responsibility (for action)	Responsible level

For knowledge to be realized, first, we need to attend to our attending and what gives us curiosity, delight, anxiety, and so on. Secondly, we need to advert to our intelligence, what is it we do not understand yet, the dissatisfaction with current explanations, the puzzled search for new understanding, the release when we receive insights, and our efforts to express what it is that we have understood. Thirdly, we need to attend to our reasonableness, whether our understanding fits the evidence, whether it is coherent or true, whether something will work or not. Finally, we need to attend to the responsibilities of our action. We move from one question to another in a conscious and dynamic manner. Enactment of these process imperatives may be construed to constitute authenticity on the part of the researcher (Coghlan, 2008b). It is grounded, not in any thesis or grand theory, but in the recognizable operations of human inquiry and action.

A further challenge within the field of action and collaborative research is to ground methodologies in the practical form of knowing that seeks to enhance the practice of communities, organizations, and individuals in the everyday world, where interests and concerns are human living and the successful performance of daily tasks and discovering immediate solutions that will work (Susman & Evered, 1978; Gibbons et al., 1994; Schon, 1995; Reason & Torbert, 2001). Understanding actions in the everyday world requires inquiry into the constructions of meaning that individuals make about themselves, their situation and the world, and how their actions may be driven by assumptions and compulsions as well as by values (Marshall & Reason, 2007; Melchin & Picard, 2008). In a similar vein, large systems and groups hold their own shared meanings, which direct their actions (Schein, 2004). The collaborative dynamic of action research and collaborative management research involves engagement with others in conversation as to the insights that they have into situations, how those insights differ, the priorities that different stakeholders may have and how to negotiate collaborative action.

A second element of working within the domain of practical knowing that poses challenges to research methodology is that in the everyday practical world, no two situations are identical. Time has passed; the place has changed. We remember differently. A remembered set of insights is only approximately appropriate to the new situation. We may have insights into situations that are similar, but not identical. In order to move from one setting to another, we must grasp what modifications are needed and to decide how to act. Organization development and change through action research and collaborative management research is located in the world of practical knowing where inquiring into the practical world of the everyday needs to be able to accommodate the changing nature of data where situations are not identical and shift as a consequence of intervention.

THE GENERATIVE INSIGHT AND APPLICATION OF THE GENERAL EMPIRICAL METHOD ACROSS MODALITIES OF ACTION RESEARCH AND COLLABORATIVE MANAGEMENT RESEARCH

Each modality within action research and collaborative management research is based on an insight. I refer to this form of insight as a generative insight as it constitutes the foundational understanding that has led to the particular framing of each modality, and which generated further insights and methods of working within each modality. Building on Gergen (1978), Bushe (2010) applies the notion of generativity to organization development and change and argues that "it occurs when a group of people discover and create new ideas that are compelling to themselves and others and provoke new actions."

While there are many modalities within the broad approach that we call action research and collaborative management research, this paper focuses only on seven of them. This selection is one that I, as the author, have made. There may be criticisms of this selection and queries as to why others have not been included. My main criterion, which included the exigencies of space, has been to stay within those approaches that work within the field of organization development and change. Even within this perspective I have had to be selective. Accordingly, I have selected not to include approaches that work mainly within the field of community development and social transformation, participatory action research being the notable instance of such an approach. I have focused on action learning, action science, appreciative inquiry, clinical inquiry/research, cooperative inquiry, developmental action inquiry, and learning history. Each of these is based on generative insights that give each modality its own distinctive character and emphasis. While some of these modalities have been compared previously, particularly in terms of their philosophical basis (Raelin, 1999; Shani, David, & Willson, 2004), this exploration works from the recognizable operations of human knowing. Through focusing on generative insights and how the general empirical method may be applied, it is hoped that readers will receive their own insight into these action modalities and, thereby, discover for themselves how to engage with them (Table 2).

Table 2. Generative Insights and the General Empirical Method across Action Modalities.

	Generative Insight	General Empirical Method
Action learning	There can be no learning without action and no (sober and deliberate) action without learning. Those unable to change themselves cannot change what goes on around them.	L = P + Q. Subjecting experience to questioning insight in the company of peers and taking action.
Action science	People are unaware of their theories-in-use. Being able to systemically analyze reasoning and behavior to identify causal links can produce actionable knowledge.	Testing privately held inferences and attributions in action.
Appreciative inquiry	When people focus on what is valuable in what they do and try to work on how this may be built on, it leverages the capacity of metaphors and conversation to facilitate transformational action.	Attending to insights from power of positive questioning, leading to action.
Clinical inquiry/ research	When researchers who gain access to organizations at the organization's invitation in order to be helpful and to intervene to enable change to occur, this is the most fruitful way of understanding and changing organizations.	Helping clients attend to their experience, have insights into that experience, make judgments as to whether the insights fit the evidence, and then to take action.
Cooperative inquiry	Each person is a *co-subject* in the experience phases by participating in the activities being researched and a *co-researcher* in the reflection phases.	Continuing cycles of experiences being shared, questions asked, insights generated, meanings articulated and tested in action, leading to further questions and insights, tested, understood, and acted on.
Developmental action inquiry	Learning to inquire and to act in a timely manner contains central and implicit frames that each person acts out of in given periods of time.	Inquiring-in-action through attending to the four territories of experience.
Learning history	Capturing what individuals and groups have learned and presenting it through the jointly told tale enables readers to learn about organizational dynamics.	Attending to and discussing one's own questions and insights through reading the experience and insights of others, leading to shared insights.

Action Learning

The generative insight that underpins action learning is found in Revans' two statements: "There can be no learning without action and no (sober and deliberate) action without learning" (Revans, 1998, p. 83); "Those unable to change themselves cannot change what goes on around them" (Revans, 1998, p. 85). Grasping this insight is at the heart of understanding what action learning is about, how it works and what it seeks to achieve. Central to action learning is a distinction between puzzles and problems. *Puzzles* are those difficulties for which a correct solution exists, and which are amenable to specialist and expert advice. *Problems*, on the other hand, are difficulties where no single solution can possibly exist because different people advocate different courses of action in accordance with their own value systems, past experience, and intended outcomes.

Revans (1971) describes three processes central to action learning, what he refers to as a *praxeology* of human action.

- A process of inquiry into the issue under consideration – its history, manifestation, what has prevented it from being resolved, what has previously been attempted... Revans calls this process *System Alpha*.
- Action learning is science in progress through rigorous exploration of the resolution of the issue through cycles of action and reflection. He calls this *System Beta*.
- Action learning is characterized by a quality of group interaction, which enables individual's critical reflection, and ultimately the learning. This is the essence of action learning and Revans calls it *System Gamma*.

These three processes emphasize how action learning involves engagement with real problems rather than with fabrications, and is both scientifically rigorous in the confronting the problem and critically subjective through managers learning in action. Participating managers take responsibility for and control of their own learning and so there is minimal use of experts. Revans (1971, 1998) outlines a scientific method: observation/survey involves collecting and classifying what seems to go on; theory/hypothesis generation involves suggesting causal relationships between those happenings; test/experiment involves taking action on the basis of those causal relationships; audit/review involves asking if that action has gone as expected and review/control involves rejecting, changing, or accepting the emergent causal relationships. While the practice of action learning is demonstrated through many different approaches, two core elements are consistently in evidence: participants work on real organizational problems that do not appear to have clear solutions; and participants meet on equal terms to report to one another and to discuss their problem and progress (O'Neil & Marsick, 2007).

The general empirical method is embedded in enacting in Revans' learning formula, L = P + Q. L stands for learning, P for programmed learning (i.e., current knowledge in use, already known, what is in books, etc.) and Q for questioning insight. The questioning and reflective process is enacted through the scientific method. Experience in both the past and present is subjected to questioning with a view to gaining insights into what is going on regarding the problem at hand, why it is happening and what might be done about it. Implementation of Revans' scientific method through the praxeology of systems alpha, beta, and gamma provides a process through which the learner, in the company of peers in an action learning group, engages in critical inquiry into experience, gains insights, takes risks in taking action on the problem, which sets up further experiences for reflection and so the process continues.

Action Science

Action science describes, "research capable of explaining phenomena, informing practice and adhering to the rational aims of science, while avoiding the 'inner contradictions' characteristic of normal science techniques in the social realm" (Friedman & Rogers, 2008, p. 252). The generative insight for understanding action science is that we are unaware of our theories-in-use and how they implicitly guide our behavior, which are likely to contribute to ineffectiveness. Being able to systemically analyze and document patterns of behaviors and the reasoning behind them in order to identify causal links can produce actionable knowledge, that is, theories for producing desired outcomes (Argyris, 2004). In Argyris' (1987) view, practice-oriented scholars became so client-centered that they failed to question how clients themselves defined their problems and ignored the building and testing of propositions embedded in their own practice. On the theoretical side, scholars conducted research that met the criteria of rigor of normal science but was disconnected from everyday life. Action science assumes that learning is the first and primary objective for the researcher, the clients and the system, and that knowledge produced should be put into empirically testable propositions, which in turn may be organized into a theory. Therefore, action science should take account of the way people learn, the way research is conducted, and how theory is created.

There are three implications to be noted for the general empirical method (Argyris, Putnam, & Smith, 1985).

1. Knowledge must be designed with the human mind in view, that is, taking account of the limited information-seeking and processing capabilities of human beings in the context of taking action in complex situations.
2. Knowledge must be relevant to forming purposes as well as achieving them.
3. Knowledge must take account of the normative dimension, the value questions related to the formation of purposes.

The general empirical method lies at the heart of action science. The process of inquiry into our theories-in-use requires attention to the operations of knowing, which involves testing privately held inferences and attributions and how they lead to ineffective strategies and behaviors. What action science is addressing is the operation of movement from insight to judgment. Its techniques, such as the ladder of inference, the left and right hand column method, and treating facts as hypotheses, provide ways of focusing on the distinction between what I infer/attribute and what I know. So I may ask myself, is my insight an inference/attribution? On what evidence am I forming a judgment about what is going on and what I choose to do? Action science challenges us to engage in self-reflection and to attend to the knowing on which we base our actions. So I may ask myself, what is the evidence of my understanding? How have I come to understand in that way and not in another? How do I know that my understanding is true? Action science poses similar questions. What are my espoused theories and my theories-in-use and can I express them in a way that I can't squirm out of them? How can I become more aware of my skilled incompetence, how my reasoning functions to protect myself and how I become blind to my blindness? How do I cover up inconsistent messages that I produce, deny producing them, and make that denial undiscussable and make the undiscussability of the undiscussable itself undiscussable?

Appreciative Inquiry

Appreciative inquiry is built on the generative insight of inquiry as positive, that is, if people focus on what is valuable in what they do and try to work on how this may be built on, then it leverages the generative capacity of metaphors and conversation to facilitate transformational action (Ludema & Fry, 2008; Bushe, 2010). This insight is itself made up of several insights that Reed (2007) outlines as assumptions underpinning appreciative inquiry.

- In every organization something works somewhere.
- What we focus on becomes our reality and the language we use creates our reality.
- Reality is created in the moment and there are multiple realities.
- The act of asking questions influences by getting people to think in new ways, which may lead to acting in new ways.
- People have more confidence and comfort to journey to the future when they carry forward parts of the past.
- If we carry parts of the past forward they should be what is best about the past.
- It is important to value differences.

As Reed points out, these assumptions are the outcomes of long processes of research that have produced practical guidelines (Cooperrider & Srivastva, 1987). In other words, the above assumptions are themselves insights that have been explored and verified by judgment.

The two cycles that appreciative inquiry utilize: the four *D*s (*D*iscovery, *D*ream, *D*esign, *D*elivery) and the four *I*s (*I*nitiate, *I*nquire, *I*magine, *I*nnovate) enable researchers and practitioners to move from experience to selected action and to attend to and receive insights into understand the power of positive questioning. Accordingly, each step of the cycles involves experience, understanding, and judgment. For instance, the *discovery* step involves inquiry into the experience of what works well, insight into how and why it is successful, affirmation by judgment, and then creation of the *dream* to build on it. And so the general empirical method continues in the other steps of the cycles.

Clinical Inquiry/Research

Clinical inquiry/research is grounded in the generative insight that when researchers gain access to organizations at the organization's invitation in order to be helpful and intervene to enable change to occur, which is the most fruitful way of understanding and changing organizations (Schein, 1987, 1995, 2008). As such, it is synonymous with process consultation, whereby the consultant creates a helping relationship with a client, which enables the client "to perceive, understand, and act on the process events that occur in the client's internal and external environment in order to improve the situation as defined by the client" (Schein, 1999, p. 20). There are several accompanying core insights. The issues that clinical researchers work on are important. They accept the assumption that unless they attempt to change the system they cannot really understand it. The primary sources to organizational data are not what is "out there" but are in the effects of and responses to intervention.

There are three basic assumptions underlying Schein's notion of clinical inquiry/research.

- Clinical researchers are hired to help. The research agenda comes from the needs of the client system, not from the interests of the researchers.
- Clinical researchers work from models of health and therefore are trained to recognize pathological deviations from health.
- Clinical researchers are not only concerned with diagnosis but have a primary focus on treatment.

Through being present in a helping role, the clinical inquiry/researcher is noticing how data are continuously being generated as the change process proceeds. While it may not be clear what these data might mean, the researcher's mode of inquiry enables the client to explore, understand, and act upon the events as they emerge. In this way, the clinical researcher's data are "real-time," generated in the act of managing change, and not data created especially for the research project.

Schein's (1999) definition of process consultation as helping clients "to perceive, understand and act" may be reframed in terms of the general empirical method as helping clients attend to their experience, have insights into that experience, make judgments as to whether the insights fit the evidence and then to take action (Coghlan, 2009). Observation of clients in action and subsequent conversations between clinical researchers and clients seek to bring out experience (through pure inquiry) test insights and form judgments about that experience (through diagnostic inquiry) and then make decisions and take action (through confrontive inquiry). As Coghlan (2009) argues, clinical inquiry/research makes demands on clinical researchers to apply the general empirical method to themselves by being attentive to data, intelligent in understanding, reasonable in making judgments, and be responsible in making interventions.

Cooperative Inquiry

Heron and Reason (2008, p. 366) define cooperative inquiry "as a form of second person action research in which all participants work together in an inquiry group as co-researchers and co-subjects." The participants research a topic through their own experience of it in order to:

1. Understand their world to make sense of their life and develop new and creative ways of looking at things.
2. Learn how to act to change things they might want to change and find out how to do things better.

Heron (1996, p. 1) puts it, "it is a vision of persons in reciprocal relation using the full range of their sensibilities to inquire together into any aspect of the human condition with which the transparent mind-body can engage." The generative insight for understanding cooperative inquiry is how each person is a *co-subject* in the experience phases by participating in the activities being researched and a *co-researcher* in the reflection phases by participating in generating ideas, designing and managing the project, and drawing conclusions.

The general empirical method operates in cooperative inquiry as participants' experience is brought to the group and exposed to questioning. Group members inquire into how individuals construct the meanings of these experiences. Further questions are asked. As the group explores the experiences of its members, further insights are generated and meanings are articulated. So there are continuing cycles of experiences being shared, questions asked, insights generated, meanings articulated and tested in action, leading to further insights, tested, understood, and acted on. An important element of cooperative inquiry is that it works with the different ways of knowing, so experience and insights may be expressed in different forms.

Developmental Action Inquiry

Developmental action inquiry is an action science, "a kind of scientific inquiry that is conducted in everyday life…that deals primarily with 'primary' data encountered 'on-line' in the midst of perception and action" (Torbert, 1991, p. 220). The generative insight that developmental action inquiry adds to action science is that learning to inquire and to act in a timely manner contains central and implicit frames that each person acts out of in given periods of time.

Torbert adds the developmental dynamic of learning to inquire-in-action by emphasizing that as we progress through adulthood we may intentionally develop new "action-logics" through stages of ego development (Torbert & Associates, 2004; Torbert & Taylor, 2008). Developmental theory offers an understanding of both our own and organizational transformation through a series of stages of development so that we gain insight into our own and organizational action logics as we take action.

The general empirical method is applied through process of inquiry-in-action through attending to the four territories of experience: the outside world, our own sensed behavior and feelings, the realm of thought, and vision/attention/intention (Torbert & Taylor, 2008). It engages reflection on experience through a series of inquiry loops and enables insight into taken-for-granted assumptions about how we engage with the outside world, how we think, how we make judgments, what our intentions are, and how our action strategies are grounded. Enacting the four "parts of speech" – explicitly stating the purpose of speaking for the present occasion (*framing*); explicitly stating the goal to be achieved, asserting an option, perception, feeling or proposal for action (*advocating*); telling a bit of the concrete story that makes the advocacy concrete and orients the others more clearly (*illustrating*); and questioning others to understand their perspectives and views (*inquiring*) – provides a process that facilitates insight into the purpose of a particular communication and seeks to diminish ambiguity.

Learning History

"The goal of a learning history is to increase participation in a dialogic reflection on past action for creating desired future practices" (Bradbury & Mainmelis, 2001, p. 342). The learning history presents the experiences and understandings in the own words of those who have gone through and/or been affected by the change in order to help the organization move forward and to contribute to our understanding of the social dynamics of organizational change. Rather than presenting the univocal voice of a single author or group of researchers, the learning history presents concurrent, multiple, and often divergent voices in an organizational story. Presenting the jointly told tale is enabled by the format, whereby columns of narrative text are juxtaposed with interpretative voice of participants (often disagreeing) and the voice of the learning historian. The generative insight underpinning the learning history is that by capturing what groups have learned and presenting it through the jointly told tale readers may learn about organizational change. Readers are encouraged to attend to the questions that arise from their engagement with the text as they choose which column to read first and how they might switch back and forth from participants' narrative and learning historians' comments, and to the insights they receive from reading multiple voices and perspectives.

A learning history is both a product and a process. It is built around four elements: multi-stakeholders' co-design around notable accomplishments, insider/outsider teams leading reflective interviews, distillation, and thematic writing, and validation and diffusion with original participations and salient others (Roth & Bradbury, 2008). Roth and Bradbury (2008) ground the content and process of the learning history approach in insights from theories of learning and theories of social construction, which emphasize the importance of history as an informant of organizational awareness, learning, and preferred action.

The general empirical method is enacted through both conversations and written texts. Hearing and reading the multiple voices and perspectives within the process of a learning history enable insight into the insights of others and through conversation the possibilities for new shared insights to emerge, on which judgments may be reached and actions planned and taken.

Illustration

In a collaborative research initiative that was focused on developing network learning in the supply chain (Coghlan & Coughlan, 2005, 2008), a choice of action learning as the appropriate action modality was made. Action learning was selected on the basis that it offered the managers of the participating firms in the supply chain the opportunity to engage in shared action and inquiry on pertinent issues in their commercial relationship. A contributing factor in the choice of action learning was the managers' familiarity with learning-in-action in the area of quality management through the Deming plan-do-check-act cycle. This prior experience and knowledge of cycles of action and learning provided the opportunity to build action learning skills within a familiar perspective, while at the same time develop collaborative learning skills in action. One particular supply chain relationship provides an interesting example of action learning (Coughlan & Coghlan, 2009).

One supplier delivered pump components to the system integrator. For several years, one low-cost, high-volume component part, a plastic insert, had been problematic. The issue originated during the injection molding process when vacuum bubbles occurred as a result of material shrinkage during the molding process. Despite many attempts the supplier had not been able to resolve this issue and, despite quality inspections and a high resulting internal scrap rate, defective inserts were delivered to the system integrator. The defective components melted in service with a severe knock-on effect for end users. Instead of penalizing the supplier for poor performance, the system integrator and the supplier agreed to initiate a collaborative improvement initiative to tackle the issue. Despite several joint efforts the issue got worse, as evidenced by an increasing scrap rate. Two insights rescued the situation. One insight was to replace the material from which the insert was made and the other was to change the design of the insert, which involved changes in a mating part manufactured by another supplier.

The operational issue between the two firms was effectively a puzzle, that is, it was a technical issue that had a technical solution, if the experts could only find it. At the same time, this technical puzzle was embedded in an interorganizational problem, which was framed in terms of how the participating firms in the supply chain could become a learning network. The quality of the action learning process through which the participating firms engaged in developing shared goals and vision, mutual interdependence, and joint work and activities was paramount. At the same time, the researchers needed to know the distinction between problems and puzzles in action learning and not get trapped by the demands and details of the technical puzzle so as to remain focused on the bigger picture of the aims of the initiative, namely to develop network learning in the supply chain.

DISCUSSION

What does this exploration and application of the general empirical method to the modalities of action research and collaborative management research offer us? First, rather than viewing it as an effort at intellectual imperialism that seeks to mandate a single method to the exclusion of all others, it seeks to provide insight into these multiple modalities and to illustrate how each modality engages the recognizable operations of human knowing. This illustration seeks to facilitate understanding of the generative insight underpinning each modality and how our engagement in each modality draws on what we know and on how we inquire into what and how others come to know. Second, it enables insight into similarities and differences in emphases between the modalities and the possible trade-offs we may make in adopting one modality over or in conjunction with, another. Third, it seeks to provide insight into contemporary challenges in action research and collaborative management research in the field of organization development and change.

Enacting the General Empirical Method in Action Modalities

Table 3 illustrates how the operations of human cognition – experience, understanding, and judgment – and then action enable us to receive insight into each action modality from the perspective of the engaged inquirer. At its core, applying the general empirical method to each modality is a matter of being attentive to experience and observable data, questioning that experience with a view to receiving insights/understanding in seeking possible explanations of that experience, and forming judgments on the explanations, which provide the best understanding of the experience. Engaging this method requires the dispositions to perform the operations of attentiveness, intelligence, and reasonableness, to which responsibility is added when we seek to take action.

Each of the modalities is grounded in experience: a problematic situation or a developmental opportunity as a possible stimulus, the experience of working to engage collaboratively with others to enable change to take place, and to generate actionable knowledge and the experience of our own consciousness as we think and feel in action. In action learning there is the experience of confronting a problem for which there is no evident solution. Action science and developmental action inquiry are grounded in experiences of ineffectiveness through the disparity between one's espoused theory and theory-in-use. In appreciative inquiry, it is the experience of seeking to generate transformational change. In cooperative inquiry there is the experience of co-inquiring with others and taking action on an issue of concern. In clinical inquiry/research it is the experience of working to build a helping relationship with a client in order to help the client in order to improve a situation as defined by the client. The experience of reading multiple voices in the learning history provides an experience from which questions arise.

Each experience is subjected to inquiry, to a search for insight or understanding into the identified experience. In action science and developmental action inquiry, inquiry into outcomes may lead to inquiry into actions, possibly into goals and into intentionality in order to uncover reasoning behind actions. In action learning, insight into how the problem has been faced previously without success and understanding of perceived causal

Table 3. Enacting the General Empirical Method in Action Modalities.

	Attentiveness to Experience	Intelligent Questions for Understanding	Reasonable Questions for Reflection	Responsible Questions for Action
Action learning	Confronting a problem for which there is no evident solution	*System Alpha* questions: What is the history of this problem? What has been attempted previously? *System Beta* questions: How do I collect and classify what seems to go on? What causal relationships exist between events? Have events gone as expected? *System Gamma* questions: What am I learning?	Do I accept/reject, or change emergent causal relationships?	What actions will I take to address the problem?
Action science	Experiencing ineffectiveness	Are the outcomes of my actions what I intended? What actions did I take? What was the reasoning behind my actions? What are my theories-in-use?	How can I test that the knowledge produced can be put into empirically testable propositions?	How do I behave out of my theory-in-use?
Appreciative inquiry	Developing strategy and change	What is positive in the current situation? What works well in the present situation that can be developed?	Has what has been selected generated energy for change?	What actions will I take?
Clinical inquiry/ research	Build a helping relationship with client in order to improve a situation as defined by the client	How can I be helpful to the client's needs?	Have I checked that my understanding fits with what the client is intending?	What actions will I take?

Cooperative inquiry	Co-inquiring and taking action on an issue of concern	How do I understand my own experience that I bring to the group? How do I understand the experience of the other participants as they present it?	Does my understanding fit the evidence?	What actions will I take to address on my issue of concern?
Developmental action inquiry	Learning to act in a timely manner	Are the outcomes of my actions what I intended? What actions did I take? What was the reasoning behind my actions? What are my action logics? Do these inquiry loops provide insight into my stage of development?	Do my inquiry loops confirm my insight into my action logics?	How do I behave out of my action logics?
Learning history	Reading a account of a jointly told tale	How credible do I find the story? How might these related perspectives help further action?	Do these insights fit and make sense?	What actions might I take?

relationship between forces in tackling the problem enable action strategies to be developed and experimental action taken. In appreciative inquiry, insight into what has worked well facilitates the creation of positive strategies. In cooperative inquiry, engagement in the group facilitates insights into one's own and others' experience. In clinical inquiry/research, insight into how the relationship is being helpful to the client (or not) and enabling insight in the client is central. In reading a learning history, insight into the convergences and divergences across the multiple voices provides the basis for further questions.

Each insight must be subjected to some sort of verification, where as we reflect on how each insight has illuminated inquiry and we check that our insights are reasonable in fitting the evidence. For instance, in action science and developmental action inquiry, we may check if the inquiry into action, goals, and intentionality confirmed insight into theory-in-use or action logics. In clinical inquiry, the client's response may indicate the degree of helpfulness. Finally, the question remains as to what appropriate action accompanies the judgment. What do we choose to do next?

Similarities, Differences, and Possible Trade-Offs

I have illustrated how each action modality engages with the operations of human knowing – experience, understanding, and judgment. It may be noted that each modality has its own emphasis, for example, addressing a practical problem in action learning, generating transformational change in appreciative inquiry, building a helping relationship in clinical inquiry/research and so on. At the same time, while each modality has its own particular emphasis, other aspects are not ignored. For instance, while cooperative inquiry is strong on the insights of participants as co-subjects and co-researchers, it also emphasizes cycles of action and reflection and the enacting different forms of knowing. Appreciative inquiry, while focusing in the generative capacity of the positive stance, also provides a context for collaboration.

Choosing a particular action modality involves the consideration of four factors (Shani & Pasmore, 1985). First, there is the context, both external and internal, in which the issue for development (or the problem to be addressed) is located. Understanding the context with this complexities and forces for and against change is a critical consideration. Second, there is the quality of relationships between organizational members and researcher and between the organizational members themselves that becomes the foundation for collaborative inquiry and action. For example, if a group has no history of shared inquiry, then selecting an appropriate action modality needs to build from that reality. Third, how the action-oriented inquiry may be conducted needs to be considered. Issues of structuring the inquiry fall into this category. Fourth, the dual outcomes of action research are some level of sustainability (human, social, economic ecological) and the development of self-help and competencies out of the action and the creation of new knowledge from the inquiry (Docherty, Kira, & Shani, 2009).

Insights from considering these four factors set the choice of action modality. In some contexts, the internal context may demand a focus on operational action to address an elusive problem and so the choice of action learning may fit, as illustrated in the above example. In another context, where a group seeks to explore professional practice, a modality such as cooperative inquiry may be appropriate (e.g., Reason, 1998). Rather than treating the action modalities as being all the same or using only one modality to address all contexts, the key is to have insight into the context and into the insights that underpin each modality. Table 4 provides a guide as to how a particular modality might be selected and to the challenges in working with the four factors.

Are there trade-offs across the modalities? In what Reason and Torbert (2001) call first-person practice in which the focus of inquiry is personal and professional practice, action science and developmental action inquiry play a significant role. In engaging in collaborative inquiry with others, what Reason and Torbert (2001) call second-person practice, action learning, cooperative inquiry, and appreciative inquiry provide valuable frames. Of course, working in collaboration with others may evoke personal learning and so the individually oriented inquiry modes, such as developmental action inquiry, provide insights into one's collaborative styles and behavior. Where the emphasis is on systemic change, the first- and second-person modes of action and inquiry attempt to work in harmony in order to achieve desired ends and to generate actionable knowledge.

Philosophical Implications

There are also some philosophical implications that enable us to relate the general empirical method to the issues discussed earlier regarding the turn from modernism. Understanding consciousness as a quality in the operations of human knowing, rather than a form of perception, is at the heart of the general empirical method.

Table 4. Factors for Considering an Action Modality.

Action Modality/ Factors for Consideration	Context	Quality of Relationships	Quality of Action-Oriented Inquiry	Outcomes
Action learning	When there are organizational *problems* for which there are no single solutions and engagement in action and in peer learning	Creating and maintaining a climate of trust and willingness to participate in group of peers to engage with one another	Subjecting experience to questioning insight in the company of peers and taking action.	Problems addressed and personal learning internalized for addressing future problems
Action science	When thinking processes have been shown to be ineffective in achieving desired outcomes	Creating a trusting climate to enable individuals to explore their theory-in-use	Testing privately held inferences and attributions in action.	Effectiveness in action and testable actionable theory generated
Appreciative inquiry	When positive thinking has the potential to generate transformational action	Creating a climate for participants to engage in generative conversation	Attending to insights from power of positive questioning, leading to action	Transformational change
Clinical inquiry/ research	When ODC consultants work to be helpful to clients	Building a relationship between client and consultant so that the consultant can be helpful as the client needs it	Helping clients attend to their experience, have insights into that experience, make judgments as to whether the insights fit the evidence, and then to take action	Effective change and personal learning

Cooperative inquiry	When individuals who share a common search agree to meet to explore their experience and to take action	Creating and maintaining a climate of trust and willingness to explore together	Engaging in cycles of action and reflection in the group	Personal empowered learning and action
Developmental action inquiry	When leadership development is at heart of transformational change	Building a supporting climate for individuals to engage in self-reflection and transformation	Inquiring-in-action through attending to the four territories of experience	Organizational and personal transformation
Learning history	When there has been a complex transformational change from which learning may be drawn for future action	Creating openness to respect multiple and often conflicting voices and perspectives on the same events	Attending to and discussing one's own questions and insights through reading the experience and insights of others, leading to shared insights.	Learning from the past to carry into the future

- By encouraging us to note the immanent dynamisms of our efforts to understand and of how new experiences and insights change our understanding, the general empirical method challenge assumptions that knowing is a matter of abstracting unchanging concepts from experience and placing them in current logical positions.
- By making us aware that inquiry and insights are not simply more sophisticated sense perceptions, the general empirical method challenges assumptions that inquiry is a matter of getting outside of self "in here" to integrating existing world of things "out there."
- By making ourselves aware of how our self-understanding changes as we move from an earlier perspective of questions to a later larger perspective of still further questions, the general empirical method challenges the subjectivist tenet that we already have a self. The self, at least the self-responding to the desire to know, is a dynamic activity of consciousness yet in progress Though inquiry and reflection of our own practice as inquirers, we realize the "self" as an intelligent center of dynamic questions, the fuller range of questions proportionate our capacity to inquire and to resolve.

Implications for Contemporary Challenges in Organization Development and Change

Contemporary discussion on the current state of the field of organization development and change includes a contrast between "dialogic OD" and "diagnostic OD" (Bushe & Marshak, 2009). "Diagnostic OD" is framed in terms of an approach that gathers data in order to compare an organization with a set of prescriptions or desired future state, with implicit assumptions that objective data may be used in a process of diagnosis and subsequent intervention. In contrast, "dialogic OD" focuses on the multiple experiences and perspectives within an organization and the need to create conversational opportunities in order to build new realities.

Buono and Kerber (2008) make an important distinction between three approaches to change: directed change, planned change, and guided changing. In "directed change" the focus is diagnostic: have tightly defined goals and a command approach by leadership in order to achieve change quickly. In "planned change" the focus is also diagnostic as change leaders define clear goals, have a plan to achieve them that includes flexible engagement and participation. Such approaches are likely to be useful in limited or focused change initiatives, such as continuous operational improvement. "Guided changing" is dialogic and involves collaborative exploration of the expertise and creativity of organizational members as organic change merges and evolves.

The general empirical method applies to "diagnostic OD" in directed and planned change. Inquiry into problems and puzzles in action learning, for example, conform to the diagnostic focus on seeking insights that tend to be grounded in systemic causality. At the same time, the general empirical method works with both data of sense and data of consciousness and does not treat objects without taking into account the corresponding operations of the subject and does not treat a subject's operations without taking account of the corresponding objects. As such, it is congruent also with "dialogic OD" through its focus on exploring insights and forming critical judgments about individuals' and groups' interpretations and frames of reference. In each of the action modalities explored above, the emphasis is on exploring subjective experience and how the participants construct the meaning of the situations in which they find themselves, which they seek to change, and how they frame and implement action strategies.

The general empirical method provides a perspective on assessing the quality of action research and collaborative management research in terms of dimensions of real-life action, the quality of collaboration, the quality of inquiry in action and sustainability (Shani & Pasmore, 1985; Levin, 2003; Reason, 2006; Coghlan & Shani, 2008; Pasmore et al., 2008; Coghlan & Brannick, 2010). Attending to and inquiring into experience in the realm of practical knowing grounds the engagement with real-life issues. As a collaborative process it enables inquiry into individual and shared actions, co-inquiry into what these actions might mean and a search for shared insights, and so to generate further questions and ultimately affirm shared judgments and take joint action. Cycles of attending to experience, understanding, and judgment, both individually and collaboratively constitute a reflective process through which insights may be identified and corrected and so learning becomes explicit. The outcomes of engaging in the general empirical method are that the knowledge generated be understood to be actionable and transportable and adaptable to other settings.

CONCLUSIONS

As the field of organization development and change settled into the twenty-first century and becomes comfortable with both diagnostic and dialogic approaches, it is expanding its range of modalities of inquiry (Coghlan & Shani, 2010). Within the modalities of inquiry there are diversities of action modalities. The aim of this chapter has not been to minimize or deflect diversity or to create a single overarching method. It has been, rather, to direct the action research and collaborative management research community of inquiry and practice to reflect on the multiple action modalities so as facilitate insight into each modality and to clarify how the operations of our cognitional structure are operative within each modality in order that we may better understand what we are doing. In this chapter I have sought to identify common ground across the multiple modalities of action research and collaborative management research through articulating and exploring a general empirical method that is grounded in the recognizable structure of human knowing. The general empirical method enables us to appropriate our own conscious reality as existential subjects. As conscious subjects we can attend, inquire intelligently, judge reasonably, and decide freely and act responsibly. As conscious existential subjects we can accept and confront the fact that it is up to us to decide that our actions will be responsible, our judgments reasonable, our investigations intelligent, and we advert to data of both sense and consciousness. We bring the general empirical method to the process of action research and collaborative management inquiry where we reflect on individual and shared actions, co-inquire into what these actions might mean, seek shared insights, generate further questions, and ultimately affirm shared judgments and take action.

ACKNOWLEDGMENTS

I thank Paul Coughlan, Aoife McDermott, Joe Raelin, Peter Reason, Bill Pasmore, Patrick Riordan, Rami Shani, and the members of the action research/cooperative inquiry doctoral seminar (Vivienne Brady, Geralyn Hynes, Marian Hennessey, David O'Brien, and Denise O'Brien) for their helpful feedback in developing this paper.

REFERENCES

Argyris, C. (1987). Reasoning, action strategies and defensive routines: The case of OD practitioners. In: R. W. Woodman & W. A. Pasmore (Eds), *Research in organizational change and development* (Vol. 1, pp. 89–128). Greenwich, CT: JAI.

Argyris, C. (2004). *Reasons and rationalizations*. New York: Oxford University Press.

Argyris, C., Putnam, R., & Smith, D. (1985). *Action science*. San Francisco: Jossey-Bass.

Bradbury, H., & Mainmelis, C. (2001). Learning history and organizational praxis. *Journal of Management Inquiry*, *10*(4), 340–357.

Buono, A., & Kerber, K. (2008). The challenge of organizational change: Enhancing organizational change capacity. *Revue Science de Gestion*, *65*, 99–118.

Bushe, G. R. (2010). Generativity and the transformational potential of appreciative inquiry. In: D. Zandee, D. L. Cooperrider & M. Avital (Eds), *Organizational generativity: Advances in appreciative inquiry* (Vol. 3). Bingley, UK: Emerald.

Bushe, G. R., & Marshak, R. J. (2009). Revisioning organization development: Diagnostic and dialogic premises and patterns of practice. *Journal of Applied Behavioral Science*, *45*, 348–368.

Coghlan, D. (1997). Organizational learning as a dynamic interlevel process. In: M. A. Rahim, R. T. Golembiewski & L. E. Pate (Eds), *Current topics in management* (Vol. 2, pp. 27–44). Greenwich, CT: JAI Press.

Coghlan, D. (2008a). Exploring insight: The role of insight in a general empirical method in action research for organization change and development. *Revue Science de Gestion*, *65*, 343–355.

Coghlan, D. (2008b). Authenticity as first person practice: An exploration based on Bernard Lonergan. *Action Research*, *6*(3), 351–366.

Coghlan, D. (2009). Toward a philosophy of clinical inquiry/research. *Journal of Applied Behavioral Science*, *45*(1), 106–121.

Coghlan, D., & Brannick, T. (2010). *Doing action research in your own organization* (3rd ed.). London: Sage.

Coghlan, D., & Coughlan, P. (2005). Collaborative research across borders and boundaries: Action research insights from the CO-IMPROVE project. In: R. W. Woodman & W. A. Pasmore (Eds), *Research in organizational change and development* (Vol. 15, pp. 277–297). Greenwich, CT: JAI.

Coghlan, D., & Coughlan, P. (2008). Collaborative research in and by an interorganizational network. In: A. B. Shani (Rami), S. A. Mohrman, W. A. Pasmore, B. Stymne & N. Adler (Eds), *Handbook of collaborative management research* (pp. 443–460). Thousand Oaks, CA: Sage.

Coghlan, D., & Shani, A. B. (Rami). (2008). Collaborative management research through communities of inquiry. In: A. B. Shani (Rami), S. A. Mohrman, W. A. Pasmore, B. Stymne & N. Adler (Eds), *Handbook of collaborative management research* (pp. 601–614). Thousand Oaks, CA: Sage.

Coghlan, D., & Shani, A. B. (Rami). (2010). Editors' introduction: Organization development – Toward a mapping of the terrain. In: D. Coghlan & A. B. Shani (Rami) (Eds), *Fundamentals of organization development* (Vol. I, pp. xxiii–xxviii). London: Sage.

Cooperrider, D. L., & Srivastva, S. (1987). Appreciative inquiry in organizational life. In: R. W. Woodman & W. A. Pasmore (Eds), *Research in organizational change and development* (Vol. 1, pp. 129–170). Greenwich, CT: JAI.

Coughlan, P., & Coghlan, D. (2009). Reconciling market requirements and operations resources: An opportunity for action learning. *Action Learning: Research and Practice*, *6*(2), 109–120.

Crossan, M., Lane, H. W., & White, R. E. (1999). An organizational learning framework: From intuition to institution. *Academy of Management Review*, *24*(3), 522–537.

Dewey, J. (1933). *How we think*. Lexington, MA: Heath.

Docherty, P., Kira, M., & Shani, A. B. (Rami). (2009). Organizational development for social sustainability in work systems. In: R. W. Woodman, W. A. Pasmore & A. B. Shani (Rami) (Eds), *Research in organizational change and development* (Vol. 17, pp. 77–144). Bingley, UK: Emerald.

Friedman, V. J., & Rogers, T. (2008). Action science: Linking causal theory and meaning making in action research. In: P. Reason & H. Bradbury (Eds), *Handbook of action research* (2nd ed., pp. 252–265). London: Sage.

Gergen, K. J. (1978). Toward generative theory. *Journal of Personality and Social Psychology*, *36*, 1344–1360.

Gibbons, M., Limoges, C., Nowotny, H., Schwartzman, S., Scott, P., & Trow, M. (1994). *The new production of knowledge*. London: Sage.

Heron, J. (1996). *Cooperative inquiry*. London: Sage.

Heron, J., & Reason, P. (2008). Extending epistemology within a cooperative inquiry. In: P. Reason & H. Bradbury (Eds), *Handbook of action research* (pp. 366–380). London: Sage.

Kanaris, J., & Doorley, M. (2004). *In deference to the other*. New York: State University of New York Press.

Kolb, D. A. (1984). *Experiential learning*. Englewood Cliffs, NJ: Prentice-Hall.

Ladkin, D. (2005). The enigma of subjectivity: How might phenomenology help action researchers negotiate the relationship between 'self', 'other' and' truth'? *Action Research*, *3*(1), 108–126.

Levin, M. (2003). Action research and the research community. *Concepts and Transformation*, *8*(3), 275–280.

Lonergan, B. J. (1988). In: F. Crowe & R. Doran (Eds), *Collection. The collected works of Bernard Lonergan* (Vol. 4). Toronto: University of Toronto Press (Original publication, New York: Herder, 1967).

Lonergan, B. J. (1992). In: F. Crowe & R. Doran (Eds), *Insight: An essay in human understanding. The collected works of Bernard Lonergan* (Vol. 3). Toronto: University of Toronto Press (Original publication, London: Longmans, 1957).

Ludema, J., & Fry, R. (2008). The practice of appreciative inquiry. In: P. Reason & H. Bradbury (Eds), *Handbook of action research* (2nd ed., pp. 280–296). London: Sage.

Marshall, J. (1999). Living life as inquiry. *Systemic Practice and Action Research*, *12*(2), 155–171.

Marshall, J. (2001). Self-reflective inquiry practices. In: P. Reason & H. Bradbury (Eds), *Handbook of action research* (pp. 433–439). London: Sage.

Marshall, J., & Reason, P. (2007). Quality in research as 'taking an attitude of inquiry'. *Management Research News*, *30*(5), 368–380.

Mathews, W. (1981). Method and the social appropriation of reality. In: M. Lamb (Ed.), *Method and creativity: Essays in honor of Bernard Lonergan* (pp. 425–441). Milwaukee, WI: Marquette University Press.

Melchin, K., & Picard, C. (2008). *Transforming conflict through insight*. Toronto, Ont.: Toronto University Press.

Meynell, H. (1998). *Redirecting philosophy: Reflections on the nature of knowledge from Plato to Lonergan*. Toronto, Ont.: University of Toronto Press.

Miller, N. (1994). Participatory action research: Principles, politics and possibilities. In: A. Brooks & K. E. Watkins (Eds). The emerging power of action inquiry technologies. *New Directions for Adult and Continuing Education*, *53* (Fall), 60–80.

O'Neil, J., & Marsick, V. (2007). *Understanding action learning*. New York: American Management Association.

Pasmore, W. A., Woodman, R. W., & Simmons, A. L. (2008). Toward a more rigorous, reflective, and relevant science of collaborative management research. In: A. B. Shani (Rami), S. A. Mohrman, W. A. Pasmore, B. Stymne & N. Adler (Eds), *Handbook of collaborative management research* (pp. 567–582). Thousand Oaks, CA: Sage.

Raelin, J. (1999). Preface. *Management Learning*, *30*(1), 115–125.

Raelin, J. (2009). Seeking conceptual clarity in the action modalities. *Action Learning: Research and Practice*, *6*(1), 17–24.

Reason, P. (1998). Cooperative inquiry as a discipline of professional practice. *Journal of Interprofessional Care*, *12*, 419–436.

Reason, P. (2006). Choice and quality in action research practice. *Journal of Management Inquiry*, *15*(2), 187–203.

Reason, P., & Bradbury, H. (2008). *Handbook of action research* (2nd ed.). London: Sage.

Reason, P., & Torbert, W. R. (2001). The action turn: Toward a transformational social science. *Concepts and Transformation*, *6*(1), 1–38.

Reed, J. (2007). *Appreciative inquiry: Research for change*. Thousand Oaks, CA: Sage.

Revans, R. W. (1971). *Developing effective managers*. London: Longmans.

Revans, R. W. (1998). *ABC of action learning*. London: Lemos & Crane.

Roth, G., & Bradbury, H. (2008). Learning history: An action research practice in support of actionable learning. In: P. Reason & H. Bradbury (Eds), *Handbook of action research* (2nd ed., pp. 350–365). London: Sage.

Schein, E. H. (1987). *The clinical perspective in fieldwork*. Thousand Oaks: Sage.

Schein, E. H. (1995). Process consultation, action research and clinical inquiry: Are they the same? *Journal of Managerial Psychology*, *10*(6), 14–19.

Schein, E. H. (1999). *Process consultation revisited: Building the helping relationship*. Reading, MA: Addison-Wesley.

Schein, E. H. (2004). *Organizational culture and leadership* (3rd ed.). San Francisco: Jossey-Bass.

Schein, E. H. (2008). Clinical inquiry/research. In: P. Reason & H. Bradbury (Eds), *Handbook of action research* (2nd ed., pp. 266–279). London: Sage.

Schon, D. A. (1995). Knowing-in-action: The new scholarship requires a new epistemology. *Change*, *November/December*, 27–34.

Shani, A. B. (Rami)., David, A., & Willson, C. (2004). Collaborative research: Alternative roadmaps. In: N. Adler, A. B. Shani (Rami) & A. Styhre (Eds), *Collaborative research in organizations* (pp. 83–100). Thousand Oaks, CA: Sage.

Shani, A. B. (Rami)., Mohrman, S. A., Pasmore, W., Stymne, B., & Adler, N. (2008). *Handbook of collaborative management research*. Thousand Oaks, CA: Sage.

Shani, A. B. (Rami)., & Pasmore, W. A. (1985). Organization inquiry: Towards a new model of the action research process. In: D. D. Warrick (Ed.), *Contemporary organization development: Current thinking and applications* (pp. 438–448). Glenview, IL: Scott Foresman.

Susman, G. I., & Evered, R. D. (1978). An assessment of the scientific merits of action research. *Administrative Science Quarterly*, *23*, 582–601.

Torbert, W. R. (1991). *The power of balance*. Thousand Oaks, CA: Sage.

Torbert, W. R. Associates. (2004). *Action inquiry*. San Francisco: Berrett-Koehler.

Torbert, W. R., & Taylor, S. S. (2008). Action inquiry: Interviewing multiple qualities in attention for timely inquiry. In: P. Reason & H. Bradbury (Eds), *Handbook of action research* (2nd ed., pp. 239–251). London: Sage.

ART OR ARTIST? AN ANALYSIS OF EIGHT LARGE-GROUP METHODS FOR DRIVING LARGE-SCALE CHANGE

Svetlana Shmulyian, Barry Bateman, Ruth G. Philpott and Neelu K. Gulri

ABSTRACT

*This chapter analyzes the success factors, outcomes, and future viability of large-group methods. We have used an exploratory action research approach focusing on eight variously purposed large-group methods (America*Speaks*, Appreciative Inquiry, Conference Model®, Decision Accelerator, Future Search, Participative Design, Strategic Change Accelerator/ACT (IBM), and Whole-Scale™ Change). We interviewed nine leading practitioners and creators for each method, as well as six clients who had played key roles in most of these methods' execution at their organizations, asking them to reflect on the current practices and outcomes and the future of each respective large-group method, as well as the methods as a group of interventions. Based on our findings derived through theme and content analysis of interviews, we purport that both the Art (excellence in method execution) and the Artist (the right facilitator) are necessary for achieving desired outcomes of the large-group methods. We stipulate that critical elements of the Art include these*

Research in Organizational Change and Development, Volume 18, 183–231

ISSN: 0897-3016/doi:10.1108/S0897-3016(2010)0000018010

five common elements (or five "I"s): having the right Individuals *in the room; aiming the method at resolving the right* Issue*; having* Intentional *process (including pre-work, intra-method process, and follow-up); having the right* Information *in the meeting; and using the right* Infrastructure *(such as appropriate physical space, technology, etc.). We suggest that while these elements of Art are important, the simultaneous requisite role of the Artist is to manage the tension between the rigidity of the Art (the 5 "I"s) and the emerging human dynamics occurring between the large-group method process and the associated evolving client objectives. That is, to achieve desired outcomes, the execution of large-group method needs to be both highly premeditated and ingenious. We supplement our findings with client case descriptions and quotes from the practitioners and conclude that these large-group methods are particularly appropriate for resolving a variety of issues facing today's organizations operating under the conditions of high technology saturation, interdependence, globalization, economic downturn, and others – and that this, with some exceptions, will likely remain the case in the future. However, the future use of these methods will be challenged by the availability of Artists who can execute the methods so they lead to desired outcomes. We close with discussion of open questions and directions for future research.*

INTRODUCTION

Is it the Art or the Artist? The Metaphor

Listening to a good symphony performance can be an incredibly exciting experience. So what brings about an unforgettable orchestral performance? Jennifer Hambrick, a WOSU Classical Music radio station host, provides one answer in her blog, stipulating that great music is born out of "arriving at the essence of the human experience that gave birth to the music." This beautiful quote is both the embodiment of and a disguise for many elements that go into making a great musical performance. In Jennifer's (and our) view, both the *Art* of making music (the musicians' skills, the concert hall, the score itself, etc.) and the *Artist* (the conductor and his interpretation of the piece) are essential in producing the magical effect. With regard to what we call *Art*, Hambrick continues, "I can attest to the many aspects of orchestral musicians' work that directly affect the overall sound of a performance … Every orchestra does have its own *sound*." This *sound* is indeed influenced by various components. The *sound* begins with picking the right *piece* that works for the type, size, and proficiency level of the orchestra. An orchestra itself must include properly trained and assembled group of *musicians* able to work together. The intentional and intense *process* of individual pre-work and group rehearsals would lead up to the performance. The right *information* must be provided to each musician in the form of musical scores, the description of the piece intention, and the conductor's interpretation. The *physical* components of performance need to be in place – an orchestra pit must be acoustically tested, the instruments used must be free of broken parts, and the orchestra hall should meet the standards of the audience and performers.

Regarding the *Artist*, Hambrick continues: "With most recordings, the difference between good and great lies not entirely in what the players in the compared orchestras are doing differently from each other, but first and foremost in the various conductors' interpretations of the music and how the conductors lead the orchestras to play out (literally) those interpretations ... Whatever the conductor does on the podium will directly affect how the musicians in the orchestra play and how the orchestra sounds." It is indeed the *Artist* who brings together all these potentially disparate elements that collectively amount to a unified artistry and harmony. He is able to flexibly manage the tension between the intended rigidity of the art and the emerging dynamics and the mood of the audience and the orchestra.

It is then both the *Artist* and the *Art* that come together to create a magical musical experience. Atik, who spent time studying the dynamics of orchestras, noted, "You have sometimes a hundred people, sometimes more, on the stage who develop ... I would say an energetic field, a psychological energy field which is very strong and has an existence of its own. And the conductor has to be forming that field and be part of it" (Atik, 1994).

Large organizational systems undergoing substantial change are at least as complex as orchestras creating musical performances; they represent some the same dynamics that occurs in large orchestras. In this chapter, we consider elements of *Art* in executing large-group methods for organizational change (such as using the method to address the right issue, including the right individuals, following the intentional process, having access to the right information and proper physical infrastructure) and stipulate that it is only in combination with the great *Artist* (the method facilitator) that these elements can amount to their desired outcomes (including people and organizational changes as well as long-term benefits) – just like these same aspects come together in creating a beautiful symphony.

The chapter begins with the background and context for this research and the questions we were pursuing in this chapter. It continues with a brief overview of the large-group methods, and proceeds with the findings from the research questions. We conclude with the conceptual model for large-group method effectiveness (which includes the key success factors and the outcomes of these methods), and insights regarding the projected future relevance for use of the large-group methods and implications for managers and practitioners. Future research directions are also discussed.

Research Context: Contributions and Limitations

Before summarizing the findings and conclusions of our research we would like to briefly discuss the context of this research, which both enhances the contribution that this inquiry makes to the field of organizational change – and limits our findings. This chapter, as do all such papers, articles, and books, has a history of its own and owes its existence to many players. It also occurred at a point in time that may have influenced our findings.

First, in early 2009 William Pasmore approached this research team with the idea that while there had been a lot of activity, publications, and stories about the use of large-group methods for enacting large-scale change in the late 1990s and early 2000s (including the most recent volumes by Bunker & Alban, 2006; Holman, Devane, & Cady, 2007), little summative analysis has been written that would inform practitioners, academics, and researchers on the primary questions that have formed the basis of this chapter: *What is the current state of large-group methods? Do they work? Is the use of these methods growing or declining?* And finally and probably most importantly, *is there a future for these methods or are they simply a fad that will disappear as all fads eventually do?* William's questions are intriguing and to the point. As practitioners we have all seen fads come and go, usually doing more damage than good, hurting rather than helping the credibility of our profession and, of course, our clients. On the other hand, if large-group methods for approaching organizational change lead to powerful and lasting effect, it is important to track the evolution of the method (as a group). It is also important to identify factors that lead to success as well as challenges that, unaddressed, could consign these methods that would potentially create sustainable change to our profession's historical landfill. These are, of course, ambitious questions, and we do not propose that we have answered them perfectly or completely. Rather, this chapter serves as another data point, a snapshot in time intended to provide a "current-state point of view," with no pretense of providing the final word. However, we are much encouraged to be a witness of the *2010 version* of the large-group methods (in which many methods we have reviewed seemed to have gained characteristics already different from those described even in the most recent literature, such as Holman et al., 2007). However, we also realize that these questions will remain, despite our efforts, central questions for future research.

Second, the members of our research team came to this task with our own histories, our own experiences, and our own biases. We are an "inter-generational," diverse group with different levels of experience in the field of organizational change, different ages, different countries of origin, and different cultural and religious backgrounds. Our experience with large-group methods runs the gamut of "considerably experienced" to "no experience" (including one member of the team who had a personal and professional relationship spanning decades with several of the practitioners interviewed and is a past and present partner with three of them – most of our team, however, had never met the interviewees). As to our biases, which we fully acknowledge, we made every attempt to hedge them with whatever intellectual integrity we possess, basing our dialogue and conclusions on the data itself – while grounding it with our passion for understanding of what works in our field. To the extent that we have misinterpreted or misrepresented data, or misunderstood interviewees, we will make an advance apology – the errors are solely the authors'.

Third, the group of practitioners and clients we interviewed has certainly influenced our findings. While we attempted to choose methods representing various types of interventions, our decisions about which methods to include were also limited by our knowledge of these methods and access to the practitioners who use them. Our practitioners are, without doubt, a stellar group – all are masters of change in their own right and have experimented with, adopted, and adapted these methods over long careers. As a group they have seen what works and what doesn't; all are also master consultants. We are deeply indebted to them for making themselves available for these interviews, revealing the "secrets" of their trade, and reviewing the drafts of our analysis making sure that we have correctly interpreted their inputs – ultimately providing an invaluable contribution to this chapter. All are both enthusiastic about participating and passionate about what they do. All have helped their client organizations achieve outstanding, lasting results using not just the methods attributed to them here, but many other change techniques and methodologies. We also owe them a debt of gratitude for reaching out to their clients and enabling interviews with the ultimate "users" who we would otherwise not have had access to (all of whom we found to be equally enthusiastic and passionate about the projects we focused on, as well as frank in discussing these projects' successes and limitations). The clients have had not only the passion but also the courage to try innovative approaches to enacting lasting change in their organizations. These *pragmatic risk-takers* were totally honest with us about their experiences – ultimately confirming one of our long-held beliefs that at the end of the day, all else being equal, it is great clients that make great projects. It is important to note that while we have been given examples of applications of large-group methods around the world, in the end, given the scope of this chapter, we have decided to focus our findings on North American practice of large-group methods.

Last, it should be mentioned, as it may have influenced perceptions of the current and future state of the use of these methods, that the period in which this research occurred is perhaps the most challenging for all types of organizations in the past 50 years. We conducted these interviews while deep in the throes of the "Great Recession." Businesses and other organizations have been, at least while this research has been taking place, retrenching and cost-cutting, and very few are taking any risks. At the same time, the dominance of technology and the internet as a defining force, which Marvin Weisbord noted in our interview with him and Sandra Janoff as probably "the wildcard" when it comes to the future form these methods take, is advancing at an ever-increasing pace.[1] Technology that was not available in the late 1990s and early in this century is creating questions future research will have to answer. While many of the large-group methods we studied are technology enabled, and America*Speaks* has effectively conducted meetings of 10,000 on three different continents using internet-based audio and video, the rest are basically "face to face," based on the principle of getting the "whole system in the room," or at least as much representation of the whole as possible. When the room is the internet, things may well change and new forms of large-scale methods may well take the place of those we studied.

In summary, while our research was truly exploratory, our backgrounds and initial ideas landed us to starting research with some initial hypotheses and hunches – but, as it often happens in organizational change projects themselves, we ended up in an entirely different place than we started. Initially, we were focused on the group of methods themselves, but through the interview process we began to understand that the methods were really only tools in the hands of what we began to understand as the other two critical components, the *Artists*, and of course, the *Clients.* While they are all innovative, powerful tools based on solid principles, summarized in our *Five I's* conceptual model (presented in this chapter's Conclusions), they remain tools that, as our music metaphor indicates, are only techniques without which the master musicians cannot produce a symphony. Thus, as biased as our views are, through our literature research, interviews, and internal dialogue we began to understand that the answers to the basic questions William Pasmore proposed were far more complex than a simple yes, no, or maybe.

Research Questions

What are Large-Group Methods?

Bunker & Alban maintain that "large group interventions for organizational and community change are methods for involving the whole system, internal and external, in the change process" (Bunker & Alban, 1997, p. xv). They suggest that common elements of such large-group methods include (a) understanding the need for change, (b) analyzing current reality and deciding what needs to change, (c) generating ideas about how to change existing processes, and (d) implementing and supporting change to make it work (Bunker & Alban, 1997). Over time, many methods for generating large-scale change have emerged (Holman et al., 2007). The range of known large-scale change methods, and their usage, over the course of 50 years serves as testimony to the fact that leading change is an ever-present need in organizations. "These large group methods have been used in change efforts concerning (1) changes in strategic direction, (2) acceptance and implementation of quality programs or redesign projects, (3) changes in relationships with customers and suppliers, and (4) changes in structures, policies or procedures" (Bunker & Alban, 1997, p. xvi).

Much has been written about these methods to describe the key processes and methodology (Bunker & Alban, 1997; Bunker & Alban, 2006; Holman et al., 2007, and many others). Large-group methods are seen as a means for engaging participation among large numbers of stakeholders. By facilitating dialogue and discourse among key constituents, large-scale change methods seek to deliver better decisions and plans for change that all parties can support. Theoretical underpinnings for large-scale change methods range from Lewin's (1947) representation of change and Schein's (1987, 1988) thinking about change as cognitive restructuring to Revans' (1978) conceptualization about action learning and many others.

The Research Questions
In light of the context described in the previous section, the purpose of this research was twofold: (1) to understand *how* large-group methods deliver results they promise, and (2) to understand *whether* the large-group methods would work as intended *today* and, if so, whether they would remain effective in the *future*. To understand the answer to these two broad exploratory questions (the *how* and the *whether*), our goal was not to resolve these questions for *each* of the large-group methods, but rather, use each specific method we studied as the unit of analysis in order to draw conclusions about these methods and their inherent particulars and ultimate effectiveness as a class of methods for driving large-scale change in organizations.

METHOD

Selecting Large-Group Methods

Eight large-group methods were chosen from more than 60 methods in use today (Holman et al., 2007). Specifically, we have considered eight large-scale change methods to represent various types of change methods engaging whole systems (Holman et al., 2007). The change methods include *Adaptable methods* (methods "used for a variety of purposes, including planning, structuring and improving" (Holman et al., 2007, p. 22) – for example, Appreciative Inquiry, Whole-Scale™ Change, Conference Model®, Future Search, and Decision Accelerator); *Planning methods* (methods used "to help people shape their future together" (Holman et al., 2007, p. 24) – for example, America*Speaks*); *Structuring methods* (methods used to "redefine relationships and/or redesign work practices" (Holman et al., 2007, p. 25) – for example, Participative Design); and *Improving Methods* (methods used to "increase effectiveness in processes, relationships, individual behaviors, knowledge and/or distributive leadership" (Holman et al., 2007, p. 26) – for example, Strategic Change Accelerator (IBM's "ACT"). We purposely have not considered *Supportive Methods* ("practices that enhance the efficacy of other change methods" (Holman et al., 2007, p. 27) because we aimed to study the main methods of promoting organizational change. It is important to note that the classification above differs somewhat from the classification offered by Holman et al. (2007). This new classification has been vetted with leading practitioners of the above-mentioned interventions and reflects the most current understanding and application of large-group methods. This revised classification also underscores the previously referred to dynamic nature of large-group methods as these interventions continue to find new forms and applications demanded by modern organizations, ultimately turning nearly all (or maybe all) large-group methods into *Adaptable Methods* used to address a great range of issues and to solve a great variety of problems (even our *2010 version* has us classify majority of the methods we have considered as *Adaptable*). While we did not get a chance to consider interventions beyond the eight large-group methods listed below, we feel that our exploratory research uniquely unveils this evolving dynamics of the use of large-group methods. Below are brief descriptions of the eight large-group methods we have considered (Phillips, 1995) (Table 1).

Adaptable Methods
The Appreciative Inquiry Summit is defined by Ludema, Whitney, Mohr, and Griffin (2003) as "typically a single event or series of events that bring people together to: (1) discover the organization or community's core competencies and strengths, (2) envision opportunities for positive change, (3) design the desired changes into the organization or community's systems, structures, strategies, and culture, and (4) implement and sustain the change and make it work" (Ludema et al., 2003, pp. 12–13). The method is based on the premise that organizations grow in the direction of what they regularly and consistently focus their attention upon. To enable a strong organization, the topic of inquiry, according to Appreciative Inquiry principles, should be at the intersection of honest curiosity and the direction in which the organization wants to move – thereby generating the "information" and energy needed to create higher levels of performance beyond that which could be obtained by stopping with fixing a past problem or weakness. The goal of Appreciative Inquiry is to not only identify the positive core of the organization (i.e., its many assets, resources, strengths, and opportunities) but to leverage that positive core in creating the most desired future. This approach enables a form of "grounded visioning" – imagining a desired future which is based on the best of what already exists today, and stimulates participants into designing innovations in strategy, structure, processes, services, or relationships which ultimately turn the visions into new results. The Appreciative Inquiry Summit method includes a 5D model known as Define (identifying the strategic topic(s) to inquire into), Discover (exploring success story highlights), Dream (envisioning what might be, the results, and the impact), Design (of new strategies, structures, processes, services, or relationships), and Destiny (collaborating in implementation to develop and continually evolve the organization). The Appreciative Inquiry Summit is

Table 1. Summary of Eight Large-Group Methods for Large-Scale Change.

Name	Type	Size	Preparation	Events	Follow-up	Cycle	Practitioner Training	Special Resources
Appreciative Inquiry	Adaptable	20–2,000	1 day–many months	1 day–many months	3 months–1 year	As needed, continuous	Self-study	None
Whole-Scale™ Change	Adaptable	10–10,000	2–4 days per event	Several 2–3 day events	1 month–1 year	As needed	General	One logistics assistant per five tables
Conference Model®	Adaptable	40–7,000	1–3 months	Three 2 day events	6–12 months	As needed	General	None
Future Search	Adaptable	40–100+	3–6 months	2.5 days	As needed to purpose	Periodic	General	None
Decision Accelerator	Adaptable	15–100+	2 weeks–2 months	0.5–3 days	30–90 days	As needed	In-depth	Rolling white boards, sound systems, IT support, "crew" space
America*Speaks*	Planning	100–10,000	6–12 months	1 day	3–12 months	As needed	In-depth	Polling system, wireless groupware, one networked laptop, one facilitator table
Participative Design	Structuring	15–200	2 weeks–many months	1–3 days	Active adaptation via redesign	As needed	In-depth	None
Strategic Change Accelerator/IBM ACT	Improving	15–100+	2–4 weeks	2–5 days	30–90 days	As needed	In-depth	None

Note: This table has been adapted from the excerpt from the table presented in *The Change Handbook* (Holman et al., 2007). Changed and additions have been made based on the interviews conducted for this research.

just one of eight methodologies ("forms of engagement") which fall under the larger umbrella of Appreciative Inquiry. Other Appreciative Inquiry methods ("forms of engagement" – Ludema et al., 2003) include, whole-system inquiry projects over a period of time, and small-group activities that stand alone or support larger initiatives (Cooperrider & Whitney, 2007).

The Whole-Scale method was developed in the 1980s at Ford Motor Company when leaders were seeking to move its management culture from hierarchical to more participative. The method, which consists of a series of small- and/or large-group interactions, enables an organization to undergo a paradigm shift. It has been used successfully in designing organizational structures and changing organizational processes (James & Tolchinsky, 2007). The method is based on the principle that once the organization members experience a paradigm shift, they see the world differently and are ready to act to transform the organization toward the new and shared vision (Dannemiller & Jacobs, 1992). Whole-Scale™ Change applies a combination of action learning and accelerators to drive the change (James & Tolchinsky, 2007). Using participants that represent all organization levels, functions, or geographies, Whole-Scale™ Change creates a microcosm of the organization in order to discuss and deliver change. The method then supports participants in developing structures and relationships that enable that vision, and in aligning leaders and employees so that change can be implemented in a collaborative manner.

The Conference Model® engages people in system-wide change through a series of integrated conferences and walkthroughs (Axelrod & Axelrod, 1998). The Conference Model® is an elegant application of Axelrod's four engagement principles: Widen the Circle of Involvement, Connect People to Each Other, Create Communities for Action, and Promote Fairness which lend its uses to such diverse applications as redesigning organizations and processes, developing new organizational cultures, creating team-based organizations, and creating organizational futures (Axelrod & Axelrod, 2007). The Conference Model® includes up to three conferences (ranging from 30 to hundreds of participants at all organizational levels): Vision Conference (where vision themes are developed by participants), Technical Conference (where current organizational barriers are identified), and Design Conference (where vision themes, disconnects, beliefs, and behaviors are combined to design criteria for the new process or organization). Walkthroughs are mini-conferences that are used to connect people who were unable to attend a conference to the change process and solicit their feedback. Walkthroughs are critical to success because they provide a mechanism for involving the whole system (Axelrod & Axelrod, 1998; Axelrod, 1992).

The Decision Accelerator is generally used as "organic work system for sustained innovation and change work within a single organization".[2] As the title would suggest, this method accelerates decision-making and operational effectiveness by engaging critical stakeholders in a highly focused way, and is a tool to help organizations solve critical business issues faster, while at the same time building commitment through a high-involvement/high-commitment process (The Sapience Decision Accelerator (n.d.)). It brings participants together to examine problems and create solutions in a "purpose built-environment".[2] Decision Accelerator has its origins in the work of Trist and Emery (1965), with adaptations by organizations as diverse as the US Army in the 1980s, companies like Hewlett Packard in the 1990s and early 2000s and consulting firms like E&Y/Cap Gemini.[3] The method has been used successfully in strategic planning, merger strategy and implementation, innovation management (from conception to rapid prototyping and final design) and many others.[2] What seems to separate the Decision Accelerator from other methods we examined is the importance placed on the "intentionally designed laboratory environment"[4] and the attention paid to the infrastructure and design of the meeting room itself. The infrastructure typically includes the use of mobile white boards, music, graphic artists, video, a dedicated "real-time knowledge capture" support team (within the room) and other elements that seem to create high degrees of information flow, which in turn creates high degrees of adaptation, innovation, focus, and action. The unique physical environment created for a Decision Accelerator has been described to the authors as "somewhere between a meeting and a rock concert" in terms of the planning required, its use of music, the "crew" support team, and the energy generated.[2,4] Finally, it is important to note that Decision Accelerator is only considered a large-group method when the Decision Accelerator implemented as a one-time event. However, more often Decision Accelerator is seen as an organizational model and work system which mobilizes the network and serves as an open systems planning process in preparation for further work systems network nodes executing to plan. In that, Decision Accelerator has evolved in some cases into a full strategic change process and "high-speed information processing environment" that in at least one case seems to have taken the leap of creating a whole new way of working – a new work system based on collaboration, innovation, and speed.[4]

Future Search was developed by Weisbord and Janoff (2005) as a means to help a system transform its capability for action and has been used for a wide variety of applications. According to Weisbord and Janoff (2010), such applications include developing strategic plans, redesigning product supply chain, developing environmental sustainability plans, creating collaborations among former antagonists to commit to the organizational renewal during an economic recession, creating and implementing plans for improvements, and many others. The intention of the Future Search method is to enable consensus, build commitment, and enable planning. The approach posits that by supporting mutual learning, multiple stakeholders can co-create future-oriented solutions to difficult issues they face today. The Future Search is suited to complex systems and issues such as communities, institutions, schools, and other entities to make and implement plans, restructure organizations, and solve social, economic, and technological problems (Weisbord & Janoff, 2007). The process allows participants to explore the current state of the larger environment, understand the driving need for change, and collaborate to create a future through action planning together. As such, the Future Search conference requires a high level of engagement by participants, and is based on the belief that people support what they help create. There are seven underlying principles that must be adhered to in order for the event to be successful (Bunker & Alban, 1997). These principles include working with the "whole system in the room"[5]; the need for participants to think globally and act locally; recognizing common ground; self-managing nature of the group; expertise resides within the total group; focus on developing an ideal future scenario (rather than problem-solving); and the belief that change involves the whole person: mind, body, and spirit. These principles are now also grouped into four ideas – having the whole system in the room; experiencing the whole system before focusing on any part; focusing on the future and seeking common ground; and enabling people to take responsibility for their own learning and action (Holman et al., 2007).

Planning Method

The America*Speaks* method aims to create a forum for citizens to provide input toward decisions that affect their community (Lukensmeyer & Brigham, 2002). The method's premise is based on the underlying concern that, for a variety of reasons, citizens are increasingly excluded from public decision-making processes. The America*Speaks* method seeks to address this concern and simultaneously influence public officials to make informed decisions. Large-scale forums, such as the 21st Century Town Hall Meeting, provide a means to engage hundreds or even thousands of participants. The method focuses on discussion and deliberation among participants, rather than presentations or speeches. Prior to the event, each participant receives a discussion guide with information about the issues under consideration. On arrival, participants are grouped at tables of 10 or 12 and instructed to begin. As they address the issues, they are supported by a trained facilitator who provides process support and keeps participants focused on the task. Through the use of wireless technology and groupware computers, America*Speaks* collects input and polling data from each discussion group in real time. Within minutes, the organizers can provide reporting in real time to participants in service of further discussion or decision-making (Lukensmeyer & Brigham, 2002). Ultimately, voting results are compiled into a set of collective recommendations that are provided to participants, decision-makers, and the news media.

Structuring Method

Participative Design is example of a Structuring Method where work groups redesign their own work. The method begins at the bottom of the organization and works its way up. Participative Design was developed in response to difficulties encountered in implementing traditional Socio-Technical Systems design process (Emery & Devane, 2007). This alternative approach asks employees to design, control, and coordinate their own work. The underlying assumption is the idea that participants are most familiar with their work and tasks, and best able to develop and implement efficiencies in performing that work. The method has been used successfully to design organization structure, improve operational processes, and increase quality and customer satisfaction levels (Emery & Devane, 2007). The Participative Design process includes the following phases: (1) Education (educational workshops which include employees at all levels, at which senior management comes up with minimum critical specifications against which all designs that are developed must be measured); (2) Analysis (redesign workshops where senior management briefly shares the minimum critical specifications and the work-unit participants analyze how the job is currently done and assess how much this falls short of meeting the specific critical human requirements); (3) Redesign (drawing the existing work flow and organizational structure and then the redesigned organizational elements for better ways of accomplishing the work); and (4) Implementation (interim meetings between work groups to get feedback and learn from their efforts, to develop measurable goals and targets and other impacts of redesigned work) (Emery, 1995).

Improving Method

The Strategic Change Accelerator/IBM's ACT (Accelerate Change Together), is a large-scale change process for addressing issues that impact organizations across geographic and functional boundaries (Phillips, 1995). The method specifically seeks to move participants and issues rapidly from problem identification to solution to execution. The method was originally developed for IBM as an adaptation of GE's highly successful WorkOut initiative. The premise for the approach was to minimize "silo mentality barriers" and simultaneously address critical business issues and needs. IBM's CEO, Lou Gerstner, wanted to move quickly to a fully integrated, rapid-acting, truly global IBM. ACT was created to drive critical strategic solutions across geographic, functional, business, and traditional "organizational silos" (Phillips, 1995). ACT can be customized to meet the situation and needs of any organization seeking to reposition itself. The method begins with a strategy and planning component, where executive sponsors and key stakeholders define the scope for the session, and the issues to be addressed. Following the planning phase, a business meeting is organized where participants are grouped into teams and develop potential solutions. The participant teams present their recommendations for solutions to a leadership cadre of sponsors and decision-makers. Each recommendation is accompanied with a detailed set of action steps and a "champion" that represent the framework for implementation. The leadership team makes immediate decisions to accept, reject, or gather more data for each recommendation (about 90% of solutions are accepted at that point of the meeting).[6] The remainder of the session is devoted to mapping out implementation plans and strategies for the chosen solution(s). The ACT method seeks (a) to develop creative solutions to critical strategic issues, (b) enable rapid decisions that might not otherwise be possible due to silo-bound chains-of-command, (c) assure full commitment to decisions stemming from the input of all participants, and (d) position the organization to quickly execute recommendations (Phillips, 1995).

Participants

To better understand the current use, antecedents of success, and outcomes of each large-scale method, an interview was conducted with the leading practitioner (and sometimes inventor) of the method, as well as the clients holding high-level positions in their respective organizations that have experienced a particular method (clients were interviewed for six out of the eight methods described in this chapter). The practitioners were selected by the research team through professional networks, based on availability. The clients were then introduced to the research team by the practitioners and were sought to represent prominent successful implementations of a particular large-group method and have been interviewed based on their availability.

Procedure

The researchers conducted an hour-long interview with each practitioner and 30- to 45-minute interviews with clients of the large-scale methods, using a standard interview guide that covered the history of the method, the antecedents of method success, and common method outcomes (please see appendix for interview guides). Each interview has been transcribed and also recorded in order to ensure that practitioner and client comments are represented accurately. The recorded interviews were sent to those interview participants who requested the audio file.

Analysis

After all practitioner and client interviews were completed, the research team compiled all transcribed notes and documents provided by the interviewees (such as web site links, publications, white papers, etc.). The qualitative data was analyzed to determine themes describing success factors and outcomes of the eight large-group methods. Both exploratory theme analysis and content analysis have been used to develop the findings. First, the researchers have looked at all qualitative data we collected and developed a list of emerging themes. The themes were then grouped in categories corresponding our research questions (such as evidence of large-group methods success or failure, success factors and inhibiting forces for large-group methods, future of large-group methods, etc.). Upon conducting this exploratory analysis, the team has gathered for a group analytical session and, informed by background readings, our original research questions, and the emerging themes have developed a Conceptual Model for Successful Large-Group Method (presented later in this chapter). After completion of the session, three team members were tasked with content analysis of interviews. These team members worked systematically through each interview transcript grouping comments into their assigned framework elements (so each model element has only been worked on by one researcher), synthesizing comments into findings, and picking representative quotes from both practitioners and the clients to exemplify the findings. In conducting this analysis, the researchers have moved between interview transcripts and the background literature to ensure that the categories presented mutually exclusive and complete framework of factors relevant to large-group methods (adhering to single-factor categorization of comments). The analysis was then consolidated and reviewed by the senior members of the research team to ensure that the comments were classified appropriately (and singly) into the model element, that coding was consistent between the researchers, and that the categories were interpreted correctly. The senior team members made revisions to this analysis and finalized the category titles and assignment of comments. We have also kept track of comments that did not fit into any category of the developed framework and included these thoughts in the reflections on the future of the large-group methods and future research directions.

Finally, in our exploratory analysis, we have tried to control various biases common for qualitative research. First, we believe that the diversity of our team (in terms of ages, experiences, countries of origin, etc.) has, to a degree, helped us to control for uniform individual biases in findings. Second, we have asked the practitioners both about success factors and limitations of large-group methods – and have also interviewed both practitioners and the clients. This approach also helped us gather varying perspectives on the questions we pose this avoiding uniformity of respondents' biases. Third, we have also encouraged the interviewees, many of whom are themselves renowned theoreticians and researchers, to genuinely share their insights in the interest of furthering the field of organizational development. Because we found that many of the interviewees have readily shared both advantages and limitations of the large-group methods, we believe that we have been able to diminish positive bias in results sufficiently for this exploratory research.[7]

FINDINGS

Do They Work: The Outcomes of Large-Group Methods

Based on the interviews we conducted, both of practitioners and of clients, we conclude that without a doubt these methods work as advertised. Across the board we were given examples of how these methods delivered on client expectations, both in terms of "hard results" (such as cost savings, process efficiencies, customer satisfaction ratings increase, cycle time improvements, etc.) as well as creation of organizational "social capital."[4] As a whole, this group of methods, with all of their iterations and future combinations, may be the most powerful way to enact sustainable change – because "with all of the complexities and need for stakeholder buy-in to make anything happen, they may be the only way."[2] Let us now review some examples of large-group method outcomes.

Holman et al. (2007) and the contributors to their *Change Handbook* discuss a wide variety of outcomes dealing with *People*, *Organizational systems*, and *Long-term sustainable change* that are driven by the use of large-group methods. These themes are uniformly confirmed by the practitioners and clients interviewed for this chapter. For example, one practitioner cites "three kinds of outcomes that we track on every project: (1) individual; (2) policy change, planning process, and budget changes; and (3) evidence of cultural change, which is our language of large scale sustainable change."[8] Clients seem to support the notion that these methods "fare extremely well against all three of those, if done correctly."[9] Let's consider these three types of outcomes in more detail.

People

Individual Motivations. In discussing the outcomes of large-group methods, the outcomes related to individuals' motivations resulting from directly influencing change building blocks are the first ones that many practitioners and clients address because "once [employees] begin to understand the system in which [they] work and [they] have a voice in changing that system, [this] directly impacts motivation."[10] These findings are consistent with much literature purporting that large-group methods achieve the desired outcomes mainly through affecting people – and do so by impacting group energy, intrinsic motivation, and high emotional engagement (e.g., Bunker & Alban, 1997; Bunker & Alban, 2006; Holman et al., 2007, and many others). More specifically, the people-related outcomes of large-group methods, it seems, have to do with high participation of stakeholders – which leads to high levels of information internalization, high motivation to act upon developed plans, and high commitment to decisions. "People feel more empowered at the end of these sessions ... Six months later they could still quote facts about social security … People will say *this is democracy in action*."[8] Large-group methods view people as "*social capital*" (initially a Decision Accelerator term) and an asset to be managed through trust. Clients of large-group methods in particular seem to support the notion that large-group methods have a commitment level built into them, whereby employees "are doing change instead of having change done to them … this is powerful because you have stakeholders co-authoring change."[9] Thus this "co-authored" impending change is not simply followed – it is embraced. Many large-group method clients and practitioners agree that resistance to change often happens when employees feel that the impending change does not embrace old practices and customs that made these employees successful in the past. In contrast to this dynamic, large-group methods "invite people to identify exactly what has made them successful in the past, and it asks them to build on that, and to carry the best of the past forward. So it gives [employees] confidence, that even though the future is going to be somewhat different than in the past, they are still going to use those things that matter most deeply to them."[11] In sum, the concept of social capital – its creation, relevance, and use – is probably a research topic of its own. Suffice it to say that the power of getting most or all key stakeholders in the same room at the same time and dealing with issues they care about, with the information and authority necessary to act, is without doubt an effective way to create lasting, meaningful change.

Relationships. Many clients and practitioners noted that having people work with each other so closely and intensely for several hours or days creates special bonds and relationships that employees take back to their day-to-day work – which ultimately results in people working better together (making large-group methods into "*mega-teambuilding*" activities of sorts). These methods "build bridges within the organization that are essential for the ongoing implementation of change and new ideas."[11] The trust and relationships that result from the large-group methods are some of the essential outcomes produced as a result: "You stop being that hated other department. It is the building trust and connections with people that help work get done."[10] The client interviews seem to support the exact notion that practitioners put forward and agree that the large-group methods impact individuals "because you have the whole system in the room; it forces the dialogue to get outside the whole silo of conversation"[12] and because "the supporting dynamic is built in … [so participants] don't feel as alone and as disconnected as with other methodologies."[13]

Utilizing the "Whole Person". Most importantly, large-group methods do not appear to compartmentalize individuals into the tasks they are working on directly as part of their daily routines. Instead, they utilize the whole experience of individuals to produce higher level outcomes. Additionally, they lead individuals through a process of personal self-discovery and appeal to the "self-actualization" level of individuals' motivation (the top level of Maslow's hierarchy of needs, Maslow, 1943). Participants leave the experience "feeling valued for what they have created in their life"[14] and "bringing about individual change."[13] Maslow's self-actualization level includes morality, creativity, spontaneity, problem-solving, lack of prejudice, and acceptance of facts – all of the factors called upon by large-group methods from their participants – which enable discovery of "new information … new ways of relating to one another … learning and action at a new level."[15]

Limitations of Large-Group Methods. While large-group methods produce potent people-related outcomes, they are not without limitations. It is important to note that large-group methods are essentially systemic and structural interventions and therefore do not address individuals' personality constraints with the change directly – but nonetheless provide unique and often never before experienced opportunities for growth to employees. "We don't work on behavioral characteristics, but offer [people] opportunities to do things that they have never done before when the task and goal is so important to them."[8]

Further, some practitioners and clients warn that continuous use of usually effective large-group methods within the same organization may lead to over-sensitization of individuals to the process of these interventions – ultimately decreasing the usefulness of the methods, especially at the individual level. The practitioner states: "Given the topic, sometimes the same people show up to many different sessions, generating a risk for individual burn out … participants may become desensitized/over-exposed to methodology."[16] The client confirms, "The other problem is … burnout. People think they can anticipate what's coming next … so you have to continually challenge the facilitator team to keep it fresh for the stakeholders and keep them engaged."[9]

Finally, practitioners note the importance of following up on commitments made in the meetings associated with large-group interventions because "lack of follow-through is like breaking a psychological contract" and results in potential negative outcomes of the process.[17]

Organizational Systems

"Hard" Results. *The Change Handbook* lists a multitude of outcomes that individual large-group method result in, such as process and structural improvements, cost savings, product innovations, and many others (Holman et al., 2007). Our interviewees confirm that when large-group methods are well executed, "they are immensely powerful when changing business structures … whether or not they are mapped cleanly or thoroughly – but this is powerful because you have stakeholders co-authoring change."[13] One group of outcomes that is influenced through the use of large-group methods deals with specific "hard" measurable results (such as cost reduction, revenue generation, etc.). Below are just a few examples of "hard" results obtained through the use of the various large-group methods.

Dick Axelrod describes effects of the Conference Model®: In the Calgary Health System, the wait time has been reduced by between 10 and 40 percent, depending on the sub-specialty. For example, in the diabetes, hypertension, and cholesterol center, the wait time was reduced from 96 days to 4 days (Bichel, Erfle, Wiebe, Axelrod, & Conly, 2009). The client of Conference Model® confirms, "By the end of the process, about 2–2.5 years, we saw very early returns and the employee satisfaction returns went up early. Even though we weren't tracking performance improvement we knew we would see significant increases in productivity. We had reduced our cost by $700 million. Morale had gone up. It was way above what it was before the strike. The change process … was an absolute essential ingredient."[18]

IBM has used the Strategic Change Accelerator method to literally transform the corporation. In a presentation that Lou Gerstner made to his worldwide management council in the fall of 1996, ACT was credited for "[general] cost savings of over $700 m, revenue increases of over $900 m; and inventory carrying cost reductions of over $1.2b" in the first year alone. Lou Gerstner was hold to say to his leaders that if they have not been using ACT, he would question their management skills.[6]

Joel Fadem and Stu Winby used the Decision Accelerator process in a project called Right Track at Alegent Health. As of October 2008 over 180 Decision Accelerators on a variety of issues and challenges, from strategic to operational, were conducted. The process was credited with producing strategies that essentially inverted Alegent's performance though reducing costs, increasing revenues and, notably, patient quality outcomes. At the same time Decision Accelerator has created what can fairly be described as a "collaborative culture," a new way of working within Alegent. Using the Decision Accelerator Alegent created projects that helped it achieve the health care industry's top "Combined HCAHPS and CMS Quality Ranking" during 2006–2007, unseating the Mayo Clinic, for the first time, as number one (HCAHPS Scores Innovation Design Lab Case Study, 2007).

America*Speaks*, which most clearly has the largest scope and scale of any of the methods we looked at, has achieved what can only be described as heretofore "unheard of" results in highly politically charged environments. In its work with the State of California, America*Speaks* was able to totally alter the state's budget priorities and helped to create policy changes that probably would never have occurred otherwise. And, of course, almost anyone who is in this field already knows about their work with the City of New York post-9/11, when they brought over 5,000 citizens together to talk about how the city should proceed in rebuilding the site where the Twin Towers once stood.[8]

Product and Process Innovations. Other types of organizational outcomes of large-group methods deal with process and organizational changes. For example, the Appreciative Inquiry Summit process "allows people to generate and rapidly prototype structure and process innovations."[19] Whole-Scale™ Change is used for process and structural redesign (and at times for both simultaneously while "keeping different pieces aligned and integrated").[20] And yet another possible "process" outcome has to do with building consensus required for moving long range plans forward where large-group methods "allow to build a sense of community."[15] The Future Search client echoes this sentiment: "The Future Search gave us a way to tear down the silos and begin to communicate more effectively and to a larger group of people because we could get them all to dialogue at one time."[12]

Process, structures, money aside – how about averting human disaster? A Future Search was credited by the *New York Times* in an article published in 2005, quoting a Federal Aviation Administration executive who participated in creating a "minor miracle" by helping the FAA avert what was otherwise believed to be an impending catastrophe in air traffic control during the summer of 2005, by bringing together representatives of the FAA, airlines, unions, major US airports, and other key stakeholders to examine and solve the problem (Bunker & Alban, 2006). As is the case with most large-group meetings we examined, this was the first time those who all shared a part of the problem and, consequently, part of the solution had ever been in the same room together at the same time.

Long-Term Sustainable Change

Benefits Realization. Long-term sustainability of large-group methods is on the forefront of the agenda of practitioners (and is certainly a leading concern of large-group methods clients). Based on the interviews conducted by the research team, we have seen strong evidence that the large-group methods have a great potential for producing a long-term sustainable change. "Having done all kinds of different things … I would give [this large group method] high marks to set up conditions for long-term change."[13] Practitioners also note large-group methods' long-term impacts: "The Process Outcomes seem to last."[21] "Cultural change happens …. Any citizen in any neighborhood in the city could see commitments made in the summit by dollars in program areas. The citizen could see the same data as the mayor – that is system change."[8]

Creating Adaptable Systems. One of the key elements of creating long-term sustainability appears to be a focus on creating adaptable systems rather than simple one-time problem solving. To that effect, many practitioners and clients point to a particular large-group method transition from a one-time event to a "way of getting the work done," in which large-group methods may become "a culture ... a way to mobilize and get a lot of work done."[22] The clients confirm that exact notion that "to become culturally embedded in how we get certain work done here"[23] creates sustainability: "We have implemented the design, but needed to make changes to it. You're constantly adapting your organization."[24] Dick Axelrod speaks about "widening the circle" of the Conference Model®, thereby intentionally creating larger groups of change which reach critical mass leading to sustainability.[10]

How do They Work? The Art of Large-Group Methods

Having considered the desired and probable outcomes of large-group methods, we would now discuss the necessary ingredients of success – or, as we would describe them later, the five "I"s that represent the *Art* of large-group method – and the characteristics of an Artist driving the method implementation.

The Right Issues

Client Situation. The city of Calgary in Canada used Dick Axelrod's Conference Model® to reduce the time between seeing a primary care physician and the referral to a specialist. The primary task was reducing the wait time, which is a very specific operational challenge. However, the task was linked to a higher strategic purpose: to improve the health care system in Calgary, making the Conference Model® large-group method a particularly appropriate way to address this challenge because it required involving a wide group of organizational stakeholders, developing connections between the various groups of stakeholders, creating networks of stakeholders aimed at specific actions linked to issues – and doing all of the above in a fair and equitable way (all characteristics of the Conference Model®).

Key Issues. What do we want to accomplish in this "meeting," "summit," or "event"? What is the purpose of all of us gathering in one room for hours or days Based on the theme analysis of clients' and practitioners' interviews, it appears that to be successful, the large-scale methods need to be aimed at the right issues. The right issues need to be clear, central to the organizational life, and linked to a greater organizational purpose – or, as Bunker and Alban also suggest, the issues addressed must be systemic and they must affect a large number of people across all layers of an organization (Bunker & Alban, 1997).

Issues as Key Imperatives. "It is necessary to create a connection between people and the purpose. The task itself must be clear; however the greater purpose should also be recognized. The issues that are tackled must be perceived as important, real and tangible in order to gain momentum."[10] While the task may be an important short-term consideration, the purpose of the large-scale method is to allow participants to think more systemically with a long-term approach in mind. For example, Ludema et al. (2003) maintain that the Appreciative Inquiry Summit task should be clear, simply articulated, and of strategic significance. Often, the central task is highlighted in the title of the "event" to ensure participants are aware of its purpose – for example "An Inquiry Into Optimal Margins for Our Company" or "An Inquiry Into a Care Delivery Model For Patients, Providers and Economic Sustainability."[11]

The task of the "meeting" should allow individuals to have knowledge of the whole product or service. At times, "workers only see a small part of the [organization's] final product and meaning is often denied to them"[21] Large-group methods close this gap and allow individuals to see how their contributions fit into the larger picture. For example, the key principle of Future Search is to focus the task on the future, rather than issues or problems of the past. In other words, the task should focus on creating common ground that allows the organization to move forward toward future aspirations. Additionally, aligning individual futures with organizational aspirations further supports the greater purpose of the entire system.

Issues and Sponsor Commitment. The common sentiment among practitioners and clients of large-group methods is that without proper follow-through with the key players, the "event" or method is simply a gathering of key stakeholders. "We don't do this work until it is legitimately linked to decision-making."[8] Practitioners of large-group methods tend to agree with Kotter's (1995) ideal for managing change in that sponsors of the large-scale methods (and large-scale change) in organizations must have the authority to provide resources toward tasks and action items that stem from the "event." For example, in the case of IBM's ACT, in addition to providing resources, sponsors, and decision-makers should be actively involved with the follow-through or implementation of action items that arise from the event – and without this level of commitment, no change will occur.[6] Similarly, for Future Search, resolved issues will not be incorporated into the organization's future unless sponsors and decision-makers fully endorse the change.[15] Other large-group methods have similar dynamics around stakeholder follow-through.

The Right Individuals

Client Situation. Future Search has been implemented at FAA and is widely believed to avert various issues in air traffic control during the summer of 2005, by bringing together representatives of the FAA, airlines, unions, major US airports, and other key stakeholders to examine and solve the problem. This convening of diverse stakeholders representing the "whole system" was critical in finding the solutions.

Key Issues. What kinds of individuals need to be engaged in the large-group method in order for it to reach the desired objectives? Based on the theme analysis of both client and practitioner interviews, it appears that, to be successful, large-scale methods need to engage the whole system (including a multitude of internal and external stakeholders), secure hands-on participation and sponsorship of the executive leaders, and juxtapose stakeholder groups and sub-groups so that interdependent parties have an opportunity for close interaction during the process.

Individuals as Members of a Whole System. Future Search pioneers Marvin Weisbord and Sandra Janoff suggest that one of the fundamental principles in large-scale change is to get all of the right people in the room.[15] Practitioners concur that event planning must include detailed evaluation of potential participants in the process. The right people include those who have the expertise to contribute to discussions, the authority to provide meaningful direction, and the resources to support decision outcomes. Once these individuals are together in one room, the "wholeness" of the system can be explored (Whitney & Cooperrider, 2000). A system's ability to experience its "wholeness" enables a feeling of togetherness and belonging among members and the opportunity for learning. "Multiple groups in the room have a much greater chance of identifying new possibilities, increasing efficiencies and identifying opportunities to work more effectively across teams or transfer process from one group to another."[21]

"If you're working changing a system and you only have half the stakeholders in the room, you're missing some very key voices, which detracts from the process."[11] When internal and external stakeholders are brought together, it allows for different voices, perspectives, and experiences to be shared across borders within an organization. When all layers are brought into one room, the silos are broken and one layer cannot point fingers at the other layer, making it less of an "us" vs. "them" and more of a "we or us" change initiative. "You get a sense that you are connected to a goodness that comes from the power of the whole. You realize you really need one another" (Whitney & Cooperrider, 2000, p. 15).

Alternatively, another potential failure of large-group methods occurs when autonomous or independent units with no related task sit in a room. Iterative knowledge sharing is more likely to occur with participants who view themselves as interdependent with other areas of the organization. Although there may be individuals who are not advocates of the upcoming change, it is important that all stakeholders, both internal and external, are involved in the cause or issue in some capacity.

Much of what practitioners describe experiencing is represented in Wells' (1990) discussion of the five levels of group process: intrapersonal, interpersonal, group-as-a-whole, intergroup, and interorganizational process. As such, the whole-system process is not without risks. "When you go large group, you go public in a very big way and that may scare people … There is certainly a higher risk when all stakeholders are in one room, however there is potential for great change, when *each* stakeholder takes responsibility for a portion of the change initiative."[10] When a public commitment is made, a certain level of accountability exists after the "event" is over and everyone returns to business as usual; public commitments engender responsibility (Whitney & Cooperrider, 2000). For example, a Future Search client, in speaking about participation of customers and suppliers in the process, stated that by including "suppliers and customers, [it] made the whole process much richer … and critical to the success … change was effected on their side as well … I think sometimes you don't want to expose your dirty side. The dangerous thing is that we only like to see ourselves as we like to see ourselves; [in this process], we get a complete view of who we are and what we are doing."[12]

Individuals as Leaders of Change. "Proper organizational sponsorship is a critical success factor for large-scale change … With a committed sponsorship leader or committee, the organization is likely to feel that the change effort is of the utmost importance."[12] Essentially, the "tone at the top" dictates how the change will be perceived throughout all layers of the organization. Burke (2002) describes change leaders as individuals with a high tolerance level for ambiguity, as well as the ability to delegate or take control as situations merit. High-level executives need to model the desired behavior, which impacts employees' perception of the change. For example, in IBM's ACT, high-level executives, titled "change masters," also identify other people who can potentially be change enablers throughout the organization.[6]

Many practitioners agree that a large-scale change effort will always be more successful if the sponsor can assist with the implementation of the change. This sponsor(s) has the resources (e.g., additional human capital or funding) for the follow-through and therefore can ensure that the change is sustainable. For example, for Decision Accelerator, the key to sustaining the change is to have sponsorship that is committed to implement the change because they have the authority to apply the methodology to appropriate issues.[4]

The Intentional Process

Client Situation. A government agency within the national security community utilized Paul Tolchinsky's Whole-Scale™ Change methodology to assist with redesigning the training and education initiatives in the organization. With the assistance of the Whole Scale methodology, the organization was able to move the organization from a bureaucratic structure to a training-centric system. Following the specific process prescribed by the Whole-Scale™ change methodology of small and large groups allowed for a structured process for key stakeholders to discuss the future state of the organization.

Key Issues. Porras and Robertson (1992) describe organization development as "planned, behavioral science-based interventions in work settings for the purpose of improving organizational functioning and individual development." Intentional process is essential in ensuring that all development objectives can be met. The elements of such an intentional process include the careful planning and pre-work, adherence to methodology and underlying principles during the event, and thorough post-event follow-through. An intentional process during the event, in particular, encourages participants to experience both subject immersion and intensity of engagement. Intentional process, in this sense, seeks to raise motivation levels and can lead to greater post-event outcomes.

Intentional Process in Pre-Work

Underlying Principles. While each large-group method has its own unique set of underlying principles, practitioners agree that following the "principles" of a large-scale method is critical in achieving success. For example, in the case of Future Search, "organizations that observe the principles, will have success."[25] For America*Speaks*, events will not be meaningful unless four guiding principles are closely followed: "The challenge in sustaining this work is great; however, the key is to embed this work into the system on an ongoing basis."[8] This shift to a new process in an organization can only begin with an event where the guiding principles are strictly observed.

Following the Prescribed Process. Creating an event plan, process, or agenda as prescribed by methodology is crucial. Schein (1987) discusses that determining settings, methods, time schedules, and goals are essential tasks. Each large-scale method has different components involved in the process agenda; however, the common collective theme is the need to have details discussed and documented prior to the event.

For example, Bernard Mohr, pioneer of Appreciative Inquiry, stresses the importance of having the summit planning group actually engage in Discovery, Dream and Design in their own planning work for the larger summit – thereby giving them an experiential preview of the summit itself. Mohr also suggests that the time to establish "boundaries or givens" is in the planning of the summit and not in the middle of it. "The outcomes of an Appreciative Inquiry Summit are never known in advance, just as the outcomes of any conversation are never known in advance. You can structure, frame and set some boundaries, but even within that structure and frame and boundaries, the Appreciative Inquiry Summit method is fundamentally a method of social innovation. By definition innovation is something we haven't had before and we can't predict it … and of course, the extent to which the people that have access to controlling the resources and influence and authority within the system are comfortable with that, has a direct bearing on the outcome of and use of the method."[11]

Marvin Weisbord and Sandra Janoff point out that cases where Future Search has not been as successful have been due to an organization attempting to reduce costs by reducing time requirements or compromising on number or experience level of facilitators.[15] Joel Fadem, practitioner of Decision Accelerator, speaks of the process agenda as a script of all the fine points that should occur in the event. Sponsors and key decision-makers should review and refine the script many times before the event occurs. Fadem states that the script should include information regarding attendees, human infrastructure (i.e., facilitators and external consultants), time boundaries, structure of small and large-group meetings, and the process for follow-through of action-items derived in the meeting.[22] IBM/ACT requires a planning team prior to the event to organize key stakeholders, issues to be discussed, and small- and large-team sessions.[6] Participative Design requires the creation of a design team to work on preparation for the event. America*Speaks* has process walk-through sessions prior to the event to make sure all details are thought of as they relate to process and human infrastructure. Consultants and facilitators present at the event are recruited based on their skill set as it relates to conflict resolution and meditation.[8]

Intentional Process in Delivery

Creativity Supported by Structure. Marshak (2006) points to five dimensions – political, inspirational, emotional, mindset-driven, and psychodynamic – that can facilitate or derail change at the individual or group level. Practitioners and clients alike describe managing these dynamics within the event structure to support creativity and change. "The process grew out of the meeting itself; we started with a clean slate and dreamed where we wanted to be," says a client who used the Appreciative Inquiry Summit process. He describes the ability of the Appreciative Inquiry Summit to allow for creativity through the structured use of the phases of the methodology.[26] Bernard Mohr, pioneering practitioner of Appreciative Inquiry, describes why starting an Appreciative Inquiry Summit with Discovery using the "paired interview technique" is important: "the intention at the start of the summit is to create new relationships within the system, relationships across boundaries of hierarchy or departmental silos, so that in the process of answering the inquiry questions, people build new kinds of connections, which become the essential 'fuel' for the implementation process."[11] Similarly, Marvin Weisbord and Sandra Janoff, practitioners of Future Search, discuss the underlying principles as a structure to house the creativity and innovative thinking that the participants bring to the event. The principles are simply the blueprint to allow the participants to focus on a common ground and think of future solutions for the issue(s) at hand.[15] Don de Guerre, Participative Design practitioner, also discusses the concept of working within the framework of six psychological principles, but allowing for space to discuss creative options as they relate to process and design improvements in the organization. "Participative Design is a participative action research process whereby work is not changed unless individuals have the 'elbow room' to discuss alternatives."[21]

Intensity and Immersion. Conducting meetings in special settings for the purpose of generating change has its roots in the T-group intervention

(Highhouse, 2002). The intensity of the large-group process that participants are engaged in allows addressing issues in compressed timeframes without being interrupted by work. Practitioner Dick Axelrod notes regarding the Conference Model®, "We are working on something that is tangible and we are affecting people's jobs. Something they care about a lot. Nitty gritty stuff. It's more than just creating a vision – it's getting into the basics of how we do work and I think it taps into how to improve work ... taps into that in a kind of profound way. In a visceral way, they begin to understand where they sit in the system, how they impact others in the system and there is a community that builds and wants to do something about it."[10]

Intentional Process in Post-Work

The third stage in Lewin's (1947) change model points to the need for establishing a system or process that will solidify the new desired state. Many large-group methods include an important implementation component that includes follow-up processes that need to occur after the event is over. Many practitioners believe that the sustainability of the change effort lies in the follow-through processes, which need to be discussed prior to the meeting.[20] For example, the Conference Model® shares the same underlying belief related to follow-through of momentum created in the event. Dick Axelrod, practitioner of Conference Model®, discusses the concept of collaborative loops; where the system learns to design their own large groups after the event. The collaborative loops allow the system to learn of a different way to convene whereby the long-term sustainability concern is thought of as a process issue prior to the event.[10]

The Right Information

Client Situation. Beginning in 2005, Alegent Health Systems leveraged the Decision Accelerator to facilitate collaboration across the multiple stakeholders in this large and complex health care system. To drive results, Alegent needed to enable dialogue among patients, physicians, community agencies, hospital staff groups, and others. In speaking about the Decision Accelerator's capabilities, the Alegent client highlighted the importance of bringing the right information into the room so that information sharing and immersion can take place. "The more you can bring the topic and experience to life, the more engaged [participants] will be in the process, and the conversations will be richer."[9]

Key Issues. In all the large-group methods we studied, access to the "right" information is essential to the critical thinking that needs to take place.

To arrive at well-justified solutions, participants need access to comprehensive, relevant, and accurate information in order to carefully and thoughtfully generate ideas and process options. As such, the "right" information needs to be both deep and broad. Information may be supplied to participants; at other times, information is generated by participants themselves. In all methods, information serves as the leveling element that enables participants to contribute, develop a shared perspective, and jointly create a new reality.

Facts and Figures as Information. Some methods emphasize that information is that which is sourced from facts and figures data. In this sense, information can be gathered prior to or developed during the process of a large-group method. Business and marketplace information, organizational financial performance data, and human capital data are key information sources that may support event objectives. Additionally, empirically driven data captured during a method's execution is important information to cycle back into the system for decision-making.

For example, the "Participative Design process is a participative, action research process."[21] Information is collected from system members. Their individual knowledge of and experience within the system is collected during the method's execution. This approach ensures a thorough understanding of the problem domain. Similarly, the Decision Accelerator requires a rapid inspection of information brought into the system by key stakeholders. Information is either brought into the environment through tacit knowledge or created by collective conversation. The Decision Accelerator method in some respects "acts as a big information processing machine."[4] Practitioners hypothesize that information processing in this fashion is more than a method, but fundamental to the way work is accomplished. Information used in the IBM/ACT method includes data collected prior to the event. In some cases, information is a collection of key business issues. In other cases, information is a collection of process maps ready for analysis and consideration. In this method, participants are asked to discuss, evaluate, and make decisions based upon business information.[6] America*Speaks* events carry this idea forward from organization-level intervention to broad scale public events. An essential concern addressed with this method is the importance of providing participants with access to neutral information. America*Speaks* produces a participant guide which contains information that enables participant education prior to the event, to alleviate the concern whether "a community in the US [can] get enough information to behave democratically."[8] During the event, software assists in collecting information, providing a real-time feedback loop that enables both small-group discussion and large-group decision-making.

Emotional Experience as Information. Other methods assume that information is a blend of, or the intersection between, fact and figures data and the human experience. For these methods, both types of information represent key inputs to and outputs from events.

Historical and current information about the session topic is fundamental for a successful Future Search conference. Sharing and discussing this kind of information creates common ground and is essential to action planning. During a Future Search conference, participants discuss how they are addressing key trends now and what they want to do in the future. As such, the Future Search method supports discovery of new information (Weisbord & Janoff, 2007).

Similarly, the Appreciative Inquiry Summit, one method within the larger practice of Appreciative Inquiry, also assumes that information exists within participants (Cooperrider & Srivastva, 1987; Cooperrider & Srivastva, 1999). The method relies upon inquiry to vocalize that information and bring it forth into the system for evaluation. Bernard Mohr maintains that "historically, we have thought of the process of data collection or inquiry or research as something [that] comes prior to change in human systems … the rethinking that Appreciative Inquiry has brought to the table (is … the awareness that change begins at the instant of the first question)."[11]

Paul Tolchinsky describes information as a key component of the Whole-Scale™ Change method, which depends in part on the sharing of information so that participants in the organization can make thoughtful decisions, both individually and collectively as a system.[20] The Conference Model® practitioners recognize the role information access plays in enabling transparency. "In a visceral way, [participants] begin to understand where they sit in the system, how they impact others in the system and there is a community that builds and wants to do something about it."[10]

The Right Infrastructure

Client Situation. The executive of the Vision Council was trying to enable a community of eye health care professionals, manufacturers, and suppliers achieve a goal: to develop a public health message that all could agree to and support. There had been many attempts at crafting a unified eye health message with no success. As a result of using the Appreciative Inquiry Summit method, not only were they able to come to agreement on the essence of a public health message, they also agreed upon structures and funding needed to carry forward the execution of that message. The latter outcome, a legal entity (the formation of which was concluded within just months of the summit), was unexpected. "You cannot do something like this virtually. You can do follow up things but the meeting was so important. You have to have the face to face."[27] This outcome demonstrates how the Appreciative Inquiry Summit method, its infrastructure, and its approach enable collaboration and accelerated social innovation.

Key Issues. Both physical spaces and networking technologies permit large numbers of stakeholders to be actively engaged. Both infrastructure elements serve to support the collection and analysis of data, as well as enable decision-making and planning. Technology, in particular, has added value to large-group methods in the same way it has enhanced human productivity and effectiveness in other domains. A variety of technological tools have been used in lieu of physical space or in concert with physical space. Ultimately, adequate infrastructure enables group process, and some methods leverage infrastructure more than others to create an environment where change can take place.

Infrastructure as "Container". Some large-scale methods use infrastructure to establish a "container" (Green & Molenkamp, 2005) where events can take place. The "container" holds participants together in some fashion for an agreed upon period of time. At a basic level, infrastructure includes facilities to house the attendees, meeting space for large- and small-group interaction, and electronics for communication vehicles. In this respect, infrastructure plays a valuable but supporting role in providing logistical support and facilitating interpersonal relationships and collaboration.

Paul Tolchinsky commented that "you can't use high technologies effectively unless you have ways for people to connect on an emotional level."[20] The Whole-Scale™ Change methodology includes both in-person group sessions and technology-supported communications to encourage participation and engagement. The Conference Model's® approach is similar, using a series of large-group events and walk-through events over time, based on an organization's needs and change plan. "You have to create connections between people and the purpose. You have to promote a sense of equity and fairness in what's going on."[10]

Infrastructure as Enabler. Some methods further leverage the "container" to create enabling conditions for group-level patterns and ideas to surface. In this respect, infrastructure functions to elicit group dynamics that dislodge historical norms, support idea generation, and optimally convince participants to change.

For example, the Decision Accelerator leverages physical space, flexible furniture, and tools to enable collaboration across organizational levels and roles. The method creates "a new social physical model ... not the historical downstream planning process."[4] Similarly, the Appreciative Inquiry Summit method stipulates that participants move between various groupings during the summit from groups of two, to groups of six to eight and then larger and larger groupings: These various groupings allow for integrating conversations at many levels "you can structure, and you can frame and you can set some boundaries, but even within that structure and frame and boundaries, the Appreciative Inquiry Summit method is fundamentally a method of social innovation, and by definition innovation is something we haven't had before and we can't predict it. Therefore, having the chance for all members of the system to be in dialogue on all aspects of the preferred future is essential to creating actions to which everyone can commit."[11]

In addition to physical space and technology, the America*Speaks* methodology leverages a highly skilled human infrastructure to ensure that all voices are heard. America*Speaks* uses technology infrastructure to bring people into public policy-making, and human infrastructure of trained facilitators – "people who are capable of process consultation, conflict resolution and mediation" – to enable dialogue and ensure the legitimacy of event outcomes.[8]

How do They Work? The Artist as a Conductor of Large-Group Methods

Holman et al. (2007) suggest that mastery of any whole-system change method is a lifetime's work. For the practitioners interviewed for this chapter, that idea is quite literally true. These practitioners are members of an elite group of "*Artists*" and pioneers in large-scale change methodology. Whether driven by a fundamental desire to help people, a deep calling toward social action, or simply dissatisfaction with the status quo, these practitioners innovated and created new ways of implementing change. Burke (1997) maintains that organization development as a field was founded on both humanistic values and ethical concerns for democracy and social justice. In our discussions, the practitioners shared their ideas about what makes large-scale change methods, in particular, so successful. In truth, however, it seems insufficient to discuss the "art" without thinking about the "artist" and his or her contribution to the art.

Consider Schein (1999) and his description of three distinct types of consultation: the expert consultant, the doctor/patient model of consultation, and the process consultant. He writes that the expert consultant is a valued advisor and provider of expertise. He goes on to describe the doctor/patient model of consultation, where the physician asks questions and provides a diagnosis and prescription. He closes with a description of process consultation, where a helping relationship is created as a medium for change. The practitioners we interviewed could be viewed as consultants functioning in all three capacities, and yet, this representation may be simply a baseline description of their capabilities. These practitioners possessed the critical capabilities and experience needed to manage the consulting process, conduct analysis and diagnosis, design appropriate interventions, facilitate and perform process consultation, develop client capability, and evaluate organization change. "There is this intersection between whatever the situation might require, whatever the consultant bias is towards a particular methodology, and whatever the client can tolerate."[10]

Worley and Varney (1998) compiled an extensive record representing the body of knowledge, skills, and competencies needed for practitioners in the organization development and change profession. As this chapter focuses on large-scale change methods and the "artists" who brought them to life, we turn our focus specifically to facilitation, where the artists' unique characteristics and abilities are critical to successful delivery of large-scale change.

Consultant as Seeker

Paul Tolchinsky describes how he "was looking for how can we speed the organization design process and how [he] could be get more participation" in the process.[20] Collaborating in the development of the Whole-Scale™ Change method was the outcome of a need for a new way of doing things. Perhaps this process of continual questioning reflects how the "artists" we interviewed are so innovative in their work. The large-group method consultants we spoke to possess passion, a sense for risk-taking, creativity, and a willingness to experiment. In talking about large-group methods practitioners emphasized that "everyone pushes the boundaries. [Practitioners] are continually validating the parameters. Do these principles make sense to leaders and to the consultants that guide people?"[15]

Consultant as Agent

Consultants often play a special role during the large-group method facilitation that is both different from and similar to other roles that consultants usually play in the Organizational Development world. Facilitators must "enable learning at a new level"[15] by "paying attention to the individual's journey and the organization's journey" and "how you allow the individual to work on individual dynamics and organization dynamic."[20] Bernard Mohr recognizes how a consultant influences outcomes. As a leading practitioner of the Appreciative Inquiry Summit method, Mohr argues that "objectivity in inquiry is a false premise. There is no such thing as an objective question. All questions are an intervention, which move the system into one direction or another. Every question therefore has within it the seeds of the system's future"[11] Carolyn Lukensmeyer argues that we "need those skills and use those skills for the common good."[8]

In sum, the ability of an *Artist* to be both premeditated (in competently executing every complex detail of the method) and ingenious (in sensing when the changes could be made in real time in order to better meet client objectives) is crucial. This is something that practitioners describe as "delivery agility"[22] as the critical factor for a competent facilitator: "You need to plan an event very well, and then be able to completely change in process if you need to, in order to be productive ... The initial premise was to create the conditions for some new thinking to show up in these sessions. Stimulate people's thinking. You can't guarantee that a powerful effective idea or thinking will occur, but you *have to* create the conditions where that kind of outcome could happen ... At the end of each day, [there is] a lot of review and rewrite, sometimes even in the middle/during the event. Agility is essential. The facilitator's experience is critical."[22]

CONCLUSIONS

Summary of Findings: The Conceptual Model for Successful Large-Group Methods

Based on the findings described above, below is our suggested conceptual model for successful large-group method that emerged from our findings. First, we suggest that a successful intervention results in three key outcomes critical for the long-term sustainable organizational success, including *People* who are motivated to change, are committed to the changes, and are empowered with new interdependent relationships formed as a result of large-group methods participation; *Organizational* outcomes, including "hard outcomes" (such as cost savings, revenues, increases in numerically measured customer and employee satisfaction, etc.), as well as changes in

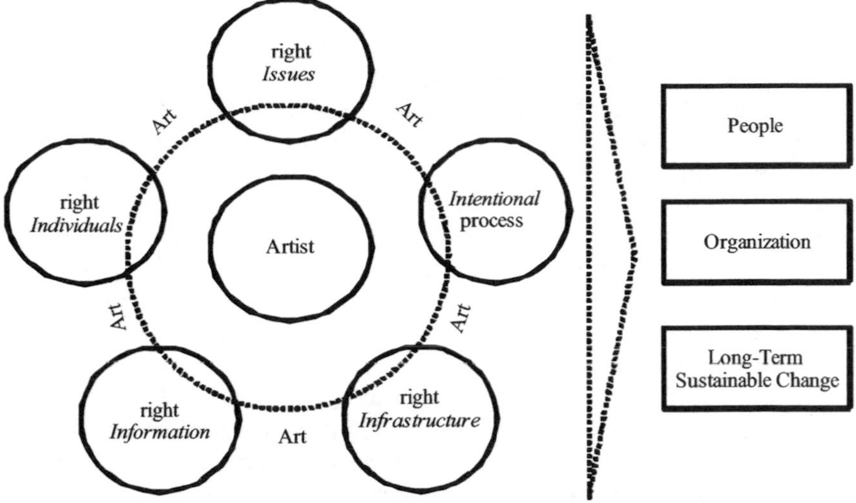

Fig. 1. Conceptual Model for Successful Large-Group Method.

processes, structures, and other organizational aspects aligned to the organizational change objective; and long- and short-term realized benefits that result in the *Long-Term Sustainable Change*.

We also purport that both the *Art* (excellence in method execution) and the *Artist* (the right facilitator) are both necessary for achieving the desired outcomes of the large-group methods. Furthermore, we stipulate that critical elements of Art include the following five elements (or five "I"s): having the right *Individuals* in the room, aiming the large-group method at resolving the right *Issue*; having *Intentional* process (including structured pre-work, intra-method process, and follow-up); having the right *Information* in the meeting; and utilizing the right *Infrastructure* (such as specifically appropriate physical space, technology, etc.). We suggest that while these elements of the Art are important, the simultaneous requisite role of the Artist to flexibly manage the tension between the intended rigidity of the Art (the 5 "I"s) and the emerging human dynamics of the large-group method and associated evolving client objectives is critical (Fig. 1).

Is there a Future for Large-Group Methods?

So, to summarize, we know that they work. There is clear and abundant data throughout many cases included in this chapter – and many that are not – and throughout the testimonies of our "panel of experts" and clients, much of which, for space and other limitations, we are simply unable to include. And while we purposely avoided deep research into the question of "sustainability," as that has been a topic of several other research papers in this series, we strongly believe that the results produced by these methods are "sustainable," at least under any reasonable definition of that word in today's environment. At the very least they are as sustainable as any other set of methods that we believe is out there. Of course, to some degree, the same could be said and has been documented for many other methods that are available today. Six Sigma Quality and Lean Manufacturing projects have been shown to achieve significant impacts and, in many cases, have been shown to have lasting results. And we would be negligent if we did not mention the many successful socio-technical system projects that have occurred over the years, particularly since many of the large-group methods that we examined were identified by our practitioners as having their roots in the work of Emery and Trist (e.g., Emery & Trist, 1965). We also believe we understand the elements that make these methods successful, as represented by our simple model above. *But is there a future for them?*

To answer this question is of course like reading a crystal ball. We have all seen highly successful methods last for a time and then almost disappear, replaced by what some would call a fad and others would call their salvation. As to our group of practitioners and clients we must admit that we were surprised at the diversity of opinion that we heard from those we interviewed on this question (because due to our own enthusiasm about these methods, we expected everyone to say "yes").

Surprisingly, the answer was not one that we would call anything close to consensus. Some practitioners felt that given the complexity of the issues, and the need for stakeholder buy-in which seems to only be increasing every day, the "flattening" impact of the internet on our society, and the emergence of Web 2.0 tools, there is simply no other option for creating sustainable changes in organizations than "continuously expanding the circle"[28] – and this is exactly what the large-group methods do. Further, as many of the practitioners of large-group methods indicated, the methods themselves seem to continue adapting to these changes (e.g., the previously mentioned example of the seven underlying principles of Future Search (Bunker & Alban, 1997) that have now been consolidated into four that includes the elements of the seven – but also some new nuances (Holman et al., 2007)). Weisbord and Janoff, in commenting on the impending evolution of large-group methods, stated that: "Now everyone is integrating-a lot of practitioners tailor make interventions for clients."[15] As we have previously mentioned, many of the methods themselves have *adapted* to the changing organizational conditions by becoming *Adaptable Methods* (i.e., methods used for variety of applications), regardless of what type of issue they have been originally designed to help solving (and the number of Adaptable Methods is likely to continue to grow). Yet, at the same time, many of our research participants (both clients and practitioners) felt that the use of these methods, at least over the last 18 months or so, is not increasing but may well be decreasing with frequency of use (due to the "method fatigue" described earlier in the section regarding the limitations of "People" outcomes of large-group methods).

Further, it may well be, as we indicated from the outset, that the difficult economic times that mark the period in which this chapter is being written are having an impact on the perceptions regarding future use of large-group methods. Some of our research participants raise a concern that to some clients these methods seem risky as they are not convinced that the benefits outweigh the costs. And ultimately, as several of our practitioners noted, and as other studies have shown, the client, and their willingness to take the risks, give up control, and turn solutions to problems over to "the group," is critical. These types of leaders, these types of clients, are still a rare commodity in our world and are that much rarer today when, during the time of crisis, many managers default to traditional ways of solving problems. It may be, as several practitioners have suggested to us, that there will ultimately be no choice, that the democratization of our society, brought about by powerful tools such as the internet, will ultimately determine the outcome.

However, we see even a greater risk to the future of large-group methods. This risk goes back to our original question that ultimately formed the title of this chapter. Is it the *Art* (method) or the *Artist* (practitioner)? The answer, of course, is that it is both, and in addition it is the *Client*. And herein lies the problem and the challenge for the future existence of these methods: *the Art cannot be separated from the Artist*. While this may be a function of the group of methods we looked at, it is clear that the amount of skill required to perform the *Art* has come from many years of practice. Our group of practitioners are consultants who may well be at the very height of their consulting prowess, that share the attention to detail, the capacity to listen and respond to their clients, and the ability "to turn on a dime" when necessary.[2] At the same time only a few methods of those we looked at have so far been extended into a formalized teaching and learning environment. For example, the Future Search is being advanced through the establishment of the Future Search Network (FSN). Further, since 1991 beyond the boundaries of the FSN, Weisbord and Janoff have trained over 3,600 people in Africa, Australia, Asia, Europe, and the Americas to implement Future Search with hundreds more practitioners having replicated Future Search experience in many of the world's cultures.[15] Additionally, there is a large community of practitioners that has embraced Appreciative Inquiry and the Case University graduate program promotes wide practice and institutionalization of this large-group method. The new Artists (and the new Art) of participative design are also coming from the M.A. in Human Systems Intervention at Concordia University in Montreal. However, while these are very hopeful signs of the Art of the large-group methods being shared beyond the network of experienced practitioners (Artists), to our knowledge, and this may well be an error on our part, as we did not explore this question deeply with our group of practitioners, few other methods include with it the intention of creating a significant number of artists of similar skills (outside the immediate consulting practice surrounding the *Artist*). In other words, there is no *Academy of Art* yet established that an aspiring consultant, who wishes to gain these skills, can turn to – neither is there a place to go, a business school, that teaches aspiring leaders how to sponsor and lead large group based change processes from inside the organizations. So where, we ask, will our future *Artists*, both consultants and clients, come from? And will they, as those before them, have to continuously recreate and reinvent the wheel of large-group methods? Or is there a better way?

These questions, of course, will eventually be answered by the "next generation" and we do have some level of hope and trust that at the same time there is what appears to be a great proliferation of different change methods, as identified in *The Change Handbook* (Holman et al., 2007), there will always emerge a group of great *Artists*, both managers and consultants, who can take things to the next level. The real question, of course, is how long can the future wait and what will we have lost in our own lack of knowledge transfer from this generation of managers and practitioners to the next?

Implications for Practice and Future Research

Through our research into the questions posed in this chapter, we conclude that these large-group methods are powerful and are particularly appropriate for resolving a wide variety of issues facing today's organizations that operate under such prevalent conditions as technology saturation, increasing interdependence and globalization, economic contractions and expansions, and others that may come to mind – and that this will remain the case in the future. Given the speed of issue resolution resulting from the whole class of large-group methods and their obvious associated cost effectiveness, these methods should continue to be ever more attractive than traditional "expert-based" methods for improving overall organizational effectiveness in a sustainable way. We also conclude that the future use of these methods will be challenged by the availability of "Artists," practitioners and mangers alike, who can apply these methods so that they lead to desired outcomes. The limitations posed by perceived risk and the natural inclination that most managers have toward maintaining control within a small group of decision makers will also continue to be a barrier to the use of these methods. The implications for the practice of organizational change and development should be clear, as should the implications for business schools who wish to create leaders capable of leading and sustaining large-scale change.

Practitioners will need to develop beyond the basic skills that are taught to them in even some of the best academic institutions. In addition to basic consulting skills, they will need to develop the skills to plan and lead these types of events and processes, as well as a variety of capabilities to support large-scale change over time. And they will need to have the opportunity to develop these skills under the tutelage of those who already possess them. A solid definition of this "craft" needs to be developed and a system to support its development needs to be created. To the extent that this can become more formalized, the *Art* will have a greater likelihood of successful continuation and expansion, the creation of the *Artists*. As almost all of our practitioners and clients suggested in one way or another, the need is there. It will be up to the practitioners themselves, in addition to institutions of higher education, foundations, or other future or existing institutions, to create the capacity to meet the need. Much the same can be said for aspiring leaders, managers, and business schools.

As to the future research, our team has only scratched the surface of the answers to the ambitious research questions we have posed in the beginning of this chapter. More formalized empirical study into these questions is needed. More specifically, we suggest the following as some potentially interesting and fruitful questions to address. First, how many companies currently use large-group methods and to what extent they are being successful? To what extent is the use of these methods expanding or contracting? Second, a study of practice is needed to understand what are the skills and capabilities required to plan, lead, manage, and provide effective consultation to leaders and sponsors of change at this level. Third, conversely, we need to look at the characteristics of clients that have greater propensity to use the large-group methods effectively – and, even more importantly, at how do we turn a client that may not have great propensity for succeeding with large-group method into a client that has an outstanding chances of being successful with it. Fourth, to what extent can these types of events be conducted and these methods applied utilizing the internet in new and creative ways and to what extent are benefits, such as the creation of "social capital," either limited or potentially enhanced through the use of these technologies? As several of our practitioners put it, to what extent is what we are learning in face to face, smaller settings scalable to larger and larger systems and is there a way to use technology to accomplish that? Fifth, we feel it would be important to understand what creates the breaking point between transformation at the individual level, which typically seems to occur using these methods, and true long-term organizational transformation. Finally, as we mentioned before, our findings focus on North American practice of large-group methods – expanding this research to include international perspective from clients and practitioners would be a great contribution to the field of studying large-group methods.

In coming back to the metaphor that we began this chapter with, our team has been privileged to be led by the hands of *Artists* to "look behind" the curtain of an orchestra creating a beautiful symphony that the large-group methods represent for organizations undergoing organizational change. And in that quick backstage tour, we have seen that no one facet of large-group method in particular is a critical prerequisite for the successful outcomes of these interventions. Instead, it is the interaction of multiple elements within the "symphony" of a large-group method that all work together toward the change in human and organizational systems (e.g., right *Individuals* with the right *Information*; right *Issues* within the right *Infrastructure*, etc.). This conclusion takes us back to the systemic view of organizational performance and, we hope, will provide critical input in further use and adaptation of large-group methods, as long as the essence of these methods (the *Art* and the *Artist*) remain at the core of how these methods are implemented because, as Jennifer Hambrick, a WOSU Classical Music radio station host, put it, "in that essence live the human and the divine" (Hambrick, 2009).

NOTES

1. Marvin Weisbord and Sandra Janoff interview, November 27, 2009.
2. Joel Fadem interview, November 21, 2009.
3. Some of these companies worked with Decision Accelerator based on a model developed by MG Taylor Corporation, which was founded in 1979 and offered several Decision Accelerator-type "built-environments" in various parts of the United States and offered these spaces to clients to support their collaborative work processes.
4. Stu Winby interview, December 1, 2009.
5. This is a fundamental condition for success Marvin Weisbord first advocated in Chapter 13 of Productive Workplaces (Weisbord, 1987).
6. Chuck Phillips interview, November 3, 2009.
7. This positive bias could have occurred because, in theory, both the practitioners and the clients we have spoken with may have had some vested interest in telling us a positive story about their work.
8. Carolyn Lukensmeyer interview, November 10, 2009.
9. Decision Accelerator client interview, November 9, 2009.
10. Dick Axelrod interview, November 9, 2009.
11. Bernard Mohr interview, November 11, 2009.
12. Future Search Client interview, December 8, 2009.
13. Whole-Scale™ Change client interview, December 8, 2009.
14. Bernard Mohr interview, November 11.
15. Marvin Weisbord and Sandra Janoff interview, October 27, 2009.
16. Joel Fadem, interview, October 21, 2009.
17. Paul Tolchinsky interview, October 12, 2009.
18. Conference Model® client interview, December 3, 2009.
19. Bernard Mohr states interview, November 11, 2009.
20. Paul Tolchinsky interview, November 12, 2009.
21. Don de Guerre interview, October 21, 2009.
22. Joel Fadem interview, October 21, 2009.
23. Decision Accelerator client, December 1, 2009.
24. Participative Design Client interview, December 5, 2009.
25. Sandra Janoff interview, October 27, 2009.
26. Appreciative Inquiry client interview, November 24, 2009.
27. Appreciative Inquiry client interview, November 9, 2009.
28. As Dick Axelrod so elegantly describes it – see Footnote 16.

ACKNOWLEDGMENTS

The authors would like to express our appreciation to Dick Axelrod, Joel Fadem, Don de Guerre, Sandra Janoff, Carolyn Lukensmeyer, Bernard Mohr, Chuck Phillips, Paul Tolchinsky, Marvin Weisbord, and Stu Winby, and managers and executives in the client organizations that have experienced large-group methods interviewed for this research for sharing their insights, comments and ideas that contributed to the development of this chapter. The authors would also like to express their gratitude to William Pasmore who approached this research team with the idea that lead to development of the research questions that have formed the basis of this chapter.

REFERENCES

Atik, Y. (1994). The conductor and the orchestra: Interactive aspects of the leadership process. *Leadership & Organization Development Journal, 15*(1), 22–28.

Axelrod, E., & Axelrod, R. (1998). The conference model: Engagement in action. *Organization Development Journal, 16*(4), 21–28.

Axelrod, E., & Axelrod, R. (2007). The conference model. In: P. Holman, T. Devane & S. Cady (Eds), *The change handbook: The definitive resource on today's best methods for engaging whole systems* (pp. 207–211). San Francisco, CA: Berrett-Koehler.

Axelrod, R. (1992). Getting everyone involved: How one organization involved its employees, supervisors, and managers in redesigning the organization. *Journal of Applied Behavioral Sciences, 28*(4), 499–509.

Bichel, A., Erfle, S., Wiebe, V., Axelrod, D., & Conly, J. (2009). Improving patient access to medical services: Preventing the patient from being lost in translation. *Healthcare Quarterly, 13*, Special Issue October 2009.

Bunker, B., & Alban, B. (1997). *Large group interventions: Engaging the whole system for rapid change*. San Francisco, CA: Jossey-Bass, Inc.

Bunker, B., & Alban, B. (2006). *The Handbook of large group methods: Creating systemic change in organizations and communities*. San Francisco, CA: Jossey-Bass, Inc.

Burke, W. (1997). The new agenda for organization development. *Organizational Dynamics, 26*(1), 6–20.

Burke, W. (2002). *Organization change: Theory and practice*. Thousand Oaks, CA: Sage Publications, Inc.

Cooperrider, D., & Srivastva, S. (1987). Appreciative inquiry in organizational life. *Research in Organizational Change and Development, 1*, 129–169.

Cooperrider, D., & Srivastva, S. (1999). *Collaborating for change: Appreciative inquiry*. San Francisco, CA: Berrett-Koehler.

Cooperrider, D., & Whitney, D. (2007). Appreciative Inquiry: A positive revolution in change. In: P. Holman, T. Devane & S. Cady (Eds), *The change handbook: The definitive resource on today's best methods for engaging whole systems* (pp. 73–88). San Francisco, CA: Berrett-Koehler.

Dannemiller, K., & Jacobs, R. (1992). Changing the way organizations change: A revolution of common sense. *Journal of Applied Behavioral Science, 28*(4), 480–498.

Emery, F. (1995). Participative design: Effective, flexible and successful, now!. *The Journal for Quality and Participation, 18*(1), 6–10.

Emery, F., & Trist, E. (1965). The causal texture of organizational environments. *Human Relations, 18*, 21–32.

Emery, M., & Devane, T. (2007). Participative design workshop. In: P. Holman, T. Devane & S. Cady (Eds), *The change handbook: The definitive resource on today's best methods for engaging whole systems* (pp. 419–435). San Francisco, CA: Berrett-Koehler.

Green, Z., & Molenkamp, R. (2005). *The BART system of group and organizational analysis: Boundary, authority, role and task*. Retrieved December 30, 2009 from http://www.akriceinstitute.org/

HCAHPS Scores, M. Joshi, Network for Regional Healthcare Improvement Summary. Alegent Health Decision Accelerator-Innovation Design Lab Case Study, Executive Summary, Center for Effective Organizations, Fall 2007.

Highhouse, S. (2002). A history of the T-group and its early applications in management development. *Group Dynamics: Theory, Research, and Practice*, *6*(4), 277–290.

Hambrick, J. (2009). *The difference between good and great*. Retrieved December 20, 2009 from http://www.wosu.org/blogs/classical/?p = 2543

Holman, P., Devane, T., & Cady, S. (Eds). (2007). *The change handbook: The definitive resource on today's best methods for engaging whole systems*. San Francisco, CA: Berrett-Koehler.

James, S., & Tolchinsky, P. (2007). Whole-Scale Change. In: P. Holman, T. Devane & S. Cady (Eds), *The change handbook: The definitive resource on today's best methods for engaging whole systems* (pp. 162–178). San Francisco, CA: Berrett-Koehler.

Kotter, J. P. (1995). Leading change: Why transformational efforts fail. *Harvard Business Review*, *73*(2), 59–67.

Lewin, K. (1947). Group decision and social change. In: T. M. Newcomb & E. L. Hartley, et al. (Eds), *Readings in social psychology* (pp. 197–211). New York: Henry Holt.

Ludema, J. D., Mohr, B., Whitney, D., & Griffin, T. J. (2003). *The Appreciative Inquiry Summit: A practitioner's guide for leading large-group change*. San Francisco, CA: Berrett-Koehler.

Lukensmeyer, C., & Brigham, S. (2002). Taking democracy to scale: Creating a town hall meeting for the twenty-first century. *National Civic Review*, *91*(4), 351–366.

Marshak, R. (2006). *Covert processes at work: Managing the five hidden dimensions of organizational change*. San Francisco, CA: Berrett-Koehler.

Maslow, A. H. (1943). A theory of human motivation. *Psychological Review*, *50*(4), 370–396.

Phillips, C. (1995). *ACT!: IBM white paper* (unpublished manuscript).

Porras, J., & Robertson, P. (1992). Organizational development: Theory, practice and research. In: M. D. Dunnette & L. M. Hough (Eds), *Handbook of industrial and organizational psychology* (2nd ed., Vol. 3, pp. 719–822). Palo Alto, CA: Consulting Psychologists Press.

Revans, R. W. (1978). *The ABC of action learning*. London: Lemos & Crane.

Schein, E. H. (1987). *Process consultation: Vol. 2. Its role in organization development* (2nd ed.), Reading, MA: Addison-Wesley.

Schein, E. H. (1988). *Process consultation: Vol. 1. Its role in organization development* (2nd ed.), Reading, MA: Addison-Wesley.

Schein, E. H. (1999). *Process consultation revisited: Building the helping relationship*. Boston, MA: Addison-Wesley Publishing Co., Inc.

The Sapience Decision Accelerator. (n.d.) Retrieved January 26, 2010, from http://www.sapienceoc.com/index.php?option = com_content&view = article&id = 14&Itemid = 12

Weisbord, M. (1987). *Productive workplaces: Organizing and managing for dignity, meaning, and community*. San Francisco, CA: Jossey-Bass Publishers.

Weisbord, M., & Janoff, S. (2005). Faster, shorter, cheaper may be simple; It's never easy. *The Journal of Applied Behavioral Science*, *41*(1), 70–82.

Weisbord, M., & Janoff, S. (2007). Future search: Common ground under complex conditions. In: P. Holman, T. Devane & S. Cady (Eds), *The change handbook: The definitive resource on today's best methods for engaging whole systems* (pp. 316–330). San Francisco, CA: Berrett-Koehler.

Weisbord, M., & Janoff, S. (2010). *Future search: An action guide to finding common ground in organizations and communities* (3rd ed.). San Francisco, CA: Berrett-Koehler.

Wells, L. (1990). The group as a whole: A systematic socioanalytic perspective on group relations. In: J. Gillette & M. McCollom (Eds), *Groups in context*. Reading, MA: Addison-Wesley.

Whitney, D., & Cooperrider, D. L. (2000). The Appreciative Inquiry Summit: An emerging methodology for whole system positive change. *Journal of the Organization Development Network*, *32*(1), 13–26.

Worley, C., & Varney, G. (1998, Winter). A search for a common body of knowledge for master's level organization development and change programs. *Academy of Management Newsletter*, 1–4.

APPENDICES

Appendix 1: Large-Group Methods Research Interview Participants

I. Decision Accelerator

Practitioners: Joel Fadem – Joel Fadem and Associates, Stu Winby – Sapience Organizational Consulting
Client: Senior Executive – Alegent Health

II. Strategic Change Accelerator/IBM's ACT

Practitioner: Chuck Phillips – Sapience Organizational Consulting

III. Appreciative Inquiry

Practitioner: Bernard Mohr – Innovation Partners International
Client: Senior Executive – The Vision Council

IV. America*Speaks*

Practitioner: Carolyn Lukensmeyer – America*Speaks*, Inc.

V. Future Search

Practitioners: Marvin Weisbord, Sandra Janoff – Future Search Network
Client: Chairman Emeritus – Haworth, Inc.

VI. Whole-Scale™ Change

Practitioner: Paul Tolchinsky
Client: Project Manager – United States Intelligence Agency

VII. Conference Model®/Collaborative Loops

Practitioner: Dick Axelrod – Axelrod and Associates
Client: Senior Executive-Boeing, Inc.

VIII. Participative Design

Practitioner: Don de Guerre – Associate Professor at Concordia University in Montreal.
Client: CAO – City of Winnipeg, Canada

Appendix 2: Practitioner Interview Guide

I. History and experience of using the large-group method

1. Please describe your history and experience with using the [method]?

II. Success factors using the large-group method

2. Please describe a project where the [method] was used successfully. Why do you think it worked so well on this project?
3. Please describe a project where the results were not what you would consider successful and what you would have changed if you could. Why do you think the results were not as successful?
4. In general, where/under which conditions is the [method] successful (i.e., quality of the method execution itself, participation of stakeholders, focus on designing self-adaptive systems rather than a specific static organizational form, etc.)?
5. In general, to what extent does long-term success rely on the quality of the large-group method vs. other factors such as strong leadership sponsors, project management, action planning, and execution?
6. Do you believe these success factors we just discussed are specific to the [method] – or are similar to other large-group methods?

III. Outcomes of using [method]:

7. In your opinion, do large-group methods of the type you are describing "work" in terms of:

   7a. Developing individual's motivations to change? Why or why not?
   7b. Changing actual processes, structures, technologies – and making those aligned with changes objectives? Why or why not?
   7c. Creating long term, sustainable large-scale change? Why or why not?

IV. Future of large-group methods:

8. What do you think is the future of these types of interventions is in comparison to those in the quality/performance improvement field such as LEAN or Six Sigma?
9. In your opinion, how well do these methods work in today's organizations under such prevalent conditions as high technology saturation, globalization, economic downturn?
10. Is there a future for these large-group methods?

Appendix 3: Client Interview Guide

I. History and experience of using the large-group method

1. Please describe your history and experience with using the [method]?

II. Success factors using the large-group method

2. Was the [method] used successfully in your organization? Why do you think it worked so well on this project?
3. [if applicable] Have you experienced a project where the results of using the [method] were not what you would consider successful? Why do you think the results were not as successful?
4. In your view, to what extent did you feel the long-term success rely on the quality of the large-group method vs. other factors such as strong leadership sponsors, project management, action planning, and execution?

III. Outcomes of using [method]:

5. In your opinion, did the [method] "work" in terms of:

   5a. Developing individual's motivations to change? Why or why not?
   5b. Changing actual processes, structures, technologies – and making those aligned with changes objectives? Why or why not?
   5c. Creating long term, sustainable large-scale change? Why or why not?

IV. Future of large-group methods:

6. In your opinion, how well do these methods work in today's organizations under such prevalent conditions as high technology saturation, globalization, economic downturn?
7. Is there a future for these large-group methods?

THAT'S NOT HOW I SEE IT: HOW TRUST IN THE ORGANIZATION, LEADERSHIP, PROCESS, AND OUTCOME INFLUENCE INDIVIDUAL RESPONSES TO ORGANIZATIONAL CHANGE

Robert M. Sloyan and James D. Ludema

ABSTRACT

The purpose of this research was to understand the sensemaking processes people use to determine their responses to organizational change initiatives as they unfold overtime. Based on a longitudinal comparative case study of five business units in a $900-million manufacturing organization in the United States, it shows that people continuously assess how the initiatives will enhance or diminish their individual and organizational identities using four kinds of trust: trust in the organization, trust in leadership, trust in the process, and trust in outcomes. The complex dynamics among these "four trusts" and their influence on responses to change are described. A four trusts model is proposed to help change leaders formulate specific trust-building strategies to increase the probability of success of organizational change initiatives. Implications for research and practice are discussed.

Research in Organizational Change and Development, Volume 18, 233–277

ISSN: 0897-3016/doi:10.1108/S0897-3016(2010)0000018011

INTRODUCTION

Resistance to change has been extensively researched in the organizational sciences ever since Coch and French (1948) first addressed the issue in their seminal article, "Overcoming Resistance to Change." Until the 1990s, resistance was almost universally accepted. It was treated as a pervasive, if not inevitable, human characteristic that led to low organizational performance and needed to be overcome by managers, primarily through the application of rewards and punishments (Dent & Goldberg, 1999). More recently, researchers have questioned these assumptions. They propose that reactions to change are multidimensional and complex (Merron, 1993); that people resist loss of status, pay, or comfort more than change itself (Dent & Goldberg, 1999); that responses to change can be understood as moving on a continuum with commitment at one end and aggressive resistance at the other (Coetsee, 1999); that negative responses to change may be motivated by positive intentions (Piderit, 2000); and that support for change is temporary and variable based on evolving individual and contextual factors (Fisher & Howell, 2004). Rather than accepting resistance as inevitable, researchers have begun to explore a wide range of responses to change.

Within this body of research, much has been done on the antecedents, types, and consequences of different responses to change but little on the sensemaking processes people use to determine their levels of support for change initiatives as they unfold overtime. Following Weick (1995), we define sensemaking simply as how people make a sense of the world in which they live. This involves interpreting information and assigning meaning (Schwandt, 2005), usually by fitting information into a schema, a pre-existing structure for the understanding and allocation of meaning (Poole, Gioia, & Gray, 1989; Stein, 1992; Thomas, Clark, & Gioia, 1993). A clear understanding of these dynamics is important from a theoretical perspective because people take an active part in regulating their levels of support for change initiatives by making sense of them. They discuss them, have feelings about them, judge them, compare them to other experiences, and choose courses of action related to them (Bartunek, Rousseau, Rudolph, & DePalma, 2006). They make appraisals and construct explanations regarding the necessity of the change, its probability of success, and the effect it will have on their individual and organizational well-being, and based on these appraisals, they respond with varying levels of cognitive, emotional, and behavioral support (Msweli-Mbanga & Potwana, 2006; Oreg, 2006; Piderit, 2000). To explore these processes in the context of an emerging change initiative will provide additional insight into the dynamic interplay of identity, sensemaking, and responses to organizational change.

This research also has important practical implications. Some argue that 70% of change initiatives fail (Beer & Nohria, 2000). This is particularly true of large-scale change initiatives (e.g., mergers and acquisitions, organizational redesigns, and enterprise-wide IT migrations) that alter formal structures, work systems, beliefs, and social relationships (Huy, 2001; Watzlawick, Weakland, & Fisch, 1974) and tend to be impersonal, high risk, uncertain, slow, disruptive, and seldom fully implemented (Mintzberg & Westley, 1992). These initiatives require people throughout the organization to make shifts in the interpretive frameworks that give meaning to their behavior and sustain their organizational arrangements (Bartunck & Moch, 1994; Egri & Frost, 1991; Gersick, 1991; Greenwood & Hinings, 1993), and yet their complexities make it difficult for change leaders to predict when these shifts will occur and how best to influence them. A better understanding of the relationship between identity, sensemaking, and responses to change will provide change leaders a conceptual framework for determining how and when to intervene to lead change more effectively.

RESPONSES TO CHANGE

Resistance to Change

The idea of resistance to change is often credited to Kurt Lewin (1951) and his work with force-field analysis, but the first published reference is based on Coch and French's (1948) classic study of the Harwood Manufacturing Corporation. Coch and French (1948) attributed resistance to both individual and contextual factors (Bernerth, Armenakis, Field, & Walker, 2007). Lewin (1951) held a similar view. He understood the person as a complex energy field in which behavior could be conceived of as a change in some state of the field (Marrow, 1957). The status quo represented equilibrium between barriers to change and drivers of change. Weakening the barriers or strengthening the drivers was required to unfreeze the status quo and begin the change process (Dent & Goldberg, 1999). Lewin's (1951) early work put psychological processes at the center of attention, with forces for change battling against individual resistances such as habits and routines and dislike of insecurity and the unknown (Coch & French, 1948; George & Jones, 2001). His later work emphasized contextual factors such as roles, attitudes, behaviors, and norms, all of which could cause the system to be at equilibrium or disequilibrium. In this analysis, resistance to change was seen as a systems phenomenon with individual psychological factors being only one part (Dent & Goldberg, 1999).

During the 1950s, resistance to change quickly became a pervasive topic in management studies, but analyses of its systemic and contextual dimensions were rare. Emphasis was placed on psychological factors and on strategies managers could use to overcome resistance in individual employees. Dent and Goldberg (1999) attribute this, in part, to the time period:

> The 1950s was also a time when the percentage of union membership in the United States reached its zenith, and it was common for managers to think dichotomously of labor verses management. We suggest that by the end of the decade, the idea of resistance to change had become crystallized into what can be called received truth. By definition, received truth is accepted without question. (p. 39)

From the 1950s well into the 1980s, resistance to change was understood primarily as a personality trait that was inevitable, pervasive, and difficult to change. Much research was done to develop and validate incentive systems to help managers overcome the resistance of their employees (Dent & Goldberg, 1999).

Challenging Resistance

During the 1990s, researchers began to challenge traditional views of resistance and explore a wider range of responses to change. Davidson (1994) proposed that resistance had come to include "anything and everything that workers do which managers do not want them to do, and that workers do not do that managers wish them to do" (p. 94). He argued that resorting to such a residual category of analysis obscured the multiplicity of different actions and meanings that merit more precise analysis in their own right. Similarly, Dent and Goldberg (1999) claimed that typically people do not resist change, per se. They may resist loss of status, loss of pay, and loss of comfort, but these are not the same as resisting change. To insist that people inevitably resist change dichotomizes and oversimplifies responses to change and leads to unproductive and often exploitive actions within organizations.

Piderit (2000) demonstrated that responses to change are characterized by three distinct yet related dimensions: emotional, cognitive, and intentional. Resistance to change is represented by the set of responses to change that

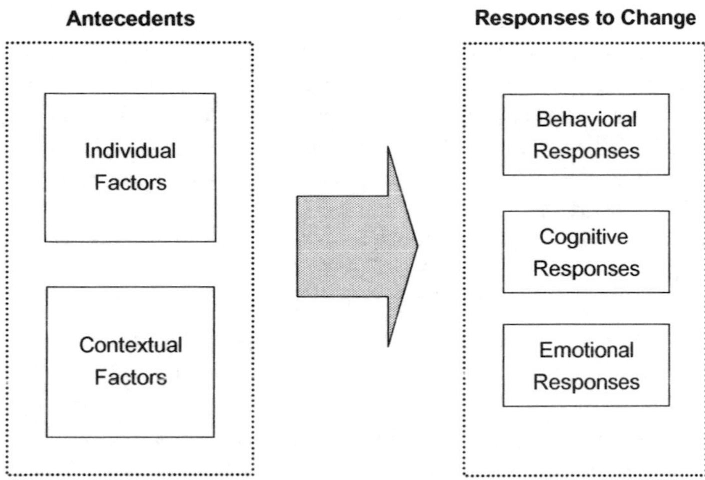

Fig. 1. Antecedents of Emotional, Cognitive, and Behavioral Responses to Change.

are negative along all three dimensions, and support for a change is represented by a set of responses that are positive along all three dimensions. Responses to a change initiative that are neither consistently negative nor consistently positive can be understood as cross-dimensional ambivalence in employees' responses to change and are more prevalent than are pure resistance or commitment. Oreg (2006) built on Piderit's (2000) work and earlier work by McGuire (1985) and identified individual and contextual antecedents that lead to that different forms of emotional, cognitive, and behavioral responses to change (see Fig. 1). Oreg's (2006) framework provides a starting point for our research.

Behavioral Responses to Change

Studies of behavioral responses to change are common in the resistance to change literature and usually focus on negative attitudes and counter-productive behaviors such as hostility, sloppy effort, fawning and submissiveness (Zander, 1950), defiance or omission (Ashforth & Mael, 1996), deception (Shapiro, Lewicki, & Devine, 1995), turnover (Probst, 2003), workplace deviance (Robinson & Bennett, 1995), denial (Scott & Jaffe, 1988), and cynicism (Wanous, Reichers, & Austin, 2000). Managers often perceive resistant behaviors as negative because they see employees who resist as disobedient (Watson, 1982). However, depending on its motivation, resistance can play a positive role in organizational change efforts by helping to ensure that the changes are appropriate, well thought out, and likely to achieve their intended results. It can encourage a search for alternative approaches and synthesis of conflicting opinions (Waddell & Sohal, 1998). As Maurer (1996) puts it, "Resistance is what keeps us from attaching ourselves to every boneheaded idea that comes along" (p. 57).

Some behavioral responses to change are motivated by an individual's belief that they are acting in the best interest of the company. Voice, as a response to dissatisfaction, can be a constructive response to problems that need to be corrected (Farrell, 1983; Hirschman, 1970; Van Dyne & LePine, 1998), and opposition can be an attempt to act in accordance with ethical principles (Milgram, 1965; Modigliani & Rochat, 1995). Similarly, many positive behaviors have been associated with responses to change, including compliance behavior (Sagie, Elizur, & Greenbaum, 1985), prosocial behavior (George & Bettenhausen, 1990), conscientious behavior (Yoon, 2009), sportsmanship (Yoon, 2009), cooperation (Herscovitch & Meyer, 2002), championing (Herscovitch & Meyer, 2002), and taking charge (Morrison & Phelps, 1999). Thus, individual responses to change cannot be understood simply by studying behaviors. Underlying motivations require an understanding of cognitive and emotional processes.

Cognitive Responses to Change

A person's response to change is influenced by appraisals about how a situation or event will affect his or her level of well-being (Lazarus & Folkman, 1984). Decisional balance models suggest that people prepare for action when they perceive the benefits of change to outweigh the anticipated risks (Prochaska et al., 1994). Many studies have focused on the role of schema in these assessments (Bartunek & Moch, 1984, 1987). George and Jones (2001) elaborate:

> People develop schemas for stimuli or concepts that they come across repeatedly. Once a schema has been developed for a concept, whenever stimuli that are encountered fit or are related to the concept, the schema is activated and used to interpret information. (p. 421)

When confronted with change, people use schema to interpret the change and alter their mind-sets only if they see the point of the change and agree with it (Lau & Woodman, 1995; Lawson & Price, 2003; Msweli-Mbanga & Potwana, 2006). If they believe that something is wrong and needs to change

(Armenakis & Harris, 2002), and if they see a reasonable probability of success, they are usually willing to change (Lau & Woodman, 1995). However, research has shown that even when cognitive appraisals support a willingness to change, emotional factors can act as a deterrent.

Emotional Responses to Change

Organizational change often triggers intense emotions (Bartunek, 1984). In some cases, these emotions are negative and can lead to resistance (Isabella, 1990; Kanter, 1983; Cox, 1997). For example, loss or anticipated loss of control, routines, traditions, status, and relationships can lead to fear (Neck, 1996), frustration (Coch & French, 1948), anxiety (Argyris & Schon, 1978), resentment (Kruger, 1996; Strebel, 1996), grief (Perlman & Takacs, 1990); and depression (Vakola, Tsaousis, & Nikolaou, 2003). Some have compared these emotions to the grieving process associated with major traumatic events such as death and dying (Bridges, 2009). Eriksson (2004) argues that in environments of rapid and continuous change, these negative emotions can be exacerbated by an emotional residue of fatigue and lethargy left over from past change initiatives.

Positive emotions can also be associated with change. Building on Ryan and Deci's (2000) self-determination theory, Quinn and Dutton (2005) propose that when people feel their basic needs of autonomy, competence, and relatedness are being met, it creates energy in the sense of being eager to act and capable of action. Fredrickson (1998, 2001) suggests that these conditions activate positive emotions and the enhanced thought–action repertoires associated with them. For example, interest leads to investigation, exploration, and learning; joy to play, imagination, and experimentation; hope to transforming problems into opportunities, rebounding quickly after setbacks, and persevering in finding solutions; and pride to camaraderie, cooperation, and prosocial behavior. As Kanter (1983) observes, "Change is disturbing when it is done to us, exhilarating when it is done by us" (p. 64).

Individual Antecedents

Consistent with the early works of Coch and French (1948) and Lewin (1951), recent research on responses to change demonstrates that they are influenced by individual and contextual antecedents. For example, at the individual level, studies have shown that resistance may occur because it increases the anxiety of real or imagined consequences (Morris & Raben, 1995; Smith & Berg, 1987), including threats to personal security (Bryant, 2006) and confidence in ability to perform (Morris & Raben, 1995; O'Toole, 1995). Oreg (2003) identified six sources of resistance based in personality: (1) reluctance to lose control, (2) cognitive rigidity, (3) lack of psychological resilience, (4) intolerance for the adjustment period involved in change, (5) preference for low levels of stimulation and novelty, and (6) reluctance to give up old habits.

Other studies have focused on specific traits as predictors of individual responses to change. Miller, Johnson, and Grau (1994) argued that people with a high need for achievement view change more favorably because they believe it will help them achieve their goals. Personal resilience and positive self-concept have been associated with higher levels of acceptance and ability to cope with change because they buffer people from negative emotions and amplify the benefits of positive emotions, such as hope, optimism, and perseverance (Wanberg & Banas, 2000). Studies have shown that people with high internal locus of control (Lau & Woodman, 1995) and high risk tolerance (Judge, Thoreson, Pucik, & Welbourne, 1999) are more resilient because they are excited by the prospect of change and believe that they can influence its outcome, while people who are risk averse (Slovic, 1972) and intolerant of ambiguity (Budner, 1962) favor conventionality and resist change because they fear loss of control.

Contextual Antecedents

The wider organizational context can encourage or discourage change and strengthen or diminish sources of resistance (Armenakis & Harris, 2002; George & Jones, 2001). Population ecologists view inability to change as a function of institutionalized routines and practices embedded in organizational structure and culture (Hannan & Freeman, 1984). Existing industry patterns and organizational systems, structures, processes, routines, and sunk costs contribute to inertia and push organizations toward greater reliability and predictability which, in turn, acts against change (Waddell & Sohal, 1998). Similarly, punctuated equilibrium theorists point to macro forces as the source of inertia. Here the system itself is providing the resistance. It is the institutionalized routines and practices embedded in organizational structure, culture (Schein, 2004), and organizational identity (Hatch & Schultz, 2002) that are reinforcing the status quo.

Other contextual factors are embedded in the change process itself. Through a variety of experiments, Coch and French (1948) concluded that groups that were allowed to participate in the design and the development of the changes have much lower resistance than those that do not (Dent & Goldberg, 1999). People who believe that they have some control over the change events are better able to cope with the changes (Lau & Woodman, 1995). Similarly, providing information about a change has been shown to reduce resistance (Miller et al., 1994; Wanberg & Banas, 2000). Others have examined the role of procedural justice. The perception of fairness within the process itself will impact the individual's acceptance of the change (Greenberg, 1990). Studies of organizational justice suggest that although both outcomes and process influence people's responses, procedural aspects are most likely to influence employees' behavioral responses (Crino, 1994).

METHODS

Since the purpose of our research was to understand the sensemaking processes people use to determine their responses to organizational change initiatives, we elected to use a longitudinal comparative case study design. Case studies are appropriate when the focus is on a contemporary phenomenon within some real-life context and when "how" and "why" questions are being asked (Eisenhardt, 1989; Miles & Huberman, 1994). Comparative case studies provide a strong base for theory building because they allow researchers to select categories or dimensions, and then look for within-group similarities coupled with intergroup differences (Eisenhardt & Graebner, 2007; Yin, 2003). Combining comparative case studies with longitudinal designs is a particularly effective combination because it allows researchers to "catch reality in flight," study long-term processes as they unfold, and return to embeddedness as a principle of method (Pettigrew, 1990).

When we began our research, Rob was a senior leader at Apex, a $900-million, 4,500-employee manufacturing organization in the United States, and Apex had just launched an enterprise-wide change initiative called "Project Optimize." The purpose of Project Optimize was to create a new shared services organization that would be responsible for accounts payable, payroll, and IT for all five Apex business units. Along with the new organization, Apex was installing a common enterprise resource planning (ERP) system designed to help Apex manage its resources (materials, human resources, finance, etc.) more effectively and efficiently. By migrating each individual business unit onto a common ERP system, Apex hoped to achieve synergies in budgeting, forecasting, production scheduling, inventory management, accounts payable, and financial reporting.

Not surprisingly, Project Optimize (which included both the new shared services organization and the new ERP system) was controversial. Historically, business units at Apex were highly autonomous, each focusing on a separate set of products and markets and each managing its own resources, processes, and information. At the time of launch, there was considerable skepticism within the business units about the value of Project Optimize and about the deeper motives of corporate headquarters in implementing it. Many people believed that corporate leaders simply wanted to exercise a higher level of control over the business units. Others believed that the complexity of Project Optimize would siphon off valuable time and money, inhibit the ability of the business units to be entrepreneurial, decrease performance across the system, and ultimately fail. Corporate leadership was struggling with how to roll out Project Optimize in a way that would produce commitment on the part of the business units and increase its chances of success.

This was an ideal setting for a longitudinal comparative case study. First, it allowed us to explore Project Optimize in its real-life context and to ask questions about "how" and "why" people at Apex made sense of Project Optimize. Second, it allowed us to look for within-group similarities and intergroup differences across five separate and highly autonomous business units. Third, it allowed us to "catch reality in flight" by examining the forces and factors that influenced people's sensemaking processes overtime and the impact these factors had on their responses to change.

Insider/Outsider Research Team

We conducted our research as an insider/outsider team. As an executive at Apex, Rob was the insider, and as a university professor, Jim was the outsider. This provided the advantage of insider access to people, information, and contextual understanding while tempering some of its inherent biases (Bartunek, 2008). It also allowed us to focus attention on both rigor and relevance (Bartunek, Trullen, Bonet, & Sauquet, 2003) by addressing the demands of quality required by the research community and of practical applications required by organizational members at Apex (Roth, Shani, & Leary, 2007). Rob collected all the data, and we shared in the design of the study, analysis of the data, and writing.

Participants

Rob, along with human resources personnel in the five Apex business units, identified and invited 33 people to participate in the study, all of whom accepted. To gain a diversity of perspectives, they were selected to represent a cross-section of the employees affected by Project Optimize. They included five representatives from the corporate offices (the CEO, the CFO, a Senior Manager, and two people working in the new Apex shared services organization), three people working on implementation of the new ERP system, and five representatives from each of the business units (in most cases, the Business Unit Leader, a Senior Manager, two Managers, and one Individual Contributor). Twenty one were men and twelve women. They ranged in age from 30 to 59, with an average age of 43.3 and in years of service from 1 to 28, with an average of 11.2.

Data Collection

We relied on three sources of data – participant observation, semistructured interviews, and monthly change logs. This allowed us to triangulate our findings and strengthen our assertions (Eisenhardt, 1989; Yin, 1994). The participant observation was conducted by Rob over the 18 months of the study, from April 2007–October 2008. During that time, he sat in dozens of meetings and participated in hundreds of formal and informal conversations about Project Optimize. He listened for and asked questions about how people were making sense of the change process and how that affected their level of support for the changes they were being asked to implement. He took hundreds of pages of field notes following the guidelines of Spradley (1980).

Rob conducted 74 semistructured interviews over three rounds using the responsive interviewing model outlined by Rubin and Rubin (2005). Each interview was digitally recorded and transcribed verbatim. Round one was conducted from April–June 2007, round two from November 2007–February 2008, and round three from May–August 2008. Questions included: What do you think of Project Optimize? How's it going? What's working and what's not? How are you feeling about the change process and how it's unfolding? Do you think it will succeed? What will be its impact, positive and negative? What have you heard others say about Project Optimize and the change process surrounding it? What are you saying about it? What are your biggest concerns about Project Optimize? Do you support it? Are others supporting it? Why or why not? Is there anything else you would like to tell me about Project Optimize and the change process? For rounds two and three, Rob created a short questionnaire based on Piderit's types of responses to change: cognitive, emotional, and intent (see appendix). This tool allowed him to assess the interviewee's acceptance levels during the interview, ask clarifying questions, and invite them to explain any shifts from their previous responses.

The monthly change logs were emails sent to Rob by participants highlighting their thoughts, feelings, and observations regarding the Project Optimize change process. Each month Rob initiated the correspondence by sending an email asking for the participants' reflections. He relied on various combinations of the questions used in the interviews. Although completion of the change logs waned as the study progressed (e.g., 87% completed their log for May, 2007 while only 52% responded in May, 2008), they provided an extremely rich source of data, revealing significant shifts overtime in patterns of sensemaking and support for Project Optimize.

Data Analysis

Data was analyzed in three rounds using the conventions of grounded theory (Glaser & Strauss, 1967; Strauss & Corbin, 1998). During the late summer and fall of 2007, Rob's field journal, the interview transcripts, and the participants' monthly change logs from round one were content analyzed. Ten core categories emerged (see Fig. 2). We were surprised to discover that participation, peer influence, and communication were not among them given their importance in previous studies of responses to change (Coch & French, 1948; Ford & Ford, 1995). Using the technique of theoretical sampling recommended by Strauss and Corbin (1998), we decided to add questions about participation, peer influence, and communication to our interview guide for round two.

During the spring of 2008, Rob's field journal, the interviews, and the participants' monthly change logs from round two were content analyzed. Based on this analysis, the ten categories from round one were reduced to seven (see Fig. 2). A central category also began to emerge: trust. We began reviewing the literature on trust to enhance out theoretical sensitivity (Strauss & Corbin, 1998) and then went back to the data. We discovered that, across the business units, people continuously assessed how Project Optimize would enhance or diminish their individual and organizational identities using four kinds of trust: trust in the organization, trust in

Fig. 2. Development of Coding Categories.

leadership, trust in the process, and trust in outcomes (see Fig. 3). They actively used these four trusts to regulate their support for the process.

To gain a deeper understanding of these dynamics, in round three we asked all 33 participants to continue with their monthly change logs but, consistent with the process of theoretical sampling (Strauss & Corbin, 1998), interviewed only the 12 that we felt would give us the greatest insight into our research questions. They included three people at each of the business

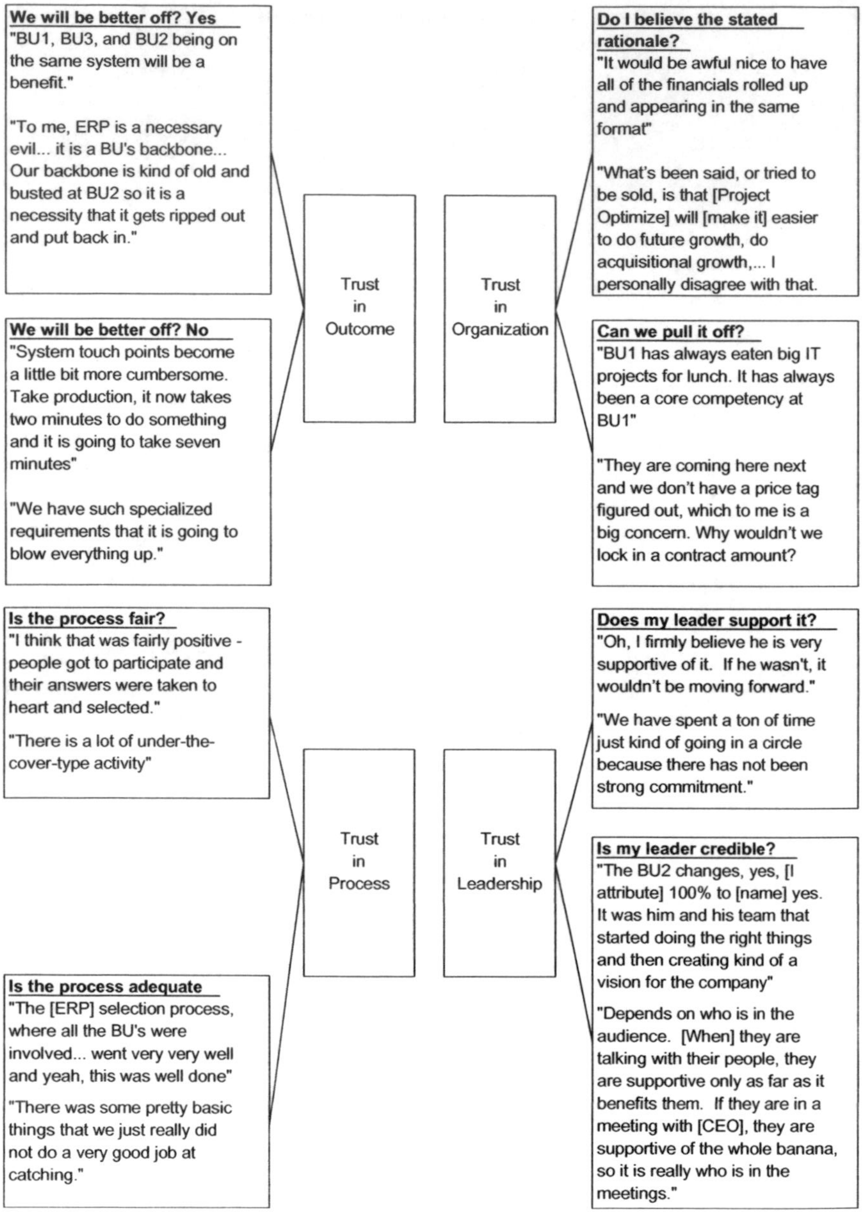

We will be better off? Yes
"BU1, BU3, and BU2 being on the same system will be a benefit."

"To me, ERP is a necessary evil... it is a BU's backbone... Our backbone is kind of old and busted at BU2 so it is a necessity that it gets ripped out and put back in."

We will be better off? No
"System touch points become a little bit more cumbersome. Take production, it now takes two minutes to do something and it is going to take seven minutes"

"We have such specialized requirements that it is going to blow everything up."

Trust in Outcome

Trust in Organization

Do I believe the stated rationale?
"It would be awful nice to have all of the financials rolled up and appearing in the same format"

"What's been said, or tried to be sold, is that [Project Optimize] will [make it] easier to do future growth, do acquisitional growth,... I personally disagree with that.

Can we pull it off?
"BU1 has always eaten big IT projects for lunch. It has always been a core competency at BU1"

"They are coming here next and we don't have a price tag figured out, which to me is a big concern. Why wouldn't we lock in a contract amount?

Is the process fair?
"I think that was fairly positive - people got to participate and their answers were taken to heart and selected."

"There is a lot of under-the-cover-type activity"

Is the process adequate
"The [ERP] selection process, where all the BU's were involved... went very very well and yeah, this was well done"

"There was some pretty basic things that we just really did not do a very good job at catching."

Trust in Process

Trust in Leadership

Does my leader support it?
"Oh, I firmly believe he is very supportive of it. If he wasn't, it wouldn't be moving forward."

"We have spent a ton of time just kind of going in a circle because there has not been strong commitment."

Is my leader credible?
"The BU2 changes, yes, [I attribute] 100% to [name] yes. It was him and his team that started doing the right things and then creating kind of a vision for the company"

"Depends on who is in the audience. [When] they are talking with their people, they are supportive only as far as it benefits them. If they are in a meeting with [CEO], they are supportive of the whole banana, so it is really who is in the meetings."

Fig. 3. The Emergence of the Four Trusts.

units who had implemented the new ERP system, one at the remaining business units, one from Apex Corporate, and two from the ERP implementation team. We interviewed them with two objectives in mind: (1) to better understand how trust was built and how the four trusts interacted and (2) to better understand how individual and organizational identity influenced sensemaking and trust building.

FINDINGS AND ANALYSIS

Our findings can be summarized in three major points. First, as people made sense of Project Optimize, they did so through the lens of four distinct yet related kinds of trust: trust in the organization (Apex), trust in leadership, trust in the process, and trust in outcomes (see Fig. 4). Trust in the organization was influenced by the perceived intent of the changes and by the perceived competence of Apex to implement them effectively. The key question people asked themselves was: "Do I understand and believe the rationale for change?" Trust in leadership was influenced by perceived levels of support by corporate and business unit leaders and by the amount of resources dedicated to the projects. The key question was: "Does my leader support the change, and is he or she credible?" Trust in the process was influenced by perceptions of representation and procedural justice. The key question was: "Is the process adequate and fair?" Trust in outcomes was influenced by experience with similar initiatives in the past and by the anticipated impact on individuals, business units, and the organization as a whole. Key questions were: "Will we be better off, and is it achievable"? To the extent that the responses to these key questions were positive, they enabled trust and increased support for Project Optimize. To the extent that they were negative, they eroded trust and diminished support for the initiative.

Second, levels of trust were directly related to individual and organizational identity. Not surprisingly, people evaluated Project Optimize based on the perceived impact it would have on their autonomy, authority, security, success, and workload. Different business units, functions, and levels in the organization interpreted different aspects of the change initiative differently based on the impact they believed it would have on them.

Third, trust was an emergent state that evolved over the course of the change initiative as people made sense of shifting events, interactions, and observations. As a result, responses to change were highly dynamic, advancing, and retreating along a continuum similar to that described by

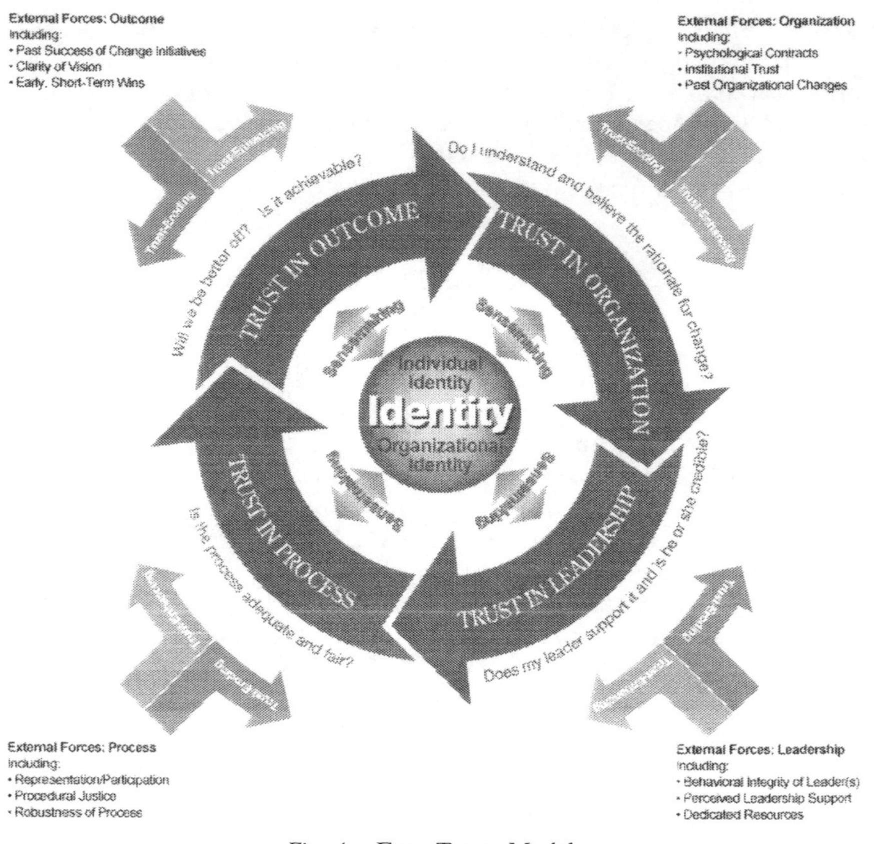

Fig. 4. Four Trusts Model.

Coetsee (1999). Based on their levels of trust, people moved back and forth among at least seven different response zones: aggressive resistance, active resistance, passive resistance, apathy, support, involvement, and commitment.

TRUST

Trust is essential for managing change because trust is necessary for risk taking, and risk taking is integral to organizational change (Bartlett & Ghoshal, 1995; Simons, 1999). Trust influences performance, including group performance (Dirks, 1999, 2000; Kegan & Rubenstein, 1973), job satisfaction (Muchinsky, 1977; Rich, 1997), and commitment

(Brockner, Siegel, Daly, Tyler, & Martin, 1997); perceptions, including perceived accuracy of information (Roberts & O'Reilly, 1974) and perceptions of fairness (Fulk, Brief, & Barr, 1985); and acceptance, including goal acceptance (Oldham, 1975), decision acceptance (Tyler & Degoey, 1996), and compliance with decisions (Kim & Mauborgne, 1993). Trust has also been conceptualized as an emergent state (Burke, Sims, Lazzara, & Salas, 2007) and a history-dependent process that accumulates and builds incrementally over the course of a relationship (Child, 2001; Jones & George, 1998; Lewicki, McAllister, & Bies, 1998). When a trustor takes a risk with a trustee that leads to a positive outcome, the trustor's perceptions of the trustee are enhanced (Mayer, Davis, & Schoorman, 1995).

Definitions of trust vary, but a uniting factor is the idea that trust develops from an individual's perceptions about another person or entity's trustworthiness (Clark & Payne, 2006). Robinson (1996) defines trust as a person's "expectations, assumptions, or beliefs about the likelihood that another's future actions will be beneficial, favorable, or at least not detrimental to one's interests" (p. 576). Mishra (1996) defines it as "one party's willingness to be vulnerable to another party based on the belief that the other party is (a) competent, (b) open, (c) concerned, and (d) reliable" (p. 265). Mayer et al. (1995) summarize the literature on factors that lead to trust and conclude that ability, benevolence, and integrity appear frequently and seem to explain much of trustworthiness. Building on these perspectives, for the purpose of this study, we defined trust as a person's expectation or belief about: (1) the likelihood that another's future actions will be beneficial, or at least not detrimental, to their interests, and (2) the competence of the other party. We view trust as a categorical schema people use to select certain information to pay attention to and then decide how to interpret that information (Taylor, 1999). We found that four kinds of trust were used consistently as a categorical schema as people at Apex made sense of Project Optimize: trust in the organization, trust in leadership, trust in the process, and trust in outcomes.

Trust in the Organization

Scholars have shown that trust is enhanced when people believe their organization will put self-interest aside and act in favor of other orientation or collective orientation (Zucker, 1986). The organization assumes an anthropomorphic identity (Maguire & Phillips, 2008) as people personalize their relationship with the social system that they are embedded

(Kramer, 1999). At Apex, trust in the organization was comprised of two subcategories: intention and competence. Many people were suspicious of Apex's intentions for implementing Project Optimize. They were afraid that the centralization of information was a power move on the part of Apex corporate to better control the business units. When asked about the reason for Project Optimize, one business unit leader said: "…so corporate can see our numbers any time they want." This was considered problematic because, historically, each business unit was highly autonomous, and an entrepreneurial spirit was encouraged. Business unit leaders were rewarded, recognized, and promoted for entrepreneurial success. They were afraid of losing their autonomy, freedom to innovate, and opportunities for personal advancement. One business unit leader put it this way:

> What they're trying to sell is the ease of doing future growth through acquisitions and being able to add value to those acquisitions and bring them into a common platform that is already established. Personally, I don't buy it. I think it will get in the way of our ability to grow because decisions will be made by the wrong people using the wrong information at the wrong time.

Others were concerned that Project Optimize would streamline work for Apex corporate leaders but make it more difficult for the business units. It would siphon off valuable time and money and decrease performance across the system. A business unit manager put it this way:

> Finance, the CFO, wants balance sheet and income statements coming from the same software, but I think people are concerned about Apex getting all of the data because they know that it's going to be another 50 questions that, you know, will take us another 50 hours to answer.

Similarly, many participants were skeptical about Apex's ability to implement Project Optimize competently. Much of the skepticism was based on previous experiences of failure. For example, one business unit leader talked about a previous software implementation that failed because Apex corporate did not follow through on execution at the business unit level. He said: "We had to implement estimating [software] twice in our business unit because corporate's high-level vision was fine, but the detailed user interfaces were unusable for our estimators." After the first stage of Project Optimize (IT Shared Services) faltered, concerns about competence grew. A business unit manager said:

> The only thing is, sometimes the Apex people don't understand that there are little quirky things within each business unit. Some of those things are going to come out when we implement the next stage, and just like with the IT Shared Services, they won't know what to do.

Some believed that Apex's inconsistency in execution was a result of their refusing to take responsibility for the changes they initiated. A business unit leader said:

> The problem is, if they [Apex] have control and authority, that is fine, but without them taking the reins and taking the responsibility, it's no good. I have seen that happen before so many times where they want control, but they are not willing to make the investment in time and attention to get the job done.

The perception on the part of many members of the business units was that Apex remained at the "30,000 foot level" and was unwilling to "get their hands dirty." These people believed that ultimately the changes would not be fully implemented. As a result, they withheld their support.

The lack of trust in Apex and the consequent ambivalence toward Project Optimize can be explained in part by research on institutional trust and psychological contracts. Institutional trust develops when individuals generalize their trust to large organizations or institutions made up of people with whom they have low familiarity, low interdependence, and low continuity of interaction (Lewicki & Benedict-Bunker, 1995; Maguire & Phillips, 2008). While the actions of highly visible role models (e.g., leaders) play an important role (Kramer, 1999), trust in the organization remains a separate assessment. Institutional trust is comprised of a set of socially learned and confirmed expectations people have of the organizations and institutions in which they live and work (Barber, 1983) and is dependent on the expectation that the organization will act with predictability and goodwill (Costigan, Ilter, & Jason, 1998; Maguire & Phillips, 2008). Clearly at Apex, this was not the case. Many people were skeptical about Apex's intentions to act with goodwill and its capacity to act with a positive predictability that would ensure successful execution of Project Optimize.

Psychological contracts lie at the foundation of employment relationships (Rousseau, 1990). They are held by employees and represent employees' beliefs about the reciprocal obligations between them and their organization rather than any specific agent of the organization (Sims, 1994). Psychological contracts are perceptual and idiosyncratic in nature and are based on perceived promises, where a promise is defined as any communication of future intent (Rousseau, 1989). Employees' beliefs about the obligations underlying their employment relationships are not necessarily shared by agents of the organization (Lucero & Allen, 1994). Change initiatives often cause a loss of organizational trust because they violate psychological contracts by shifting responsibilities, workloads, titles, reporting relationships, reward structures, and other implicit or explicit agreements between employees and the organization. This was clearly the case with Project Optimize. It altered the psychological contracts Apex had with members of the business units by changing long-established patterns of power, authority, responsibility, autonomy, workflow, reward, and opportunities for success in the marketplace. Some of these changes were clear and explicit, while others were uncertain, and they led to a lack of organizational trust and ambivalence toward the Project Optimize process.

Trust in Leadership

Research suggests that people are willing to align their attitudes, values, assumptions, and commitments with those of the organization when they trust the integrity and credibility of their leaders (Kouzes & Posner, 1992; Simons, 1999). Trust in leadership can compensate for the lack of information and uncertainty that often accompany organizational change initiatives, thereby reducing speculation and unwarranted reservations (Weber & Weber, 2001). At Apex, trust in leadership was comprised of three subcategories: leadership credibility, leadership support, and dedication of resources. Credibility was dependent on past experiences with the leader and his or her perceived level of trustworthiness overtime. One business unit president was seen as particularly trustworthy because of his reputation of honesty, willingness to listen, and success. People liked the way the business unit had changed over the previous five years and attributed the changes to him. One of his business unit managers explained it this way:

> We trust [our business unit president] because he is willing to share information and keep his door open both ways. He's willing to go in and say, "Hey, we are having a heck of a time with this and this is why. Can you help us figure it out?" This allows people to say, "Oh my gosh, we have been doing this for years, and here's an idea that would fix that."

The credibility this business unit president earned by being willing to share information, admit he did not have all the answers, and listen to feedback, carried over into Project Optimize. Another of his business unit managers said:

> He is fully supportive. He's concerned with resources, conflicts, and priorities, of course, but he sees the value of what we are trying to accomplish, and if he sees the value and he says he's supportive, you can take that to the bank.

Similarly, people regulated their responses to Project Optimize based on the perceived level of support of their leaders. Actions, comments, and gestures were scrutinized. An individual contributor talked about how his lack of support for Project Optimize was directly related to the perceived lack of support on the part of his business unit leader team. He said they claimed to be supportive but demonstrated otherwise:

> We had to do those four-hour training sessions, and we have not done them for a year. Like, okay, obviously that is not a priority, because we have not gotten support from the leadership group to say, yes, we can pull people off the line to do that training.

In other cases, people felt they were getting mixed messages from their leaders. Often during our interviews, people responded with a roll call of leaders and their perceptions, for example, "John Smith loves the project, but Mary Jones thinks it is stupid." A member of the ERP team said:

> You have the business unit president saying one thing, and you have people on his leadership team when the business unit president isn't around saying another thing. It's a total non-starter. Are we doing this thing or aren't we?

Particular attention was paid to the level of resources dedicated to Project Optimize. Apex business unit leaders had great discretion on how to allocate resources, and for many people, how their leaders used this discretion was the "ultimate proof" of support. For example, a business unit manager wrote the following passage in his monthly change log:

> We held the ERP project kickoff meeting with the business unit team as well as reps from Apex corporate and the software company representatives. The general plan and timelines were presented again, but what I saw and heard from others was that the real value was in seeing the amount of support and firepower that's being dedicated to this project. There was an Apex team, specialists from the software company, people specializing in training, people specializing in project management, the governance committee, and so on. There was a "whatever it takes, we're going to do this" atmosphere.

Trust in leadership and its impact on responses to organizational change can be explained in part by research on behavioral integrity, transformational leadership, and organizational citizenship behaviors. Leadership actions trigger varying degrees of trust or lack of trust based on their level of perceived behavioral integrity (Morgan & Zeffane, 2003). Behavioral integrity is the perceived degree of congruence between the values expressed by words and those expressed through action. It is "the extent to which a manager 'walks her talk' and, conversely, the extent to which she 'talks her walk'" (Simons, 1999, p. 90). When leaders act in consistently congruent ways, they create a sense of trustworthiness that can have a positive impact on the affective, cognitive, and intentional components of responses to change (Oreg, 2006).

Herold, Fedor, Caldwell, and Liu (2008) found that transformational leadership was positively associated with change commitment under conditions of high personal job impact. This is true because transformational leaders give individual consideration to followers' needs, provide intellectual stimulation and encouragement for their ideas, appeal to their sense of values, help them see a higher vision, and encourage them to exert themselves in the service of achieving that vision (Bass, 1985; Burns, 1978; Herold et al., 2008). These characteristics are associated with leadership outcomes, including organizational citizenship behavior (OCB), that is, behavior not prescribed by a person's job description but directly or indirectly beneficial to the organization (Organ, 1990; Rousseau & Parks, 1993; Simons, 1999). When leaders take the time to develop trusting, supportive relationships with team members, team members are more committed to the team and more willing to advance change activities to ensure team success (Burke et al., 2007). People who receive leadership support and encouragement are more likely to act voluntarily in supporting organizational change initiatives (Vanyperen, Berg, & Willering, 1999). This proved true at Apex. When people believed in the integrity of their leaders and saw them clearly and consistently supporting Project Optimize, especially with the dedication of resources, they grew in their acceptance of the initiative and invested time and energy into helping it succeed.

Trust in the Process

Much research has linked participation with acceptance of change (Coch & French, 1948; Homans, 1951; Lewin, 1951; Cooperrider & Srivastva, 1987; Pasmore, 1994; Kotter, 1995; Wanberg & Banas, 2000; Ludema, Whitley, Mohr, & Griffin, 2003). Weisbord's (2004) assertion that "people support what they help to create" reflects the idea that when people are actively involved in producing change, they are more likely to trust it, accept it, and invest time, energy, and resources into making it successful. At Apex, trust in the process was comprised of two subcategories: representation and procedural justice. People who were most accepting of Project Optimize felt that the process was "fair" and that everyone's "voice was heard." Interestingly, they were less concerned about participation in the process than they were about having their interests well represented. For example, one business unit manager, who was not directly involved in the implementation, expressed support throughout the process because he felt well represented by his colleagues. He said:

> I've been supportive of Project Optimize all along because I feel like we are well represented on the governance committee. [Our business unit president] and [our business unit leader] are on it. If it was a governance committee made up only of people from the other business units and the corporate offices, I might worry a little bit.

Another business unit manager expressed support for the process because his project leader consulted him and his colleagues and then brought their input to the Project Optimize core team. He said:

> I was only on one committee. We studied where to invest our time in terms of receiving material coming into our business unit. [Our project leader] met with us, and we brought up some scenarios – the pros and cons – and where we could save time more efficiently and all that. [Our project leader] took down all the notes and brought them to the core team, and we got what we needed. That was a positive.

Procedural justice was also a critical factor in determining how people responded to Project Optimize. In contrast to distributive justice which focuses on the fairness of outcomes, procedural justice addresses the fairness of the procedures used to achieve outcomes (Greenberg, 1990; Robbins, Summers, & Miller, 2000). At Apex, people constantly monitored Project Optimize to ensure that the process was fair. For example, one of the senior leaders at Apex corporate talked about the importance of including all relevant stakeholders. He said:

> There were 31 people who cast votes [on which ERP system to use], and it was unanimous. I think the inclusion of everyone was really important and went very, very well. There was a lot of effort put into that so that everyone had a seat at the table and would know that the process was fair.

In contrast, later in the process, a project team was formed ostensibly to select and purchase maintenance software. Behind the scenes, however, one business unit had already determined the software, and the other business units would be forced to adopt it. The project team was formed to create the illusion that all stakeholders were being consulted. Not surprisingly, when people found out about the deception, they were angry and began to withdraw their support, not only for the maintenance software project, but for the entire Project Optimize initiative. A business unit manager explained it this way:

> There is a lot of under-the-cover-type activity, where we kind of already have choosen [the software], but then we are going to pretend this big team exists that is going to choose. Sue got chosen to be on it. Her boss, a maintenance manager, said, "I need you

> to go up and participate on this team. Here are our requirements. Make sure the system you are looking at meets these requirements." I think it came out in about week three or four that the system had already been selected. I think it came out by accident, and it rolled back negatively, very negatively, especially for Sue. She wasn't happy that she had wasted all this time. She said, "they could have just sent me a note, sent me a copy of the system and asked 'will this work' and be done with it. Don't pretend there is this team. It's BS."

This business unit manager had been actively involved in other aspects of Project Optimize that in her words "went well," but after hearing about the maintenance software project team, she rated her support for Project Optimize very low in comparison to other participants.

Perceptions of procedural justice often had historical roots. Throughout the change process, members of the smaller business units expressed suspicion that the largest business unit, business unit 4, would determine the course of events to their detriment. They pointed to past instances of "favoritism" to justify their concern. An ERP team member explains:

> There are a lot of people really wondering at this point how far Project Optimize is going to go across the organization. Is it going to be like it was last time and basically stop at business units 1 and 2? What happens when it gets to business unit 4? What's truly going to happen? Is business unit 4 going to end up with what they have now – and that's just basically pulling financials out of it – or are they ultimately going to commit to full implementation?

The ERP team member was referring to a software migration done eight years earlier in business units 1, 2, and 4. After significant investments of time and money, business units 1 and 2 succeeded in implementing the new software, but business unit 4 implemented only some of the modules. Business unit 4 then forced business units 1 and 2 to revert back to the old software for the modules it failed to implement. This perceived breach of procedural justice had a negative effect on some people's willingness to support Project Optimize.

These findings suggest that procedural justice can serve as an important proxy for participation in large-scale change initiatives. While participation gives people direct influence on the change, can reduce feelings of fear and uncertainty (Bordia, Hobman, Jones, Gallois, & Callan, 2004), and is likely to improve trust (Clark & Payne, 2006), procedural justice has been shown to increase perceptions of fairness and acceptability of outcomes (Lind & Tyler, 1988). When change leaders enact fair procedures, such as providing voice, people are willing to cooperate by investing resources, time, and energy in the collective (De Cremer & Tyler, 2007). This is true because perceived fairness influences people's judgment about the trustworthiness of leaders and about their willingness to follow (Tyler & Lind, 1992). When they perceive the process to be conducted in a procedurally just manner, they are likely to view the proposed changes as legitimate; whereas, when they perceive the process to be procedurally unjust, they are likely to doubt the integrity of leadership and the intended changes (Korsgaard, Sapienza, & Schweiger, 2002). People who feel they are treated in a procedurally just manner are more likely to reciprocate with organizational citizenship behaviors and with support for organizational change initiatives (Korsgaard et al., 2002).

Procedural justice becomes particularly important when outcomes, past or present, are perceived as unfavorable (Brockner & Wiesenfeld, 1996; Cropanzano & Folger, 1989). Whereas favorable outcomes may generally satisfy people, unfavorable outcomes elicit a greater need for explanation and thus focus people's attention more strongly on the procedures used to arrive at the outcome (De Cremer, 2005). According to referent cognitions theory (Folger, 1986), outcomes that are negatively discrepant are necessary but not sufficient antecedents for the expression of resentment toward the party deemed to be responsible for the outcomes. The recipient of the outcomes also needs to believe that the expression of resentment is justifiable in light of the depriving party's behavior. If the depriving party acted in a procedurally fair manner, recipients have fewer reasons for reacting negatively to the adverse outcomes (Brockner et al, 1994). Simply put, the perception of procedural justice makes the outcome more justifiable; therefore individuals are more likely to accept the changes regardless of outcome.

Trust in Outcomes

People are more likely to react positively to change where it most closely and beneficially affects their work, including status, responsibility, involvement, job satisfaction, and work/–family balance (Morgan & Zeffane, 2003). During a change initiative, people continuously assess whether the change initiative will be beneficial for them and for the organization and whether they and the organization have the capacity to achieve their goals. In the early phases of Project Optimize, many people were optimistic about its anticipated benefits. They affirmed the advantages of moving to one system and replacing current systems, which were antiquated and inadequate. One business unit leader said:

> This whole ERP implementation will be a big benefit, because a lot of the business units are so intertwined. We'll be able to leverage a lot of those synergies and take advantage of being sister companies.

Some felt that one system would provide common tools, facilitate the sharing of information and best practices, and potentially reduce their workload. A business unit manager said:

> From a scheduling perspective and even from an inside sales perspective, a lot of what we do is on Excel spreadsheets. I refer to our current system as an Atari 2400. The technology is way outdated. For one of my employees to go in and look up a customer's order, it can sometimes take four software systems to figure out what they are looking for!

Many people knew that transferring to shared services and a new ERP system would be difficult, but they supported it and described it as a "necessary evil" or something that "must be done."

Others were pessimistic about outcomes. People in the business units were afraid that as functions became centralized, many tasks would "fall between the cracks," become "orphaned," and result in more work for them. For example, a business unit accounts payable manager said:

> In the new centralized system, we will not have an accounts payable person here at the business unit, but somebody is going to have to pick up the slack. Somebody is going to have to manage those reports, and it will be one of two people; either the supervisors – which will pull them away from managing – or we some pseudo-finance person. But the bottom line is that it will fall back on our shoulders here in the business units.

People in the business units were also concerned about the loss of control and service that would result from having the common systems in an offsite location. An ERP team member said:

> Unfortunately a common model assumes a perfect world, which does not exist on the manufacturing floor. Someone is going to screw up in receiving, and someone is going to screw up in deliveries, and those types of things. Where are the touch points when the server and the people managing it are in [another state 500 miles away]? Back to the business unit, I think you have too many cases where service levels will be harmful to the business unit.

People were concerned about how their needs would be prioritized against the needs of the other business units and how response times would be affected when the shared services organization was "hundreds of miles" rather than "a few steps" away or "right down the hall."

Some people were concerned about job security, particularly within the finance function. They quickly understood how their jobs could be affected long before any changes were announced. A business unit finance person puts it this way:

> I guess before all of this, I was pretty happy with the company and pretty happy with my role here, but as this is going along, I think it is a lot of hours and you are not guaranteed a job at the end. You almost feel like maybe you are working yourself out of a job.

> Everybody is a little apprehensive about the whole shared services, and what is actually going to be going to Apex, and what is going to be staying here, and what impact that will have on our livelihoods.

Past ERP experiences, positive or negative, had a positive influence on peoples' trust in outcomes. Over the previous 10 years, Apex had initiated five ERP implementations in individual business units and one across multiple business units. Three were outright successes, and two (including the multiple business unit attempt) failed to be fully implemented. Not surprisingly, past successes gave people confidence and increased comfort with Project Optimize. One business unit leader put it this way:

> ERP has been perceived as a major change throughout Apex except at [our business unit] where we had a very successful ERP implementation six years ago. For us it's like, "Oh! We get to do that again? Okay we know how to do that. We've got almost the same team of people in place, we know what the methodology is, we have a strong project management environment…piece of cake." There is a lot less trepidation here than there is at other business units.

Counterintuitively, some business units that had been through failed ERP attempts were nevertheless confident about their ability to implement the ERP system associated with Project Optimize. For example, an individual contributor told the story of lessons learned from his business unit's failed attempt:

> Last time, we kind of felt like we were strong-armed into it, and it was a disaster. There was a pretty good commitment to the project on the part of management, but we had the wrong guy running it, and it was a very large task, and I think that the people who were on the project were overwhelmed with it. It dragged on and on, and of course the dollars were mounting, and there was a lot of pressure on us to get it done, and the whole thing was mess. But, boy did we learn a lot in the process! I'm not too worried about Project Optimize because now we know what not to do.

The impact of trust in outcomes on responses to organizational change can be explained in part by expectancy theory. Expectancy theory (Vroom, 1964) suggests that people are willing to support change initiatives when they feel a sense of valence and efficacy. Valence is the importance, attractiveness, desirability, or anticipated satisfaction with outcomes. It represents the appraisal process through which people examine a proposed change effort, seeking out the potential personal gains and losses or organizational benefits that will emerge for them as a result of successful change (Brown, 2007). To the extent that valence is positive, people are more likely to support the initiative. Efficacy is the perceived capacity to produce the desired effect. During organizational change, high efficacy decreases the perceptions of difficulty and increases efforts, improving the chance for successful change (A. A. Armenakis, Bernerth, Pitts, & Walker, 2007), while low efficacy represents the self-perception of incapability and an overmagnification of difficulty level (Meichenbaum, 1977), leading to self-fulfilling ineffectiveness (Bandura, 1982; Brown, 2007).

The findings of expectancy theory are supported by those of hope and image theory. Hope is defined as a positive motivational state based on a clear sense of goals (goal-directed determination), agency (confidence in the capacity to achieve the goal), and pathways (planning to meet the goal) (Snyder, 2000; Snyder et al., 1991). To the extent that people have a desired goal in mind and believe they have the capacity to achieve the goal, they will invest cognitive, emotional, and behavioral energy into achieving it (Ludema, Wilmot, & Srivastva, 1997). Similarly, image theory (Beach & Mitchell, 1987) suggests that people possess three decision-related images that constrain the decisions they can make: an image of how things should be, an image of the goals they must pursue to satisfy the demands of the first image, and an image of the strategies (behaviors) needed to achieve those goals. Positive images of the future support commitment to organizational change initiatives by creating an affirmative emotional climate of heightened optimism, hope, care, joy, altruism, and passion and by provoking confident and energized action (Srivastva & Cooperrider, 1990). Positive images of the future not only influence acceptance of outcomes but catalyze action to achieve them.

IDENTITY

How people at Apex responded to Project Optimize was influenced by their individual, work, and organizational identities. This is consistent with Weick's (1995) assertion that sensemaking is grounded in identity and the process social identity construction (Brown, 2001). In a work setting, people develop a work identity comprised of organizational, occupational, and other identities that shape the roles they adopt and the ways they behave when performing their work (Walsh & Gordon, 2008). Work identity is conceptualized in terms of a person's position or role within an established set of categories that define an industry, social network, or labor market (Corley et al., 2006) – for example, their department, profession, or work group – and their position within these categories influence their responses to change (Greenwood & Hinings, 1996). At Apex, acceptance of Project Optimize varied by function, level, and business unit. For example, 83% of the people in finance functions discussed job security, yet this concern was rarely mentioned by those outside of finance. Similarly, higher level employees (business unit presidents and leaders) talked about the power dynamics between Apex corporate and the business units and about the advantages and disadvantages of Apex remaining a holding versus becoming more of an operating company, while lower level employees never mentioned it. Work identity clearly impacted people's interpretations of the change initiatives.

Organizational identity also played an important role. Organizational identity refers to those attributes of the organization that members perceive as central, enduring, and distinctive (Albert & Whetten, 1985). It is formed by a process of ordered interorganizational comparisons and reflections upon them overtime. People use their interpretation of organizational identity as a guidepost for measuring the importance of change initiatives, their meaning, and ultimately their acceptance level. At Apex, organizational identity revolved around the business units, and significant differences among business units became evident. Responses to change were surprisingly consistent with business unit organizational identity. For example, the ERP system was implemented simultaneously at business unit 1 and business unit 2. These two business units were located in the same community and shared the same parking lot, but their identities and their responses to the ERP implementation were vastly different.

The organizational identity of business unit 1 centered on quality. It produced highly engineered products that must meet extreme safety standards, that required long lead times (up to a year) to create, and were so complex that only a few other companies in the world could compete with them. It had a highly trained workforce with low turnover and long tenure and had been widely respected in the building industry for over 50 years. Its members prized accuracy, precision, and "careful, thorough evaluation" over everything else. The organizational identity of business unit 2 centered on speed and flexibility. Throughout this study, its members made very little mention of products. They talked about creating a "great place to work" and focused on internal issues such as the employment relationship and their "intense, fast-paced, challenging, and rewarding" environment.

When these two business units were asked to implement the ERP system, they responded in ways that were consistent with their organizational identities. Business unit 1 took a deliberate and methodical approach, which was a source of frustration for the ERP implementation team. One member put it this way:

> Trying to get BU1 to [commit to] a date is a completely foreign concept. They have no idea what the hell a date means, why we should set it, or if it is even important. They don't care because this is their process and they're going to take their time doing it.

In contrast, a manager at business unit 1 was comfortable with deliberate and methodical approach and chafed against pressure to accelerate it:

> It's going like a typical implementation. You get some things figured out and you run into walls on other things. From my perspective, if you take out the schedule or hard deadline, it is going fine.

During Project Optimize, changes consistent with organizational identity were perceived as evolutionary and easily accepted, while changes inconsistent with identity were perceived as revolutionary and quickly rejected (Hargadon & Douglas, 2001).

TRUST AS AN EMERGENT STATE

Trust is an emergent state (Burke et al., 2007) that can be developed or broken due to specific interactions and can be linked to specific situations. It evolves overtime as people make sense of unfolding events and interactions, and as it evolves, it affects responses to change (Isabella, 1990; Jones & George, 1998; Lewicki et al., 1998). At Apex, when IT Shared Services was implemented, people began complaining about services levels almost immediately, and their dissatisfaction diminished trust in the organization and reduced their support for Project Optimize overall. For example, a business unit manager said:

> I don't see a lot of support for Project Optimize these days. Most of it is driven by poor service-level agreements that we've seen with IT Shared Service. People are like, "Our history has shown that we did not do that well, so now we are talking about putting finance into a shared service environment? Give me a break."

A similar decline in trust and acceptance occurred when the board of directors changed the implementation timeline for the ERP system. In an attempt to cut costs, the original five-year timeline was shortened to three. This forced the ERP implementation team to sacrifice functionality and scope to meet the deadlines. One ERP team member said:

> We keep on focusing on the dates, and we have never told people, "guess what, to hit those dates, you are going to have functionality gaps and you are going to have to live with it." They think we are going to hit those dates and deliver everything they already have, and no one has told them that, "no, this is going to be a step back for a number of years." It's a joke.

The aggressive timeline and sacrifices in functionality also diminished trust in the organization at the business unit level. One business unit leader said:

> This is typical of IT, re-scoping as a project management tool to stay on schedule. That's not possible in the building business. If it is a 50-story building, you can't say, "well, I am not going to get done on schedule so I am only going to do 40 stories," but apparently you can get away with that in IT. We had envisioned a new project breakdown structure as part of the new ERP, and I can see that getting slowly eroded, and it is going to end up getting scoped out.

Similar declines in trust and acceptance levels occurred after an update meeting where a business unit president was perceived as bored, while trust and acceptance levels increased when a notoriously incompetent IT Help Desk employee resigned and was replaced with a person perceived as more competent.

Weick (1995) points out how making sense of unfolding events and interactions is often done retrospectively. Whatever is now, at the present moment, and under way determines the meaning of whatever has just occurred:

> People who know the outcome of a complex prior history of tangled, indeterminate events remember that history as being much more determinant, leading "inevitably" to the outcome they already knew. Furthermore, the nature of these determinant histories is reconstructed differently, depending on whether the outcomes are seen as good or bad, then antecedents are reconstructed to emphasize incorrect actions, flawed analysis, and inaccurate perceptions, even if such flaws were not influential or all that obvious at the time. (Weick, 1995, p. 28)

A crucial property of sensemaking is that human situations such as change initiatives are progressively clarified, but this clarification often works in reverse. It is less often the case that an outcome fulfills some prior definition of the situation; it is more often the case that an outcome develops that prior definition.

This was certainly true at Apex. Trust fluctuated throughout Project Optimize as people continuously re-evaluated the changes under way. For example, once IT Shared Services had been implemented in all five business units and the new ERP system had been implemented in two of them, the ERP system was found to have significant limitations, and people became increasingly critical of the process that had been used to select and implement it. Some now felt that the software choice was a mistake, and they blamed the ERP selection team for not doing their due diligence and the ERP software company for "overselling" and even lying during their demonstration sessions. Once people felt that the process delivered a suboptimal outcome, their trust in the process was compromised. Regarding the ERP selection team's lack of due diligence, one business unit leader said:

> We need something that has a very robust scheduling system with the ability to move forward and backward. We just found out that [our new ERP system] can't do that. We cannot mass forward schedule things, which is essential to our business.... But the most frustrating thing, I just found out, is that somebody knew about this ahead of time and didn't tell us.

Regarding deception on the part of the software company, an ERP team member said:

> I was not involved, but from what I understand, [our new ERP provider] just did one heck of a good sales job, and the other vendors performed poorly. [Our new ERP provider] came in with lots of bells and whistles and oohed and ahhed and told us everything we wanted to hear. But then when you start implementing, you find, oh geez, they lied! All of the glitches and problems are things they told us it could do. So, yeah, I'm not near as positive about it now as I was then.

For these people, their retrospective sensemaking diminished their trust in the process. The "unanimous" decision to go with the new ERP service provider was no longer mentioned. The conversation shifted to blaming the ERP selection team for "not asking the right questions" and "not knowing what to look for" and the ERP provider for "lying" and "promising anything."

TRUST BUILDING AND RESPONSES TO CHANGE

To view trust as an emergent state invites change leaders to develop specific trust-building strategies designed to increase the probability of positive responses to change. Following Coetsee (1999), we propose that responses to change are highly dynamic, advancing, and retreating along a continuum of at least seven different response zones (see Fig. 5). Aggressive resistance is extreme and usually involves vicious behavior such as purposely committing errors, destruction, theft, sabotage, and violence. Active resistance is characterized by strong but not destructive behavior, such as blocking or impeding change by voicing strong opposing views, working to rule, slowing down activities, protests, and personal withdrawal. Passive resistance includes holding negative perceptions and attitudes, voicing opposing views, and engaging in regressive behavior such as threats to quit. Apathy represents a transition point between rejection and acceptance and includes

Aggressive Resistance	Active Resistance	Passive Resistance	Apathy	Support	Involvement	Commitment

Adapted from Coetsee (1999)

Fig. 5. Responses to Change as a Continuum.

perceptions and attitudes that are neutral and behaviors characterized by "passive resignation." Support is the weakest form of acceptance. It reflects cognitive agreement with the change but no action. Involvement combines cognitive support with willing cooperation and participative behavior. The strongest form of acceptance is commitment. It is seen as the willingness of employees to use or direct their energy and loyalty for the benefit of the organization to such an extent that a strong emotional link and attachment is created (Allen & Meyer, 1990; Mayer & Schoorman, 1992). Commitment entails more than just a higher degree of involvement; it requires strong cognitive, emotional, and behavioral investment (Piderit, 2000).

Change leaders can help move people toward commitment by creating alignment among the four trusts: trust in the organization, trust in leadership, trust in the process, and trust in outcomes. The four trusts are distinct though clearly interrelated. Movement in one area will affect the others and the whole. For example, if an individual interprets a process as unfair, it reduces trust in process. As a consequence, it will also reduce trust in outcome because the person may question whether their image of the future will be realized. Similarly, trust in the organization and trust in leadership may suffer as the organization and its leaders are associated with the unfair process. A further consideration is that trust builds incrementally but can erode instantly. This is true for each of the four trusts. A trust-eroding event will have a more dramatic effect than a similar trust-building event. Additionally, a particularly strong trust in one of the four trusts cannot offset a strong distrust in another. Therefore, change leaders must ensure that all of the four trusts are aligned as any one of them can harm acceptance.

To build trust in the organization, change leaders are advised to communicate the rationale openly, frequently, and honestly throughout the change initiative. If there are past issues that have created cynicism or past change initiatives that have failed, they need to be acknowledged and shown why the current initiative is different. Individuals do not begin each change initiative anew. A person's entire history with the organization affects their current trust level. Due to this history and the number of possible interactions, trust in organization is the most difficult of the four trusts to effect. It is not likely to be created through one initiative. Nevertheless, change leaders can increase trust through open communication, honoring commitments, and delivering promised results.

Similar to trust in organization, trust in leadership is an emergent process that can begin long before a change initiative is announced. Leaders are advised to consider every interaction as an opportunity to increase trust. It is essential to demonstrate trustworthiness (e.g., benevolence, consistency, and competency) and support of the initiative. Leaders must realize that they are always on stage especially during times of change. People will interpret everything they do and infer meaning. Leaders need to be vigilant in ensuring that their actions are consistent with their words. Further, leaders are encouraged to create more informal interactions. A conversation or a small meeting is a better opportunity to create trust than a formal presentation. Informal settings tend to be more two-way communication. Leaders can better demonstrate that they are trustworthy by listening, responding, and showing an understanding of the issues important to people in the organization. Behavioral integrity (Simons, 1999) is a critical component of leadership in both times of change and times of stability.

Trust in process is more variable than either trust in the organization or trust in leadership. Though people start each initiative with some level of bias, trust in process is more focused on the current initiative. Therefore, it is subject to more dramatic fluctuations during the initiative than are the other trusts. Change leaders are advised to not only ensure that the change process is adequate and fair, but to communicate the process throughout the initiative. The goal is transparency. Transparency ensures that people can see the process (e.g. decision-making process and people involved). Feedback mechanisms must be established to give employees a voice in the process. Additionally, feedback mechanisms surface issues earlier in the change process and increase the likelihood of success. Finally, change leaders must constantly monitor the process to ensure that it is fair, adequate, and well communicated.

Similar to trust in process, trust in outcomes can fluctuate significantly throughout the change initiative. Trust in outcome is particularly susceptible to changes in the other trusts. Change leaders should communicate the benefits of the change initiative and, when possible, augment the general, organization-wide communication with specific information for the individual or group. Employees should understand what effect the changes will have on them personally as well as the benefits for the organization. This targeted communication can help employees visualize a positive outcome. Additionally, change leaders need to build efficacy. By systematically planning for and creating short-term wins (Kotter, 1995), change leaders can influence individuals' confidence in the initiative. Change leaders must ensure that both targeted communication and short-term wins occur throughout the course of the initiative. People must believe that the future state is better and possible.

IMPLICATIONS

The comparative case study design used in this research allowed us to explore the influence of trust on responses to organizational change, but it left some interesting questions unanswered. For example, it appears as though the four trusts are distinct yet related constructs, but more precision is needed. In what ways do they overlap? Are they defined orthogonally, or are they interchangeable? How important is it to address each one separately, or can they even be addressed separately? From an intervention perspective, how does a change leader know where to start? Similarly, the evidence collected at Apex suggests that the four trusts are the key concepts that explain trust in interventions, but further research is needed to test their relative importance compared to other variables frequently associated with trust. Finally, while the four trusts model is interesting it does not clearly establish causality, only relationships. Further research is needed to build and test causal models so that the four trusts can become more useful in an intervention. For example, what are the levers a change leader needs to pull to create trust, and in what order? If identity is a moderator of the effects of trust-making efforts, how can a change leader create trust in such a way that identity enables rather than hinders trust-making efforts? Answering such questions would help build causal models that could be used by practitioners to assess the current situation in organizations and formulate specific trust-building actions to support acceptance of change.

Further study into how individuals construe organizational events is also needed. An exciting opportunity for research is a study that ties acceptance directly to organizational events within the change initiative itself. Isabella (1990) studied the interpretation of key change events but there is also a benefit to studying the smaller events within the change initiative itself (i.e., communication meetings, a negative interaction, team meetings, etc.). Acceptance levels within our study often changed after seemingly minor issues. For example, acceptance levels declined after an update meeting where a business unit president was perceived as bored. On the other hand, acceptance levels increased because an incompetent IT Help Desk employee resigned and was replaced with an individual perceived as more competent. Our study was not designed to capture the direct effect on acceptance levels from these types of events. Further research into this area can reveal how specific events can influence individual responses to change.

CONCLUSIONS

This study contributes to the literature on trust by identifying those aspects of a change initiative in which individuals must trust for individual acceptance: the four trusts. It also expands our understanding of the role of sensemaking in determining trustworthiness and connects sensemaking with individual responses to change. It supports the conceptualization of trust as an emergent state in which every action and interaction is a possibility to increase or decrease trust. People will begin a change initiative with a predetermined level of trust. Trust can be built throughout a change initiative incrementally. However, trust can be lost instantly. The goal of the change leader is positive movement. We propose that as levels of trust increase, so will acceptance. The four trusts model provides a conceptual framework for change leaders to better understand and influence individual responses to change.

REFERENCES

Albert, S., & Whetten, D. A. (Eds). (1985). *Organizational identity* (Vol. 7). Greenwich, CT: JAI Press.

Allen, N. J., & Meyer, J. P. (1990). The measurement and antecedents of affective continuance and normative commitment in the organization. *Journal of Occupational Psychology, 63*(1), 1–18.

Argyris, C. & Schon, D. (1978). *Organizational learning: A theory of action perspective*. Reading, MA: Addison-Wesley.

Armenakis, A. A., Bernerth, J. B., Pitts, J. P., & Walker, H. J. (2007). Organizational change recipients' beliefs scale. *Journal of Applied Behavioral Science*, *43*(4), 481–505.

Armenakis, A. A., & Harris, S. G. (2002). Crafting a change message to create transformational readiness. *Journal of Organizational Change Management*, *15*(2), 169–183.

Ashforth, B. E., & Mael, F. A. (1996). *Organizational identity and strategies as a context for the individual* (13). Greenwich, CT: JAI Press.

Bandura, A. (1982). Self-efficacy mechanism in human agency. *American Psychologist*, *37*, 122–147.

Barber, B. (1983). *The logic and limits of trust*. New Brunswick, NJ: Rutgers University Press.

Bartlett, C. A., & Ghoshal, S. (1995). Rebuilding behavioral context: Turn process reengineering into people rejuvenation. *Sloan Management Review*, *37*(1), 11–23.

Bartunek, J. (Ed.) (2008). *Insider/Outsider Team Research*. Los Angeles: Sage.

Bartunek, J., Trullen, J., Bonet, E., & Sauquet, A. (2003). Sharing and expanding academic and practitioner knowledge in health care. *Journal of Health Services Research & Policy*, *8*, 62–68.

Bartunek, J. M., & Moch, M. K. (1984). Changing interpretive schemas and organizational restructuring: The example of the religious order. *Administrative Science Quarterly*, *29*(3), 355–372.

Bartunek, J. M., & Moch, M. K. (1987). First-order, second-order, and third-order change and organization development interventions: A cognitive approach. *Journal of Applied Behavioral Science*, *23*(4), 483–500.

Bartunek, J. M., & Moch, M. K. (1994). Third-order organizational change and the western mystical tradition. *Journal of Organizational Change Management*, *7*(1), 24.

Bartunek, J. M., Rousseau, D. M., Rudolph, J. W., & DePalma, J. A. (2006). On the receiving end: Sensemaking, emotion, and assessments of an organizational change initiated by others. *Journal of Applied Behavioral Science*, *42*(2), 182–206.

Bass, B. M. (1985). *Leadership and performance beyond expectations*. New York: Free Press.

Beach, L. R., & Mitchell, T. (1987). Image Theory: Principles, Goals, and Plans in Decision Making. *Acta Psychologica*, *66*, 201–220.

Beer, M., & Nohria, N. (2000). Cracking the code of change. *Harvard Business Review*, *78*(3), 133–141.

Bernerth, J. B., Armenakis, A. A., Field, H. S., & Walker, H. J. (2007). Justice, cynicism, and commitment: A study of important organizational change variables. *Journal of Applied Behavioral Science*, *43*(3), 303–326.

Bordia, P., Hobman, E., Jones, E., Gallois, C., & Callan, V. J. (2004). Uncertainty during organizational change: Types, consequences, and management strategies. *Journal of Business and Psychology*, *18*, 507–532.

Bridges, W. (2009). *Managing transitions: Making the most of change*. Cambridge, MA: Da Capo Press.

Brockner, J., Konovsky, M., Cooper-Schneider, R., Folger, R., Martin, C., & Bies, R. J. (1994). Interactive effects of procedural justice and outcome negativity on victims and survivors of job loss. *Academy of Management Journal*, *37*(2), 397–409.

Brockner, J., Siegel, P. A., Daly, J. P., Tyler, T., & Martin, C. (1997). When trust matters: The moderating effect of outcome favorability. *Administrative Science Quarterly*, *42*(3), 558–583.

Brockner, J., & Wiesenfeld, B. M. (1996). An integrative framework for explaining reactions to decisions: Interactive effects of outcomes and procedures. *Psychological Bulletin*, *120*(2), 189–208.

Brown, A. D. (2001). Organization studies and identity: Towards a research agenda. *Human Relations*, *54*(1), 113–121.

Brown, S. (2007). Change recipients' beliefs and justice: The moderating role of leader-member exchange. Paper presented at the Academy of Management Proceedings, Philadelphia, PA, USA.

Bryant, M. (2006). Talking about change: Understanding employee responses through qualitative research. *Management Decisions*, *44*(2), 246–258.

Budner, S. (1962). Intolerance for ambiguity as a personality variable. *Journal of Personality*, *30*(1), 29–50.

Burke, C. S., Sims, D. E., Lazzara, E. H., & Salas, E. (2007). Trust in leadership: A multi-level review and integration. *The Leadership Quarterly*, *18*(6), 606–632.

Burns, J. M. (1978). *Leadership*. New York: Harper & Row.

Child, J. (2001). Trust-the fundamental bond in global collaboration. *Organizational Dynamics*, *29*(4), 272–288.

Clark, M. C., & Payne, R. L. (2006). Character-based determinants of trust in leaders. *Risk Analysis: An International Journal*, *26*(5), 1161–1173.

Coch, L., & French, P. (1948). Overcoming resistance to change. *Human Relations*, *1*, 512–532.

Coetsee, L. (1999). From resistance to commitment. *Public Administration Quarterly*, *23*(2), 204–222.

Cooperrider, D. L., & Srivastva, S. (1987). Appreciative inquiry in organizational life. In: R. Woodman & W. Pasmore (Eds), *Research in organizational change and development* (Vol. 1). Greenwich, CT: JAI Press.

Corley, K. G., Harquail, C. V., Pratt, M. G., Glynn, M. A., Fiol, C. M., & Hatch, M. J. (2006). Guiding organizational identity through aged adolescence. *Journal of Management Inquiry*, *15*(2), 85–99.

Costigan, R. D., Ilter, S. S., & Jason, B. J. (1998). A multi-dimensional study of trust in organizations. *Journal of Management Studies*, *10*, 303–317.

Cox, J. W. (1997). *Effects of organizational change on interpersonal relationships*. Cleveland, OH: Case Western Reserve University.

Crino, M. D. (1994). Employee sabotage: A random or preventable phenomenon? *Journal of Managerial Issues*, *6*(3), 311–330.

Cropanzano, R., & Folger, R. (1989). Referent cognitions and task decision autonomy: Beyond equity theory. *Journal of Applied Psychology*, *74*, 293–299.

Davidson, J. (Ed.) (1994). *The sources and limits of resistance in a privatized utility*. New York: Routledge.

De Cremer, D. (2005). Procedural and distributive justice effects moderated by organizational identification. *Journal of Managerial Psychology*, *20*(1), 4–13.

De Cremer, D., & Tyler, T. R. (2007). The effects of trust in authority and procedural fairness on cooperation. *Journal of Applied Psychology*, *92*(3), 639–649.

Dent, E. B., & Goldberg, S. G. (1999). Challenging "resistance to change". *Journal of Applied Behavioral Sciences*, *35*(25), 25–41.

Dirks, K. T. (1999). The effects of interpersonal trust on work group performance. *Journal of Applied Psychology*, *84*(3), 445–455.

Dirks, K. T. (2000). Trust in leadership and team performance: Evidence from NCAA basketball. *Journal of Applied Psychology*, *85*(6), 1004–1012.

Egri, C. P., & Frost, P. J. (Eds). (1991). *Shamanism and change: Bringing back the magic of organizational transformation* (Vol. 5). Greenwich, CT: JAI Press.

Eisenhardt, K. M. (1989). Building theories from case study research. *Academy of Management Review*, *14*(4), 532–550.

Eisenhardt, K. M., & Graebner, M. E. (2007). Theory building from cases: Opportunities and challenges. *Academy of Management Journal*, *50*(1), 25–32.

Eriksson, C. B. (2004). The effects of change programs on employees emotions. *Personnel Review*, *33*(1), 110–126.

Farrell, D. (1983). Exit, voice, loyalty, and neglect as responses to job dissatisfaction. *Academy of Management Journal*, *26*, 596–607.

Fisher, S. L., & Howell, A. W. (2004). Beyond user acceptance: An examination of employee reactions to information technology systems. *Human Resource Management*, *43*(2), 243–258.

Folger, R. (Ed.) (1986). *Rethinking equity theory: A referent cognitions model.* New York: Plenum.

Ford, J. D., & Ford, L. W. (1995). The role of conversations in producing intentional change in organizations. *Academy of Management Review*, *20*(3), 541–570.

Fredrickson, B. L. (1998). What good are positive emotions? *Review of General Psychology*, *2*, 300–319.

Fredrickson, B. L. (2001). The role of positive emotions in positive psychology: The broaden-and-build theory of positive emotions. *American Psychologist*, *56*(3), 218–226.

Fulk, J., Brief, A. P., & Barr, S. H. (1985). Trust-in-supervisor and perceived fairness and accuracy of performance evaluations. *Journal of Business Research*, *13*(4), 301–313.

George, J. M., & Bettenhausen, K. (1990). Understanding prosocial behavior, sales performance, and turnover: A group-level analysis in a service context. *Journal of Applied Psychology*, *75*(6), 698–709.

George, J. M., & Jones, G. R. (2001). Towards a process model of individual change in organizations. *Human Relations*, *54*(4), 419–444.

Gersick, C. J. G. (1991). Revolutionary change theories: A multilevel exploration of the punctuated equilibrium paradigm. *Academy of Management Review*, *16*(1), 10–36.

Glaser, B., & Strauss, A. (1967). *The discovery of grounded theory: Strategies for qualitative research.* New York: Aldine Publishing Company.

Greenberg, J. (1990). Organizational justice: Yesterday, today and tomorrow. *Journal of Management*, *16*, 399–432.

Greenwood, R., & Hinings, C. R. (1993). Understanding strategic change: The contribution of archetypes. *Academy of Management Journal*, *36*(5), 1052–1081.

Greenwood, R., & Hinings, C. R. (1996). Understanding radical organizational change: Bringing together the old and new institutionalism. *Academy of Management Review*, *21*(4), 1022–1054.

Hannan, M., & Freeman, J. (1984). Structural inertia and organizational change. *American Sociological Review*, *49*, 149–164.

Hargadon, A. B., & Douglas, Y. (2001). When innovation meet institutions: Edison and the design of the electric light. *Administrative Science Quarterly*, *46*, 476–501.

Hatch, M. J., & Schultz, M. (2002). The dynamics of organizational identity. *Human Relations*, *55*(8), 989–1018.

Herold, D. M., Fedor, D. B., Caldwell, S., & Liu, Y. (2008). The effects of transformational and change leadership on employees' commitment to a change: A multilevel study. *Journal of Applied Psychology*, *93*(2), 346–357.

Herscovitch, L., & Meyer, J. P. (2002). Commitment to organizational change: Extension of a three-component model. *Journal of Applied Psychology*, *87*(3), 474–487.

Hirschman, A. O. (1970). *Exit, voice, and loyalty: Responses to decline in firms, organizations, and states*. Cambridge, MA: Harvard University Press.

Homans, G. C. (1951). *The human group* (5th ed.). New Brunswick, NJ: Routledge & Kegan Paul Ltd.

Huy, Q. N. (2001). Time, temporal capability, and planned change. *Academy of Management Review*, *26*(4), 601–623.

Isabella, L. A. (1990). Evolving interpretations as a change unfolds: How managers construe key events. *Academy of Management Journal*, *33*(1), 7–41.

Jones, G., & George, J. (1998). The experience and evolution of trust: Implications for cooperation and teamwork. *Academy of Management Review*, *23*, 531–546.

Judge, T. A., Thoreson, C. J., Pucik, V., & Welbourne, T. M. (1999). Managerial coping with organization change: A dispositional perspective. *Journal of Applied Psychology*, *84*(1), 107–122.

Kanter, R. M. (1983). *The change masters*. New York: Simon and Schuster.

Kegan, D. L., & Rubenstein, A. H. (1973). Trust, effectiveness, and organizational development: A field study in R&D. *Journal of Applied Behavioral Science*, *9*(4), 498–513.

Kim, W. C., & Mauborgne, R. A. (1993). Procedural justice, attitudes, and subsidiary top management compliance with multinationals' corporate strategic decisions. *Academy of Management Journal*, *36*(3), 502–526.

Korsgaard, M. A., Sapienza, H. J., & Schweiger, D. M. (2002). Beaten before begun: The role of procedural justice in planning change. *Journal of Management*, *28*(4), 497–516.

Kotter, J. P. (1995). Leading change: Why transformation efforts fail. *Harvard Business Review*, *73*(2), 59–67.

Kouzes, J. M., & Posner, B. Z. (1992). Ethical leaders: An essay about being in love. *Journal of Business Ethics*, *11*(5), 479–484.

Kramer, R. M. (1999). Trust and distrust in organizations: Emerging perspectives, enduring questions. *Annual Review of Psychology*, *50*, 569–598.

Kruger, W. (1996). Implementation: The core task of change management. *CEMS Business Review*, *1*, 77–96.

Lau, C. M., & Woodman, R. W. (1995). Understanding organizational change: A schematic perspective. *Academy of Management Journal*, *38*(2), 537–554.

Lawson, E., & Price, C. (2003). The Psychology of Change Management. *McKinsey Quarterly*, *4*, 30–41.

Lazarus, R. S., & Folkman, S. (1984). *Stress, Appraisal and Coping*. New York: Springer Publishing Company.

Lewicki, R., McAllister, D. J., & Bies, R. J. (1998). Trust and distrust: New relationships and realities. *Academy of Management Review*, *23*(3), 438–458.

Lewicki, R. J., & Benedict-Bunker, B. (Eds). (1995). *Trust in relationships: A model of development and decline*. San Francisco: Jossey-Bass.

Lewin, K. (1951). *Field theory in social science*. New York: Harper.

Lind, E. A., & Tyler, T. (1988). *The social psychology of procedural justice*. New York: Plenum Press.

Lucero, M. A., & Allen, R. A. (1994). Employee benefits: A growing source of psychological contract violations. *Human Resources Management, 33*, 425–446.

Ludema, J. D., Whitley, D., Mohr, B. J., & Griffin, T. J. (2003). *The appreciative inquiry summit*. San Francisco: Berrett-Koehler Publishers, Inc.

Ludema, J. D., Wilmot, T. B., & Srivastva, S. (1997). Organizational hope: Reaffirming the constructive task of social and organizational inquiry. *Human Relations, 50*(8), 1015–1052.

Maguire, S., & Phillips, N. (2008). "Citibankers"™ at Citigroup: A study of the loss of institutional trust after a merger. *Journal of Management Studies, 45*(2), 372–401.

Marrow, A. J. (1957). *Making management human*. New York: McGraw-Hill.

Maurer, R. (1996). Using resistance to build support of change. *Journal for Quality & Participation*, 56–63.

Mayer, R. C., Davis, J. H., & Schoorman, F. D. (1995). An integrative model of organizational trust. *Academy of Management Review, 20*(3), 709–734.

Mayer, R. C., & Schoorman, F. S. (1992). Predicting participation and production outcomes through a two-dimensional model of organizational commitment. *Academy of Management Journal, 35*(3), 671–684.

McGuire, W. J. (Ed.) (1985). *Attitudes and attitude change* (3 ed., Vol. 2). New York: Random House.

Meichenbaum, D. H. (1977). *Cognitive-behavior modification: An integrative approach*. New York: Plenum Press.

Merron, K. (1993). Let's bury the term "resistance". *Organizational Development Journal, 11*(4), 77–86.

Miles, M. B., & Huberman, A. M. (1994). *Qualitative data analysis: An expanded sourcebook* (2nd ed.). Thousand Oaks, CA: Sage.

Milgram, S. (1965). Some conditions of obedience and disobedience to authority. *Human Relations, 18*(1), 57–76.

Miller, V. D., Johnson, J. R., & Grau, J. (1994). Antecedents to willingness to participate in a planned organizational change. *Journal of Applied Communication Research, 22*(1), 59–80.

Mintzberg, H., & Westley, F. (1992). Cycles of organizational change. *Strategic Management Journal, 13*, 39–59.

Mishra, A. K. (1996). *Organizational responses to crises: The centrality of trust*. Thousand Oaks, CA: Sage Research.

Modigliani, A., & Rochat, F. (1995). The role of interaction sequences and the timing of resistance in shaping obedience and defiance to authority. *Journal of Social Issues, 51*(3), 107–123.

Morgan, D. E., & Zeffane, R. (2003). Employee involvement, organizational change and trust in management. *International Journal of Human Resource Management, 14*(1), 55–75.

Morrison, E. W., & Phelps, C. C. (1999). Taking charge at work: Extrarole efforts to initiate workplace change. *Academy of Management Journal, 42*(4), 403–419.

Morris, K., & Raben, C. (Eds). (1995). *The fundamentals of change management*. San Francisco: Jossey-Bass.

Msweli-Mbanga, P., & Potwana, N. (2006). Modelling participation, resistance to change, and organizational citizenship behaviour: A South African case. *South African Journal of Business, 37*(1), 21–29.

Muchinsky, P. (1977). Organizational communications: Relationships to organizational climate and job satisfaction. *Academy of Management Journal, 20*, 592–607.

Neck, C. P. (1996). Thought self-leadership: A self-regulatory approach towards overcoming resistance to organizational change. *International Journal of Organizational Analysis (1993–2002), 4*(2), 202.

Oldham, G. (1975). The impact of supervisor characteristics on goal acceptance. *Academy of Management Journal, 18*, 461–475.

Oreg, S. (2003). Resistance to change: Developing an individual differences measure. *Journal of Applied Psychology, 88*(4), 680–693.

Oreg, S. (2006). Personality, context, and resistance to organizational change. *European Journal of Work and Organizational Psychology, 15*(1), 73–101.

Organ, D. W. (Ed.) (1990). *The motivational basis of organizational citizenship behavior* (Vol. 12). Greenwich, CT: JAI Press.

O'Toole, J. (1995). *Leading change: Overcoming the ideology of comfort and the tyranny of custom*. San Francisco: Jossey-Bass.

Pasmore, W. A. (1994). *Creating strategic change: Designing the flexible, high-performing organization*. San Francisco: Jossey-Bass.

Perlman, D., & Takacs, G. J. (1990). The ten stages of change. *Nursing Management, 21*(4), 33–38.

Pettigrew, A. M. (1990). Longitudinal field research on change: Theory and practice. *Organization Science, 1*(3), 267–291.

Piderit, S. K. (2000). Rethinking resistance and recognizing ambivalence: A multidimensional view of attitudes toward an organizational change. *Academy of Management Review, 25*(4), 783–794.

Poole, P., Gioia, D. A., & Gray, B. (1989). Influence modes, schema change, and organizational transformation. *Journal of Applied Behavioral Science, 25*(3), 271–289.

Probst, T. M. (2003). Exploring employee outcomes of organizational restructuring: A solomon four-group study. *Group and Organization Management, 28*(3), 416–439.

Prochaska, J. O., Velicer, W. F., Rossi, J. S., Goldstein, M. G., Marcus, B. H., Rakowski, W., et al. (1994). Stages of change and decisional balance for 12 problem behaviors. *Health Psychology, 13*, 39–46.

Quinn, R. E., & Dutton, J. E. (2005). Coordination as energy-in-conversation. *Academy of Management Review, 30*(1), 36–57.

Rich, G. (1997). The sales manager as a role model: Effects on trust, job satisfaction, and performance of salespeople. *Journal of the Academy of Marketing Science, 25*(4), 319–328.

Robbins, T., Summers, T. P., & Miller, J. L. (2000). Intra- and inter-justice relationships: Assessing the direction. *Human Relations, 53*(10), 1329–1355.

Roberts, K. H., & O'Reilly, C. A. (1974). Measuring organizational communication. *Journal of Applied Psychology, 59*(3), 321–326.

Robinson, S. L. (1996). Trust and breach of the psychological contract. *Administrative Science Quarterly, 41*(4), 574–599.

Robinson, S. L., & Bennett, R. J. (1995). A typology of deviant workplace behaviors: A multidimensional scaling study. *Academy of Management Journal, 38*(2), 555–572.

Roth, J., Shani, A. B., & Leary, M. M. (2007). Facing the Challenges of new capability development within a biopharma company. *Action Research, 5*(1), 41–60.

Rousseau, D. M. (1989). Psychological and implied contracts in organizations. *Employee Responsibilities and Rights Journal, 2*, 121–139.

Rousseau, D. M. (1990). New hire perceptions of their own and their employer's obligations: A study of psychological contracts. *Journal of Organizational Behavior*, *11*(5), 389–400.

Rousseau, D. M., & Parks, J. M. (1993). The contracts of individuals and organizations. *Research in Organizational Behavior*, *15*, 1–43.

Rubin, H. J., & Rubin, I. S. (2005). *Qualitative interviewing: The art of hearing data* (2nd ed). Thousand Oaks, CA: Sage.

Sagie, A., Elizur, D., & Greenbaum, C. W. (1985). Job experience, persuasion strategy, and resistance to change. *Journal of Occupational Behavior*, *6*, 157–162.

Schein, E. H. (2004). *Organizational culture and leadership* (3rd ed.). San Francisco: Jossey-Boss.

Schwandt, D. R. (2005). When managers become philosophers: Integrating learning with sensemaking. *Academy of Management Learning & Education*, *4*(2), 176–192.

Scott, C. D., & Jaffe, D. T. (1988). Survive and thrive in times of change. *Training and Development Journal*, *42*, 25–27.

Shapiro, D. L., Lewicki, R. J., & Devine, P. (1995). When do employees chose deceptive tactics to stop unwanted change? In: R. J. Lewinski & B. Shepard (Eds), *Research on negotiation in organizations* (Vol. 5, pp. 155–184). Greenwich, CT: JAI Press.

Simons, T. (1999). Behavioral integrity as a critical ingredient for transformational leadership. *Journal for Organizational Change Management*, *12*(2), 89–104.

Sims, R. R. (1994). Human resource management's role in clarifying the new psychological contract. *Journal of Human Resource Management*, *33*, 373–382.

Slovic, P. (1972). Information processing, situational specificity, and the generality of risk taking behavior. *Journal of Personality and Social Psychology*, *22*, 128–134.

Smith, K. K., & Berg, D. N. (1987). *Paradoxes of group life*. San Francisco: Jossey-Bass.

Snyder, C. R. (2000). *Handbook of hope: Theory, measures, and applications*. San Diego, CA: Academic Press.

Snyder, C. R., Harris, C., Anderson, J. R., Holleran, S. A., Irving, L. M., & Sigmon, S. I. (1991). The will and the ways: Development and validation of an individual-difference measure of hope. *Journal of Personality and Social Psychology*, *60*, 570–585.

Spradley, J. P. (1980). *Participant observation*. Fort Worth: Harcourt Brace.

Srivastva, S., & Cooperrider, D. L. (1990). *Appreciative management and leadership: The power of positive thought and action in organizations*. San Francisco: Jossey-Bass.

Stein, D. J. (1992). Schemas in the cognitive and clinical sciences. *Journal of Psychotherapy Integration*, *2*, 45–63.

Strauss, A., & Corbin, J. (1998). *Basics of qualitative research: Techniques and procedures for developing grounded theory*. Thousand Oaks, CA: Sage.

Strebel, P. (1996). Why do employees resist change?. *Harvard Business Review*, *74*(3), 86–92.

Taylor, S. S. (1999). Making sense of revolutionary change: Differences in members' stories. *Journal of Organizational Change Management*, *12*(6), 524–539.

Thomas, J. B., Clark, S. M., & Gioia, D. A. (1993). Strategic sensemaking and organizational performance: Linkages among scanning, interpretation, action, and outcomes. *Academy of Management Journal*, *36*, 239–270.

Tyler, T. R., & Degoey, P. (1996). Trust in organizational authorities: The influence of motive attributions on willingness to accept decisions. In: R. M. Kramer & T. R. Tyler (Eds), *Trust in Organizations* (pp. 331–356). Thousand Oaks, CA: Sage.

Tyler, T. R., & Lind, E. A. (Eds). (1992). *A relational model of authority in groups* (Vol. 25). New York: Academic Press.

Vakola, M., Tsaousis, I., & Nikolaou, I. (2003). The role of emotional intelligence and personality variables on attitudes towards organizational change. *Journal of Managerial Psychology*, *19*(2), 88–110.

Van Dyne, L., & LePine, J. A. (1998). Helping and voice extra-role behaviors: Evidence of construct and predictive validity. *Academy of Management Journal*, *41*(1), 108–119.

Vanyperen, N. W., Berg, A. E. V. D., & Willering, M. C. (1999). Towards a better understanding of the link between participation in decision-making and organizational citizenship behavior: A multilevel analysis. *Journal of Occupational and Organizational Psychology*, *72*(3), 377–392.

Vroom, V. H. (1964). *Work and motivation*. New York: Wiley.

Waddell, D., & Sohal, A. S. (1998). Resistance: A constructive tool for change management. *Management Decision*, *36*(8), 543–548.

Walsh, K., & Gordon, J. R. (2008). Creating an individual work identity. *Human Resource Management Review*, *18*(1), 46–61.

Wanberg, C. R., & Banas, J. T. (2000). Predictors and outcomes of openness to changes in a reorganized workplace. *Journal of Applied Psychology*, *85*(1), 132–142.

Wanous, J. P., Reichers, A. E., & Austin, J. T. (2000). Cynicism about organizational change: Measurement, antecedents, and correlates. *Group & Organization Management*, *25*(2), 132.

Watson, T. J. (1982). Group ideologies and organizational change. *Journal of Management Studies*, *19*, 259–275.

Watzlawick, P., Weakland, J., & Fisch, R. (1974). *Change; principles of problem formation and problem resolution*. New York: WW Norton & Company.

Weber, P. S., & Weber, J. E. (2001). Changes in employee perceptions during organizational change. *Leadership & Organizational Development Journal*, *22*, 291–300.

Weick, K. E. (1995). *Sensemaking in organizations*. Thousand Oaks, CA: Sage.

Weisbord, M. R. (2004). *Productive workplaces revisited*. San Francisco: Jossey-Bass.

Yin, R. K. (1994). *Case study research: Design and methods* (2nd ed.). Newbury Park, CA: Sage.

Yin, R. K. (2003). *Case study research: Design and methods* (3rd ed., Vol. 5). Thousand Oaks, CA: Sage.

Yoon, C. (2009). The effects of organizational citizenship behaviors on ERP system success. *Computers in Human Behavior*, *25*(2), 421–428.

Zander, A. (1950). Resistance to change: Its analysis and prevention. *Advanced Management Journal*, *15*(1), 9–11.

Zucker, L. G. (1986). *Production of trust: Institutional sources of economic structure 1984–1920* (Vol. 8). Greenwich, CT: JAI Press.

APPENDIX. SURVEY OF RESPONSES TO CHANGE

Shared Services

	Agree	Somewhat Agree	Not Sure	Somewhat Disagree	Disagree
This change will be good for the organization					
I believe that I can personally benefit from this initiative					
This initiative is causing me some anxiety or fear					
I had a bad feeling about this initiative					
I am actively supporting this project					
I voiced my concerns to management (if applicable)					

ERP

	Agree	Somewhat Agree	Not Sure	Somewhat Disagree	Disagree
This change will be good for the organization					
I believe that I can personally benefit from this initiative					
This initiative is causing me some anxiety or fear					
I had a bad feeling about this initiative					
I am actively supporting this project					
I voiced my concerns to management (if applicable)					

Source: Adapted from Piderit's (2000) types of responses to change.

THE IMPACT OF TRUST ON THE ORGANIZATIONAL MERGER PROCESS

Paul Michalenko

ABSTRACT

This is a qualitative study of eight merged organizations. They consist of a unique sector, namely Catholic men's religious provinces. The study attempts to determine characteristics of successful mergers by understanding the processes and dynamics of mergers when membership needs to be involved and in some cases give approval of the merger. Regardless of the initiation of the merger or the processes utilized it appears that three factors and one result bring about success. A clear mission-driven purpose, authentic leadership, and inclusive engagement are essential elements of any process. They set the path for building trust among members and organizations, which may result in organizational renewal.

INTRODUCTION

The researcher began this study wishing to explore what made mergers more successful in a unique category of organizations – Catholic men's religious provinces. There were no criteria on how success would be experienced or defined, but assumed that some organizations experienced greater

Research in Organizational Change and Development, Volume 18, 279–314

ISSN: 0897-3016/doi:10.1108/S0897-3016(2010)0000018012

satisfaction with their merger outcome than others. The goal was to explore change processes that these organizations engaged to understand which of these change processes accomplished the more successful merger results.

Research on implementing change as a process has its roots in the early work of Lewin (1947), wherein he conceptualized change as progressing through successive phases called unfreezing, moving, and freezing. Building on this early work, Judson (1991), Kotter (1995), Galpin (1996), Armenakis and Bedeian (1999), and Armenakis, Harris, and Feild (1999) have described multi-phase models for change agents to follow in implementing changes.

The Judson (1991) model of implementing a change is comprised of five phases: (a) analyzing and planning the change; (b) communicating the change; (c) gaining acceptance of new behaviors; (d) changing from the status quo to a desired state; and (e) consolidating and institutionalizing the new state.

Kotter (1995) recommended eight steps for change agents to follow in implementing fundamental changes in how an organization operates: (a) establishing a sense of urgency by relating external environmental realities to real and potential crises and opportunities facing an organization, (b) forming a powerful coalition of individuals who embrace the need for change and who can rally others to support the effort; (c) creating a vision to accomplish the desired end result; (d) communicating the vision through numerous communication channels; (e) empowering others to act on the vision by changing structures, systems, policies, and procedures in ways that will facilitate implementation; (f) planning for and creating short-term wins by publicizing success, thereby building momentum for continued change; (g) consolidating improvements and changing other structures, systems, procedures, and policies that are not consistent with the vision; and (h) institutionalizing the new approaches by publicizing the connection between the change effort and organizational success.

In a third attempt to offer guidance for successfully implementing change, Galpin (1996) proposed a model comprised of nine wedges that form a wheel. As a foundation for each wedge in the model, Galpin (1996) stressed the importance of understanding an organization's culture as reflected in its rules and policies, customs and norms, ceremonies and events, and rewards and recognition. The Galpin *wheel* consists of the following wedges: (a) establishing the need to change; (b) developing and disseminating a vision of a planned change; (c) diagnosing and analyzing the current situation; (d) generating recommendations; (e) detailing the recommendations; (f) pilot testing the recommendations; (g) preparing the recommendations for rollout; (h) rolling out the recommendations; and (i) measuring, reinforcing, and refining the change.

Armenakis et al. (1999) proposed two models that incorporate elements of both Lewin's (1947) work and Bandura's (1986) social learning theory. The first model considers creating readiness for change so that resistance is minimized. The objective of the second model is to facilitate the adoption and institutionalization of desired change. The operational mechanism underlying both models is the basic change message being conveyed. As argued by Armenakis et al. (1999), to be effective, such a message should incorporate five components: (a) discrepancy (i.e., we need to change); (b) self-efficacy (i.e., we have the capability to successfully change); (c) personal valence (i.e., it is in our best interest to change); (d) principal support (i.e., those affected are behind the change); and (e) appropriateness (i.e., the desired change is right for the focal organization). The logic behind both models is to convert the constituencies affected by a change into agents of change. Of special interest to both change agents and change researchers are the influence strategies that Armenakis et al. (1999) identify as being useful for transmitting change messages. These include (a) persuasive communication (e.g., speeches by change agents and articles in employee newsletters); (b) active participation by those affected (e.g., vicarious learning, enactive mastery, and participative decision making); (c) human resource management practices (e.g., selection, performance appraisal, compensation, and training and development programs); (d) symbolic activities (e.g., rites and ceremonies); (e) diffusion practices (e.g., best practice programs and transition teams); (f) management of internal and external information; and (g) formal activities that demonstrate support for change initiatives (e.g., new organizational structures and revised job descriptions).

Cooperrider and Srivastva (1987) approached the organizational change process from a positive approach. With a focus on "appreciative inquiry" they provide a four-phase process: (a) discovery – appreciate the best of what is; (b) dream – imagine what could be; (c) design – determine what should be; (d) destiny – create what will be. Their process focuses on what is right with the organization rather than the problem. It also requires getting the whole system in the room to best understand the "positive core" of the organization and determine the future direction.

In addition, the processes can be implemented in different ways. The process consultation (Schein, 1999) approach is where the organization is actively involved in identifying the problem and generating a remedy. Other organization process approaches could involve confrontation meetings, or intergroup relations interventions either through a microcosm group or intergroup conflict negotiation (Cummings & Worley, 2005). Large group interventions (Bunker & Alban, 1997) are another mechanism for engaging in change processes. These processes include *Open Space Technology* (Owen, 1997), *Future Search* (Weisbord & Janoff, 2000), *The World Café* (Brown & Isaacs, 2005), and *The Appreciative Inquiry Summit* (Ludema, Whitney, Mohr, & Griffin, 2003).

What these change processes have in common is that they engage the members of the organization at a variety of levels. The merger of two or more organizations is probably the most radical change an organization can engage. In the decision and process to merge, are there processes and results that contribute to successful merger?

RESEARCH METHOD

A comparative case study approach (Eisenhardt, 1989; Yin, 2003) was chosen to guide the research. The intent was to build a grounded theory (Glaser & Strauss, 1967; Strauss & Corbin, 1998) that provided at least a partial answer to the question: "What makes mergers more successful in some men's religious communities than in others?" Eight merger organization cases were chosen for the study and the researcher embarked on listening deeply "to what the research participants (had) to say" (Auerbach & Silverstein, 2003, p. 15). He also wanted to leave room for serendipitous findings and for the research question and research focus to shift after the data collection had begun.

Data Collection

As a practitioner in the field of merging religious institutes, the researcher studied past and present clients for whom he was the organizational consultant and facilitator of the merger process. In addition, he also studied other merged organizations that employed other or no consultants. The organization's time lines range from having legally merged eight years ago to those currently completing the process of merging.

The sources of data include:

- Participant observation: Journal notes taken while facilitating the merger process in the organizations that were clients and as observer at meetings of others (Spradley, 1980).
- Interviews: Between three and seven members of each of the merged organizations were interviewed. Those interviewed were from different

premerger organizations and represent different populations (leadership, membership, member of the transition committee, etc.) (Creswell, 2007; Rubin & Rubin, 2005; Yin, 2003).

- Archival documents: A documentation review of the history of the decision to merge and the discussions that led to the choice of consultant and process (Creswell, 2007; Yin, 2003)
- Review of Internet correspondence, chat room discussions, and minutes of meetings/gathering that are posted (when utilized).

The organizations studied were identified in a variety of ways. A personal invitation to be a part of the study by the researcher based upon an existing or previous consultant relationship. In addition, the Conference of Major Superiors of Men (CMSM), a coordinating agency of men's Catholic religious congregations in the United States, issued an invitation through their members' Internet server to participate in this study. The director of CMSM also encouraged certain leaders of men's religious congregations who have been through merging processes to volunteer for the study. The final selection of the eight organizations was based on a willingness to participate, access to members for interviews, openness to share archival information, and opportunities for participant observation. The organizations were also limited to English-speaking groups in North America.

Table 1 charts the organizational cases, the number of provinces (distinct organizations) merging, the researcher's relationship/involvement with specific organizations, when the data were collected, the number of interviews, the participant observer hours as well as any archival or electronic data that were used in the study.

Implications for Merger/Acquisition Research

The most compelling reason why firms enter into a merger is the belief that by combining with other organizations they might be better able to reach their strategic goals more quickly and more economically (Buono, 2003). This reason could apply to both for-profit and not-for-profit as well as religious congregations. The difference is in the articulation of the strategic goals. For-profit goals are about achieving corporate growth, economies of scale, vertical integration, and diversification normatively tied to financial returns (Buono, 2003). Not-for-profit (Golensky & DeRuiter, 2002) and religious congregations' goals involve financial considerations as well but they are also often tied to other dimensions of organization life such as more effective witness, ministry, service, outreach, and future planning.

Table 1. Data Collection of Merger Cases.

Organization and Number of Members	Number of Provinces Merging	Researcher's Relationship to Organization	When Data Was Collected	Interviews	Participant Observation	Archival Data	Electronic Correspondence
A-300	Three	Organization consultant after decision to merge	One year after merger decision	Four	As facilitator for six months – 49 h	Previous records of meetings leading to merger	Minutes of planning meetings
B-250	Two	Organizational consultant leading to merger decision	During merger process	Three	As facilitator for seven months – 29 h	Previous legislation leading to merger conversation	Minutes of planning meetings
C-100	Two	Organizational consultant leading to merger decision	During merger process	Four	As facilitator for six months – 20 h	Previous records of meetings leading to my being retained	Minutes of planning meetings
D-130	Two (plus others)	Organizational consultant leading to merger decision	During merger process	Six	As facilitator for seven months – 25 h	Had previous documents from prior consulting	Minutes of planning meetings
E-325	Four	Organizational consultant leading to merger and post merger	Seven years after the merger	Four	As post merger facilitator – 10 hours	Received materials documenting merger process	Correspondence
F-160	Two (one had previously merged)	Organizational consultant during aspects of the merger	During the merger process	Four	As facilitator for decision making event – 35 h	Received previous documentation	Minutes of meetings and correspondence
G-600	Four	Researcher	Seven years after merger	Four	None	Previous records of premerger meetings	Correspondence
E-400	Three	Researcher	During merger process	Seven	As observer to planning meetings – 12 h	Intranet documentation	All material was available electronically

The research material on secular mergers is troubling. Cartwright and McCarthy (2005) quote statistics that "83% of all deals fail to deliver shareholder value and an alarming 53% actually destroy value" (p. 253). Despite seemingly favorable strategic, financial and operational assessments research suggests that mergers have less than a 50–50 chance of success (Buono & Bowditch, 2001; Pritchett, 1997). Executive turnover within the first five years is 70% (Cartwright & Schoenberg, 2006). Organizations experience "merger syndrome" where members feel stressed, angry, disoriented, frustrated, confused, and frightened (Marks & Mirvis, 1992, 1998). Most of corporate mergers are driven by leadership that has a unique perspective on the corporation's strategic goals and economic future, but sometimes fail to factor in the merger's impact on people and their performance. The negative effects may include increased uncertainty, a rise in stress and a decrease in satisfaction, commitment, and desire to stay with the organization and a lessening in perceptions of the organization's trustworthiness, honesty, and caring (Schweiger & Denisi, 1991).

Habeck, Kroger, and Tram (1999) write that the worst mistake is to leave employees without a sense of the goals and objectives of the merger. Communication is vital for employee understanding and buy in and early integration. Another pitfall from their perspective is that the merging organizations get caught in the details.

In the other extreme is a preoccupation with the psychological effects of a merger on employees. Brajkovich's (2001) executive commentary on Marks and Mirvis (2001) psychological preparation for mergers cautions about the concentration on the internal integration of a merger, which often results in the loss of an outward focus and the "dynamics of external excellence." Forgetting about the purpose of the merger, to increase strategic advantage has as much to do with merger failures as does ignoring the human side of mergers.

Some mergers are successful. Marks and Mirvis (2001) write that strategic and psychological preparation throughout the process encourages a positive result. An articulated strategic intent with clear criteria that leads to a careful search for an appropriate partner supports success. Attention to the psychological mindsets and opportunities for members involved in a merger to dialogue, express their hopes and concerns and learn coping tactics through workshops, facilitates the merging process. Another essential is commitment from top leadership "to set the proper tone, articulate principles of the integration and bring these principles to life in their own actions" (Marks & Mirvis, 2001). Other literature stresses the need for "strategic fit" (Stahl & Sitkin, 2005), which takes into consideration organizational culture, dominance, management style, and the social climate (capacity to build trust).

Case Studies Compared across Categories

The data were collected from the eight organizations and coded by the researcher and another coder (Table 2). A number of categories and subcategories concerning the merger processes emerged. The first category was the context of the merger process. Subcategories included data about the interaction of the organizations prior to merger and the nature of this interaction (positive–negative, leadership–membership, etc). Size differential of the organizations was another subcategory. What impact would smaller and larger groups have on the process? Though all the cases were clear that it was a merger between equals not all had the same number of members or resources. Who initiated the merger was yet another subcategory. Some of the mergers were initiated from outside forces, others from internal leadership or membership.

The second category had to do with the purpose of the merger. These varied from pragmatic resource and personnel allocation to lofty desires to renew or reanimate themselves as organizations. All were concerned about future viability should they remain as they were. A third category was the role of leadership in the merger process. A subcategory noted the interorganizational leadership collaboration during the process. Another focus was the role of an interprovincial steering committee for the merger process. The last subcategory was the role of an outside facilitator in the merger process.

The largest category was the engagement processes. A number of subcategories emerged under this category. The assembly or retreat of all the members in the merger process was a consideration and how often that occurred. Whether relationship building intentionally took place at the assemblies/retreats. Other focuses of gatherings especially on structural or financial issues. Were the members engaged in creating a new unified vision for the merger? Indicators whether appreciative/positive organizational processes were utilized. What communication mechanisms were utilized to keep all the members aware of what was happening? Were straw ballots utilized to access the organizations readiness to merge? Were other area groupings convened either by geography, age, or interest to further dialogue among members? Were invitations extended to other stakeholders during the process? Were there outside presenters educating the members on issues that impacted the merger? Indicators whether trust was present or enabled throughout the process.

Table 2. Categories Compared across Cases.

Categories	A	B	C	D	E	F	G	H
Context								
History of Interaction	Positive	Positive but limited	Positive at leadership level	Positive especially with coworkers	Formation	Positive long history	Positive at Leadership level	Limited
Size differential	One larger province of three	Equal size	Two larger provinces of four	One larger province of three	One slightly larger	Equal size	Two larger of the four	One larger
Initiation	International chapter (positive)	International leadership (distrustful)	International leadership (forceful)	International leadership (positive)	Members (positive)	Province leadership (resistance)	Province leadership (positive)	International leadership (forceful)
Purpose	For more effective ministry, diminishment, Canadian province bankrupt	Best effective use of resources (people, money, buildings) for the mission	Best way of mobilizing human resources for mission, diminishment	Insuring the future of the mission	An act of unity and an act of mission, reduction in numbers	Addressing the conventual presence on the East coast and visioning for the future	Refounding (spiritual renewal) and restructuring (realignment of structures)	Disagreement in purpose between the two –diminishment or greater clarity of mission
Leadership	Collaborated with each other	Collaborated with each other	Too forceful then realigned	Confusion/action	Avoidance	Supportive/divisive	Collaborated with each other	Conflictual
Interprovincial steering committee	Yes for various events	Yes	Yes as a tactic to enhance process	Yes with fulltime project director	Yes but was ineffectual	Yes, but was too forceful	Provincials were the committee	Councils were the committee until conflict
Facilitator	Yes	Yes	Yes	Internal	No then yes	Yes	Yes	For parts of the process (conflictual)

Table 2. (*Continued*)

Categories	A	B	C	D	E	F	G	H
Engagement processes								
Assembly/retreat of all members	Yes – 4 ×	Yes – 1 ×	Yes – 1 ×	Yes – 2 ×	Yes – 3 ×	Yes – 1 ×	Yes – 1 ×	Yes – 3 ×
Fostered relationship building	Yes	Yes	Yes	Yes	Yes	Yes	No	No
Focused on structural/ financial elements	No	No	No	Yes	Yes	Yes	Yes	Yes
Discussed vision	Yes	Yes	Yes	Yes	Yes	Yes	Yes (leadership's)	No
Appreciative processes	Yes	Yes	No	No	Yes	Yes	No	No
Communication mechanism	Email	Mail	Mail	Intranet	Mail	Mail	Mail	None
Straw ballot	Yes	Yes	Yes	Yes	Yes	Yes	no	Yes
Regional/age/ interest groups	Yes	No	Yes	Yes	Yes	Yes	Yes	No
Utilized outside presenters	Yes	No	Yes	No	Yes	No	No	Yes
Invited laity to be part of the process	Yes	No	No	Yes	No	No	No	No
Description of trust	Growing trust built over six years	Growing trust modeled by leadership	Slowly grew through conversations especially the smaller groups concern about being absorbed by the larger	Used humor to minimize and appreciate differences	When signs of movement were visible trust increased towards leadership and each other	Despite the long-term relationship there seemed to be suspicion	No opportunity to investigate trust among members, fear and possessiveness emerged later	Distrust among leaders and some members, wanted assurances

Unique aspects	Made the decision first and then worked out the details over time	Both provinces were initially in dialogue with other merger partners that did not move forward	Provincials were perceived as moving too fast	Dedicated project director who managed an intranet server for communication, clear involvement with lay co-workers	Momentum began with the grassroots membership, a large number of foreign members work and reside in the states	Provincials were driving the merger but not everyone was following, utilized a survey for feedback	It seems the provincials (and facilitator) were isolated from the concerns of the grassroots membership	One province had merged with another province six years earlier, lacked spiritual motivation for merging, corporate model
Descriptions of results	Described as "unity, sense of direction, new relationships, restructured hearts"	Described as a sense of hope, possibilities for the future	Described as fantastic spirit, culture of vocations, energy, and hope for the future	Described as new life and vitality, assurance that the mission will continue	Described as a greater awareness of international and cross-cultural membership as well as reconciliation and hope	Articulated a common vision	They restructured, but with discontent among some, no renewal of spirit	They made the decision, but felt they had no other choice
Indications of renewal	"Something transformative had happened to them"	"A renewed sense of the charism and a revived sense of hope for the future"	"There is new energy, hope and a willingness to embrace the future yet unknown"	"New life and vitality"	"Members have been reconciled and feel they have a new start"	"Focusing on the vision for Conventual Franciscan life on the East coast"	"Missed an opportunity"	"Merger is not a time to renew community life and spirit"

A further category highlighted aspects about the merger process that were unique to a particular organization. Another category noted the responses to how members described the "results of the merger." The last category collected statements about indications of renewal or transformative change as a result of the merger process. These last two categories served as indicators with the level of satisfaction or success in regards the merger results.

EMERGING FACTORS FOR SUCCESSFUL MERGERS

Using the research data organized into categories, certain factors emerged that could indicate what facilitates successful mergers. First, regardless of how the concept of merger came about or what past interactions were, a clear mission-driven purpose for merger that connects with the organization's founding purpose is essential for a merger to be successful. Second, leadership throughout the merger process must act authentically. Authentic actions by leaders are described as focused on the purpose for merger, actively engaged in the process, utilizing people and resources toward the process, and getting out of the way when their involvement is preventing effective dialogue. Third, inclusive engagement of all members in articulating the purpose, connecting it to a common vision, dialoguing about future possibilities, and building transparent relationships is critical.

What was further discovered is that these key factors alone do not predict success. What brings about successful mergers is how these key factors build trust within and between the different organizations' members. An agreed-upon, clear mission-driven purpose sets the stage for positive motivation to embark on the merger process. Leaders foster interorganizational trust through their positive behaviors, clear communication and inter-organizational relationships – in other words, through acting authentically. Three organizational leaders contemplating a merger engaged a consultant to facilitate their meetings. Their instructions to her were "if you begin to hear a lot of 'Bsing' we want you to call us on it." They were aware of their desire for merging as well as their own hesitation and ambivalence regarding the restructuring process but did not want to be an impediment to the process. At their very first meeting, the two leaders approaching the possibility of merger made a pact with each other. They promised that they would not place any conditions on the merger; everything was up for discussion. Institutions, locations, current financial structures – all were open for discussion, with agreement that there would be no covert wrangling going on behind the scenes. Engagement processes that provide opportunities to build both intermember trust and a common trust in a shared vision of the future accelerate the merger process. A high sense of trust can propel the members and possibly the whole organization into a renewal experience. Members of one organization committed themselves to four gatherings of all the members involved in the merger. During these events they told stories of their life and work. They entered into rituals together, dreamed of the future, and at the last gathering they were astonished by the unity they felt. Old organizational boundaries had collapsed. They describe this experience as an enlivenment, an emergence of hope for the future, a greater clarity of purpose, a sense of oneness. When this happens members are more generous, willing to move, change work positions and build relationships with others. They become more attractive to others, fostering a welcoming culture, and openness to creating a new work culture with others.

The reverse is also true. When the merger process did not have a clear, articulated purpose that members could embrace, there was mistrust and questioning why a merger was necessary or where the idea came from. The four leaders were convinced a merger of their four organizations was the right direction. They were new in their role as leaders and aware of the interminable previous discussions about merger by past administrations. They committed to moving forward. What they were not aware of was the mistrust among members of the different organizations. Some members were fearful of the financial condition of another organization. Another organization was perceived as more traditional in leadership style and culture. Some of the past leaders were not convinced that the timing of merger was right and undermined the process. Two other leaders were of opposite personalities, one an aggressive lawyer and the other a laid back nurturer. The demands of merging overwhelmed one and frustrated the other. One of the leaders, in the midst of merger discussions, tried to embark on a construction project before the merger without consulting the other leader. The news of this stopped merger conversations until international leadership and a consultant (also the researcher) intervened.

When leaders did not keep the purpose/vision as the focus or behaved inauthentically (conflictual, deceitful, noncommunicative, etc.) with other leaders and members, the merger process suffered. Engagement processes that never helped members build trusting relationships by sharing stories of value or never facilitated a dialogue about what a shared vision of the future would look like ended up with administrative restructuring but missed obtaining renewed hope and an enlivened spirit. One merger steering committee gathered all the members from four organizations at an assembly. They used the time to give reports from working committees on different aspects of their life. Because there were different practices the anxiety increased, especially when it came to the monthly amount paid to each member. They focused on the details without first discussing the big picture, a vision for the future of a new merged province.

The cases followed similar steps in the restructuring processes. The paradoxical finding is that some organizations were able to perceive a lack of trust or conflict present in one of the steps of the merger process. They identified it and adjusted the process. Others were not able to perceive the lack of trust or chose not to focus on the conflict and just plowed forward. Two leaders were verbally attacked at a meeting the year after a decision to move forward was agreed. It was obvious that nothing had happened. It also became obvious that the two leaders were not communicating and certainly not in agreement with each other. They argued about bringing in a consultant to assist them. Finally, after the strong feedback from members the leaders sprung into action, hired a consultant and made themselves available to move the merger process forward.

The process of merging provinces of Catholic men's religious communities is not a linear process. It is more like a dialogue or conversation that gets initiated and then grows, including more members in the conversation as it goes along. This methodology of growing inclusion means that you repeat steps already taken. If along the way the conversation breaks down, the process is slowed or even stuck. This can happen especially when the purpose of the merger is not clear, when leadership is not leading the process effectively or when engagement processes have not effectively included the members.

Two similar organizations had two very committed leaders moving the merger process forward. However, they were aware that members of their inner circle were not as equally supportive of the idea. Instead of dealing with the resistance they engaged a separate commission to move the process forward, acting covertly and keeping their associates in the dark. When they got wind of the activities and plans the two leaders and the commission were confronted, and a stalemate occurred. A consultant (also the researcher) mediated a conversation between all parties where the levels of mistrust were articulated. The confronting members were added to the commission as an attempt to include them in the preparation of an assembly of all the members. The tension, mistrust. and suspicion permeated the assembly even though a high majority of the members were ready for merger.

When engagement processes are successful, the conversation grows and takes on an energy of its own that lasts far beyond the formal decision to merge. Four leaders were ready to merge their organizations when they recognized high levels of resistance to their "pushing" restructuring.

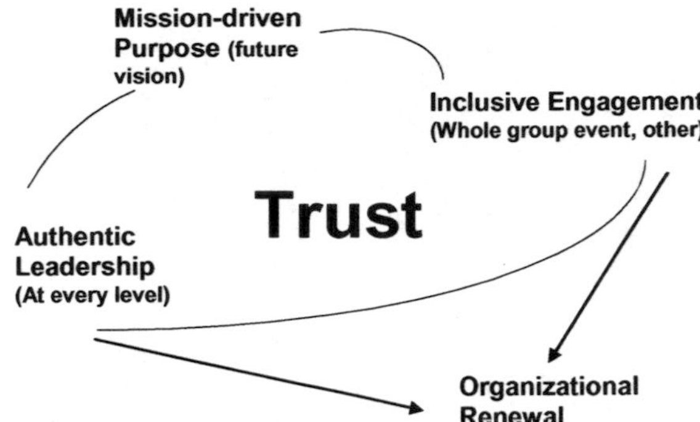

Fig. 1. Process in Mergers of Men's Religious Organizations. *Note:* Three key elements that spiral throughout the process, increasing member ownership and building organizational renewal.

They got out of the way, handing the work of merger conversations to a committee of respected members. Trust was restored by freeing up the conversation. Six years later, they still report a growing energy and spirit for the future of their new organization. They have consistently attracted new members throughout those years in higher proportion than most similar organizations.

Underlying the whole process is the building of trust at every level of the process. If merger partners begin with low trust at the beginning, perhaps because of previous histories, and this low level of trust is not addressed, the process can be sabotaged at an inopportune time. The diagram above graphically shows the process mergers can take (Fig. 1). The three key elements continue to interact and reinforce each other, building trust and including more members in the conversation. When trust is not built the process can slow or stop at any point.

Causal Relationships

Assessing the element of trust in the relationship between merger partners allowed authentic leadership to adjust the process and engage new processes to build trust (Fig. 2). This perception could have been from previous interaction. In some of the cases, perceived radical differences in cultures created fear of having to operate by another organization's values. Leaders characterized the differences with metaphors and made them public. One organization was nicknamed the Mavericks (they are unique and always

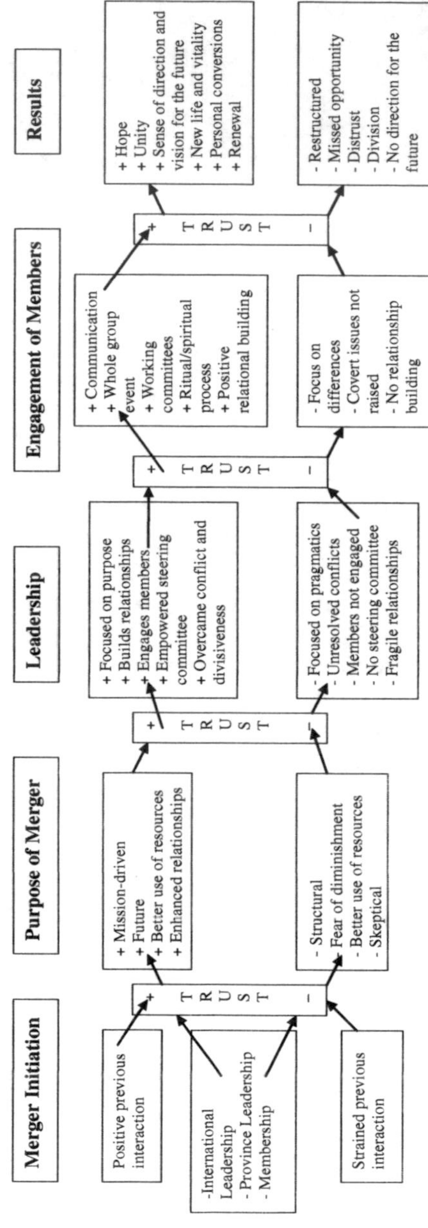

Fig. 2. Casual Relationship of Key Elements of Merger Process.

do things differently). Another was named the Marines (they are disciplined and follow orders from the top). The third was more difficult to name, they were somewhere between the Mavericks and the Marines. The metaphors created a humorous and safe way of addressing differences as well as the gifts each organization brought to the merger. Fear of cultural differences was replaced by trust and the merger was then able to move forward and look at a common purpose for merging.

Purpose of Merger

When the reason for the merger was for structural and pragmatic reasons alone, the motivation to merge translated into self-preservation and survival. The fear of diminishment communicated a strong message of negativity, blame, and failure. These organizations require a value and mission-driven reason for the merger. Realities within and without the organization cannot be ignored. However, the purpose for merger must be intimately connected to the organization's founding vision. Asking the question, "Why should we exist into the future?" is important. It is not about numbers or ages. Most of these groups were founded and refounded with only a few members. Merging provides an opportunity to revisit and reanimate the vision for a new time, resulting in a hoped for vision of a different future and mutual trust that, working together, these organizations could attain. This clarity of purpose is discerned by all the members, not just leadership or the merger coordinating committee. It connects with authentic leadership and inclusive engagement as both the invitation and the mechanism for engaging in conversations about the purpose for a merger. It sets the stage, direction, and motivating force for the merger process. In the absence of a compelling reason to merge, alternative motives are assumed. These motives focus on financial inequities and the need for monies or the inability to fulfill pension requirements. These and other assumptions fuel gossip and add suspicion and distrust to the process.

Three organizations embraced a common vision for restructuring as "an urgent call to transform minds and hearts to facilitate new life in mission and ministry." This vision permeated all their conversations and became a mantra of sorts. It engaged members for personal renewal but also for greater effectiveness in service. They lived into their articulated and shared vision. Another organization, on the other hand, had no vision other than to get the administrative restructuring done with the least amount of interruption to their lives. One of the partners in a merger had a "strategic plan" and was not interested in starting over with a merger partner who they felt would not value their plan. The merger process was plagued with tension.

Authentic Leadership

Authentic leadership emerges from a collection of attributes that leaders embody. Leaders in the mergers of the organizations studied have shown authentic leadership when they have focused on what is best for the future of the organization's vision, lived out in their situation over and above their own personal issues. These leaders had the freedom to ask the hard questions about the future, transparently communicate the reality of personnel and resources, and hold before their members a hopeful future. They were able to balance the mission/cultural focus of merging with the business/financial realities. Having done their research, they were not promising more than what was realistic, but were also not letting bottom line concerns dictate their future. Authentic leaders both led and walked with the member's ongoing conversations about a clear purpose for the merger and their involvement in creating the new. They modeled authenticity in the way in which they engaged with leaders and members of merger partners as well as with their own members (especially those who may not have agreed with them). Authentic leaders were sensitive to the fears and concerns of the most vulnerable members and provided assurance. They could see when they were blocking the process because of their role or personality and got out of the way. They recognized the emergence of tension or conflict and took the responsibility as leaders to deal and resolve the conflictual issues. Authentic leaders chose the members with the right gifts and reputation to steer the merger process. They supported the merger steering committee and interrelated with them. They were not threatened by the success or creativity of the merger committee. Authentic leadership invested in facilitation, intranet providers, and other resources that fostered communication and built trust among those engaged in the merger process.

Authentic leadership plays a pivotal role in successful mergers. How leaders enter into the merging process has an impact on the organizations involved (Sitkin & Pable, 2005). *Managers'* expectations during initial stages of cooperation – in terms of the level of trust and distrust that they hold toward their partners – have a major impact on the development of these relationships in later stages. This stems from their influence on formal coordination and control, interorganizational performance, and the favorability with which managers interpret the behavior of their partners (Vlaar, Van den Bosch, & Volberda, 2007). Trust and distrust develop along self-reinforcing paths; starting conditions leave strong imprints on the development of cooperative relationships. The way the process begins will have an influence throughout the merger and into the future. Leaders can influence the success of a merger by the decisions and actions they make.

Inclusive Engagement

Inclusive engagement broadened the conversation so that every member had an opportunity to ask questions and give their opinion. Engagement was gradual, often beginning with a small group and broadening to include others. Whole group events, where all the members were engaged in cross organizational dialogue in the same place, were essential to inclusive engagement for these groups. One organization with three merger partners held four such events. Another group felt that if they had held more than one whole group event the process of merging would have gone more quickly. The focuses of successful whole group events were dialogues around the purpose of merger and processes to build relationships and trust among members. Members needed the opportunity to envision the future possibilities, see the agreement among diverse stakeholders, and build relationships with members who shared common values. When this occurred there was a gradual internalization of the new entity they were moving toward. When the engagement was focused on outside speakers or structural and pragmatic differences in organizational cultures, members left the events with more questions, more concerns and a greater fear of differences overall.

Positive Inclusive Engagement

Two mergers that had the highest indicators of success utilized positive/affirmative processes as they dialogued about a possible merger. Other mergers also utilized these processes. Two mergers did not use these particular processes but were also more successful than others. They did engage in storytelling, ritual remembering, focused conversations, and "time to just talk." Creating a positive climate and focusing on positive conversations seemed to create positive communication, relationships, and emotions that were contagious (Cameron, 2008), though some more than others. Some of the differences can be correlated with other factors. Past interaction of the merging groups and their experience of trust over suspicion as well as the perceived effectiveness of the leaders by the members colored the effectiveness of positive processes. When the members thought that the leaders had an "agenda" it was difficult for them to enter into positive/appreciative approaches. Interviewees in the more successful merged organizations recounted how they had focused on what they had in common rather than their differences.

Four of the organizations utilized aspects of "appreciative inquiry" (Cooperrider & Srivastva, 1987) for parts of their merger process. Their assemblies became appreciative summits (Ludema et al., 2003) where they engaged each other in conversations, inquiring into the positive core of their organization. Others did positive storytelling to work through cultural differences and build positive relationships. When a positive approach was utilized in the early conversations of mergers, the impact was felt throughout the process. Frederickson's "broaden and build theory" holds that "the momentary unpredictability characteristic of positive states over time yields resilience that allows people to flexibly adapt to inevitable crises" (Frederickson, Tugade, Waugh, & Larkin, 2003).

Positive emotions can also predict whether people will flourish or languish as individuals, relationships or large organizations.

> Human flourishing is optimal functioning characterized by four key components: (a) goodness, indexed by happiness, satisfaction, and superior functioning; (b) generativity, indexed by broadened thought-action repertoires and behavioral flexibility; (c) growth, indexed by gains in enduring personal and social resources; and (d) resilience indexed by survival and growth in the aftermath of adversity. (Frederickson & Losada, 2005, p. 685)

The organization with the most indicators of success utilized positive/appreciative processes in assemblies as well as regional gatherings. When it came to their first legislative assembly as a new entity they were faced with a shortage of members who could attend the meeting and therefore legally operate as a group of the whole. They had to resort to a delegate meeting where the decision making power resided in a much smaller group. This first appeared to the members as a step back, a lack of inclusion. The elected delegates' first action was to state that they would abide by all the decisions that are made by the whole group. They gave their political power over to the 140 members gathered. This spontaneous surrender to the conversations of the larger group had become normative. They met the crisis and responded with resiliency modeling their growth in trust and relationship as a result of the merger process. The meeting progressed and the group was able to discuss and agree upon significant criteria as their future focus, empowering leadership to positively lead them into their new future. Cooperrider and Sekerka (2003) indicate that positive organizational change involves three stages: the elevation of inquiry, the fusion of strengths, and an activation of energy.

> There are movements toward inclusion and intimacy, as well as changes in affect, language and awareness. New patterns of communicating and relating emerge, which appear to ellipse and dissipate prior means. As participants let go of the problem focus, there is room for positive conversation. This is especially notable when people collaboratively create a new vision, name their idea, and map out how it can come to fruition. (Cooperrider & Sekerka, 2003, p. 232)

The organization described is a case study on the theory of the change possibilities that can be accomplished through consistent positive inquiry, recognition, and fusion of members' strengths and the resulting energy.

TRUST

An insight that emerged from the research data was the role that trust played in the merger process. At every step of the process trust or the lack of trust was mentioned. It became clear that there was a correlation between the elements of the process and trust.

> Simply put, trust means confidence. The opposite of trust – distrust is *suspicion*. When you trust people you have confidence in them – in their integrity and in their abilities. When you distrust people, you are suspicious of them – of their integrity, their agenda, their capabilities, or their track record. It's that simple. We have all had experiences that validate the difference between relationships that are built on trust and those that are not. These experiences clearly tell us the difference is not small; it is dramatic. (Covey, 2006, p. 5)

Rousseau, Sitkin, Burt, and Camerer define trust as a "psychological state comprising the intention to accept vulnerability based upon positive expectations of the intentions or behavior of another" (1998, p. 395). Conversely, distrust can be defined as negative expectations of another's intentions or behavior (Lewicki, McAllister, & Bies, 1998; Sitkin & Roth, 1993).

In reviewing the data, the researcher discovered positive and negative indications of trust at various stages of the merger process (Table 3). In two of the cases trust was experienced throughout. This does not mean that there were not differences among members but that the differences did not dominate the process or stop the process. In others it was experienced as a negative

Table 3. Indicators of Trust in the Merging Process (from Data Collected).

Trust Throughout Merger Process	A	B	C	D	E	F	G	H
Initiation/ previous interaction	Positive trust with international leadership and across provinces T	Positive trust between provinces, skeptical of international leadership T	Positive trust between provincials and international leadership T	Positive trust with some concern of different sizes of provinces	Positive trust, with some past negative experiences, member initiated	Positive trust and interaction with some suspicion	Positive trust between provincials and most members T	Philosophical and ethnic divisions for years – strongly pushed by international leadership
Purpose	Common purpose from members T	Common purpose from members T	Grew into a common purpose after concerns were addressed	Common purpose from members T	Common purpose from members T	Common purpose from members T	Common purpose articulated by leadership	Did not agree upon the purpose for merging
Leadership	Worked effectively, avoided conflict T	Began with no – nonnegotiables, worked effectively together T	Distrust between members and leaders – moving too quickly, created a new steering committee	Conflict among leaders that led to an appointment of a project director who got the process back on track	Leaders did not follow through; new steering committee and facilitator got process back on track	Provincials and councils in conflict over merger process and timeline	Provincials were the steering committee and not aware of conflict with some members	Major conflict between provincial councils over decisions and style, members became involved in the conflict
Engagement	Four assemblies grew trust T	One assembly surfaced trust T	One assembly and other small group gatherings created trusting conversations T	Two assemblies and transparent communication grew relation-ships and trust T	One assembly and yearly retreats built trust after a confrontation of leaders T	One assembly addressed issues and surfaced suspicion	One assembly that focused on structural issues and differences	Two assemblies that were input and educational
Results	Unity, something transformative had happened T	Revived sense of hope for the future T	New energy, hope and a willingness to embrace the future yet unknown T	New life and vitality, assurance that the mission will continue T	Reconciled members, cross-cultural awareness, hope T	Sense of moving forward, a common vision but more information needed	Restructured with some discontent and tension	Made the decision with the need for assurances from each other (lack of trust)

Note: T indicates the acknowledgement and presence of trust between merging provinces.

initially, but actions by authentic leadership or the inclusive engagement process were able to build trust. Leadership of three of the mergers all experienced or created conflict and confusion either among themselves or with members. Two of the organizational leaders solved the issue by getting out of the way. They created another committee to steer the process or secured a project director to lead the process. In another organization the leaders did the opposite; they finally got involved and secured competent resources in a consultant and better working committee. These interventions impacted the perceived results of the merger. They moved a mistrusting atmosphere to a greater trusting one. In another case where trust was not present at any level of the merger process the decision to move forward was made but the memory of the last assembly was a shouting match of "what more do you want from us?", indicating a tremendous amount of frustration.

The cases where distrust was more operative than trust were also identified as the least successful. Those where trust was mentioned at every step were also seen as the happiest with their results. The two areas where trust seemed to break down were with leadership and in relation to previous interaction/initiation of the merger. In three of the cases leadership was able to recognize the lack of trust and seek to restore it. One leadership group realized that another group needed to be steering the merger and not themselves. They appointed "respected" and "trusted" members to lead the process. This shift restored trust and removed the threat that leadership was forcing the merger process. Another leadership group found themselves in conflict about how to move forward. They identified a mutually agreeable "project director" and assigned him to lead the process full time. This got the process back on track and fostered transparent communication. The third leadership group simply dropped the ball. They expected the steering committee to move forward but the committee fell apart. Members challenged leadership for their inactivity and lack of movement. The leaders hired an outside consultant, created a new steering committee, and promised to be available to the merger process putting it back on track. Trust was restored by authentic leadership, knowing the reality and making the appropriate adjustments.

Central to trust and implied in both definitions is risk and vulnerability (Stickel, 1999). Risk means that one side of the trusting relationship could experience a negative outcome if the other side is untrustworthy. "The risk of negative outcomes must be present for trust to operate, and the trustor must be willing to be vulnerable. In the absence of risk, trust is irrelevant because there is no vulnerability" (Stahl & Sitkin, 2005, p. 84). In the mergers studied, the more successful mergers had a positive expectation that something better would occur. Even with differences in size, culture, and resources the hoped for outcome overshadowed the possible vulnerability of being subsumed by the other. This occurred by acknowledging the differences but also by highlighting the similarities and gains.

Rousseau et al. suggests a "bandwidth" of trust; within that bandwidth trust can take on one of three forms or mix several forms together. They describe "calculus-based trust" which is based on rational choice, an economic exchange, and the perception that an action performed will be beneficial. Then there is "relational trust" that results from repeated interactions over time. "Reliability and dependability in previous interactions with the trustor give rise to positive expectations about the trustee's intention" (Rousseaue et al., 1998). Emotion often enters into this trust because of the interaction and attachment that evolves, creating reciprocated interpersonal care and concern. The third form is "institutional trust" where there are societal controls that support the development of trust. This trust can foster or inhibit relational and calculus-based trusts. It can provide a safe context, which monitors possible harm or it can give rise to too rigid controls that undermine trust. In any event, their study on trust "leads us to conclude that context is critical to understanding trust"(Rousseau et al., 1998, p. 42). When relational trust was built, creating interpersonal care and concern among the members for some greater purpose, the mergers resulted in renewing and emotional experiences. When calculated benefits or institutional parameters were the focus, the mergers were less successful.

Trust seems to play a key role premerger, during the process of merger, and in the integration process following a merger (Stahl & Sitkin, 2005). The authors draw upon the large body of research on intra- and interorganizational trust. Their research indicates that trust is important in a number of ways: it can improve the quality of employee work performance, problem solving, and communication, and can enhance employee commitment and citizenship behavior. Manager–subordinate relationships can be improved by trust as can the implementation of self-managed work groups. Trust can increase the organizations' ability to adapt to complexity and change. Further, trust can decrease agency and transaction costs by limiting the need for monitoring and control and, ultimately, can provide firms with a competitive advantage (Stahl & Sitkin, 2005). Covey (2006) writes that when trust is high, the dividend you receive is like a performance multiplier, elevating and improving every dimension of your organization and your life. High trust is like the leaven in bread, which lifts everything around it. In a company, high trust improves communication, collaboration, execution, innovation, strategy, engagement, partnering, and relationships.

In your personal life, high trust significantly improves your excitement, energy, passion, creativity, and joy in your relationships with family, friends, and community. Building a culture of trust among members and leaders can have far-reaching effects during the merger of men's Catholic provinces. It appears that trust releases an untapped energy among members in an organization that has a significant impact on the future of that organization.

Five characteristics are offered by Stahl and Sitkin (2005) that affect trust in a merger.

- Takeover friendliness, which is interpreted as a cooperative mode versus a hostile takeover.
- Power equality between the organizations that does not result in a domination or superiority–inferiority attitude. Power asymmetry is important.
- Relative target firm performance that will provide greater assurance and hope for the members of a combined new entity.
- Cultural similarity where shared values or other similarities facilitate the development of trust
- Positive interaction history where trust has evolved over time and reinforces norms of equity.

In their research they discovered that not all five are equally important. The attractiveness of the performance and policies of the other organization rated first. Secondly, the interaction history influenced respondents trust decisions (Stahl & Sitkin, 2005). This can be related to premerger positive interaction of the cases used in this study along with a clear mission-driven purpose that is shared by all the members as indicators of success.

In the two less successful cases, there were issues between leaders and among members of the different provinces that were not or could not be surfaced. Marshak (2006) refers to these as "covert processes." He writes that there are six dimensions that are always involved in organizational change: reasons, politics, inspirations, emotions, mindsets, and psychodynamics. Reason is "overt"; the remaining five are frequently "covert" despite their impact on change. He describes "covert processes … to mean any hidden or unconscious dynamic" (Marshak, 2006, p. 1). The logical reason for a merger is often the easiest to determine. Financial and people resources can be explained with numerical facts. Yet, there are other dimensions that are not as easy to explain that can certainly affect trust. Politics of an organization often have to do with people's own needs and what they will get out of or not get out of – a planned merger. "Inspiration speaks to the aspects of people that want to do good things, want to be part of something bigger than themselves, and want to see their values, hopes and dreams fulfilled" (Marshak, 2006, p. 8). Change automatically brings with it emotion. Often it is negative emotions of fear, anger, or sadness. When these are not made overtly they can undermine trust. Mindsets are people's "paradigms or worldviews that prevent people from imagining possibilities that exist out of their unexamined assumptions" (Marshak, 2006, p. 12). Lastly, there are psychodynamic responses to change that remain covert. These are unconscious defenses against anxiety that get triggered by organizational change. In the two mergers that were less successful there are indications that covert processes were at work. In one merger one organization considered the other organization to be administratively inept, they wanted assurance that none of their members would serve in a leadership capacity in the new entity. This could not be said publicly, but the tension this mindset caused was palpable. In another merger one organization had a fear of losing its identity should they join with three others. They were critical of financial handlings of another organization and the conservativeness of another. These unarticulated feelings created an underground fear causing this group to quietly tolerate the process, but when it came for them to decide they raised strong objections, which came close to sabotaging the merger. The processes of these two mergers did not allow the organizations to allow the rational and especially the covert processes to emerge in a safe and trusting way. An absence of addressing the inspiration, the emotion, and the psychodynamic left their process unfinished and the members feeling as if they had missed something. In the end, it is not about eliminating the covert processes but accounting and adjusting for them. In the more successful mergers anxiety about cultural differences were made overt through humor and stories. The differences were seen as complementary and enriching as opposed to threatening.

Trust Leading to Member Self-Determined Decision

Unique to the merger/restructuring processes of these men's religious congregations is the fact that in most cases the members get a democratic vote for pursuing this direction. Another unique aspect is that the members are merging their entire lives not just their work lives. A majority or consensus of individual members was needed to go forward. Some of the groups reached consensus while others settled for a majority. Negative voices were present in most of the discussions yet they varied by organization. The spiraling effect of buy-in, beginning with a small group and spreading to an ever-increasing larger population as meetings progressed, seemed a pattern. Some groups spontaneously reached a unanimous decision. When trust was high the decision came easily. Trusting relationships mitigated the risk and vulnerability of a merger. When there was a lack of trust of leaders or members of another organization the process inched along until there was a breakthrough in increased trust or an outside force drove the process to a conclusion.

These merger processes are decisions of "self-determination," accomplished member by member. Ryan and Deci (2000) developed a self-determination theory to explore what makes human beings proactive and engaged or alternately passive and alienated. Their discovery is that self-determination is largely a function of the social conditions in which people develop and function. There are factors that support or forestall the natural processes of motivation. They have identified three psychological needs that are the basis for self-motivation. These needs are autonomy, competence, and relatedness. Autonomy (not to be confused with individualism) suggests an inner endorsement of one's actions. The more autonomous the behavior, the more it is endorsed by the whole self, and where the action is seen as that which one is responsible for. Autonomy gives people the choice to create, and to lead. Competence supports autonomy with a sense of having the skills, abilities, and capacity to succeed. Competence helps the person realize that the action is attainable and one has the necessary resources to engage in it. The third element is relatedness, the sense of belonging and connectedness to others. The action has an impact on others who will benefit and with those others, and I will benefit as well. The action will result in a greater good for all involved. When the inclusive engagement processes for the mergers built upon the members' ability to create the future, engage their skills and competence, and build relational connections across province boundaries, they were ready to say yes to a merger.

Research indicates that motivation that is more authentic (self-authored and endorsed) results in greater performance, persistence, creativity, and self-esteem (Ryan & Deci, 2000). When the members of the organizations studied felt as if they were being coerced to choose restructuring, tremendous resistance was experienced. One merger process had to create a new steering committee with members that were "trusted" by the membership and begin the dialogue anew because of the strong feeling of the merger being pushed from the top down. This new steering committee saw their role as facilitating a conversation among the members so they could choose freely by seeing the benefits of such a decision. They created the container for autonomy, competence, and relatedness among the members so that a determination to move forward could happen. The successful mergers were ones where the members felt empowered, included and given the resources in the context of communal dialogue to decide the course of events. They personally became convinced that merger was the right decision for them and for their organization.

Trust and Self-Determination in the Cases Researched

In all eight mergers there were multiple occasions where trust was a factor. It appeared especially within the key factors of merging; clarity of purpose, leadership roles, and engagement processes. Stories were told about suspicion of international leadership's motivation for the initiation of a merger. Previous histories were recounted where possible merger partners remembered inequities in past dealings and questioned the reason for the merger. Leaders often backed off from dealings with other leaders, dropped the ball, or attempted to make last minute decisions before the merger, creating trust tension. Members distrusted leaders or merger coordinating committees. Some felt the facilitator was not objective in the process. The merger partners were not equal in size or resources, which raised concern about being taken over. Financial accounting processes were different, with one organization allowing the local community more control while others had a more centralized system, and this impacted trust. Cultural differences expressed in spiritual practices as well as other personal and community practices were threatening. Lastly, the perceptions of the members themselves toward each other often held unprocessed assumptions and fantasies. With all these possibilities of a breakdown in trust (and more) what allowed some to claim that their merger was a success? What blocked others from experiencing success?

Connecting Purpose/Charism with Authentic Leadership and Inclusive Engagement that Built Trust

It appears that the organizations that entered into engagement processes of deep exploration and conversation about their core "meaning" experienced a renewal of their initial calling. Those who ignored these conversations in lieu of more pragmatic discussions and encounters missed an opportunity for renewal of their charism. The most successful merger focused on positive and appreciative storytelling of their core meaning in action, what it meant to have restructured minds and hearts, what new life in mission would look like. These conversations revived memories of success and "best practices" and built connections and relationships among the merger partners. They found themselves living what they professed. Other provinces did not focus on their charism and along with not building trusting relationships they failed to revive a sense of purpose and hope among the members. One organization professed to be gentle, loving, humble, relational, inclusive, and merciful men. None of these qualities were included in their merging dialogue. Had they been included, the process and results would certainly have been different.

At the core of the organizations studied are foundational stories, histories, and purposes for increasing the meaning of life for themselves and for others. When they revisited their purpose and applied it to the possible vision for a merger, they not only rewrote their future vision but began to live into it.

INTERPRETATIONS OF RESULTS

For these organizations, their founding story is all important. It holds their vision, the reason for their existence. In all cases it is outward and mission focused, yet calling for an ongoing renewal of the members. Focusing on their founding purpose and reframing it for the future created change. Some referred to the merger process as a reeducation process, a return to their formational experience. For many it was the first time in generations that they had become so focused on who they were and what difference they were meant to be in the world. Their founding vision became something that they actually reappropriated. It became alive and full of meaning for them in the process of the merger. Sammon (2003), writing about religious men in the United States, indicates that these organizations have been experiencing an identity crisis for more than 30 years. Religious life had become ambiguous. Their self-understanding had become too all encompassing. For some of the cases the merger process provided an experience for clarity and direction, not only at an intellectual level but at an emotional and spiritual level. It led in some to a personal and organizational renewal. For the successful mergers this was the advantage and gift of the merger.

Individual Conversion and Organizational Renewal: A Result of a Successful Merger

The members of successful mergers speak of themselves as being changed, and the organization being changed by the process of merger.

The engagement of the members in conversations of purpose, value, and meaning, along with the building of deeper relationships, led to renewal personally and organizationally. Robertson, Roberts, and Porras (1993) write that the nature of the work setting, the central role of individual behavior, and organizational outcomes are intimately connected features. "Change in individual organizational members' behavior is at the core of organizational change" (Robertson et al., 1993, p. 6). One way of evaluating individual change is through "conversion stories," where individuals tell their stories and indicate a marked shift in perception of themselves and the organization. Bryant and Cox (2004) used this methodology to understand how employees talked about their experience of organizational change. They examined pre- and postconversion stories. Conversion stories are defined as a change that leads an individual from "one view point to another" (Snow & Machalek, 1983, p. 169), from an "old" way of life in order to embrace a new and much better life (Zinnbauer & Pargament, 1998). Marlett (1997) suggests three factors for conversion: a deconversion from what one believes a faith toward what one is being converted to, and the continuities between the two. It involves a person's preexistent behaviors and attitudes. A change in the worldview of the person determines the conversion. Conversion requires a letting go so as to embrace something else. Mergers require that members let go of many aspects of a previous identity. Size, geography, ethnic roots, leadership structures, and relationships are but a few of the areas that are relinquished. What makes this possible is a "conversion" to embrace something new, to see the future different from the past and probably most of all an enkindling of hope.

Rambo (1993) writes, "a stage model is appropriate in that conversion is a process of change over time, generally exhibiting a sequence of processes, although there is sometimes a spiraling effect – a going back and forth between stages" (pp. 16–17). The stages he proffers begin with "context," an awareness of thc environment in which you find yourself. "Crisis" provides an opportunity for a new option. "Quest" is the human condition that seeks solutions to problems and strives for meaning and purpose. "Encounter" brings people together to search together. "Interaction" provides intense levels of learning at both the intellectual and spiritual level. "Commitment" is the decision to surrender along with an empowerment to the new possibility. "Consequence" is when the conversion calls for new actions, new sense of mission and purpose significantly different than before. Each of the merger processes went through stages, described earlier as cyclic or spiraling. When they were faithful to the process a new commitment and new actions by members and the organizations resulted.

A greater consciousness develops by intentionally reexamining the roots, purposes, memories, and founding stories of the organization. Members begin to remember and explore why they are a member and perhaps begin a process of recommitting to each other, the founding charism and religious values. The spiral stages of dialogue can create not only a new awareness but generate new energy, hope, and excitement for the future.

In the stories of the men interviewed, the high moments of the restructuring processes were ritual moments that took place in whole event gatherings. The combination of ritual moments with the visual realization that these are all the members – the future gathered – had a stirring effect. Interviewees recounted stories and experiences of standing for a straw vote and recognizing that everyone was standing. Testimonies given by older members and younger members and realizing a common bond. Discussions about what kind of preferred future they envisioned to realize that another confrere imagined the same, even though they just met. Retelling the story of their life to a new listener and coming to the awareness of the patterns that had been present leading to a sense of trust of the future as well. Some members who were disenfranchised or burned out found new possibilities, freedom, and a new start in a restructured organization.

Though much of the process of restructuring/merger involves a focus on the positive and strengths of the members and organizations, it also involves a letting go, a reconciling of the past, a deepening trust, and a common vision of the possibilities for the future. Most of all, it requires risk. Risk is an essential aspect of trust. Risk is found in these organizations' founding stories, which have their roots in a renewal experience of their founders and early members. Restructuring was another invitation to risk (and therefore trust) for the members and organizations. The risks involved an awareness of diminishing numbers, resources, and unequal power bases. Only an experience of self-surrender helped some of the organizations embrace the risk. In an initial meeting between two leadership groups looking to merge their organizations, the leaders began with stating, "there are no non-negotiables" for us, as we begin "everything is up for discussion!" That spirit created trust immediately. In another merger one organization was bankrupt because of litigation. The other two organizations saw it as a nonissue, but rather a reason to merge, so as to continue to minister in their geographic area. Other organizations that were not as open or chose not to explore the possibility of renewal settled for insurance against the risks. They negotiated leadership models, finances, and ministry commitments so as to minimize the merger impact. It was more difficult for them to "recrystallize" around something new.

Organizations moving toward restructuring or merger can settle for rearranging structures and not pursue renewal. Pragmatic realities slightly modified but still recognizable, are safer than totally new ways of being in relationship and in mission. The organizations that had a history of independent ministries staffed by their members had a greater task of redirecting the focus of the members to a corporate vision for the future. Their attitude was, It's alright to restructure but don't bother me. Groups with a greater corporate sense of their mission, perhaps because of investment in institutions or a clearer focus of their ministry seemed more pliable on how the ministry could look differently in the future. The institutions became a challenge and an opportunity. There was concern for staffing and funding into the future. The opportunity was to imagine new ways of staffing and new collaborative relationships with coworkers and other organizations.

Organizational Renewal

Mitchell Marks (2007) writes "The capacity for a transition to disrupt the current equilibrium and jar people from their status quo – that is, to unfreeze them – also gives transitions the potential to be an impetus for renewal at both the organizational and individual levels" (Lewin, 1947, p. 723). Facilitating renewal for Marks involves empathy for those experiencing the transition, engagement by involving the members in the transition, energy in identifying new creativity, and possibilities and enforcement, the facilitating of consistent adaptation. These steps in a posttransition context continue the renewal process.

Bridges (2003) believes that there is a developmental course to organizational life – that there are normal stages all organizations go through – and each has corresponding behaviors. When an organization encounters "problems" it is not a matter of fixing the organization but rather taking the organization back "to the start of its life cycle" (Bridges, 2003, p. 87). This involves the recovery of the youthful vigor that the organization had earlier in its lifecycle.

Bridges describes the organizational life cycle as beginning with "dreaming the dream," then "launching the venture," "getting organized," "succeeding," and "becoming an institution." At this point in the developmental cycle organizations have a choice. They can close in on themselves and eventually die or take the path of renewal. This developmental cycle fits the path of the mergers described. The successful mergers and the unsuccessful mergers can be characterized by whether they had "renewed" themselves or not.

Renewal for Bridges has three characteristics:

- Redreaming the dream: a revisiting of the founding purpose and claiming a central idea upon which the organization will build its activities into the future
- Recapturing the venture spirit: freeing up the behaviors, roles, and structures from the way they had been operating to a freer more open engagement
- Getting reorganized: remodeling the structures and policies of the organization, recovering the elements of a successful organization from earlier stages.

These characteristics throw the organization into a major transition, or crisis, the alternative of closing in and dying. Mergers provide an opportunity for the path of renewal. The identified indices of mission-driven purpose, authentic leadership, and inclusive engagement are new ways of operating in old structures. They can be the development stages that lead to renewal. In Catholic men's religious congregations, the renewal is at a personal level as well as an organizational level. The two are intimately connected. There is no guarantee that all the members are capable of embarking on the renewal path. However, when a significant portion of the members makes the choice the results can bring new life, hope, and an enlivened purpose for the future.

CONCLUSION

It appears that a variety of processes facilitate organizational change and transformation and subsequently can be used for mergers of organizations. The critical learning from this research is that the processes need to focus on a common mission-driven vision, leadership involvement characterized by authentic practices, and engagement of all the members in the process. Even beyond these three areas of attention is how these processes build trust among the leadership, members, and organizations. These particular organizations, because of their life commitment, need to be part of the choice for merger. Yet choosing to merge can be a pragmatic reality based upon demographic and financial data or a choice for new life, renewal, and organizational transformation. The key seems to be in the building of trusting relationships that lead to a hope filled future vision together. When processes lead to trusting dialogue and determination of a merger a further organizational renewal can occur.

Literature on mergers and acquisitions support the need for a shared vision of the new reality and leadership who model the possibility for a new merged relationship. Engagement processes are encouraged for all employees but not always possible because of geography or organizational size. Yet, the results of this study indicate that as much positive engagement as possible, which builds interorganizational as well as intermember trust, has benefits to the success of the merger.

Further research should include applying the dynamics of these mergers to for profit organizations. Determining if there is a tipping point of involvement for larger organizations is another research possibility. Clearly, where the retention of members is critical, involvement in a merger cannot happen only at a leadership level but also include membership.

REFERENCES

Armenakis, A., & Bedeian, A. (1999). Organizational change: A review of theory and research in the 1990s. *Journal of Management*, *25*(3), 293–315.

Armenakis, A., Harris, S., & Feild, H. (1999). Paradigms in organizational change: Change agent and change target perspectives. In: R. Golembiewski (Ed.), *Handbook of organizational behavior*. New York: Marcel Dekker.

Auerbach, C. F., & Silverstein, L. B. (2003). *Qualitative data*. New York: New York University Press.

Bandura, A. (1986). *Social foundations of thought and action: A social cognitive theory*. Englewood Cliffs, NJ: Prentice-Hall.

Brajkovich, L. F. (2001). Executive commentary on Mitchell Lee Marks and Philip H. Mirvis, Making mergers and acquisitions work: Strategic and psychological preparation. *Academy of Management Executive*, *15*(2), 92–94.

Bridges, W. (2003). *Managing transitions* (2nd ed.). Cambridge, MA: Perseus Books.

Brown, J., & Isaacs, D. (2005). *The world café*. San Francisco, CA: Berrett-Koehler Publishers.

Bryant, M., & Cox, J. W. (2004). Conversion stories as shifting narratives of organizational change. *Journal of Organizational Change Management*, *17*(6), 578–592.

Bunker, B. B., & Alban, B. T. (1997). *Large group interventions*. San Francisco, CA: Jossey-Bass.

Buono, A. F. (2003). SEAM-less post-merger integration strategies: A cause for concern. *Journal of Organizational Change Management*, *16*(1), 90–98.

Buono, A. F., & Bowditch, J. L. (2001). *The human side of mergers and acquisitions*. Washington, DC: Beard Books.

Cameron, K. (2008). *Positive leadership*. San Francisco, CA: Berrett-Koehler.

Cartwright, S., & McCarthy, S. (2005). Developing a framework for cultural due diligence in mergers and acquisitions. In: G. K. Stahl & M. E. Mendenhall (Eds), *Mergers and acquisitions*. Stanford, CA: Stanford Business Books.

Cartwright, S., & Schoenberg, R. (2006). Thirty years of mergers and acquisitions research: Recent advances and future opportunities. *British Journal of Management*, *17*, S1–S5.

Cooperrider, D. L., & Sekerka, L. E. (2003). Toward a theory of positive organizational change. In: K. S. Cameron, J. E. Dutton & R. E. Quinn (Eds), *Positive organizational scholarship*. San Francisco, CA: Berrett-Koehler.

Cooperrider, D. L., & Srivastva, S. (1987). Appreciative inquiry in organizational life. In: W. Pasmore & R. Woodman (Eds), *Research in organization change and development* (Vol. 1). Greenwich, CT: JAI Press.

Covey, S. M. R. (2006). *The speed of trust*. New York, NY: Free Press.

Creswell, J. W. (2007). *Qualitative inquiry and research design* (2nd ed.). Thousand Oaks, CA: Sage.

Cummings, T. G., & Worley, C. G. (2005). *Organization development and change* (8th ed.). Mason, OH: Thomson South-Western.

Eisenhardt, K. M. (1989). Building theories from case study research. *Academy of Management Review*, *14*(4), 532–550.

Frederickson, B. L., & Losada, M. F. (2005). Positive affect and the complex dynamics of human flourishing. *American Psychologist*, *60*(7), 678–686.

Frederickson, B. L., Tugade, M. M., Waugh, C. E., & Larkin, G. (2003). What good are positive emotions in crisis? A prospective study of resilience and emotions following the terrorist attacks on the United States September 11th, 2001. *Journal of Personality and Social Psychology*, *84*, 365–376.

Galpin, T. (1996). *The human side of change: A practical guide to organization redesign*. San Francisco: Jossey-Bass.

Glaser, B. G., & Strauss, A. L. (1967). *The discovery of grounded theory: Strategies for qualitative research*. Chicago, IL: Aldine Publishing Company.

Golensky, M., & DeRuiter, G. (2002). The urge to merge: A multiple case study. *Nonprofit Management and Leadership*, *13*(2), 169–186.

Habeck, M. M., Kroger, F., & Tram, M. R. (1999). *After the merger*. Upper Saddle River, NJ: Prentice Hall.

Judson, A. (1991). *Changing behavior in organizations: Minimizing resistance to change*. Cambridge, MA: Basil Blackwell.

Kotter, J. (1995). Leading change: Why transformation efforts fail. *Harvard Business Review*, *73*(2), 59–67.

Lewicki, R. J., McAllister, D. J., & Bies, R. J. (1998). Trust and distrust: New relationships and realities. *Academy of Management Review*, *23*, 438–458.

Lewin, K. (1947). Frontiers in group dynamic. *Human Relations*, *1*, 5–41.

Ludema, J., Whitney, D., Mohr, B. J., & Griffin, T. J. (2003). *The appreciative inquiry summit: A practitioner's guide for leading large group change*. San Francisco: Berrett-Koehler.

Marks, M. L. (2007). A framework for facilitating adaptation to organizational transition. *Journal of Organization Change Management*, *20*(5), 721–739.

Marks, M. L., & Mirvis, P. H. (1992). Rebuilding after the merger: Dealing with "survivor sickness". *Organization Dynamics*, *21*(2), 18–32.

Marks, M. L., & Mirvis, P. H. (1998). *Joining forces: Making one plus one equal three in mergers, acquisitions and alliances*. San Francisco, CA: Jossey-Bass.

Marks, M. L., & Mirvis, P. H. (2001). Making mergers and acquisitions work: Strategic and psychological preparations. *Academy of Management Executive*, *15*(2), 80–92.

Marlett, J. D. (1997). Conversion methodology and the case of Cardinal Newman. *Theological Studies*, *58*(4), 669–686.

Marshak, R. J. (2006). *Covert processes at work*. San Francisco, CA: Berrett-Koehler Publishers.

Owen, H. (1997). *Open space technology*. San Francisco, CA: Berrett-Koehler Publishers.
Pritchett, P. (1997). *After the mergers: The authoritative guide for integration success*. New York: McGraw Hill.
Rambo, L. R. (1993). *Understanding religious conversion*. New Haven, CT: Yale University Press.
Robertson, P. J., Roberts, D. R., & Porras, J. I. (1993). An evaluation of a model of planned organizational change: Evidence from a meta-analysis. In: R. W. Woodman & W. A. Pasmore (Eds), *Research in organizational change and development* (Vol. 7, pp. 1–39). Greenwich, CN: JAI Press.
Rousseau, D. M., Sitkin, S. B., Burt, R. S., & Camerer, C. (1998). Not so different after all: A cross-discipline view of trust. *Academy of Management Review*, *23*(3), 393–404.
Rubin, J. H., & Rubin, I. S. (2005). *Qualitative interviewing*. Thousand Oaks, CA: Sage Publications.
Ryan, R. M., & Deci, E. L. (2000). Self-determination theory and the facilitation of intrinsic motivation, social development, and well-being. *American Psychologist*, *55*, 68–78.
Sammon, S. D. (2003). *A revolution of the heart*. Talk given to the Conference of Major Superiors, Louisville, KY.
Schein, E. H. (1999). *Process consultation revisited*. New York: Addison-Wesley.
Schweiger, D. M., & Denisi, A. S. (1991). Communication with employees following a merger: A longitudinal field experiment. *Academy of Management Journal*, *34*(1), 110–135.
Sitkin, S. B., & Pable, A. L. (2005). The neglected importance of leadership in mergers and acquisitions. In: G. K. Stahl & M. E. Mendenhall (Eds). *Mergers and Acquisitions*. Stanford, CA: Stanford Business Books.
Sitkin, S. B., & Roth, R. L. (1993). Explaining the limited effectiveness of legalistic "remedies" for trust/distrust. *Organization Science*, *4*, 367–392.
Snow, D., & Machalek, R. (1983). The sociology of conversion. *Annual Review of Sociology*, *10*, 167–190.
Spradley, J. P. (1980). *Participant observation*. Toronto, ON: Thomson Learning.
Stahl, G. K., & Sitkin, S. B. (2005). Trust in mergers and acquisitions. In: G. K. Stahl & M. E. Mendenhall (Eds), *Mergers and acquisitions*. Stanford, CA: Stanford Business Books.
Stickel, D. (1999). *Building Trust in the face of hostility*. Unpublished doctoral dissertation. Duke University, Durham, NC.
Strauss, A., & Corbin, J. (1998). *Basics of qualitative research*. Thousand Oaks, CA: Sage Publications.
Vlaar, P. W. L., Van den Bosch, F. A. J., & Volberda, H. W. (2007). On the evolution of trust, distrust and formal coordination and control in interorganizational relationships: Toward an integrative framework. *Group Organization Management*, *32*, 407–429.
Weisbord, M., & Janoff, S. (2000). *Future search*. San Francisco, CA: Berrett-Koehler Publishers.
Yin, R. K. (2003). *Case study research design and methods*. Thousand Oaks, CA: Sage Publications.
Zinnbauer, B., & Pargament, K. (1998). Spiritual conversion: A study of religious change among college students. *Journal for the Scientific Study of Religion*, *37*(1), 161–180.

THE MATURE WORKFORCE AND THE CHANGING NATURE OF WORK

Kay F. Quam

ABSTRACT

Two major trends – demographic shifts in the working-age population, and the proliferation of web technologies – are having a profound and generally unrecognized effect on the nature and characteristics of work, and on opportunities for the mature workforce. Key features of the workplace point to seven broad work trends. These trends have significant implications for organizations and for older workers. Six interdependent organizational changes are central to the far-reaching effects on enterprises and operating approaches. These changing work characteristics require certain essential behaviors for mature workers to be successful in the contemporary work environment. Such a dynamic workplace provides opportunity to introduce new thinking and propose new models. Realigning organizational and workforce interests calls for developing solutions beyond the individual level, reorienting enterprise capabilities, and reframing of the organization development practitioner role as work ecosystem advisor. High-leverage strategies and systemic interventions, such as multiconstituent initiatives and action research, can be used to influence constructively the multifaceted world of work.

Research in Organizational Change and Development, Volume 18, 315–366

ISSN: 0897-3016/doi:10.1108/S0897-3016(2010)0000018013

INTRODUCTION

The convergence of societal and workplace trends will alter dramatically the nature of work, and opportunities for mature workers defined herein as those who are 55 years and older.

Multiple factors are influencing the work of the mature workforce, as well as how it is accomplished. This paper examines the implications of two such factors: demographic shifts and web technologies. First, the approaching retirement wave and global population trends point to an increase in the average age of the worldwide workforce, and to a marked slowing of workforce growth in the G7 countries. Second, the proliferation of web-enabled capabilities will make feasible and even drive changes to current business models and the existing workplace.

Changes already are under way. Organizations are revamping their business approaches and work processes to incorporate the advantages of new web capabilities, fueled by workforce entrants proficient in these capabilities. Simultaneously, these same organizations are confronted with the potential loss of enterprise and customer knowledge. Taken together, the continuation of these trends, and the challenges of the current economic climate are likely to accelerate the search for organizational efficiencies, and increase the need for state-of-the-art skills.

How can we avoid the same kind of messy transition that occurred in the 1990s when the advent of computers in the workplace and rising Internet use rendered the skills and jobs of many older workers obsolete? How can organizations best use mature workers in this environment? How can mature workers prepare for the new workplace?

The challenge cannot be met at the individual job level or even at the level of the single organization. The changes described above transcend organizations, and alter entire streams of work activity. The mature workforce increasingly will face a substantially different work environment. Much attention is being given to flexible schedules, healthcare, and retirement policies, while virtually no one is focusing on the changing nature of work itself, and the resulting implications for mature workers. The issues of both demand (jobs) and supply (skilled workers) must be addressed.

The growing wave of mature Baby Boomers soon will overwhelm prevailing approaches to meeting their needs in the workplace. Web technologies fundamentally will reshape the nature of work as Boomers know it. Meeting these challenges is not simply a matter of reskilling or even upskilling. Rather, what is required are new means of constructing work so that mature workers can contribute in ways that meet their desires and needs, and so that organizations can enlist the necessary people to perform in the new environment. Hence, the opportunity is ripe for fresh thinking, for fostering new approaches, for bringing in new players. Changing the dialogue and reframing existing concepts can advance a new alignment.

This paper is based on the premises that the nature and characteristics of work are changing in fundamental ways, and that these changes are altering requirements dramatically for workforce readiness and engagement. The paper examines the effects of shifting demographics and new information technologies on the nature of work as well as the ramifications for organizations and the mature workforce. Further, it presupposes that intervening with new models for both work and workforce use can affect the system, and that constructive realignment of work and mature workforce capability is essential for both organizations and older workers. Finally, it proposes strategies and advocates initiatives for influencing the world of work, and for equipping mature workers to participate productively and comfortably in this new environment.

The topics to be addressed are summarized below:

- "The Current Situation" describes two mega trends – demographic shifts affecting the working-age population, and the transformative effects of web technologies – that have largely yet unrecognized and unaddressed far-reaching implications for the nature of work and the mature workforce.
- "The Changing Nature of Work" identifies key characteristics of the changing workplace and major trends they represent. The range illustrates the profound changes in the culture, structure, processes, and economies of work. Seven broad work trends are defined.
- "Implications for Organizations" discusses the repercussions of changing work trends on business and operating approaches that directly affect the mature workforce. The relationships are displayed among six core changes that organizations are undergoing and the nine implications they represent.
- "Implications for the Mature Workforce" explains the challenges and beneficial ramifications of new organizational approaches for mature workers. Twelve implications are categorized into 6 key behaviors deemed essential to mature worker success in the contemporary work environment.
- "The Dilemma of Colliding Trends" presents the quandary posed by changing work trends, suggests that current solutions are inadequate because of outmoded assumptions, and signals an urgent need for mature worker involvement in shaping new approaches.

- "New Thinking Required" argues that integrating the mature workforce into emerging organizational practices requires developing solutions beyond the individual job level, reorienting enterprise capabilities, and reframing of the practitioner role as work ecosystem advisor. Topics worthy of further exploration and research are suggested.
- "Systemic Initiatives" calls for holistic approaches to address the dilemma resulting from changing work trends and workforce demographics, identifies a range of high-leverage strategies, points out benefits to change makers, and proposes broad-scale multiconstituent as well as more focused initiatives for systemic intervention.
- "Next Steps" provides guidance on how readers can use the perspectives and information presented in this paper to (1) target the fundamental issues facing them and (2) begin developing a set of high-leverage strategies, and crafting a systemic initiative with solid potential for productive and meaningful human, organizational, and societal outcomes.

THE CURRENT SITUATION

Mature workers are seeking flexibility as well as ways to apply meaningfully their experience, and to continue generating income in uncertain economic times, perhaps without realizing the full implication of impending work changes. Meanwhile, organizations are leveraging new web capabilities geared toward reshaping work while they are, or soon will be, facing workforce changes and skill shortages they may have underestimated.

Demographic Shifts

Much of the aging workforce views the funding of 30–35 years of retirement as daunting. Many are eager to apply their talents to fresh opportunities. Yet others face the need to shore up depleted assets. Millions of people will encounter this crossroads in the coming years as they contemplate the next phase of their lives. In 2006, the first crop of nearly 76 million American Baby Boomers turned 60 years old; each year approximately 2.9 million will cross that threshold. In the period 2004–2009, American workers reported that they planned to retire at age 65, up from age 62 in 1991. In 2009, workers reported changing their expectations about when they will retire, however, the actual age at which they stated they would retire changed little from that of 2008. Whereas the average retirement age of U.S. workers likely will continue to rise, nearly half (47 percent in 2009) left the workforce earlier than planned as a result of health changes, changes at their places of employment, and other circumstances (Helman, Copeland, & VanDerhei, 2009). Although the American workforce is projected to increase, the numbers will be insufficient to overcome workers' declining percentage of the total population (U.S. Census Bureau, 2001). Between 2000 and 2010, the growth rate is projected to equal the 1990s rate of 1.1 percent; the growth rate is projected to fall to just 0.3 percent in the following decade (Karoly & Panis, 2004). More broadly, a decline in the growth of the G7 workforce is projected through the year 2050, whereas the average age of the global workforce is projected to climb (U.N. Secretariat, 2009). At the same time, it is projected that only 30 percent of today's 21-year-old Americans will obtain college degrees, while college-level skills will be required by at least two-thirds of new jobs (Dychtwald, Erickson, & Morison, 2006).

The out-year effects of the longest recession since World War II on economic growth and associated labor demand remain to be seen. Over the next three decades there will be a labor shortage of 35 million workers if population trends and rates of economic and productivity growth continue (Atwater & Jones, 2004). A combination of economic growth below historical averages, increased productivity, and higher levels of educational attainment will be required to equalize labor demand and supply. Faced with these changes, organizations may tap the larger global workforce. However, that approach likely will encounter limitations resulting from in-country skilled work opportunities, alliance and intellectual property agreements, education and skill requirements, coordination challenges, cultural differences, and public policy.

The Transformative Effects of Web Technologies

The next-generation participatory web is reshaping work through peer-generated activity, decentralized collaboration, and new marketplaces. The shift from a more narrow online commerce focus to a broad e-business approach is changing enterprise (Landry, Mahesh, & Hartman, 2005). Widespread changes in business processes and jobs are being driven by new capabilities, such as social networking, online tools, peer collaboration, and user-driven commerce. Web-based approaches are bringing about a shift in work itself, and how it is structured and staffed. Examples are co-creation with peers and customers via technology, a high level of transparency in organizational transactions, publicly generated content, open feedback and rapid response from customers and critics, peer-generated solutions, and rapid lateral transmission and retrieval of marketplace intelligence.

The web is becoming a platform for services (rather than applications) where the user controls the data. The web enables a kind of collective intelligence, as exhibited by communal activity on eBay, user engagement on Amazon, peer production of Wikipedia, and grassroots citizen journalism. All of these changes are driving new ways to cluster work and people. Web technologies are creating fundamental transformations in enterprise models, leading to changes in business processes that in turn affect jobs, roles, required competencies, and careers. Many jobs as we know them either are being changed radically or eliminated entirely; others never previously imagined are being created.

A Similar Scenario

It might be helpful to recollect the early to mid-1990s when computer use moved into mainstream business processes, and Internet use was accelerated by email. How did mature workers adapt? Did organizations have enough younger employees to accomplish the work? What types of jobs emerged, changed, or were abolished?

A similar scenario is taking place with dramatic changes on the horizon or already underway in the way work is being performed. This time, however, there is a growing percentage of mature workers coupled with a declining global workforce in general. Then, mature workers were bypassed with little apparent consequence; now the early retirement of workers strains the federal budget because of lost tax revenue and earlier social security outlay. Reliance on developing web technologies and work forms will enable organizations to adapt to fewer numbers of workers, although certain lines of work – direct services for example – will continue to require a substantial workforce even while its work undergoes modification. As in the 1990s, mature workers with up-to-date skills will have the advantage. If slower job growth is experienced for a period of time, this advantage will grow.

The Unrecognized Dynamic

Numerous organizations have recognized these workforce challenges, and are initiating appropriate workplace practices, development options, and learning opportunities that both engage and retain mature workers (Pitt-Catsouphes & Smyer, 2005). Others are focused on encouraging mature workers to pursue fresh opportunities in business and public service.

Curiously, there are no comparable signs of recognition by organizations that new uses of the web and resulting new business models are changing the nature of work in fundamental ways. As examples of organizational changes, people are working across institutional and national boundaries using collaborative technology, the roles of the worker and consumer are blurring, the marketplace for ideas and production is changing, and the source of business value is shifting.

There is little evidence of efforts to identify and influence the repercussions of these changes, and to adequately prepare mature workers. From the perspective of the mature worker, many dimensions are changing: the definition of what constitutes a job, the means of performing a particular job, the manner in which work is segmented and distributed, the processes by which workers are engaged (and disengaged), the ways workers are grouped or group themselves, and finally, the sources and forms of remuneration. Success in this new environment requires a shift in thinking and working.

The Unanswered Need

The interests and needs of those aged 55 years and more, the effects of the demographic transformation, and the sweeping changes that web technologies bring to the workplace are beginning to gain attention. Yet not many are taking action to align these three factors – at least not on a comprehensive scale.

Novel organizations getting the press may appear far-fetched to many, however, noticeable and significant changes in work are occurring as mainstream organizations – commercial, nonprofit, even government – adopt web-based capabilities, and avail themselves of global capabilities. For example, the Spanish nonprofit NuestraCausa, is inviting the public to use MixedInk's collaborative writing tool to create a collective text of the ideas and opinions about immigration that are most popular in the community.

This transition, as with all major societal changes, will be messy. As mature workers find their way through this new world, who is stepping forward to create a roadmap that will help them determine how they will participate? Who is at the table with organizations to make sense of the new workplace requirements, and to create an enterprise approach that values and leverages the abilities of mature workers as integral to performance? How do these changes figure into the public policy debate?

THE CHANGING NATURE OF WORK

Distinctive features define the changing nature of work, and suggest broad trends that have important implications for organizations and mature workers.

The Scope of Change

New web uses are reshaping commerce and organizations in fundamental ways. These deep, long-term transformations are taking place in the culture, structure, processes, and economies of work. Entire business models together with their jobs are being threatened or disrupted, as illustrated by Tapscott and Williams (2006), and other researchers and authors:

- Peer-produced Wikipedia now rivals *Encyclopaedia Britannica*.
- Music downloads that create personal customized play lists dwarf compact disc sales.
- eBay and Craigslist are replacing and expanding upon newspaper classified ads.
- Acumen Fund has more Twitter followers than the entire subscriber base of the Chronicle of Philanthropy.
- Modular motorcycle firms, such as Lifan, collectively have overtaken industry leaders, Honda and Yamaha, nearly dominating a segment of the Asian market through use of self-organizing networks of subassemblers.
- Government use of open-source software threatens to remake the scope and influence of information technology system integrators.
- Procter & Gamble (P&G) has established a target to source 50 percent of new products and services from outside the company by 2010 through mechanisms such as InnovCentric.
- Peer collaboration in the field of pre-product research is curtailing duplicative approaches to pharmaceutical research and development while reshaping such traditional models of scientific research as mapping the human genome.
- The federal government is creating new platforms to access information and to elicit pubic participation, for example, via its blog, the Transportation Safety Administration dialogues directly with the public, and converts complaints and suggestions into service improvements.

The lack of an appropriately skilled workforce (Carnevale, 2005), and increasing demands for flexibility and self-fulfillment by both young and old workers are straining current work models, and accelerating the use of alternative work forms and methods of engaging the workforce. Organizations are moving from self-contained configurations to porous models characterized by various linking and sharing arrangements. The approach to accomplishing work is moving from structured, top-down, one-to-many direction setting and decision making to that of achieving shared outcomes through fluid, collaborative, many-to-many interactions. Work is becoming more distributed, interactive, and peer oriented. Organizations are decentralizing decision making, using new technologies to facilitate lateral communication, and building highly permeable business models that enable widespread collaboration among people both inside and outside the enterprise. Work also is becoming increasingly modular, mobile, and linked across distance and time by technology. Innovation is iterative, collaborative, and rapidly incremental. Teaming must occur across a mixture of different work arrangements. Co-creation among otherwise unconnected participants is expected via mass peer-to-peer communication and contributions. This ever-changing and complex web of hierarchical and nonhierarchical interactions poses challenges to alignment, requires sophisticated integrating capacity and social skills, and raises questions about how to set direction and create synergy. The responsibilities of management are shifting to linking and integrating modules of work and workers, negotiating knowledge-sharing arrangements, and working with new intermediaries in new marketplaces.

Trends in Work and Illustrative Characteristics

Myriad examples from the private, public, and philanthropic sectors illustrate new characteristics of the workplace. Patterns in these attributes point to trends in seven broad areas of work. These trends, defined in Table 1, are discussed next.

New Marketplaces

New marketplaces are created by new opportunities for commerce among multiple types and configurations of offerors and users, and by the assignment of value to additional categories of trade. Illustrative characteristics are

- *Direct-link markets* – eBay links buyers and sellers; B2Bpricenow provides an online trading and payment system for farmers and cooperatives;

Table 1. Trends in Work.

Trends	Descriptions
New marketplaces	New applications of products and services in new matchups between offerors and users
New or altered work streams	New or significantly changed work flows to deliver new product and service applications to existing or new marketplaces
New enterprise models	New business frameworks to interact in the changed marketplace
New work configurations	New types and arrangements of work tasks and roles
New intermediaries	New mechanisms or organizational agents to link interdependent marketplace players
New worker formations	New frameworks used by workers to operate and organize themselves in the marketplace
Reshaped role of management	Set of management tasks and practices required in the changing workplace

DonorsChoose.org provides the avenue for contributors to purchase supplies for needy classrooms.

- *Two-way solution markets* – InnovCentric provides a marketplace for scientific challenges in search of solutions; yet2.com provides a marketplace for "solutions," such as P&G's underused patent assets, in search of unsolved challenges.
- *Social capital markets* – SocialMarkets is a social marketplace portal and content manager that provides performance data to donors, and connects them to nonprofit organizations.
- *Platforms for public knowledge and feedback* – Neighborhood Knowledge California provides information on urban decay that guides community initiatives; Gov Gab is a U.S. government blog providing federal, state, and local information.

New or Altered Work Streams

New or altered work streams are driven by the development of new marketplaces, the entrance of new players in new roles, and the capability for real-time interactions. Representative characteristics are

- *Product/service peer development and production* – Wikipedia develops content through peer contributions; the California Department of Education uses peer production for educational materials; the Office of Management and Budget uses their wiki for rapid identification of budget earmarks; change.org is a network for social change.

- *Pooling of pre-product scientific development* – Large datasets are being made available to entire communities; OpenWetWare is a Massachusetts Institute of Technology project designed to share expertise, ideas, and biological data; pharmaceutical companies are sharing basic research in the Human Genome Project; the Single Nucleotide Polymorphism (SNP) Consortium has placed chemical landmarks present in human DNA into the public domain, also preempting proprietary efforts.
- *Real-time link to customers* – Microsoft, Ford, Starbucks, and Comcast use Twitter to gauge customer sentiment, build their brands, and provide access to customer service.
- *Wiki-based knowledge management and performance improvement* – The American College of Surgeons Committee on Trauma maintains a wiki that provides information in areas such as patient safety, disaster management, injury prevention, and regional trauma systems.

New Enterprise Models

New enterprise models are generated from the interplay of new types of business activity, new participants and participant roles, and additional foundations for business. Descriptive characteristics are

- *Partners in design* – Customers participate in BMW design; Lego encourages their customers to tinker with its software.
- *Platforms for participation* – Organizations, such as Google, eBay, and Amazon, provide the playing field where business value is created by large-scale participation.
- *Collaboration hubs* – Trading exchanges, such as Covisint for the global automotive industry and WorldWide Retail Exchange for the retail industry, link back offices of individual businesses solidifying enterprise-to-enterprise collaboration, and making marketplace-to-marketplace interactions possible.
- *Bases for business* – Goggle's business model demonstrates data-based rather than application-based market leverage; web services is a services-based rather than products-based business model.
- *Component/Contributor valuation* – Boeing must weigh and balance the value of multiple independent component manufacturers; organizations are exploring ways of monetizing individual contributions to mass collaborative efforts in order to encourage a reliable stream of free-agent contributions.

New Work Configurations

New work configurations are characterized by increasing variety and adaptability necessitated by the changeable and unpredictable nature of the interactive work environment. Illustrative characteristics are

- *Modularization* – Boeing builds planes with Lego block-style assembly; the Chinese firm, Lifan, builds motorcycles from subassemblies; Intel chips and Apple iPods combine components and services from multiple sources.
- *Fluid organizational designs* – An ITTools Blog contributor has recommended that organizational structures be based on assigning decision rights to individuals rather than to a boss; organization of work groups is driven by continuously matching a library of competencies to evolving business requirements.
- *Role mashups* – Roles are combined in novel ways; for example, wikis, YouTube, and online reader book reviews demonstrate the participant's dual functions of creator and consumer.
- *Peer-based internal processes* – Organizations are developing internal processes for generating business projections, and for allocating resources and time for activities such as creative projects; corporate communications are expanding to include employee bloggers.

New Intermediaries

New intermediaries play new roles to address new needs of disaggregated business components and new worker formations, link marketplace players for collective benefit, and bring together previously unconnected marketplace players. Representative characteristics are

- *Free Agent Links* – MBOPartners serves as the free agent's back office, and provides access to group benefits.
- *Many-to-Many Links* – EmergingMed connects patients and clinical trials; SmartVolunteer links skilled professionals with volunteer opportunities that take advantage of their professional expertise.
- *Interactive networks* – FindPharma is an informational and interactive network of pharmaceutical industry websites.
- *Resource Links* – TechSoup provides nonprofits a one-stop resource for technology needs including a service that provides access to donated and discounted products provided by technology partners; FlexibleResources.com is a talent intermediary that brokers new work arrangements, such as connecting executive stay-at-home moms with project assignments.

New Worker Formations

New worker formations are marked by increased levels of self-responsibility and in the variety of their arrangements. Both are driven by the disaggregation of work, the interactive marketplace and worker choice, and are aided by new intermediaries. Illustrative characteristics are

- *Free agency* – Either by choice or necessity, more individuals are selling or contracting for their products and services as entrepreneurs.
- *Guild-like groups* – Working Today provides services and advocates for independent workers in Silicon Alley (New York); Graphic Artist Guild upholds and improves professional standards, and protects rights of members.
- *Freelance teams* – Small teams, such as The Freelance Team, provides services to the publication industry; "worker pods" or collegial teams have developed into small independent contract research organizations providing services for clinical trials; InnoCentive found that solvers self-organized into solver teams to respond to posted problems.
- *Fluid, self-organized work groups* – Best Buy's Geek Squad is peer-based and self-organizing; self-organizing teams carry out IBM's Agile Software Development.
- *Collaboration contributors* – In a technique called crowdsourcing, members of the general public contribute their collective intelligence to an organization's tasks, thus providing the organization with a virtual talent pool and customer insight.

The Role of Management

Management's new role reflects new focal points and tasks required by the interconnectivity, changeability, fragmentation, and genre expansion of the marketplace and its components. Descriptive characteristics are

- *New management focus* – The aforementioned examples illustrate the need to manage distance collaborations and modular assemblies, alternative business platforms, a modular and free-agent workforce, and arrangements for sharing scientific and technical knowledge.
- *Challenges of interdependence* – Though roles may vary, large enterprises, smaller to midsized organizations, and government entities all face challenges of synchronization, integration, and alignment with interdependent organizations.
- *Management of tensions* – The shape and pace of the changes will depend heavily on the decisions organizations make in resolving the tensions

introduced by the changes themselves. Anticipating and working through these tensions are key tasks.

Key Tensions in Today's Work World

As organizations experience these work changes, they are grappling with a number of tensions inherent in a highly interconnected environment where actions in one area have ramifications in others. Further, the relevant issues and considerations in these trade-off decisions vary by organization type. Ultimately, the collective choices made by organizations and workers worldwide will shape the course and pace of work trends.

The following discussion provides a window into these decisions focusing on three key tensions from the perspective of complex enterprises, niche business-to-business organizations, and government entities. Each tension involves a balancing between two competing values.

The first tension is between the reduction of complexity through "chunking" or parceling of work, and the ability to integrate all the chunks successfully. Discussion of the organizational perspectives follows:

- Large enterprises adopting a modular approach to gain market flexibility and reduce complexity, risk, and expense, are encountering new complexities when they integrate the separately developed components into a final product. These organizations must decide how far they can extend their supply chain before the advantages are outweighed by their ability to carry out the complex collaborations necessary to coordinate work. Also, when they outsource key aspects of the business, they risk loss of the very characteristic that distinguishes the business, the comprehensive expertise to provide the complete product/service. The core question is, "How large and complex can the enterprise be before chunking is counter-productive?"
- Niche business-to-business organizations see opportunity in the modular approach. They have full responsibility for a piece of the final product or service, and are free to find innovative and efficient responses that solidify their niche, energize and make the best use of their personnel and material assets, and reduce cost for the larger enterprise. However, it is not uncommon for organizations in long supply chains to have poor lines of sight into the plans downstream in the chain. Niche organizations can be caught unaware with downstream buyer decisions that suddenly leave them with an inappropriate amount and type of inventory, idle or inadequate equipment, and excess or insufficient workforce. They become subject and party to overreactions that grow as they ripple through the

chain. The question becomes, "To what extent can niche organizations endure the risks of an extended supply chain for the sake of gaining a large body of work?"

- Government entities that dissect large, often technical, projects into subcontracts share many of the same advantages and disadvantages that complex enterprises encounter. With the loss of experienced personnel to retirements, and the challenge of competing with the commercial sector for key skills, these organizations risk having sufficiently skilled internal staff to define appropriate requirements, ensure compliance, anticipate and detect problems, and manage complex projects. Federal officials have noted that implementing participative technologies is not difficult; changing the business processes and associated policies necessary to implement these new models is. Their quandary raises the question, "To what extent and how quickly can agencies use these new approaches while addressing critical skill, policy, and process constraints?"

The second tension is between the advantages of virtual work, and the need for social interaction. Discussion of the organizational perspectives follows:

- For far-flung complex enterprises, virtual work has become a necessity with its advantages of flexibility, speed, and lower labor cost. At the same time, in-person interactions build trusted relationships, allow nuance in complex discussions, and/or provide business value such as the draw of social buzz at Apple stores. Initial and periodic in-person team meetings facilitate the launch of dispersed teams, encourage efficient informal interactions, and maintain commitment. Difficulties with translation across cultures, for example, when customers say customer service agents don't understand their problems, dilute the value of savings from offshore labor. An essential question is, "What level of social interaction must take place for virtual business to be successful?"
- For niche organizations, working electronically across distance and time zones provides efficiencies that enable them to participate in larger and more diverse markets. However, their ability to sell complex or unique products or services may be constrained when so much of the relationship is virtual. And they may be on the other end of the difficulties with translation across cultures, unable to explain or respond adequately to problems. An important question is, "When does reliance on virtual work leave our business too out of touch with our customers?"
- For government entities, attaining the benefits of virtual work can be a challenge. Successful virtual coordination of large multistakeholder projects requires shared standards, and agreements developed and kept

current through complex collaborations. Unless such collaborations are purposefully built in, strong institutional forces and organizational traditions generally lead agencies to implement new technologies without the accompanying interactions and trust building essential to achieving the intended benefits (Fountain, 2001). A key question is, "To what extent must the network of stakeholders be engaged for multi-jurisdictional, virtually connected processes, such as disaster management, to accomplish their mission?"

The third tension is between technology efficiencies, and business practices that build organizational affinity and discretionary contribution. Discussion of the organizational perspectives follows:

- In complex enterprises, the cool, detached efficiency of technology can be used to replace direct relationships that give people a sense of belonging and value. Yet the edge often goes to organizations that receive the discretionary effort of workers who personally identify with the enterprise. One result is that workers, experiencing the detachment, have moved on with colleagues to form their own small businesses, and enterprises have lost critical capabilities. Cause-driven enterprises, such as philanthropic organizations, offer an example of the power of organizational affinity. They establish a compelling mission and areas of emphasis that serve as magnets. These magnets build identification with the cause, draw voluntary effort, and serve as the organizing principle for the myriad contributions to their endeavor. The question is, "What is the appropriate balance between technological efficiency and more time-consuming behaviors that draw discretionary contribution?"
- In niche organizations, the arm's-length electronic and contractual arrangements with other supply chain or partner organizations change the nature of the relationship. On one hand, viewing all interdependent parties as customers likely promotes additional effort on their behalf. On the other hand, the organization's primary loyalty and effort is directed toward optimizing its own interests first. Both the niche organization and the enterprise customer want resource- and time-saving efficiency. The question is, "What are the agreements and behaviors regarding cooperation and incentives that are necessary to make the efficiencies worthwhile?"
- In government entities, technology promises to bring operating efficiencies. However, in these deep organizations, if the use of technology substitutes completely for human interaction, people lose the opportunity to hear or be heard, feel like cogs in a machine, and consequently may disengage from the organization. In certain settings, a compelling public

mission can mitigate alienation to some extent, but may result in either misdirected discretionary effort or voluntary effort only in emergency. An important question is, "What does it take to keep workers engaged in the presence of increased technology use?"

IMPLICATIONS FOR ORGANIZATIONS

Organizations are in the process of deciphering the work trends just discussed. To take full advantage of these trends, they are discovering that they must retool their enterprises and interactions with stakeholders. The resulting effects on business and operating approaches are far reaching, and have a direct impact on the mature workforce. Clearly, this transformation is not a distant phenomenon, but is occurring right now, with more examples surfacing daily. Fig. 1 depicts nine implications grouped into six core changes that organizations are experiencing as a result of new web-based technologies and demographic trends. These changes are interdependent – a shift in one will necessitate adjustments in the others. They also are rolling changes, and therefore in continual reciprocal adaptation. This calls for attentive monitoring by mature workers, as well as an active presence in shaping the adaptations. These enterprise-level changes and their associated implications are discussed in this section.

Reconstructing Work and the Role of the Workforce

The way work is organized and how the workforce is used to carry out that work are inextricably linked. The new work trends emerging from the use of participative technologies reflect fundamental changes in how commerce is conducted, and how the workforce is structured and secured. These changes are broad and systemic, leading to a substantial revision of the work ecosystem.

New Organizational Solutions

Even before the recent economic downturn, fast-paced organizations were finding it increasingly unrealistic to meet the growing demand for flexible work arrangements when critical expertises were scarce and many were working long hours. This lack of an appropriately skilled workforce, and the changed economic environment are driving organizations to look beyond

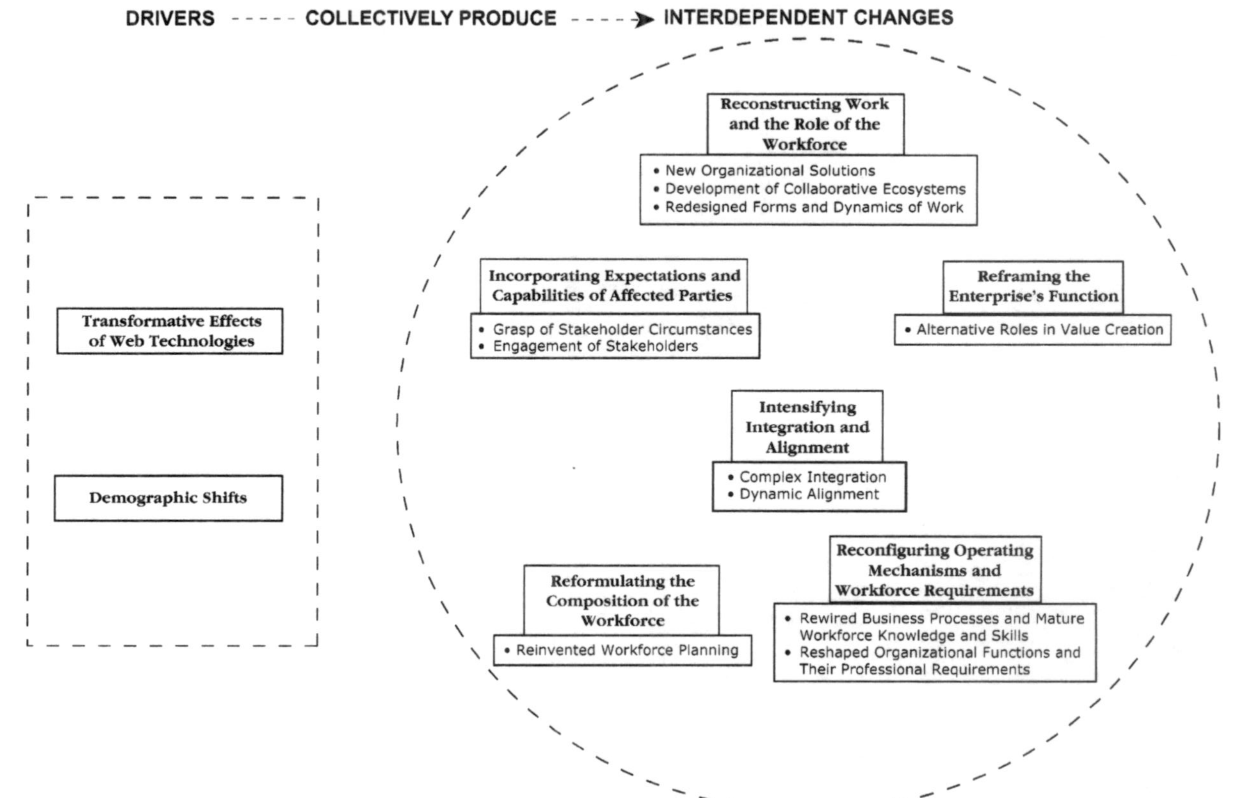

Fig. 1. The Enterprise: Interdependent Changes and Their Drivers.

the level of the individual to that of the enterprise, industry, or professional field in crafting approaches to meet mature worker and organizational needs. Organizations with foresight, including, for example, the Federal government that stands to lose large populations to retirement, also are developing strategies that contemplate declining growth in the working population.

Organizations now have workforce as well as economic and technology incentives to move toward modular work construction. Rather than solving myriad individual problems, they are carving out self-contained bodies of work that can be resourced through a combination of arrangements. These modules then can be handed over to a manager or contracted out with the freedom to compose the necessary workforce using full- and part-time, local and distant, and internal and contract resources.

At the enterprise level, organizations are partnering with others to benefit from the capabilities and knowledge of a broader workforce, and to create sharing arrangements that pool skilled resources aimed at tackling core issues. To gain access to special skills or skill clusters, organizations are engaging self-organized multifunctional clusters or single-specialty groups as well as free agents.

Development of Collaborative Ecosystems

Organizations are using a combination of internal and external self-contained interdependent performance units involving global, regional, and local entities to weave the next-generation enterprise. Whether work units are co-located, such as Sharp Electronics, or distributed, such as Apple, the trend is toward more interlacing of separate performance units. These enterprises must provide links and visibility across a many-to-many environment so that entities know where and how to plug into a stream of activity. For example, sharing arrangements of precompetitive knowledge require a primary mechanism to generate new perspectives and ideas. Enterprises also need secondary mechanisms to integrate these alternatives into business strategy. Participants must maintain a line of vision, and a sense of contributing to ultimate outcomes. The Drugs for Neglected Diseases Initiative uses open-source drug discovery as a low-cost way to engage a larger community to address orphan diseases.

Much knowledge has been gained regarding the organizational infrastructure and management required for successful team-based organizations (Mohrman, Cohen, & Mohrman, 1995; Mohrman & Quam, 2000). This information is relevant to the successful design and management of these contemporary approaches. For example, integrated design and lateral mechanisms are necessary to align and orchestrate the performance of autonomous operating units, such as Boeing's component builders.

These ecosystems are marked by internal and external connections and interactions that collectively move the system, and a continual cycle of testing and feedback that sparks learning and creative solutions. Such environments demonstrate many characteristics of organic models of organization such as a shared purpose, direction, and principles of action; the freedom of modules to self-organize to perform work; and frameworks for creativity (Coleman, 1999, Dooley, 1997). Enterprise-wide structures and processes need to be configured to enable each of these functions.

Redesigned Forms and Dynamics of Work

The way work is parceled is remaking work dynamics. For example, the use of open-source software together with technology-enabled consolidation of hosting and other functions across multiple systems are disaggregating the role of the system integrator. Not only does this change in role disrupt that business model, it forces a different concept of that work upon the workforce. As another example, service-oriented architecture is being used to facilitate interoperability among software packages to create information. This approach enables the consumer to seek the service and find the appropriate software provider for it, in contrast to seeking the provider and then searching for the service. The focus is on service, not software, requiring organizational and social skills to build visibility and trust among interdependent players providing the service.

As organizations modify the forms and dynamics of work, they are not necessarily considering the ramifications for how they use mature workers. Their approaches must go beyond case-by-case solutions to meet the broader needs of the enterprise and the mature workers. Currently, organizations are experiencing shortages of people with key skills, and are witnessing the early exodus of institutional memory, and the loss of trusted client relationships (Dychtwald, Erickson, & Morison, 2004). At the same time, they are launching totally different business models powered by new-technology natives – those for whom participative technologies are second nature – and may be bypassing much of the mature workforce. This dilemma calls for thoughtful business strategies and enlightened workforce planning that recognize the significant, even pivotal, role the mature workforce can play in business success.

Reframing the Enterprise's Function

Devising or even contemplating new ways of creating business value requires the willingness to rethink the enterprise's placement in the work stream, and to reorient the concept of its business role. A substantial shift in mindset may be necessary on the part of decision makers and those who carry out the work.

Alternative Roles in Value Creation

There are substantially altered and previously unexplored ways for enterprises to deliver value in the new world of commerce. Many organizations will choose to become adept at building platforms upon which a range of players create a valued product or experience. Examples are eBay, YouTube, and Second Life. This context-setting role focuses on providing an infrastructure for facilitating activities such as peer collaboration, social exchange, and information sharing. This role is in marked contrast to that of building and providing proprietary products and services for customers, and requires reconceiving the organization's role in creating business value.

Similarly, more organizations are assuming the role of intermediary between enterprises and a free-agent workforce in ways not previously envisioned. For example, CollabNet is a collaboration broker, and MBOPartners provides free agents access to group benefits. Mediating in a many-to-many environment is a business role quite different from that of providing one-to-many product and service delivery for which most organizations are designed. Both management and workers will be grappling with and redefining their concept of what it means to provide a product or service.

Intensifying Integration and Alignment

The more diverse and dispersed the entities and parties involved in creating and providing economic or societal value, and the more interdependent the components of product or service delivery, the more compelling the requirement for integrative and alignment mechanisms.

Complex Integration

These new organizational approaches require well-executed orchestration of independent and interdependent partner organizations, work modules, and worker formations. The enterprise structure and management processes must be in place to establish direction, and maintain a course that continuously balances stakeholder requirements and shared needs. This complex environment calls for operating practices that provide freedom for partners and modules to create, and the requirements to integrate their work into the whole. Complex collaborations of multistakeholder forums are essential for understanding component capabilities of participating entities, building trust, clarifying human and machine interfaces, and arriving at shared understanding of ultimate goals. These collaborations provide an adaptable framework for planning, making business trade-off decisions, and managing the overall effort.

Boeing's two-year delay in getting the 787 Dreamliner to production highlights the complexities of components integration, subcontractor management, and quality adherence. They acknowledge that they did not prepare adequately for the project's complexity. Their engineering force was too thin to monitor engineering issues and solutions. Flaws were not detected until assembly started. Suppliers weren't prepared to manage subcontractors. And as fuel prices rose, the expense of shipping components from distant countries fell out of alignment with cost models.

Dynamic Alignment

Projects that use large-scale integration often have long time lines that require ongoing mechanisms to coordinate, monitor, and adjust the collective endeavor. Multiple moving parts require active synchronization. Boeing's reported use of translators for 28 languages; high-resolution, close-up images of components; and a 24-hour Production Integration Center for immediate multimedia communications serves as an indicator of the level of coordination required. To reduce risk, Boeing has altered its approach, taking part of the program back in-house.

In complex systems, changes in one part of the endeavor have ripple effects on other parts of the system and on the future course of the system. For example, the Boeing delay disrupted the financial state of suppliers who may change their stance in future negotiations with Boeing, with the outcome having high stakes for both.

Multifaceted organizations are continually aligning themselves internally and with their environment. In more organic organizations, shared values and purpose serve as a "north star" that guides and aligns myriad individual decisions and actions. Action and interaction rules define core functioning while allowing experimentation and creative freedom. Active information circulation and rapid feedback build collective system awareness and learning that gives rise to self-adjusting action. Continuous environmental scanning and engagement maintain sensitivity to the environment that enables ongoing nuanced adjustments (Coleman, 1999, Dooley, 1997).

Reconfiguring Operating Mechanisms and Workforce Requirements

The business processes and functions of an enterprise are designed to fulfill the mission of the organization using available technology and human resources. If changes occur in the enterprise's role, technology and workforce use, and/or inputs or outputs, the processes and functions must be altered accordingly along with workforce requirements. Mature workers can offer unique advantages as these shifts occur.

Rewired Business Processes and Mature Workforce Knowledge and Skills
Unique new business models as well as their next-generation inventors and leaders are receiving media attention. Although these innovation leaders are important to the economy, the greater task may lie in retrofitting existing complex organizational configurations. "Green field" business units provide opportunities to start fresh with new business models. In larger established organizations, the challenge becomes transforming mainstream work processes, such as design, production/service delivery, and supply chain management, to incorporate new web capabilities while dealing with changes in the worker population. For example, in the Collaboration Project, representatives from federal agencies, working under the auspices of the National Academy for Public Administration and in collaboration with New Paradigm (now nGenera), have recognized that implementing the technology is not difficult; integrating its use into agencies' ongoing business processes is a challenge. The project's model includes as one of its key components the pivotal involvement of the Internet generation, yet does not take into account the potential contributions of the mature workforce. Consideration of the broader workforce could benefit the timely efforts of the Collaboration Project.

There has been considerable emphasis on younger workers' facility with technology-enabled business approaches. However, incorporating these approaches into ongoing concerns requires capabilities found in abundance among members of the mature workforce: extensive enterprise knowledge, professional acumen, established industry and customer relationships, comprehensive understanding of industry dynamics, and insight into business strategies. Their broad organizational understanding is particularly valuable in redesigning business processes, and in creating organizational infrastructures that put new capabilities to work across the environment.

Reshaped Organizational Functions and Their Professional Requirements
Virtually all core organizational functions and their professional requirements will experience significant change: design, production, logistics, and customer service. Corporate functions, such as business development, financial management, and knowledge management, of most organization will undergo change as well. Many may be distributed or handled in partnering entities. For example, Human Resources will work with counterparts in partner organizations, negotiate arrangements with various forms of free agency, and provide policy for new circumstances as novel as game-based work (already in use by the U.S. Army) and workplace avatars.

Reformulating the Composition of the Workforce

The time is ripe for a new perspective on the role of workforce planning in business strategy development. No longer a backwater activity, workforce planning is taking center stage because finding an appropriately skilled workforce can no longer be taken for granted.

Reinvented Workforce Planning
Workforce planning must be a key consideration in determining the viability of new business models as well as an integral component of their implementation. Organizations may find their workforce strategies splintering as a result of attempting to stem the loss of knowledgeable Baby Boomers while focusing on next-generation workers for new business models. Seeking to avoid a repeat of the 1990s dislocation, business are tapping into the pool of global workers through web-based technologies. The resulting workforce will be a combination of global and domestic resources. Sophisticated workforce planning will be required to equip an organization with appropriately skilled workers in light of demographic changes and available global resources. In addition, a level of cultural competency will be needed to integrate often nearly separate workforces into a functional organizational community.

Organizations may find that the limited availability of an appropriately skilled workforce may constrain ambitious business plans. Faulty assumptions pertaining to workforce availability and use may risk business model failure. Leveraging the native advantages of both older and younger workers seems to be an obvious necessity. Designing work to leverage their combined capabilities may be more of a challenge, and will not happen through benign neglect. The opportunity to leverage the contributions of both cohorts will be missed – or at best messy – without thoughtful workforce planning. It will require a comprehensive understanding of competency requirements, and a realistic assessment of pragmatic business models that take advantage of the full range of available workers.

Incorporating Expectations and Capabilities of Affected Parties

The marketplace increasingly is characterized by porous boundaries between organizations and their environment as well as blurring roles among customers, partners, and internal staff. The expectations and capabilities of participants within and outside an enterprise are becoming integral components of the organization's dynamics.

Grasp of Stakeholder Circumstances

Effects on the nonprofit sector illustrate new circumstances. Many of those who interact with nonprofit organizations will change. In turn, these stakeholders, such as partners and donors, will influence the nonprofit organizations to change as well so that they can continue to work effectively with these stakeholders. Nonprofit workers need to understand how new web capabilities are affecting their clients' and donors' worlds so that they can interpret needs, and formulate effective approaches.

The social services sector will be called upon to create new technology-aided solutions to existing and new problems, and be able to deal with new contexts. For example, the sector may see technology-influenced changes in client issues such as decreased face-to-face skills, and insufficient means of social interaction and support. Some may think their work will be unaffected by technologies they believe to be unaffordable. However, they risk isolation from donors and workers as well as operational inefficiencies if they do not employ new approaches that ultimately will reshape their work.

The nonprofit sector is recognizing the value of enlisting mature workers in "encore" careers, and organizations have sprung up to facilitate that transition (Freedman, 2007). Those organizations wishing to attract new workers to the field will need to be relevant in business practices.

Nonprofit organizations increasingly are using new technologies to connect to their resource and service providers, partners, and clients. Their use of web-based services and products is expanding their reach and effectiveness. The American Cancer Society's California Division, working worldwide, has conducted virtual fund-raising events on Second Life. It also has launched blogs on the worldwide fight against cancer and on futuring and innovation, and started an eCommunity project to build shared experience virtually. NetSquared provides a forum for a range of participants in social change whether they are a nonprofit, foundation, change maker, or entrepreneur. As an example, they organize "Challenges," platforms for innovators to submit technology applications that support social change such as mobile solutions to meet the needs of developing communities around the world. New Hampshire (NH) nonprofits that have banded together in the NH Center for Nonprofits provide an online core capacity assessment tool and a best practices guide.

Engagement of Stakeholders

The appropriate engagement of the various affected parties is a fundamental mechanism for accomplishing interdependent work. The organizational changes that have been presented provide the framework and examples for engaging a wide range of constituencies and types of working arrangements. As organizations make these changes, it is critical that they do not lose sight of the role of human motivation.

The performance of an organization is propelled by the energy and dedication of people – workers, partners, managers, and even customers – who attach personal significance to their work. The value of organizational performance is determined by the judgments of funders, customers, and supply- or value-chain partners. The glue of an organization is the network of relationships that create a sense of community; the goodwill and collegiality of the community facilitates its interactions.

Networked and modular organizations are challenged to foster a sense of belonging, and to maintain an awareness of the health of their greater communities. Organizations cannot assume that stakeholders automatically will embrace and unite around changes. People at the enterprise or module level adapt more readily when the changes have personal value. People attach to an organization or a worker unit where they are treated as a person, not as a cog in a machine. To engage stakeholders, management's task is to know and leverage people's capabilities and energy, and provide an enabling environment. As an aspect of that enabling environment, participative technologies can enhance an organization's ability to hear the community's "voice," facilitate connections across the network or enterprise, and provide additional options for contributing in personally meaningful ways.

In total, the organizational implications discussed in this section make clear that organizations are faced with considerable change as they anticipate and plumb customer inclinations, evaluate the changing marketplace, plot strategy, adopt enterprise approaches, configure themselves, and prepare their workforce.

IMPLICATIONS FOR THE MATURE WORKFORCE

The mature workforce is facing changing work characteristics and requirements. These changes have both advantageous and disadvantageous consequences for mature workers. This section describes the essential behaviors required for success in the new world of work. These practices are interrelated, so any changes will create a ripple effect. Fig. 2 depicts the dynamic environment of 12 implications grouped into 6 key behavioral categories.

Exercising Free Agency

Traditional employment is giving way to an era of participation and free agency. With increasing frequency, workers are finding themselves outside the traditional organizational "nest" and on their own, reaping the gains and shouldering the liabilities. Domains previously of little concern, such as intellectual property, now must be addressed.

Resourceful Self-Responsibility

The combination of peer-oriented work and self-directed participation connote a marked increase in the level of self-responsibility. New work engagement dynamics require an individual to present oneself in the marketplace, to bid to join worker assemblies, and to find supporting intermediaries. All of this constitutes more than just "finding a job." Gearing up to compete and finding one's niche in a dynamic global marketplace will be a new challenge for many.

This level of self-responsibility can be thought of as "Me, Inc." – finding business or work engagements as well as locating business support for billing, tax preparation, contracts, and benefits. Such proactive behavior also may be collective in the form of "We, Inc." – operating as a cross-disciplinary or specialty team. Although potentially exciting, this level of self-responsibility also is risky and not for the faint of heart, particularly in uncertain economic times. The emerging environment, however, is well suited to skilled mature workers seeking greater expression of identity, meaningful engagement, increased flexibility, and ongoing opportunities for learning.

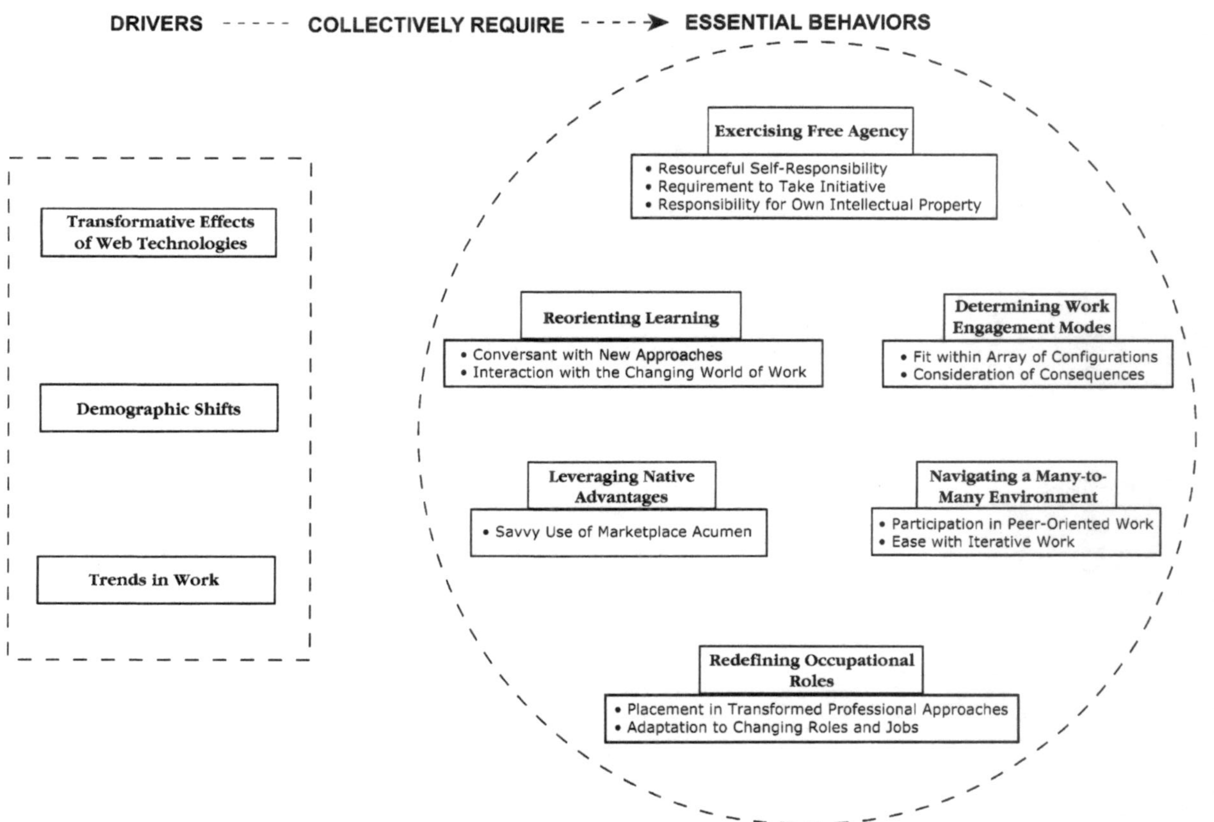

Fig. 2. The Mature Workforce: Essential Behaviors and Their Drivers.

Requirement to Take Initiative

Mature workers will be required to take initiative as independent agents amid an increasing array of worker formations and engagement options. These individuals have a lifetime of experience taking initiative in various facets of life. Many have formed strong networks and possess comprehensive understanding of their profession and industry; both provide a solid base from which to take initiative. Mature workers need to stay abreast of new modes and dynamics of work to determine how best to apply their initiative, and plug into the new environment. They will need to figure out how to be marketable in this environment. If they have previously worked as consultants, they will have a grasp of the requirements and responsibilities – as well as the advantages and drawbacks – of serving as their own agents. Others may lack this experience or a network of knowledgeable peers from whom to learn informally. If so, they may find it helpful to cultivate younger colleagues, perhaps through mutual development exchanges.

Responsibility for One's Own Intellectual Property

As people become increasingly responsible for finding work for themselves or their professional pod, they need to be alert to issues and trends pertaining to their own intellectual property. When operating as a free agent, intellectual property is an aspect of one's competitive edge. This is particularly the case for mature workers who have valuable marketable expertise. The budding efforts to compensate individual contributions to mass collaborations are intended to draw and sustain free-agent participation. Increased leverage will go to those who manage this responsibility well.

Determining Work Engagement Modes

For the duration of most mature workers' occupational lives, employment has been a relatively straightforward matter. Now they must evaluate and select among a range of alternatives and possibilities, remaining ever mindful of the consequences of each choice.

Fit within Array of Configurations

With employment relationships becoming increasingly changeable and lateral, everyone is becoming an entrepreneur. Multidisciplinary teams are self-organizing around work modules. Subject matter experts, some perhaps "guild-based," are swarming to specialized tasks. Employed workers and contract staff are working together on projects across continents and time zones. Contract project teams are integrating cross-organizational initiatives. Contributors outside employed or contracted roles, such as customers of Amazon and BMW, are engaged in work production. The result is a growing complexity of "employment" or work engagement options.

Workers will be faced with a wide spectrum of choices, and will need to find one or more workforce configurations that correspond with their interests, capabilities, individual or communal bents, and tolerance for risk. Growth in contract-based work and consultancy is expected in the near future. This increase in free-agency work will likely be accompanied by expansion of employer-like services that provide back-office support and access to benefits for specialists and self-organized teams. Lines may blur as worker assemblages become guild based or transform into small businesses.

Consideration of Consequences

This era of free agency and participation is resulting in self-direction and teaming being taken much further than ever before. A workplace made up of internal staff and semiautonomous internal teams is changing. The movement is toward an environment consisting of individual entrepreneurs and self-contained, self-directed, participative work units that have arm's length vendor/supplier or business partner relationships with the originative or coordinative organization. In this new environment, taking initiative and engaging in collaboration are not soft organizational practices. Now employing these behaviors has direct consequences for each worker's professional success or for each component of the interdependent community assembled for a particular product line or set of services. Decisions about work now extend beyond finding an employer with appealing policies and pay scales or an understanding supervisor with solid management skills. Mature workers, as self-directed free agents, must sense marketplace winds, assess collective abilities in worker assemblages, scrutinize opportunities and risks, and negotiate expected outcomes.

Navigating a Many-to-Many Environment

The work models and worker formations described above are introducing fundamental changes in the way work is performed, and the manner in which participants engage in that work. For those accustomed to the environment of the past 30 years, the more recent explosion of multidirectional activity, and the interplay among tangential work streams can be perplexing. Mature workers must become comfortable with and adept at operating in this world.

Participation in Peer-Oriented Work

Mature workers need to find their bearings in an evolving, leaderless environment that is characterized by many-to-many interactions rather than a one-to-many flow of direction and information. This type of environment is more egalitarian and lateral in its organization and execution of work. These individuals must be able to function and provide value in an environment that may feel directionless and amorphous. Mature workers may find it necessary to become engaged in this milieu to acquire their "sea legs," and to remain abreast of the ongoing changes. For example, they must learn how to find information, secure assignments, or access ways to contribute in various forums.

Ease with Iterative Work

Workers must function with ease in the development of an iterative collective "product." Some individuals may be uncomfortable, not having opportunity to fully develop their initial inputs or feeling a loss of control over the course of development or over the final product itself. Others may be hesitant to participate, wondering how best to engage in impersonal, virtual mass collaborations. Iterative work or sharing arrangements across organizations may seem counterintuitive based on mature worker experience and learned patterns, and may challenge long-standing work models.

Faceless large-scale collaborative work is different from close collegial collaboration. Mature workers may be concerned about loss of ideas, concepts, trains of thought, or lines of reasoning. Baby Boomers, perhaps at ease in participating in close-knit work teams, may find impersonal collaboration a challenge. Yet mature workers will need to find ways and places to participate in iterative work.

There is a difference between directly developing ideas or content and creating the platform for collective development and perhaps seeding it with a few ideas. Fields that require the exploration of ideas or approaches by their very nature are well suited to – and even require – a creative mix consisting of multiple perspectives. More research and development efforts fit such an iterative development-platform approach than previously thought.

Redefining Occupational Roles

Most mature workers have become adept in their chosen line of work, having gained sophisticated insight about how their work milieu functions, and how to apply their skills and knowledge. What happens when core dimensions of that professional framework, such as accepted practices, players, and rules of the road, change? Workers who stay abreast of these developments in their field can use their considerable expertise to modify their path, and to locate niches that play to their strengths and to which they can add great value.

Placement in Transformed Professional Approaches

Web technologies are having a significant impact on worker roles in certain professional disciplines, such as marketing, communications, media services, education, and scientific development. Sectors of the economy and fields of work are being affected unevenly depending, in part, on their requirement for physical presence, and technology's ability to reduce or alter that requirement. Alternative scenarios and examples of affected lines of work are discussed next.

- Work that requires worker presence will make use of technology capabilities and distant ancillary services. Examples are certain healthcare fields such as primary medical care, nursing, physical therapy, dentistry; preschool, primary, and secondary education; the skilled trades; direct social services; and agriculture.
- Work currently requiring presence ultimately may require decreased presence. This circumstance may occur in mining, corrections, security services, and law enforcement.
- Work not requiring presence will draw on the world population and technology capabilities. This approach is used in healthcare fields such as radiology and remote-control surgeries; communications/media services; information technology; marketing; higher and continuing education; and aspects of customer service.
- Certain lines of work require presence that can be widely distributed. Examples include development of tangible products, production, manufacturing, scientific research, and supply or value chain management.

As professional roles are reshaped, Baby Boomers candidly will need to assess their readiness to work differently. Have they ever served as consultants or teamed up with others possessing complementary skills to tackle a project? Have they ever found business or work online, or participated in an online community centered on a professional specialty? Do they have experience in buying or selling goods or services online, participating in online conferences, or working online with someone from the other side of the world? Mature workers who think about working in these ways are beginning to reorient their professional roles. Working as a consultant, for example, can foster the kind of mindset and allow one to gain the experience necessary to function more effectively in the new environment.

The extent of change will go farther, requiring even more adaptation. Additional questions undoubtedly will surface for mature workers: Have they ever engaged customers in creating or designing a product for them? Have they ever written a document by posting a draft for others to modify, watching (and participating) as those working on it shaped it into a collective product? Have their organizations ever entrusted them and others with the opportunity (and responsibility) to develop their own new products or services together?

Mature workers are being challenged to rethink their place within their line of work. They must be alert to the types of changes they will face, the pace of these changes, the competencies and experience they will need, and the extent and timing of these requirements.

Adaptation to Changing Roles and Jobs

It is obvious that many jobs will change significantly; others will become obsolete. Furthermore, entirely new positions will be created, such as designing and selling avatar personae, appearances, and apparel for virtual worlds. These changes in jobs, in turn, will affect line-of-work choices, career strategies, the value of specific competencies, and the nature of working relationships. Because of work modularization and free agency, worker roles may differentiate into those of specialists, integrators, and intermediaries. A person may become a peer contributor, subject matter expert, member of a worker ensemble or work module, integrator, or coordinator. In disaggregated environments, it may be more difficult to move across roles. As individuals effectively work in separate worlds, they will have relatively less informal exposure, and consequently diminished opportunity, to learn different roles. This, in turn, may lead to a narrower understanding of and decreased appreciation for the perspectives and needs of other workers.

How occupationally self-sufficient are people who have long employment histories? Those beginning to operate "Me, Inc.," and new to free agency may find it a challenge to provide for the basics, such as business development and technology support, long taken for granted as organizational members. This challenge will be further complicated by the contrasting requirements for (1) the individual entrepreneurial initiative of a free agent to secure work and (2) the collaborative spirit of a team member to perform work.

Workers will experience changes in means of obtaining work assignments as well as in competencies, working relationships, career paths, organizational tools, and the degree of initiative required to find roles and assignments. Even maintaining professional contacts can pose perplexing challenges as the dynamics in relationship networks change. For example, what is the appropriate response when a current manager or client asks to join one's LinkedIn network? When faced with such situations, many are opting to set up multiple online networks.

Nor is the role of management immune to significant changes. In addition to their expanded context-setting and linking roles, managers will encounter new challenges in attracting and sustaining the contributions of "Me, Inc." and "We, Inc.," building synergy across multiple players, and detecting and addressing issues and problems buried in the complex web of interdependent entities. As a basis for updating the course for one's career, workers need to assess their level of flexibility, and become cognizant of the adaptations they would welcome, tolerate, or abhor.

Leveraging Native Advantages

Mature workers can survive, even thrive, in this ever-changing environment by applying their "generationally honed" capabilities. They can find or develop niches where these abilities offer value or a distinct marketplace advantage to an enterprise.

Savvy Use of Marketplace Acumen

The Baby Boomer generation possesses native advantages in the marketplace: broad industry perspective, enterprise and customer knowledge, and a vast professional network. Increased use of various teaming, sharing, and partnering arrangements will require the well-developed social skills of mature workers. Broad experience that can integrate and align enterprise efforts or multiple business partners and models will prove beneficial to organizations.

Mature workers can leverage their native advantages to address businesses', industries', and professions' applications of new technology capabilities and modes of working. Such leveraging requires them to adapt these capabilities to new settings on a continual basis. Savvy mature workers will find or create places in the work stream to apply their contextual knowledge of the work environment. For example, they may develop organizational and process infrastructure to deliver products and services, and/or identify troubling patterns and root causes. The trend toward packaging more work into modules may be well suited for episodic or project work, assuming workers are comfortable with and adept in the latest technologies, and conversant with new business approaches.

Reorienting Learning

With the world of work undergoing significant reorientation, ongoing learning and adaptation are essential. The pace and nature of change dictate nimble and iterative learning. In an organizational setting, new understandings and protocols ideally evolve from the collective learning of the work community at each level of interaction (Tenkasi, Mohrman, & Mohrman, 1997).

Conversant with New Approaches

The environment will be confusing at times as transition occurs within work, professions, and whole industries. Mature workers must become versed in emerging new business and professional approaches. Rapid advances in enabling technology indicate that the learning curve will be steep and ongoing. Building professional development exchanges or forums provides opportunity to workers of comprehensive and limited experience alike for learning one another's native skills while building cross-generational relationships. Such exchanges could serve to dispel exaggerated misunderstandings across generations, and have the potential to produce innovations that uniquely combine the contributions of multigenerational participants in hard-to-replicate, competitive business approaches.

Interaction with the Changing World of Work

The world of work will remain in flux as organizations experiment with the approaches noted in this paper, and determine how to build these new practices into economically viable and sustainable entities. For example, will a business such as Wikipedia find a way of generating revenue to support growth and quality of services without alienating or losing dedicated volunteer contributors and reviewers – the heart of its success? Will "free" web-based services discover ways to produce income by providing value-added offerings, as in the case of Linux? Interestingly, this changeable state actually may ease the transition of and present an opportunity for mature workers since they may be able to continue working within current organizational models while learning new approaches. Possessing extensive industry and professional experience, mature workers are well positioned to participate in the testing and evaluation of new approaches. In this way, they can also learn during the course of the experimentation.

Workers who are in the mainstream of activity are the best equipped to stay abreast of changes, influence these changes, and ultimately find their niche. Those who are on the periphery of these changes will need to use other means to stay abreast of the nature and pace of changes, and to equip themselves accordingly. Obviously, this begs the need to create a line of sight and appropriate resources for mature workers so they can plot informed courses of action.

THE DILEMMA OF COLLIDING TRENDS

The negative repercussions resulting from the decline in the working population are now being felt. Based on October 2006 data from the U.S. Office of Personnel Management, 40 percent of federal workers will be eligible to retire by 2014 (U.S. Office of Personnel Management, 2008). Because these Federal workers have secure pension and retirement benefits, they can leave the workforce regardless of the economic situation. Workers in the commercial sector may delay retirement three to five years because of the current economic climate; however, the trend of a decreasing working-age population ultimately will prevail.

To date, mature workers looking for options and organizations facing the loss of enterprise knowledge and accomplished workers have focused primarily on remedies at the individual level. Mature workers may have migrated to a reduced workload or transitioned to new meaningful work. Organizations may be providing individual flexibility and a wider variety of employment practices. However, the number of mature workers is growing at such an accelerated rate that organizations will find it increasingly unwieldy to manage the plethora of case-by-case arrangements. Furthermore, technology advances currently under way are driving substantial changes that will continue to reshape jobs on a large scale.

At the same time, it is becoming increasingly evident that the demographic- and technology-induced restructuring of work is growing into a broad trend. New applications of technology capabilities are giving rise to additional challenges and limitations, and there is considerable trial and error testing various configurations and strategies as new business models shake out in the marketplace. It is likely that there will be a mix of these models for a period of time, Even as this condition complicates the environment, it may provide opportunities for mature workers to target industries, professions, or sectors less "whipsawed" by new approaches, and buy time for these individuals to equip themselves for the transition. Nevertheless, it is safe to say that participatory web practices will permeate the world of work and, as their use becomes the norm, virtually all aspects of work will be affected.

There is an urgent need for the interests of mature workers to be represented in public and business dialogue as the new world of work is being shaped. Meanwhile, solutions are being developed without the mature worker in mind. Not surprisingly, emergent organizations that are blazing new paths are largely geared to and powered by the Internet generation. Some authors recognize the combined potential of collaborative technologies, social networking, global business models, and the contributions of the technology-native generation, yet do not address the issues of shifting demographics or the role of the mature worker (Tapscott & Williams, 2006).

This paper argues that current enterprise initiatives, such as workplace flexibility, that are intended to address both mature workforce expectations and enterprise retention needs are insufficient because of outmoded assumptions. These assumptions ignore the ramifications of the changing nature of work, and how these changes affect requirements for mature worker success in the workplace. No longer can it be assumed that changes in the world of work will be minor or gradual, or that organizations will have infinite capacity for or will confine themselves to special arrangements for mature workers.

Organizations will seek ways to manage workload, work speed, and workforce changes through technology, a global workforce, and, of course, retention techniques such as flexible workplace practices. But new technologies and the force of the demographic shift will change the very nature of jobs. Global workforces will become competition. The specifics of these effects will vary by industry: for example, direct services still will require at least some worker presence though marketing will not be as constrained. Some of these changes will be advantageous to mature workers; others will present obstacles. Mature workers will face a twofold challenge: (1) to stay current in and to equip themselves for the changing world of work and (2) to become prepared to compete with a global workforce in certain arenas.

NEW THINKING REQUIRED

How can we avoid the same kind of difficult transition that occurred in the 1990s when computer and Internet use spread across the workplace making the jobs and skills of many older workers obsolete?

People are thinking – and rightly so – about issues such as flexible schedules, healthcare, retirement policy, and even the intergenerational workforce. Yet virtually no one is talking about work design and its implications for mature workers. The changing nature of work will necessitate higher-order solutions if this segment of the workforce is to be integrated into mainstream organizational practices. The interactive nature of these solutions will require redirection of organizational efforts. Addressing both enterprise and mature worker needs in the contemporary work environment will require an ecosystem approach by practitioners.

Beyond Solutions at the Individual Job Level

Organizations must shift their focus from solutions at the individual job level to those at the "body-of- work" level if the mature workforce is to be integrated into mainstream organizational practices. This challenge cannot be met even at the level of the single organization. These changes in the dynamics of work transcend organizations, and alter entire streams of work activity. The systemic nature of this challenge demands comprehensive approaches that unite the range of stakeholders in crafting systemic models. Piecemeal activities are insufficient.

Many jobs as we know them are being changed radically or eliminated altogether; others never previously imagined are emerging. Many organizations, certainly those operating at a fast 24/7 pace with plentiful work (and therefore jobs), cannot afford to resolve work and worker needs on a case-by-case basis. To make mature worker alternatives viable on a large scale, organizations must begin to think about defining work components at a higher level. For instance, an organization can craft a body of work that can be performed employing a variety of workforce approaches. A familiar example is the current practice of contracting for a parcel of work that a provider can accomplish using part-time and/or full-time staff, various skill combinations, and/or in-person or virtual staff. Such bodies of work are expanding to include more independent work modules, and are being staffed by a wider range of workforce alternatives, including self-organized professional clusters. The result is a movement toward a work environment of independent work units, free agents, and intermediaries.

Meeting this challenge is not merely a matter of reskilling or even upskilling mature workers. Rather, what is needed are new ways of constructing work so that mature workers can contribute in ways that meet their desires and needs, and so that organizations will have the necessary workforce to perform in the new environment. The broader organizational solutions, discussed earlier, are required.

Reoriented Organizational Capabilities

Though an important step, it is not enough for mature workers to understand how they must adapt to the contemporary work environment. The organizations that create the job opportunities and rely on that workforce must have a conscious understanding of how work is changing, and of the associated organizational and mature worker implications. As noted earlier, many organizations already are reshaping how they do work, at least in part. They may not be alert to the complementary changes that are necessary to gain the full benefits of their new approach. Neither may they have the analytical systems, enterprise structures and processes, and alignment routines necessary to support rapid change (Teece, 2007). Organizational actions to bring about change may be based unwittingly on an assumption that change can be effected simply by "telling and training." However, work ecosystems are "living" systems that, because of myriad interconnected exchanges, are too complicated to simply direct (Smith & Humphries, 2004). Rather these systems undergo change as they interact with and adapt to their environment, learn from their culture and experience, and cooperate or contend with other parties for resources and power (Dooley, 1997). Organizations may underestimate and be insufficiently equipped to realign the enterprise, and continually adapt the interdependent dimensions. Organizations need practitioners with insight into these dynamics, and the capabilities and influence to put them to use across the enterprise's environment.

The Practitioner as Work Ecosystem Advisor

As this paper demonstrates, environmental factors can have a profound effect on the enterprise and the workforce. Practitioners desiring a pivotal role in aligning organizational and workforce interests must factor in the dynamics of the ecosystem in which organizations and workers function.

Practitioners can take the following actions to put the system-wide approaches of this paper into practice:

- Introduce or reinforce a systemic approach. Use and promulgate the practice of looking for the effects any event or action might have on other aspects of this active workspace. Assess constellations of related issues. Consider the interactions and cascading effects of any actions. Provide managers with the organizational framework to support new or changed functioning including mechanisms for collaborations, linking multiple entities, and integrating diverse perspectives.
- Bring your management or client into an examination and monitoring of work trends (Table 1). Advise leaders on their implications for organizations, and the various segments of the workforce.
- Work directly on the organizational and mature worker implications (Figs. 1 and 2). For example, advise on how to reconfigure and parcel work, build multistakeholder collaborations to manage complex work environments, help mature workers and organizations use various worker formations, and educate professional associations and their members on the work changes effecting them and their profession.
- Advise and carry out the high-leverage strategies (discussed below) pertinent to the work of your organization or client.
- Identify tensions and their thresholds. Help organizations work through their analyses and strategies. Manage deliberations and weighing of alternatives.
- Initiate a learning approach. Frame efforts as action learning interventions with the dual goals of organizational progress and "learning from doing." Build sensing and adaptability capabilities into your organization or that of your client to make the learning cycle operational. Exercise the suggestions in this paper, and develop new understanding and techniques.

Practitioners themselves may need to broaden and retool their capabilities to bring the insight and skills necessary to be effective in the work ecosystem. They can take the following actions to increase their preparedness:

- Gain a system-wide perspective. Understand the role of your organization or client in the larger system. Meet the challenge of how to work with dispersed networks.
- Expand knowledge beyond the traditional organization to include work ecosystems. Participate in systemic initiatives, such as action research and multiconstituent alliances, as an agent and a learner to build capability in working with dynamic, multifaceted environments.
- Become adept with management strategies for complex systems; develop skill in creating essential organizational principles and infrastructure along with key processes and communication channels so that agents,

namely modules, teams, and individuals, can configure and collaborate to perform and integrate work (Smith & Humphries, 2004).

- Develop expertise in various change strategies. Develop and employ methods for working with planned and organic change. Adopt techniques for detecting and working with emergent change, such as environmental sensing, multistakeholder co-learning, scenario building, adaptability, and strategic intervention "nudges."
- Become a student of work trends. Be alert to new entrants and changes in the trends themselves. Look at trends in your own profession. Try out new work forms.
- Use peripheral vision to detect external events that may affect mature workers and/or the organization. Paradigm changes typically come from seemingly unrelated arenas outside one's streams of activity. For example, Wal-Mart has launched a book price war with Amazon.
- Adopt a multidisciplinary approach. Track economic and government policy issues affecting the mature workforce as well as other workforce groups. Consider how they might alter the organizational or mature workforce implications.
- Widen your scope to consider nonprofit organizations, governmental organizations, and nongovernmental organizations as well as commercial business.
- Build an influential role (formal and informal) that enables you to partner with decision-making management and external researchers to seed systemic initiatives, and leverage promising experiments across the workspace.

In volume 2 of *Research in Organizational Change and Development*, Philip Mirvis (1988) described the evolution of the practitioner's role, the content of organization development work, and the context for that work. He described the role of the practitioner through the 1960s, 1970s, and 1980s as moving from prospector to analyzer to mass marketer, respectively. In current times, describing the practitioner's role as ecosystem advisor is based on a recognition of the intertwined fates of individuals, organizations, and society. Meaningful and productive outcomes for the three are inextricably linked. Practitioners must be pragmatic and conversant in organizational environments to be viewed as relevant by decision makers. Knowledge of and sensitivity to multiple work populations is required to build a positive and enabling workplace. Practitioners must have a whole-systems view, and use integrative and aligning approaches to be effective in the heavily interdependent work environment. With no direct cause and effect in these complex systems, the practitioner's influence, and skillful selection and use of interventions that nudge the system are important capabilities.

Questions Requiring Further Research

The constructs presented in this paper are intended to catalyze further work to

- Articulate ways in which work will change
- Identify and test implications of the demographic shift, the participatory web, and the resulting trends in the nature of work
- Co-design approaches with the mature worker in mind.

The implications that are suggested in this paper raise a number of questions that require further investigation to provide organizations and mature workers with useful information and guidance.

Other topics worthy of exploration include

- To what extent, and at what pace, will the changes in work occur?
- What will be the duration of these phenomena?
- What will be the best avenues for Baby Boomers to use in finding work in this environment?
- If the mature workforce is considered in terms of five-year increments, how will cohort groups be affected differently? What issues will be pertinent? How may advantages and challenges vary by cohort? How will global solutions affect cohorts?
- How do Boomers shift gears in this environment? What factors relative to the world of work will help? Which ones will hinder them?
- To what extent will technology be tailored for ease of use by all segments of the working population, particularly as workforce shortages materialize?
- Which work design alternatives best meet the needs of organizations and the mature workforce?
- What frameworks or models can help organizations and practitioners work constructively with the organic changes driving the trends in work, and how organizations and mature workers respond to them?
- Will it be easier for subject matter experts to find a niche given the free-agent trend, and the need for knowledgeable stewards of peer production?
- Will managers be required to make even bigger leaps in mindsets and capabilities to adapt to changing roles, such as the reduction in managerial control that accompanies peer-to-peer business models and collaborative technologies? Alternatively, will many find new

opportunities applying their context-setting and alignment skills as organizations incorporate new approaches?
- What effects will the economic climate have on the scenario?
- What will be the effects of geopolitical changes and global demographic trends, such as the burgeoning highly skilled Chinese workforce?

SYSTEMIC INITIATIVES

Successful efforts will address the challenges, and leverage the opportunities identified in this paper, and anticipate others in a manner that will result in constructive outcomes for mature workers, organizations, and society as a whole. Unsettled circumstances, such as a workplace in flux, provide a favorable environment to introduce new thinking, and propose new models.

Intervening in the work and workforce dynamics described in this paper calls for a systemic approach that recognizes all facets as aspects of the dynamic whole, and that taking action on any one facet will affect the others. It will be important to engage mature workers in the development of solutions, and to facilitate collective sense making among organizations, mature workers, professional and industry groups, and policy makers.

Requirements for Comprehensive Solutions

Developing comprehensive approaches is a complex task. Effective solutions will

- Synchronize with major changes occurring in industries, be workable – even advantageous – in multiorganizational work streams, and constructively contribute to professional or field-of-work transformations.
- Address interdependencies among emerging and changing work forms, new workforce engagement formats, and worker role options.
- Take into account the unique native advantages of worker cohorts, new free-agent support services, technology tools, and other changes to workforce practices.

Although much has been written about using technology to facilitate work, there is essentially no literature that examines the effects of participatory technology and demographic trends on the nature of work, and the resulting consequences for the mature workforce. Senior workforce researchers and practitioners have expressed interest in this topic, as the scope of current studies and initiatives tends to be limited to solutions that accommodate individuals. When attention turns to workforce use of technology, the focus tends to be on the net-native population while the relevance of mature workers largely is ignored.

High-Leverage Strategies

A spectrum of high-leverage strategies can be employed to influence constructively the changes that enterprises are making, and to equip the mature workforce to function productively and comfortably in this environment. In this underinvestigated territory, there are no ready-made answers. The following suggested strategies provide avenues for exploring answers together. Fig. 3 depicts their recommended sequencing and interrelationships.

The first strategic step is to catalyze an initiative. It is important from the outset to involve mature workers in all aspects of the initiative. Understanding the changes affecting organizations and older workers along with leveraging what is known already about workable approaches are useful precursors to undertaking a series of development, testing, and policy strategies. Executing these strategies will help flesh out a roadmap of the changes, and provide insights and real-life examples for educating mature workers and decision makers. The following bullets further explain the strategies.

- *Catalyze initiatives* – Sponsoring agents can spark and catalyze initiatives that seed creative ideas, model new approaches, or scale nascent efforts.
- *Bring mature workers to the table* – It is imperative that mature workers be factored in as organizations grapple with new web capabilities and shifting demographics. The absence of mature worker representatives at the table with organizations as the new world of work is being shaped risks significant underutilization of the mature workforce or arrangements that are less than favorable for both organizations and workers.
- *Understand the dynamics of these changes and their implications* – Conduct research to understand relevant trends and suggested implications, explore key questions, and co-design innovations.
- *Build on and leverage what is known* – Studies of team-based organizations (Mohrman et al., 1995) and organizational learning (Tenkasi et al., 1997) have identified success factors for collaborative work and organizational transitions, respectively. Joint researcher/practitioner organizational

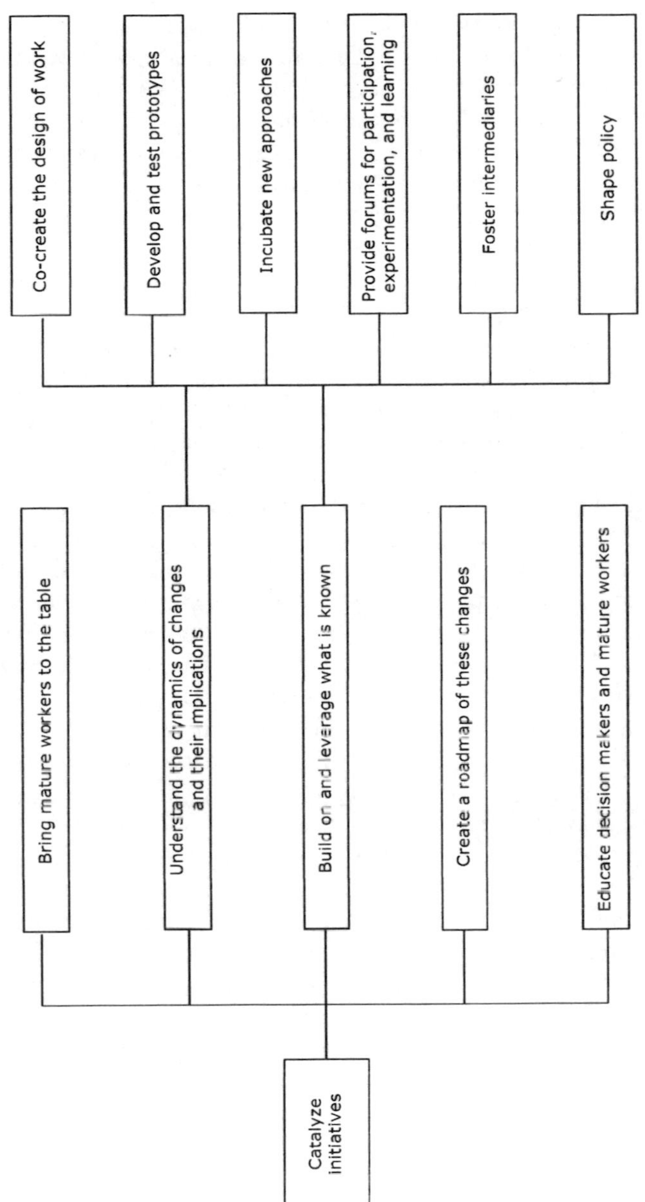

Fig. 3. Strategies to Influence Enterprise Changes and to Equip the Mature Workforce.

studies have proven useful in creating workable approaches for the new world of work (Mohrman, Gibson, & Mohrman, 2001).

- *Co-create the design of work* – Organizations' design of work needs to incorporate the use of mature worker capabilities as enterprises shape their organizational approaches to the marketplace. Constructive, workable approaches can be co-designed by organizations and mature workers.
- *Develop and test prototypes* – Pilots can be run to test new approaches. New worker and management roles can be shaped with the capabilities of the mature worker in mind.
- *Incubate new approaches* – Incubators can be used to nurture and grow promising prototypes.
- *Provide forums for participation, experimentation, and learning* – Platforms for participation can be created to benefit mature workers. For example, there could be a platform for forming peer-worker assemblies; such a platform would provide a venue to devise, shape, and propose worker formations, and might furnish the necessary infrastructure for mature workers to learn how to engage in new teaming formations. Involving mature workers in all of these aspects will harness their broad experience and wisdom in generating approaches. Use of new technology tools to develop new approaches for their circumstances will provide a learning lab or demonstration project in its own right. For example, mature workers could share and discuss opinions via blogs, capture current practices in a wiki, or use shared sites for solution development.
- *Foster intermediaries* – Intermediaries provide a support structure or conduit between independent entities for mutual benefit. New intermediaries can be formed or existing ones can be expanded or refocused to facilitate the engagement of mature workers, and enhance opportunities for participating in innovation, research and development, large collaborative efforts, knowledge sharing, and modular work.
- *Shape policy* – Policy issues will arise as organizational and worker configurations and roles change. It is important that the perspective of mature workers be represented as policies are reshaped to address the practical ramifications of these changes. For example, the variety of work-engagement modes will introduce contracting issues, while the proliferation of value-creation roles, and the growth of free agency will raise new questions regarding intellectual property.
- *Create a roadmap of these changes* – This roadmap could help mature workers determine how they will participate and afford choices for equipping themselves for the new and evolving workplace. Coupled with education about the effects of the changing nature of work on industries,

fields, and competencies, a roadmap could help provide mature workers with an understanding of their work options along with the required professional and workplace preparation required for these alternatives. It also could teach them new ways to engage with "employers," and how to form peer-worker assemblies.

- *Educate decision makers and mature workers* – Educational efforts should focus on organizational and mature workforce implications, the strategies to address them, and ways to become involved.

Benefits for Change Makers

The above strategies can be employed by mature workforce advocates to develop collectively advantageous solutions with mature workers, employers, professional associations, and others. They can serve as useful tools for employer-oriented and industry groups seeking ways to meet the dual challenges of the changing nature of work and shifting demographics. Educational institutions and professional associations will want to engage these strategic approaches to better understand and plan for the repercussions on business practices, and professional preparation and development.

Action research projects that examine the suggestions outlined in this paper draw on these methodologies to provide value to anyone seeking insight and employable approaches. These projects can be initiated and acted upon by enlightened organizational leadership. Practitioners can build the case and gain support for action research; they also may serve as internal action researchers or project managers in collaboration with outside research resources.

Taken together, these strategies provide a consortium with a comprehensive approach and the framework for generating systemic interventions to influence the multifaceted world of work.

Initiatives for Systemic Intervention

There are several considerations when selecting an approach. Initiators need to determine the scope of the effort, and how it will be addressed. This will be based in part on the set of collaborators or partners who may be engaged. Options for broad-scale or more focused approaches are described next.

Multiconstituent Initiatives
The following broad-scale initiatives leverage the engagement of multiple constituents that more accurately reflect the real world in which solutions must function.

- Consortium or Alliance Initiative – A multiorganizational initiative can provide the environment(s) and the means for vested stakeholders to grapple with issues, examine current practices, and develop ideas and approaches. They may generate initiatives to build on best practices and/or develop, test, and incubate prototypes. A range of constituents could be involved: worker cohorts, organizations, industry and professional groups, and governmental policy makers. The initiative could pull together creative organizations; sectors facing workforce dilemmas, such as the federal government; work design experts; those looking at the effects of web technologies; and perceptive and visionary mature workers. Such an initiative could engage creative thinkers and sister organizations to craft and test new approaches, and develop alternative scenarios.

  A consortium or alliance initiative could provide exchanges between organizations and mature workers on how business circumstances and work are changing, and what mature workers can bring to this situation. There would be an opportunity for organizations to consider how they can avail themselves of the native advantages of the mature workforce; meanwhile, participating mature workers would become conversant with the new approaches. Together they could identify how the needs of businesses and those of older workers can be aligned for mutual benefit. A public/private alliance or nonprofit organization could become a hub for work on this subject, or a foundation might house or support such an effort in fulfillment of its mission. The interest could be advocacy, education, social issues, economic security, public policy, or the effects of technology. Any of these could provide a platform for research.
- Action Research Project – A joint project between a research institution and a practicing organization could leverage the perspectives and expertise of both communities to produce useful findings and recommendations that may be applied more broadly (Mohrman et al., 2001). An agenda could be developed for an action research project that would draw on a range of experiences with emerging practices, and examine implications and questions, such as those indicated in this paper. The study could identify societal, governmental, and institutional factors that enable satisfying and productive use of mature workers. It also could distill key learnings for decision makers and mature workers as well as

how they might be applied. Initiatives could spring from the research as participating entities move forward with prototypes studied or generated in the course of the research.

Many of the challenges call for collective rather than arm's-length expert solutions. Many of the opportunities demand practical approaches conceived and exercised by those involved. An action research project would require a design that engages mature workers throughout the cycle of research and development of initiatives, and that is compatible with a fluid study environment. Such an approach consisting of jointly established purposes and interpretation of findings could inform both practitioners and researchers, and provide usable findings for practitioners (Mohrman et al., 2001).

Targeted Constituent Initiatives

Target initiatives, discussed next, focus on a particular constituency. These options lack the advantage of broad initiatives, with their robust approaches, but they may provide specific applications, and serve as a starting point.

- Economic Sector-Based Initiative – Nonprofit organizations could examine the extent to which they will be drawn into new technology approaches, and what this will mean for work processes, resource needs, donor engagement, and workforce readiness and recruitment. The effects of the publicized urge of mature workers to give back through work in the social services arena could be of particular interest.
- Business Association Based Initiative – Business associations likely would want to anticipate the nature and extent of changes so they might tailor products and services that equip member organizations to transition to, and succeed in, the new environment.
- Trade Association-Based initiative – A trade association likely would be interested in the implications for industry restructuring, and the resulting effects on jobs, workforce availability and preparedness, and relevant public policy. This understanding would enable the association to be ahead of the game with proactive education, solutions, advocacy, and public policy proposals.
- Professional Association-Based Initiative – A profession-oriented initiative might focus on the effects of the changing nature of work and workforce availability on the profession. This could position the association to be the organization of choice for career track information, career roadmaps, and related education and development services.

- Higher Education-Based Initiative – Academic programs concerned with professional preparation likely would be interested in keeping their curriculum and student experiences current and in step with the evolving circumstances and requirements of the workplace so as to attract and meet the expectations of mature learners and faculty.

Taking the initiative to address all of these issues is a win-win situation for organizations and mature workers.

NEXT STEPS

It is up to the reader as well as collaborators to take that initiative. This paper is intended to serve as a starting point for those who, upon grasping the ramifications of changing demographics and the contemporary world of work, wish to manage organizational and mature worker responses in ways that have optimal potential for achieving productive and meaningful human, organizational, and societal outcomes.

What challenges do you, the reader, face? What opportunities are in front of you? How can organizations best prepare for and use mature workers? How can mature workers prepare for the new workplace?

The perspectives and information presented in this paper can serve as a springboard for addressing the issues confronting readers. Study the implications for organizations and for the mature workforce (refer to Figs. 1 and 2), and then determine how they relate to your own circumstances and questions. Identify the fundamental issues that are of concern to you, and formulate your objectives. Next, walk through the section on "Systemic Initiatives" to review suggested strategies (Fig. 3). Explore how these strategies or perhaps your own ideas may be employed to develop a systemic approach geared toward your particular situation. Finally, consider the proposed initiatives to craft the game plan and framework that might best accomplish your goals.

There is opportunity to advance a new alignment. We can pull together innovative organizations, sectors facing workforce dilemmas, work design experts, those looking at the effects of web technologies, and imaginative mature workers. We can engage researchers, creative thinkers, and sister organizations to design and test new alternatives.

A range of interested parties is well positioned to lead initiatives in this arena. These parties include applied research centers; large businesses; public/private consortiums; mature worker advocacy organizations;

client/consulting firm partnerships; commerce-related, nonprofit, and public interest organizations.

A new world is emerging for the mature worker, and there is opportunity to influence it for the benefit of all.

REFERENCES

Atwater, D.M., and Jones, A. (2004). Preparing for a future labor shortage: How to stay ahead of the curve. Pepperdine University Graziadio Business Report, Vol. 7 No. 2. Available at: http://gbr.pepperdine.edu/042/laborshortage.html. Accessed on December 16, 2009.

Carnevale, T. (2005). The coming labor and skills shortage. *Training & Development*, *59*(1), 37–41. Available at: http://findarticles.com/p/articles/mi_qa5366/is_200501/ai_n21365298/pg_1?tag = artBody;col1. Accessed on December 16, 2009.

Coleman, H. J., Jr. (1999). What enables self-organizing behavior in businesses. *Emergence*, *7*(4), 33–48.

Dooley, K. J. (1997). A complex adaptive systems model of organization change. *Nonlinear Dynamics, Psychology, and Life Sciences*, *1*(1), 69–97.

Dychtwald, K., Erickson, T., & Morison, B. (2004). It's time to retire retirement. *Harvard Business Review*, *82*(3), 48–57.

Dychtwald, K., Erickson, T. J., & Morison, B. (2006). *Workforce crisis: How to beat the coming shortage of skills and talent*. Boston: Harvard Business School Press.

Fountain, J. E. (2001). *Building the virtual state: Information technology and institutional change*. Washington, DC: Brookings.

Freedman, M. (2007). *Encore: Finding work that matters in the second half of life*. New York: PublicAffairs Books.

Helman, R., Copeland, C., & VanDerhei, J. (2009). The 2009 retirement confidence survey: Economy drives confidence to record lows; many looking to work longer, Issue Brief 328, Employee Benefit Research Institute, Washington, DC. Available at: http://www.ebri.org/pdf/briefspdf/EBRI_IB_4-2009_RCS1.pdf. Accessed on December 16, 2009.

Karoly, L. A., & Panis, C. W. A. (2004). *21st Century at work: Forces shaping the future workforce and workplace in the United States*. Santa Monica, CA: RAND Corporation.

Landry, B. J. L., Mahesh, S., & Hartman, S. (2005). The changing nature of work in the age of e-business. *Journal of Organizational Change Management*, *18*(2), 132–144.

Mirvis, P. H. (1988). Organizational development: Part 1 – An evolutionary perspective. *Research in Organizational Change and Development*, *2*, 1–57.

Mohrman, S. A., Cohen, S. G., & Mohrman, A. M., Jr. (1995). *Designing team-based organizations: New forms for knowledge work*. San Francisco: Jossey-Bass.

Mohrman, S. A., Gibson, C. B., & Mohrman, A. M., Jr. (2001). Doing research that is useful to practice: A model and empirical exploration. *Academy of Management Journal*, *44*(2), 357–375.

Mohrman, S. A., & Quam, K. F. (2000). Consulting to team-based organizations: An organizational design and learning approach. *Consulting Psychology Journal*, *52*(1), 20–35.

Pitt-Catsouphes, M., & Smyer, M. A. (2005). Businesses: How are they preparing for the aging workforce? Issue Brief 2, Sloan Center on Aging & Work, Boston College, Chestnut Hill, MA. Available at: http://agingandwork.bc.edu/documents/IB02_BusinessPreparing.pdf. Accessed on December 16, 2009.

Smith, A. C. T., & Humphries, C. E. (2004). Complexity theory as a practical management tool: A critical evaluation. *Organization Management Journal, 1*(2), 91–106.

Tapscott, D., & Williams, A. D. (2006). *Wikinomics: How mass collaboration changes everything*. New York: Penguin Group.

Teece, D. J. (2007). Explicating dynamics capabilities: The nature and microfoundations of (sustainable) enterprise performance. *Strategic Management Journal, 28*, 1319–1350.

Tenkasi, R. V., Mohrman, S. A., & Mohrman, A. M., Jr. (1997). Accelerating organizational learning during transition. In: S. A. Mohrman, J. R. Galbraith, E. E. Lawler, III & Associates (Eds), *Tomorrow's organization: Crafting winning capabilities in a dynamic world* (pp. 330–361). San Francisco: Jossey-Bass.

U.N. Secretariat, Department of Economic and Social Affairs, Population Division. (2009). World population prospects: The 2008 revision, U.N. Secretariat, New York. Available at: http://esa.un.org/unpp. Accessed on December 16, 2009.

U.S. Census Bureau, Department of Commerce, Economics and Statistics Administration. (2001). Census 2000 brief – age: 2000, U.S. Census Bureau, Washington, DC. Available at: http://www.census.gov/prod/2001pubs/c2kbr01-2.pdf. Accessed on December 16, 2009.

U.S. Office of Personnel Management, Division of Strategic Human Resources Policy, Center for Workforce Information and Systems Requirements, Workforce Information and Planning Group. (2008). An analysis of federal employee retirement data: Predicting future requirements and examining factors relevant to retiring from the Federal Service, U.S. Office of Personnel Management, Washington, DC. Available at: http://www.opm.gov/feddata/RetirementPaperFinal_v4.pdf. Accessed on April 6, 2009.

ABOUT THE AUTHORS

Julia Balogun is the Professor Sir Roland Smith Chair in strategic management at Lancaster University Management School (UK) and a fellow of the Advanced Institute for Management (AIM). Julia's research and consulting centers on strategy development, strategic change and transformation. She has a particular interest in how large corporations transform themselves to both retain and regain competitive advantage in the face of declining performance and is increasingly interested in how this achieved in multinational corporations. She adopts a sociological perspective to explore strategizing in organizations, and is convenor of the EGOS standing working group on Strategy as Practice and one of the founder members of the new Strategizing, Activities and Practice Interest Group at the Academy. Her research has been published in journals such as *Academy of Management Journal, Journal of Management Studies, Organization Studies* and *Long Range Planning*. Julia serves on the editorial boards of several leading journals, including *Academy of Management Journal, Organization Science, Journal of Management Studies*, and *Long Range Planning*.

Barry Bateman is a senior strategic change and organization design consultant specializing in leading and managing large-scale organizational transformations. During a 30-year career, he has led or consulted on over 25 major transformations within large companies, multilateral institutions and government agencies. His work has been featured in books, articles, and films. From 1994 to 1998 he helped lead a major transformation at the World Bank and in 2001 he was the organizational consultant to CFO Magazine's "Transformation CFO of the Year." Barry is currently Managing Partner of Sapience Organizational Consulting, LLC, with offices in Silicon Valley and Washington, DC.

Hilary Bradbury-Huang, Ph.D., is a research associate professor at University of Southern California and director of Sustainable Business Research at the Center for Sustainable Cities. Her research, scholarly activism and teaching focus is on the human and organizational dimensions of sustainability. She co-edited the bestselling *Handbook of Action Research* (Sage, 2001, 2008) with Peter Reason and currently is editor-in-chief of the international SAGE journal, *Action Research*. Her journal articles have appeared in *Organization Science, Sloan Management Review, Journal of Management Inquiry* among others. Hilary is also founding principal of ARSECC.network, a not-for-profit organization dedicated to escalating local sustainability efforts through collaborative action research and learning: www.arsecc.net

John S. Carroll is Morris A. Adelman professor of management at the MIT Sloan School of Management and the MIT Engineering Systems Division and co-director of the MIT Lean Advancement Initiative. He taught previously at Carnegie-Mellon University, Loyola University of Chicago, and the University of Chicago. He received a B.S. (Physics) from MIT and a Ph.D. (Social Psychology) from Harvard. His research has focused on decision-making and learning in organizational contexts. Current projects examine organizational safety issues in high-hazard industries such as nuclear power, aerospace, and health care, including self-analysis and organizational learning, safety culture, leadership, communication, and systems thinking.

David Coghlan is an associate professor at the School of Business, Trinity College Dublin, Ireland and is a fellow of the college. He specializes in organization development and action research and is active in both communities internationally. He has published over 70 articles and book chapter. Recent co-authored books include: *Changing Healthcare Organisations* (Blackhall, 2003), *Managers Learning in Action* (Routledge, 2004), *Organizational Change and Strategy* (Routledge, 2006), and *Doing Action Research in Your Own Organization* (Sage – 1st ed., 2001; 2nd ed., 2005, and 3rd ed., 2010). He is co-editor of the four-volume set, *Fundamentals of Organization Development* (Sage, 2010). He is currently on the editorial review boards of: *Journal of Applied Behavioral Science, Action Research, Action Learning: Research and Practice, Systemic Practice and Action Research, Journal of Management Education, The OD Practitioner* among others.

Steven W. Floyd is a professor of strategic management and director of the Institute of Management at the University of St. Gallen (Switzerland). Dr. Floyd's research focuses on corporate entrepreneurship and the processes and practices of strategic management. His research has been published in such journals as *Academy of Management Review, Academy of Management Journal, Strategic Management Journal, Journal of Management, Journal of Management Studies, Entrepreneurship: Theory and Practice, Journal of International Business Studies, Journal of Organization Behavior, Organization Studies, Long Range Planning*, and the *Academy of Management Executive*. Dr. Floyd is a past member of the board of directors of the Strategic Management Society and a general editor of the *Journal of Management Studies*. He serves on the editorial boards of several other leading journals, including the *Strategic Management Journal, Academy of Management Journal*, and *Journal of Management*.

Neelu K. Gulri is an MA graduate in organizational psychology from Teachers College at Columbia University and has received a B.S. from Stern School of Business at New York University. With over ten years of consulting experience, she has focused on large-scale change, training and learning development, business process improvement and operational effectiveness. Additionally, she is a consultant in training in AKRI's (AK Rice Institute) group relations program.

Edward E. Lawler, III is a distinguished professor of business and director of the Center for Effective Organizations in the Marshall School of Business at the University of Southern California. He has been honored as a top contributor to the fields of organizational development, human resources management, organizational behavior and compensation. He is the author of over 350 articles and 43 books. His most recent books include *Achieving Strategic Excellence: An Assessment of Human Resource Organizations* (2006), *Built to Change* (2006), *The New American Workplace* (2006), *America at Work* (2006), *Talent: Making People Your Competitive Advantage* (2008), and *Achieving Excellence in Human Resource Management* (2009). For more information, visit http://www.edwardlawler.com and http://ceo.usc.edu.

Benyamin Lichtenstein is an assistant professor of management and entrepreneurship at the University of Massachusetts, Boston. He received his Ph.D. in organization studies from Boston College in 1998. He has published three books and nearly 50 articles, chapters, and proceedings on the areas of new venture creation, organizational transformation, and emergence; his articles have appeared in international journals such as *Organization Science, Journal of Business Venturing*, and the *Academy of Management Executive*, where he received the "Article of the Year" award in 2000. Beyond his professional work, he finds great joy playing the clarinet and being with his artist-wife Sasha and their two children, Simeon and Moriah.

James D. Ludema is a professor in the Ph.D. program in organization development and director of the center for values-driven leadership at Benedictine University. He received his Ph.D. in organizational behavior from Case Western Reserve University. He is a member of the Executive Committee of the Academy of Management's Organization Development and Change Division (2008–2013) and is author of three books and dozens of articles on leadership, strategy, and organizational change, including *The Appreciative Inquiry Summit: A Practitioner's Guide for Leading Large-Scale Change*. Jim has lived and worked in Asia, Africa, Europe, Latin America, and North America and has served as consultant to a variety of organizations including GlaxoSmithKline, Merck, BP, McDonald's, John Deere, USG, US Cellular, the US Navy, World Vision, the City of Minneapolis, and many local and international NGOs.

Paul Michalenko, ST, is a religious Brother with the Missionary Servants of the Most Holy Trinity. He has served as an organizational consultant and facilitator for many faith based, not-for-profit and for-profit organizations. Paul has a Ph.D. in organizational development from Benedictine University, Lisle, IL. His dissertation was on the restructuring of Catholic men's religious provinces. He teaches organizational change at Alverno College, Milwaukee, and is staff to the Institute for Religious Formation at the Catholic Theological Union in Chicago.

Ruth G. Philpott is an independent organizational effectiveness consultant focusing on enterprise-wide change management. She has over 20 years of corporate experience with assignments in consulting, sales, marketing, and management. Her most recent work with Fortune 500 companies includes action research and change management. She received her Master of Arts in organizational psychology from Teachers College, Columbia University.

Kay F. Quam is an organizational management consultant focused on organization design, integration, and change in complex work environments. She has experience with government agencies, non-governmental organizations, and technology, health care, and financial services organizations. She resides in Reston, VA.

Peter M. Senge is senior lecturer in organizational studies at MIT. Senge is the founding chair of the Society for Organizational Learning (SoL), a global community of corporations, researchers, and consultants dedicated to the "interdependent development of people and their institutions." He is the author of the widely acclaimed book, *The Fifth Discipline: The Art and Practice of The Learning Organization* (1990) and, with colleagues Charlotte Roberts, Rick Ross, Bryan Smith, and Art Kleiner, co-author of *The Fifth Discipline Fieldbook: Strategies and Tools for Building a Learning Organization* (1994) and a second fieldbook *The Dance of Change: The Challenges to Sustaining Momentum in Learning Organizations* (March 1999), also co-authored by George Roth. In September 2000, Senge co-authored a fieldbook on education, the award-winning *Schools That Learn: A Fifth Discipline Fieldbook for Educators, Parents, and Everyone Who Cares About Education* (2000).

Svetlana Shmulyian has a Ph.D. in organizational psychology from Columbia University. She is an Adjunct Associate Professor at the Organization and Leadership Department at Teachers College, Columbia University with special interest in behavioral research and data-based consulting methods. A principal in her firm, Shmulyian Research and Consulting Group, she provides business strategy, market research, organizational development, and employee survey services to her clients. She held internal and external consultant positions at IBM, PwC, and Arthur Andersen prior to establishing her own consulting practice.

Robert M. Sloyan is currently the vice president of human resources for a US-based manufacturing organization. In this capacity, he is responsible for all HR strategies, policies, and procedures including recruiting, benefits, compensation, training, employee development, succession planning, safety, and organizational development. Previously, he held various HR roles at SBC, Ameritech, and MetLife. He holds a PhD in organizational development from Benedictine University (2009). Additionally, he earned an MBA in finance (2001) and human resources (1994) from St. Xavier University. His research interests include organizational change, organization identity, and strategic human resources. Rob lives in the Chicago suburbs with his wife Doreen and their three boys.

Jason A. Wolf is the executive director of The Beryl Institute, a global thought leader in addressing customer service and the patient experience in health care. An entrepreneurial executive and a radical catalyst for organizational health and effectiveness, Jason has led major initiatives both as an internal organization development leader for two Fortune 500 companies and in external consulting roles working with numerous organizations in the public, private, and not-for-profit sectors. Jason is a sought after speaker in both academic and professional settings, a seasoned consultant on such topics as sustaining high performance, building cultures of service, organization change, and leadership and an author with numerous articles and publications include the upcoming *Handbook on Organization Development in Healthcare: A Guide for Leaders*. He currently serves as a professorial lecturer at American University's School of Public Affairs and has also served as a lecturer at Vanderbilt University's Peabody College. Jason was a member of the Board of Trustees of the Organization

Development Network from 1999 to 2002 and is an associate of the Taos Institute. He has a Ph.D. in organization development from Benedictine University, a M.Ed. in human resource development from Vanderbilt University, and a B.S. in foreign service from Georgetown University. He lives in Washington, DC, with his wife Beth.

Christopher G. Worley has a Ph.D. from University of Southern California. He holds a joint appointment as a research scientist in the Center for Effective Organizations at USC and as a professor of management at Pepperdine University. He is the former director of the Master of Science in Organization (MSOD) program at Pepperdine University. In addition to his articles, chapters, and presentations on strategic change and organization design, he is author of three books, including *Built to Change, Integrated Strategic Change,* and five editions of *Organization Development and Change*, the leading textbook in the field. He is a member of the Academy of Management, NTL, the OD Network, and the Strategic Management Society. He is on the editorial board for the *Journal of Applied Behavioral Science*. His recent consulting clients include Microsoft, Philips, The Hartford, and DOW. He lives in San Juan Capistrano with his wife, Debbie, and three children, Sarah, Hannah, and Sam.